Tugboat

ONE WHALING FAMILY

ONE WHALING FAMILY

EDITED BY

HAROLD WILLIAMS

Illustrated with Photographs

The Riverside Press Cambridge
HOUGHTON MIFFLIN COMPANY BOSTON
1964

W

TABLE OF CONTENTS

PART II

The Destruction of the Whaling Fleet in the Arctic Ocean in 1871. Address by William Fish Williams to the Brooks Club, New Bedford, Massachusetts, in 1902

PART III

The Voyage of the *Florence*, 1873–1874
FROM A MANUSCRIPT BY WILLIAM FISH WILLIAMS

Appendix I. One Whaling Family   385

List of Illustrations

INTRODUCTION

PART I is from the journal of Eliza Azelia Griswold Williams, who went on a whaling voyage with her husband from September 7, 1858, to October 26, 1861. Her husband, Captain Thomas William Williams, was one of the youngest whaling captains. His early voyages as master established his reputation as a "lucky captain" and a master of men. Her journal describes the life on a whaler and the places they visited. Two children were born on this voyage and they continued to go to sea with their parents for many years.

The papers of the ship for this voyage, the crew list and their stores carried on this voyage are added to show what care was required in preparation for a long voyage.

Part II is an address made by the son, William Fish Williams, before a men's club in New Bedford, Massachusetts, in which he puts the facts of the great loss of whale ships in 1871 into the record of history. He tells how Captain Williams' ship, the *Monticello*, was trapped with thirty-one others by the ice in the Arctic Ocean, and how he and his family and the crew all escaped with their lives.

Part III is the story of a voyage (1873–74) in the whaler *Florence* during which young William Fish Williams, born on his mother's first voyage, became a member of the crew and a boatsteerer, or junior officer. This voyage was one of many troubles. The son has attempted to write the true story of the American whalemen and to correct some of the misrepresentations by writers who did not understand the rigging of a whale ship. The boy knew a whale ship from stem to stern and every process of whaling. This section of the book is a record for posterity about the glory of the American seamen.

HAROLD WILLIAMS

PART I

THE VOYAGE OF THE *Florida*

1858–1861

FROM THE JOURNAL

OF ELIZA AZELIA WILLIAMS

Journal of a Whaleing Voyage to the Indian and Pacific Oceans, kept on board the ship Florida, T. W. Williams, master, commencing September 7th, 1858

SAILING DAY

In company with my Husband, I stept on board the Pilot Boat, about 9 o'clock the morning of the 7th of Sept. 1858, to proceed to the Ship Florida, that will take us out to Sea far from Friends and home, for a long time to come. I do not realize much yet that I am going away for any length of time; for this seems more like a pleasure trip just now. I fear it won't seem so long. My two Brothers are with me; Mr. Morgan, the first Mate is one of our Neighbors, makes it appear to me that we are all going back together. Mr. Fish, one of the Owners, and Mr. Robinson's Son, one of the other Owners, are on board, which makes quite a pleasant Companey. The Ship looks very fine laying off in the distance; but we do not make much headway towards her. The wind is very light; my Husband is rather impatient to get to the Ship, but he has just hailed another Boat that is near, to take us on board; now they are rowing us along quite smart; the Ship looks large as we near it; we have reached her and the men have lifted me up the high side in an arm chair, quite a novel way it seemed to me. Now I am in the place that is to be my home, posibly for 3 or 4 years; but I can not make it appear to me so yet it all seems so strange, so many Men and not one Woman beside myself; the little Cabin that is to be all my own is quite pretty; as well as I can wish, or expect on board of a Ship. I have a rose geranium to pet, that Mrs. Fish has been kind enough to send me, and I see there is a kitten on board. I think it will not all be as pleasant as it is today; the motion of the Ship I shall be a long time getting used to. The Steward has called us to dinner. With the exception of the hard bread, it would seem a good deal like a dinner at home; but the water is very poor. I think I shall be a long time getting used to that. I think I shall improve the opportunity now of writing a few words home. There is no wind and the Tug Steamer is towing us along. Mr. Fish has just given me the glass to look at the points of interest; there are not many now. The one of the greatest interest I think we have left behind; that of New Bedford. It looks beautiful from the water. One place, called Gay Head, with the naked eye has the appearance of a town, but through the glass I could see that it was an imence clay bluff, looking deserted and alone. On the opposite side of the water is Newport. We could not see the town, but near the water is a large building called the Ocean house. The Pilot has got most as far as he will go with us; kind Friends will soon leave us, and I presume they had rather go than stay here. I can not blame them, but I shall be lonely, though not alone, for I have a kind Husband with me. The Men are all quite busy on board the Ship, I hardly know at what. Now the Steamer is prepareing to leave us; all is hurry and bustle; one Man (a boat-steerer) is sick of his bargain, I expect, for he is prepareing to leave, hurrying his baggage on board the Steamer; and now the last adieus have been said; the parting kiss given, the parting tear dropped; and the Steamer is bearing kind Friends away, to be seen not again in a long time, perhaps never, by us; but we will not take a gloomy retrospect of the future, but trust in an all wise and good God, and hope for the best. The Steamer with our Friends, is fast disapearing in the distance and will soon be at home again; that dear word home; how many tender associations are connected with that one word and center about the heart, causeing it to throb every time it is brought to mind; there we have left Dear Friends, Parents, and Children, Brothers and Sisters, all near and dear to us. But I will drop the subject; it is too gloomy to contemplate, and return to the Ship. My Husband is about calling the Men together, and laying down the rules and regulations of the

Ship, that they may know what is expected of them in future. I have seen the last faint outlines of the Steamer in the distance, watched the last curl of the smoke; and now I think I will go below.

September 8th.   There is nothing of importance to write about to-day; nothing but the vast deep about us; as far as the eye can stretch there is nothing to be seen but sky and water, and the Ship we are in. It is all a strange sight to me. The Men are all busy; as for me, I think I am getting Sea sick. My Husband has just called me on deck to see the Sun set. It is a splendid sight to see the Sun set as it were in the water.

September 9th.   About the same going on today; the wind is fair, and we are leaveing home far in the distance. They are singing out from aloft, a school of Blackfish. This is a novel sight to me. There seems to be quite a number of them; they are all playing about un-contious of danger, while on board all is confution. The Men are lowering the boats to go after them. It must be sport to them, for they act like crazy Men; now I can see that the first Mate's boat has taken one, and I can see too that the fish is takeing them along in a hurry; now the seckond Mate's boat has one; the third I think won't succeed. The fish seem to be frightened, and are fast scatering. The boats have now returned, and they are prepareing to get the fish on deck. They are a queer looking fish, as black as can be, and much larger than I thought. My Husband says they are smaller much than he has seen. The Men are now takeing what they call the blubber off and the rest they thro overboard.

September 10th.   It is quite rugged today, and I have been quite sick; these 3 or 4 words I write in bed.

September 11th.   It remains rugged and I remain Sea sick. I call it a gale, but my Husband laughs at me, and tells me that I have not seen a gale yet. If this is not one I know I do not want to see one. Some of the poor sailors are sick, and I presume have wished themselves at home before this; as for me, I lay here, and hear the loud orders of the Officers on deck; the pulling of ropes, the ratling of sails and riging. In the cabin it is about as bad; the dishes and everything is on the move.

September 12th. Quite calm today, and I have been on deck some of the time, though I feel weak. I think that I shall get accustomed to the Ship's motion after a while so that I will not be sick. Ships in sight today but a good ways off. Nothing of importance today. It seems a monotonous life to me, such a sameness to it all. The Men seem to be getting their boats in readiness expecting that they may see a whale any day.

September 13th. It is calm again today, and my Husband is getting rather impatient, we get along so slow. It suits me for I am not sick when it is calm. We have frequent showers, and such show — I think I never saw; it pours down in torrents.

September 14th. More wind today, but not fair. There is quite a swell and the Ship rowles a good deal. It makes me Sea sick again; the worst sickness it seems to me that any one can have. I can hear the Men very busy over my head; now crash goes some dish. All I can think of is perpetual motion on board this Ship.

September 15th. More pleasant today. I have been on deck a short time; such a busy lot of Men. It seems to me like a good many work Shops combined; Coopers, Carpenters, Blacksmiths, and sail-makers, they are all to work at something. It makes me think that I am lazy; I have not done much yet but look on. I have seen them tack Ship. That is some excitement, the Officers giveing orders, the Men trying to obey them, but they have not learned the ropes all yet and they make a good many mistakes, though they are all called by name. I am afraid I should be a dull scholar at learning them.

September 16th. Quite calm, do not make much headway. No whale yet all anxious to see one. We are haveing beutiful moonshiny evenings; it is a beutiful sight to see the moon shine on the water. One of the boat steerers, a colored Man, has a violin, and we have some musick occationaly which makes it pleasant these nice evenings. There is a splended comet to be seen.

September 17th. Another fine day; the wind is not verry fair. Have sowed a little for the first time, helped my Husband make a sail for his boat.

September 18th. Quite pleasant. Helped to finish the sail today; then my Husband lowered his boat to try the sail. Saw a dolphin close by the boat, tryed to catch it but missed. The Men on deck tryed, the first Mate cought it but lost it again. They are a handsome fish.

September 19th. Fair wind. It is the Sabbath, and all is orderly and quiet on board; much more so than I expected among so many Men between 30 and 40. All work is laid aside Saturday night and nothing done on Sunday but what is necessary. 3 Ships in sight this morning, from mast head.

September 23rd. A beutiful day it has been and I have been on deck a good deal; I feel better up there than below, the air is so much better. There was a beutiful sight seen early this morning, a water spout. I cannot give a good description of it, as I did not see it. I am sorry that I did not. The Mate was trying to give a description of it to my Husband and me; they had not either of them ever seen one. He said it was a most singular and splended sight; he describes it as a cloud, going up to the skye from the water, from the center of which a kind of spray and drops of water could be seen and most beutiful colors, reflected upon it. At first it moved quite fast in the direction of the Ship, as if it was coming upon us; but about a quarter of a mile off it stood still; it lasted about a half hour, and then disapeared. I think I should have been frightened if I had seen it, for I have read of their being quite dangerous.

September 24th.   It has been pleasant and calm today, don't get along verry fast; quite dull, nothing worth putting pen to paper for; not even a Ship in sight. The Officers have lowered their boats to practice their Men a little.

September 25th.   It is calm and pleasant today; had a nice shower this morning. My Husband thinks that we will have a long passage to Bravo[a]. It is Saturday night, and the Men have laid aside all kinds of work, cleared up the decks, and done everything as systematic as in a hous at home.

September 26th.   The Sabbath has come around again, another week has gone; I sometimes think the time passes verry slow away, when I get thinking of home, and those Dear Children and Friend, and then think how long this voyage will be, but it is of no use to wish time away; we have the same protecting care as they at home and though denied those blessed privileges that they enjoy for a long time to come, we will trust in God that he will spare us from the dangers of the Sea, to go home in due time.

SPERM WHALES

September 28th.   A good breeze today, the wind not fair though; had a shower this morning. It soon cleared away and has been a fine day. After tea heard the cry from aloft of there blowes; then all was confution for a spell. The Men said there was a school of Sperm Whales not far off, and sure enough, in a few moments I could see them plain spouting all around; it looked queer to see them throw the white water up so high. Though it was near night, the Men lowered the boats, determined to take one or more. 4 boats were gone and I watched them through the glass to see what they would do. As they neared them I thought my Husband would stand the best chance of taking one, but the whale went down; then it seemed to me that the third Mate would take one certainly; it appeared to me that he was as near to one as he could get, and that went down. One came along close by the Ship, so close it seemed to me that one could throw a stone and hit him. I had a fine view of him; I could almost see his whole length out of water. He looked dark in the water, but he did not give me much time to look at him, for he made off with himself as fast as he could, as if he was apprehensive of danger. It is getting dark and I begin to think of the boats returning whether they take one or not. The second Mate's boat has returned; they did not take aney. The third Mate has also returned without aney. It is getting quite [dark] and I can not see the other boats. My anxiety increases with the darkness, and it is quite hazy, too; the Men have put lanterns in the riging to help them see the Ship. Now I hear my Husband's voise giveing some order to the Officers on the Ship; now he has come alongside, and has sent a boat with a lantern to assist the first Mate. The boats have both returned and the first Mate has a Sperm whale; it is small though, it is a young calf. All is confution now to get the whale fast alongside, and to get the boats back in their places. I am quite anxious to see how [the] fish looks, but it is too dark, and I think I shall have to wait till morning.

September 29th.   It is an unpleasant morning; the rain comes down in torrents. My Husband has called me on deck to see the whale. It is in the water but fast to the Ship; it is a queer looking fish, and I am afraid I shall fail in attempting to give a description. Many a better one has been given than I shall give I think; but I will try, if I fail. To begin then, I can not say that I think there is much beuty to them; there is not much form, but a mass of flesh. Their flukes and fins are hansome. They are about a mouse color. Now they have hauled him up and have commenced cutting him in, I can tell better how he looks. It looks like a monster to me and not a calf; it is quite long, and verry shiny; there does not seem to be much form to the head; it is rather flat; a large mouth, quite small eyes. I thought they had no ears as I could not see aney but my Husband tells me that they have small holes about as big around as a knitting needle; he says that their hearing is verry accute, and they have to go along as still as possible for fear the whale will hear the boats; before they get to them they take in their oars, and put up the sail in order to go still, for when they hear the least noise they go down. The Officers seem to understand exactly where to commence cutting and how to cut him all, and just where the joints are, they have handled so many. They first take the blubber off with spades with verry long handles; they are quite sharp, and they cut places and peal if off in great strips. It looks like very thick fat pork, it is quite white. They do not save aney of the body but the outside, the blubber; but the head is the greatest curiosity. They part it where there is a certain joint. They call that part the case, and it holds clear oil that they dip out like water; they think there will be a bbl and a half in this head. They have a minceing machine, that cuts the blubber up in small pieces. They have large try pots over furnaces, to try it out. They have to tend it very careful, and they have large skimmers with long handles to take out the scraps, which they burn to try the Oil. They tryed it quite fast. There has been a Steamer in sight today.

September 30th.   a good breeze today; a Merchant Ship in sight; the Oil all in casks this morning. The Men did not leave it till it was done, sometime in the night. They can't leave it when they once commence; it is necessary to try it right up as it will spoil. They had 9 bbls from that small calf.

October 1st.   fair wind today; getting everything in readiness for the whaleing season, the Cooper makeing a large tub for the minceing machine, the Carpenter makeing a box to put the spades in, and getting the signals readey for the boats; those are used in case some assistance is needed when after whales. There has been an increase on board the Ship; we have got 8 pigs in the pen.

October 2nd.   A fine breeze today; going along towards Brava now.

October 6th.   Quite pleasant, but calm and extremely warm. The Men have been breaking out Ship, as they call it; that is down between decks, where the provitions, water, coal, wood, and in fact everything they use on board the Ship, is stowed, they have to move a great maney things sometimes to get at what they want.

October 7th.   A fine day, and a good breeze. My Husband says that we will have the trade-winds now. There has been a great maney porpasses around the Ship. I never saw aney before. They are quite a large fish. The Men tryed hard to take some of them, but did not succeed.

October 8th.   It has been quite rugged today; the Ship is going along 7 knot. Some black fish close by this morning, but did not lower the boats for them. It is getting quite rugged tonight.

October 9th.   It is quite rugged today. My Husband thinks we will see land tomorrow; it will be a pleasant sight to me to see land, even though it be a bleak, foreighn Island of the Sea. There was a Ship passed us so near early this morning that the Men could be seen on deck. I would liked to have been up to have seen her; but I did see quite a curiosity this morning, a flying fish flew on board the Ship in the night. It was a beuty, about the size of a sucker, quite hansome spots on it of dark and light brown, but the wings were beutiful; it had the appearance of a thin skin with devitions of some kind of a hard sinewey substance that they could close them together when not flying. They fly up out of the water, and skim along quite a long way, and then dart under. I have one of the wings pressed.

October 10th.   It is quite pleasant; the wind fair. Passed the Island of St. Nicholas in the night. I lost sight of that, but about 4 o'clock this afternoon the cry of land was heard from aloft; in a short time my Husband pointed it out to me on deck. It looked to me like a cloud close down to the water; but I could see in a short time that it had a different look from a cloud, as peak and bluff rose up to view. In a short time the Island of St. Thiago was plain to be seen. It is a bold and rugged looking Island enough; nothing to be seen but one peak above another, reaching to the clouds it seemed, and the steep rocks comeing down to the water, where the breackers was plain to be seen. About the center of the Island one hill had the appearance of a cone. This is one of the group of Cape Verde Islands, and it seems is of some note among them, being the Capital. There are Men of War and other Ships that go in there, there is a good deal of fruit there. My Husband thinks some of going in there in the morning.

October 11th.   Quite calm; the wind died away in the night, and we can't get to the Island. Passed the Island of Fogo. It is a singular looking place; very rugged. There is a burning mountain on it; we could distinctly see the smoke comeing out of the top. The wind is too light to reach Brava tonight; it is in sight now.

October 12th.   The wind not fair to get the Ship in to harbor; concluded to row there in one of the small boats. My Husband said I could go with him, but I most repented it before we got there. It got quite rugged, and they had to go some 10 miles to get into harbor. They had the sail set and it seemed as if we flew along. I was some frightened, but made up my mind I was there, and must be calm; once in a while a great wave came, and the water would come all over us. It seemed as if it would fill the boat. My Husband sat [so as] to keep the water off from me a good deal. He told me not to be frightened, there was no danger, and I knew that the Men knew how to manage the boat. It seemed to me that we was a long time getting there, but finally reached the harbor. In rowing along beside this Island, it seemed grand and awful to look up at that imence height of rock and mountain, hardly aney vegetation to be seen up those sides, but there was signs of life there in the shape of Goats, Jackasses, and now and then a Cow or two. Those were scarse, but any number of the former all among the crags and shelveing rocks, where I suppose no human foot ever trod. So steep were those sides it seemed as if they went perpendicular up to the top, and the breackers dashing over the rocks at the foot and sounding like distant thunder, it did not seem to me that a human being inhabited that desolate looking Island, though my Husband told me that around a point of land, ahead of us, that made out into the Sea and that we was making for, was the harbor. When we got around that, we were close in to the harbor, and it seemed that the natives had seen the boat put off from the Ship. On the top of some of those highest peaks where it would make one dizzy to look almost, were some of them. We could hear them whistle distinctly. In the harbor were 2 Schooners, besides a number of little boats putting out to meet us. One of them the Health Officer. He was dressed quite neat. When they came up to us he hailed us, and wanted to know where we came from, where bound, the name of the Ship, and whether we were all well on board. My Husband told him that we was, and answered all the other questions, and gave him his papers. He could talk pretty good English. It was quite a little place when we got there. We only had to step out of the boat, and go into the custom house. It was quite close to the water. Quite a number of the natives were on the beach. They all gazed at us, as if they did not often see aney white people. I suppose that Ships do not often put into that Island unless it is occationaly that a Whale Ship puts in there for the reason that we did; to get hogs and fowls. Whilst my Husband was doing some business, they took me to the Consul's house to sit, where there were very good accomodations. There was a Schooner going to start the next morning with letters, so I sat down to finish some letters I had commenced writing home. While I sat there my Husband came in and told me that he could not get through with his business and get back to the Ship, as it was getting night. They told him that there was very good accomodations up in the City; and where could that be, thought I. Why, they said it was on top of the mountain, on top of what looked to me an inaccessible mountain; but they told us they would provide us with Jackasses to ride on, and that they never would fall, as they were so very sure footed. Now I had heard that they were the most sure footed animal that there is, and partly by the novelty of the thing, and by repeated assureances from my Husband and the Men that nothing would happen [I consented]. I was to have a side-saddle for my animal and a Man to lead him. That took off a good deal of the fear. In a few moments we were ready and started up that rugged path. Quite a number accompanyed us up to the City, that it seemed lived up there and came down to their business every day. It was 3 miles up there and as bad as it was, they told us that they could go up and back on a Jackass, in an hour. The Governor of the Island went up with us, at whose house we stopped that night. Some of the way I could hardly refrain from screaming, for it seemed to me that the poor faithful animal must fall, some places where he would have to leap down quite a ways; some places where it was so steep, I would lean forward, and hold on hard for fear of falling. My Husband was close behind, and I would look at him once in a while and laugh in spite of my fear, for he looked so comical on that little Jackass and he so tall, with his long legs come-ing most to the ground. The Governor was on a little pony. He went up that steep hill as careful as the other animals. Quite a number of the natives, Men, Women, and Children, followed us up, the most of them on foot. We met a number comeing down. They would stop and look at us till we were quite by, and laugh and talk as fast in their language, which is Portuguese. I suppose we looked as strange to them as they did to us, dressed so different as we were. They had no bonnets on, but instead had handkerchiefs put on in the form of a turban. The young Women wear very gay ones. They go barefooted all, with a few exceptions and those seem to be the first People, for I see that there is quite a distinction among them. Some of them dress quite smart, while some quite mean, hardly enough to cover them. The Men dress a good deal as they do at home, but the Women nothing like us; they wear very little cloth-ing, just a skirt and a long scarf thrown over their shoulders, pinned behind and hanging down. When they put up their arms you plainly see their chemises, so they have no waist to their dresses.

Some of them had no scarf at all on. They weave their own cloth which is by hand, and the color is principaly indigo blue. The indigo is raised on the Island. Some of their scarfs are quite pretty being clouded, blue and white. That was a strange, romantic path up that mountain; it wound around among hills, as if it was done by nature, for we went over a good deal of ground to go a little ways. In some places we would go around a hill [so] that everything would be hid from view; then suddenly come out to the very edge of the precipice, where it seemed that one misstep of the animal would dash you headlong to the foot. Then it appears to me that those natives must have picked out the path most easy of ascending, for with the exception of now and then a little level place of dirt, the whole distance was paved with cobling stones, set in such a way that it must have broken the steepness a good deal and rendered the traveling a good deal easier for Man and beast. I think the natives must have had tough feet to go up and down on those stones. A good deal of the way, on each side of the path, was planted the castor oil bean, which grown in great abundance on the Island. It is quite a high bush and makes a nice shade going up and down that mountain, for the hot suns of their climate are extreme. All among those hills, up the steep sides could be seen patches of corn, showing that they tryed to cultivate even that rough place. Some of it looked very well, too. We finally reached the top of the mountain, and lo and behold there was the City nestled away among those hills, and it was quite a place, too. The houses, a good many of them, were quite neat, all of them low, being but one story, all built of the native stone. I must say it was pleasant up there and presented quite a picturous view. The Orange, Lemon, Banana, and 2 or 3 other kinds of fruit were growing quite plentiful and were then getting ripe and the trees looked beutiful loaded with fruit. Their gardens were under a high state of cultivation; there sweet potatoes were looking nicely. They [raise] some beans, and with the exception of corn they raise no other grain, so that bread is a luxury to them. When Ships come there, they will give almost aneything for flour or hard bread. Arrived at the Governor's house, we found that he had much the nicest house, his being a story and a half high and plastered outside. [There was] a nice yard paved with stone, a piazza to the house, and seats so that one could sit there and get the cool air in the evening, for it is quite warm there. We had not much time to look around for it was most night, we had supper very soon after we arrived there. It was all strange to me; the rooms were large and airy and well furnished but with a different style of furniture from what we have. The supper consisted of soup, beans, peas, rice, and some very hard black bread; they had no tea, but they raise grapes and make their own wine. They also raise coffee. I cannot say that I relished the supper; the victuals were not seasoned to my liking. I have not spoken of the Governor's family. He had no Children at home, and his Wife was away on a visit to one of the neighboring Islands. He had a niece with him, and a little Child; he told us that one of his Daughters had died and left that child quite young. It could not then go along. It was quite pretty, as white as aney Baby. I could not talk with the Niece; she could not speak a word of English. But the Governor could talk quite well. We walked out after tea a little ways. There are some beutiful flowers growing there; roses, dahlias, and a variety of kinds; one kind that looks exactly like our oleander. I had a nice boquet given me. I have pressed some. We returned to the house quite tired with our day's adventure. The Niece showed us to our room, which was large and well furnished. The bed was very neat, the toilet table well set off with a china bowl and pitcher, brushes and combs, cologne, hair oil; and everything about the room showed a good deal of taste in the owner. My Husband sat down to write home, while I sought the pillow, tired enough.

October 13th. I got up in the morning feeling that I was in a strange place, one that I never was in before and probably never would be again. The birds were singing beautifully. In the night the crickets made me think of home and I could almost have imagined myself [there], had it not been for the braying of the Jackasses. But to return to my story. The people seemed to be stirring, so we walked out into the piazza and sat down. Very soon the Governor and his Niece came out, shook hands with us, and sat down to talk. In a few minutes a servant came in, bringing a tray with some tea and crackers. I wondered what was comeing next, but that was our breakfast. The Jackasses were got ready; the same one and the same Man to lead him was got ready for me. We took leave of the Niece and Brava City, the Governor accompaneying us down the mountain. Quite a number joined us on the way, the Women carrying kegs and calabashes of water on their heads, where they carry all their loads, I see. They fetch their water some ways it seems, and it is poor. I had reckoned on some good water, we have such awful water on board the Ship, and I thought such a mountainous place would have beautiful water; but I was disapointed. It was more frightful going down that mountain than it was going up; it was so steep it would make one dizzy to look down and see the awful height we had been up the night before. We could see the harbor below, the Ship standing in to the harbor, for she had a fair wind, and she looked beautiful. It was quite warm, but the sun was in a cloud the most of the time till we got down to the foot. We arrived safe and sound to the Consul's house, after being frightened a good deal. One of the boats had already got there to take back to the Ship whatever was to carry. I seated myself in the arm chair, while my Husband was doing his business at the custom house with the Natives. I was quite amused while there, which was some time, to see the different faces that came in there to get a peep at me. I was quite a curiosity to them. The house stood on the corner of a street, with a door opening on each side, so that every one that came down the mountain could not help seeing me from one door or the other. It seemed to me that every Man, Woman, and Child came down that morning, but I know that there did not a begining of them, for they told me that there were 7000 people on that Island. I should think that those that did come down most all of them brought something with them, thinking they might exchange with my Husband for something. Some of the Women more forward than the rest would venture in and shake hands with me, while a good maney would onley come to the door and look in at me. I had all the fruit I wanted that day, that they would bring me; but we could not talk with one another. There was one Woman that could talk very good English and we had quite a chat together. It made fun for me, for she would tell me what they would say about me, all kinds of remarks. They seemed to feel bad that they could not talk with me, but it was fun for me to see them. If I could have had one of my own folks to talk with, I should have liked it. They would talk as fast in their language and laugh as hearty, I felt like some image set up for them to look at. I did not wonder that I was an object of curiosity to them, for the Woman that talked with me said that there had been but one white woman on the Island [in] she did not know how many years. We finally left to go back to the Ship and such a crowd followed us down to the little boat, I thought they never would let my Husband off. This one wanted something and that one. My Husband had given some of them a little tobacco, so they kept begging. They are great for begging. But the boat was pushed off after a while. We left them shouting after us. There was a good breeze, and we soon reached the Ship with our load, for we had a load. We had 6 Natives that shipped to go to Sea with us, besides the Men that came in the boat, with my Husband and myself. Then we had some fruit besides other things too numerous to mention. My Husband bought a goat so I shall have some milk in my tea and coffee. The things were all got on board, we had supper, and thus ended that day, leaving Brava far behind.

October 14th. It is quite pleasant today and a fair wind. There are more hogs and hens on deck now than I wish there were. The goat and her little kid I like quite well, but I can't say the same of those black, wolfish looking hogs. We had some bananas fryed for breakfast. The Men liked them; I could not say that I did. I am not fond of them aneyway. I suppose the next land we make will be the group of Islands called Tristan da Cunha; but that will not be for a month or so.

October 20th.   Fair wind today.   There have been 6 sails in sight today; we were quite near 2 of them, so that we could see the Men on deck quite plain through the glass.   One, a large clipper Ship we could see without the glass; the Men, the Captain, also his Wife. She was looking at me, I imagine, anxious with me to see a Woman; she had the glass up to her eyes, I could see. We could almost make out her name, but not quite.

October 21st.   Fair wind. We shall soon be on the line. I shan't be sorry when we get where it is cooler for I can't endure this warm weather. A Schooner, a Brig, and a Ship in sight today.

October 23rd.   Quite a strong breeze today. Two Ships in sight not far off. Nothing new, unless it is that a hen flew over board and sailed off. It was my favorite, too.

October 30th.   Fair wind; getting some cooler. A Sail seen from mast head. Saw a great quantity of porpoises around the Ship this morning. That seems to be great fun for the Men, trying to catch them, which is not easy they are so spry; did not take aney. It is sport to see them throw themselves out of the water. They look hansome in the water; more so than they do out, I think. They are quite large. The Men eat them in cold climates but they don't think they are good here.

October 31st.   It is fair wind today. It is Sunday; all is quiet as usual. Saw some fish today, called Jumpers. They spout something like a whale, and once in a while they will throw themselves quite out of the water. I was sorry that they were not nearer that I might see how they looked. We see a plenty of little flying fish about here. They look hansome darting up out of the water, skimming along its surface, and then dieving under again.

November 1st.   A good breeze today. Saw a good maney porpoises this morning; caught one large one. They give the meat to the Hogs and hens. 2 Ships in sight; one we thought was bound to the States. We were in hopes she might come near enough to go on board, to send a letter home; but she kept off. The cry from aloft this afternoon of some spout on the lee bow. Then of course the Men were some excited. My Husband and the first Mate took the glasses and went aloft to ascertain what it was. They staid up there a good while without finding out, as it went down and they did not see it again. They came down [and] had not more than got down when the cry was "There blows." This time they felt sure it was a sperm whale. It went down again and staid 55 minutes. The Men were all anxious for it to come up, for it was getting night. At last it came up. Then there was running this way and that; 3 boats were lowered and away they went in pursuit of the whale, but it was soon sundown. Tea was waiting, but no one thought of tea then. The whale was all they wanted and they had made up their minds that it was a big one. The whale was an old fellow, I guess, for he seemed too cunning for them. He went very fast. It was getting dark, so they gave up the pursuit and returned to the Ship. They were all disappointed enough.

November 3rd. A splendid morning and fair wind; a Ship and Brig in sight. The Brig is quite near. The Island of Trinidad in sight; it is quite a small Island. It is laid down on the chart no bigger than a head of a pin. It looks to me like a barren place enough. My Husband tells me that it has once been inhabited, but is now deserted. The sun did look beautiful setting on the water tonight.

November 4th. It was very calm this morning; the water was just as smooth as glass. I have not seen it so smooth since we came out. The Island still in sight; there has been no wind to take us away from it.

November 8th. It has cleared off and is a splendid morning; 'tis quite calm. The welcome cry of "There blows" came from aloft before breakfast this morning; then all was bustle. As usual, at such times, my Husband went aloft with the glass to find out what they were. He thought they were sperm whales, but they were a good ways off and soon went down. Staid down a good while and we had breakfast in the time, keeping a Man to masthead, which they always do through the day. They change every [?] but there is one there all the daylight, to look out for whales. We had but just done breakfast when the cry was repeated. Now there was no mistake; they were sperm whales and two or three of them. Two boats were lowered and pulled lustily for them. The movements of the boats were watched from the Ship with great interest. We had to wait with patience some time; the whales were shy and went very fast through the water. Some of the time they went a good ways off. It also takes a good while to wait for them to come up after they go down. Then they come up in quite a different place. On board the Ship, they place signals to mast head in different places, and different shaped ones, made from blue and white cloth, to let those in the boats know in what direction the whales are and whether they are up or down, as it is difficult sometimes for the Men in the boats to tell, they are so low on the water and the whales change their position so often.

The Mate's boat seemed the most likely to get one; the other boat returned to the Ship. The Mate finally got fast to one. My Husband sent two boats to him to help him tow the whale to the Ship. As he was some ways off and there was no breeze to help him, it was long after dinner before they came alongside. It looked queer to me to see those three little boats, attached together with ropes, towing the whale along. Everything was in readiness on board, to make the whale fast before they got here. I went to the side of the Ship to see him after they had made him secure. It looked like a monster to me. They think he will make 40 bbls. of oil.

The sperm whale is not near as large as the right whale. They seldom yield over 80 and sometimes 100 bbls; the other kind, often 200. I could form a better idea of the whale by this than I could the one I saw before, for I was not half well then and did not view it as much as I did this one.

The Men cut this in right away; to have a good chance to see them and be out of the way at the same time, I got into my Husband's boat where I had a good view of all that was going on.

[Whales] are about a mouse color, with white spots on the belly. There are ridges all over the back, which I should think must be from age, as I did not notice any on the calf that we took before. I call them wrinkles. There were a great many marks on the back, caused, my Husband said, from fighting. They are a much hansomer fish than I had an idea they were. The flukes, or tail, and the fins are quite handsome. The jaw of a big one is frightful; their great mouth looks as if it might take in some large body. My Husband tells me that he has seen them when in the agonies of death, eject from their stomachs pieces of their food as large as a barrel. It seems that Nature has adapted a particular kind of food for each specie of whale and they frequent those parts of the Sea where their food abounds. The sperm whale eats what they call squid. It is supposed to be a living fish of some kind, and very large for there are often seen large pieces of it floating. The squid is supposed to be attracted by white objects, hence the reason the whale lies on the water still, and the squid comes darting along with great velocity, making straight for the mouth. In that way I think their food comes to them.

It must be quite an art, as well as a good deal of work to cut in the whale. He is all the time lying on the surface of the water as they work at him. He is made secure in the position they want him, at first, lying close alongside of the Ship. A Man goes right down on his back, and hooks a large stout hook into a rope that is made fast to his jaw. This is made fast up aloft by means of ropes and tackles. They have two stagings let down at the side of the Ship. The Men go down and stand on these, with their long spades, and cut. They seem to know exactly where to cut. They begin to cut a great strip. The hook is put through a hole that is cut in the end of this piece by the boarding knife. Then it is drawn up by the tackle as they cut. They do not stop till the piece goes clear around. Then it comes clear up and is let down into the blubber room where it is afterwards cut in pieces suitable for the mincing machine. They keep cutting in that way till it is all off; even the flukes and fins have a good deal of fat on them. The head they cut off and take on board in the same way that the rest is. It was singular to me to see how well they could part the head from the body and find the joint so nicely. When it came on deck, it was such a large head, it swung against the side of the Ship till it seemed to me to shake with the weight of it.

It was all done and I was glad for the Men, for it seemed to me that they must be very tired, and such a bad place for them to work. It made me tremble to see them stand there on that narrow staging, with a rope passed around their bodies and made fast to the Ship to keep them from going over, while they leaned forward to cut. Every Man was at work, from the foremast hand to the Captain. The sharks were around the Ship and I saw one fellow, more bold than the rest, I suppose, venture almost to the whale to get a bite. The huge carcass floated away, and they had it all to themselves.

November 9th. A fine morning, with a gentle breeze. My Husband has kept the Ship off through the night, thinking there might be a school of sperm whales about here, and it happened quite lucky that he did, for about 9 o'clock there was a cry of sperm whales. Three boats lowered for them, did not succeed in taking any before noon, but kept track of them. After dinner the third Mate lowered his boat, for about that time there was a great number seen in another direction. There were 4 boats off chasing those whales. I watched them through the glass all the afternoon. Some of the time I could not see the boats with the naked eye. Those that had sails up I could see distinctly, but when they get fast to the whale, they take the sail down and row. We knew from that that two of the boats were fast. Though they were a good way off, we could tell when the iron was thrown, for the whale spouted blood and we could see it plain. In a short time they seemed to be all around them. We could see them spouting all around. I should think there were more than a hundred. It was quite an exciting scene to me and mixed with a good deal of fear for the safety of those Men. It seemed to me that they were under the boats and every plunge would dash them in pieces. The Men on the Ship seemed to enjoy the fun, for they would shout and laugh; every time the whale spouted near the boat, they thought they were fast to one, and indeed it was difficult to tell when they did get fast, the whales were so thick around spouting and they were so far off. When they do get fast to one, if it doesn't die immediately, it takes the boat along with great rapidity.

Presently the first Mate came alongside with one, a cow whale. They are not as large as the males. This one, the Mate told me, had a very small calf. I must say I was sorry to hear it. The poor little thing could not keep up with the rest, the mother would not leave it and lost her life. He says they exhibit the most affection for their young of any dumb animal he ever saw. This one had a number of scars from fighting.

The boat had quite a hole stove in it near the top, by the whale. It did not render her unmanageable. It knocked the iron out of its place, and the Mate had to dodge the blow. The iron that holds the oar, I think it was. There were two boats away then, and it was fast getting night, but in a short time my Husband's returned. They had also taken one. They were made fast to the Ship, and two boats sent to the assistance of the other two that were now so far off that I could not see them. It was getting quite duskish, too. One of them, the Men knew, had got a whale, but the other one they did not know anything about. It got dark and they had no lanterns in their boats. The Men built a fire on the try works, of bits of tarred rope and scraps, which made a nice blaze. They also hung lanterns in the rigging. They holloaed to them and got the horn and blew. My Husband told me that he was not alarmed about them, for it was calm and they could keep track of the Ship, as she would not go out of the way. If they did not come till morning, they would be all right. All anxiety was at an end in a short time, by the little boats answering to the call of the Ship. Soon they came back, all of them, and the two that were away had each of them a large whale. I was glad when they came, for I was fearful of their safety, and the quiet of the Ship, before, with the fire and the occasional holloaing and blowing of the horn, made it appear an awful, solemn time to me, not being acquainted with such scenes.

My Husband tells me that I will see worse times than these before I go home; but this time is over, the 4 whales are made fast till morning, the Men are all highly pleased with their day's work and are now ready for their supper, hungry and tired enough, I think. These whales were taken in Latitude 22, 30 South and Longitude 25 West.

November 10th.   A fine morning, with a gentle breeze. All hands were up very early and at work, some trying the one that was first taken, for they had five to try out in all, and a good many were cutting in. The weather began to look squally, and before they had got half through, the wind blew a gale and the rain came down in torrents. This greatly retarded their work. I thought it was impossible for them to work at all with the waves dashing up against the Ship and those huge monsters moving up and down in the water, sometimes so covered that you could scarcely see them. But they worked on and did not cease. There was a complete din of noises on deck — the wind, the rain, the Officers shouting to the Men, the mincing machine, and altogether it was a confused place. One of the stagings gave way and pitched the first Mate into the water, but he did not seem to mind that, for he was up and to work again, wet as he was; in fact they were all as wet as they could well be. I have not seen much of their work today, it has been such a bad day. It cleared away before night and made it better for them. When I went on deck they were cutting in the last whale. There were three large heads on deck and they were about hoisting the last one on. I was glad for the Men when they got through. Such quantities of blubber as they have got in the room [besides] all the heads. I don't see when they will get it all into oil.

The Men worked away at them till night and all night too. They don't stop cutting or trying as long as they have a bit of blubber on the Ship; they never let the fire go out till they are through. One set of Men is relieved every two hours by a new set.

November 11th. A fine morning and good breeze. The Men are still at work on the heads. There is a great deal of work about and the Ship is the dirtiest place that I ever saw when they are cutting in and trying out whales, especially when there is the fat of five on board. The old mincing machine is going yet, and the great fires from the furnaces, fed by the scraps, constantly blazing.

In the afternoon the Mate came to me and wanted me to go with him and take a look down in the reception room, as he termed it. I went, and I could not refrain from laughter, such a comical sight! There the Men were at work up to their waists in blubber. The warm weather had tried out the oil a good deal and made it soft. I don't see how they could stand in among it, but they were laughing and having a good deal of fun. I had heard the Men tell about the blubber room, but I had not had the pleasure of seeing it before. They do not often have it like that; seldom have they as much blubber together in warm weather. When it is cold it does not get soft like that. The smell of the oil is quite offensive to me. They are not nearly through yet but the heads are all done. They yield a sight of oil, they do not know yet how much. The Men saved the jawbones — I suppose they intend to make something fancy from them when there is leisure. They only save the bone out of the head. It is white out of the sperm whale and black out of the other kinds.

There are Ships in sight.

November 12th. Fair wind and pleasant. On account of the work on board they have not had out much sail, so we do not go along fast. The work is progressing as far as possible. The Men think they will get through and cleaned up by tomorrow night, ready for Sunday. They are as busy as bees, some at one thing and some at another; one man almost all the time grinding spades, ever since they began to cut in the whales; some are tending the machine and as the pieces come through putting them into the try pots. One Man has a large long handled skimmer, that he skims off the scraps [with], and then he puts them into a large tub that all the time looks full though they feed them on the fire when they want them; as the pots get full they bail it off into a cooler and when it is cold, they put it into casks.

November 13th. Quite pleasant with a gentle breeze. All hands hard at work this morning; this afternoon they had a general time cleaning up. They had to use a good deal of sand to scrub and plenty of water to wash off the decks, and then I think all the grease wont come out the first time, but the deck is yellow pine and it will not soak in so bad. There are a great many casks on deck.

November 14th. This is the Sabbath day, and I think that all hands have reason to be thankful that it is and a day of rest. Though denied those great privileges that our Friends at home are enjoying today, we can enjoy quiet here and can read the Bible without being disturbed, which is a great privilege. There is no noise or confusion here today.

November 15th. It is pleasant with a fair wind today. A Ship in sight. The men are all busy as they are every day. The Cooper is driving the hoops onto the casks; they are new and shrink and have to be attended to or they will leak. They have about one hundred and fifty bbls. of sperm oil, and all hands feel pleased. They think they have been quite lucky.

November 16th. Pleasant with a good breeze. The Men are stowing away the oil below. Some are getting their boats in trim, repairing the damaged one and grinding their irons and lances ready to take more whales when they are lucky enough to see them.

November 19th. It is quite an unpleasant, uncomfortable day. It is cloudy and the air is raw and cold. It rained powerfully in the night, so that the decks are very wet. While I am writing there is a cry from aloft of "There blows." It seemed that there were right whales close by or but a short distance off. Three boats were lowered in a short time, and off in pursuit. I can hear all that is going on on deck from where I sit writing. Now that the confusion is over, I think that I will go on deck a few minutes and see them. I have been on deck and I could plainly see the whales spout, not a great way off. It is quite rugged and those little light boats danced over the waves like feathers, with their sails set, but the whales, it seemed, were too swift for them, for they were running away at a great rate. I did not stay up there long, for the wind was quite chilly. Since I came down, the boats have returned to the Ship and given up the chase.

November 20th.   It is quite a pleasant morning, but rugged. Right away after breakfast, the cry of "Land!" was heard from aloft. In a short time the Island called Inaccessible was full in view. That is rightly named, for it is a desolate place with no inhabitants. Before noon, Tristan da Cunha was in sight. There is one other I can see in the distance. There are four in the group; the largest one, and the only one that is inhabited, is Tristan da Cunha. It is quite level down to the water — for some way, it looks to be. We are quite near it. I can see the houses and the cattle grazing but not a tree is to be seen. The grass looks beautiful and green. I can count twenty houses. My Husband tell me that all the inhabitants live right there on the flat. He is going ashore, if he can, to get some potatoes and milk. They catch beautiful fish there and two boats have just gone after some. My Husband's boat has gone now.

It seems to me that it gets more rugged. The waves roll high and the Ship pitches a good deal. I am watching the boat. I have fears for them though they laugh at my timidity. The little light boat doesn't seem to touch the water at all when she goes over those gigantic waves.

The Steward and the Cabin Boy are having some sport trying to catch the birds with a hook and line. They use pork for bait. It draws the birds all around the Ship. They have several times taken a bit of the bait; but now one is caught. The Steward has drawn him up and given him to me. He is a beauty and is what they call a Cape Horn Pigeon. He is about the size of a duck, shaped something — the bill and all — like them. He is pure white on the breast and under the wings, with beautiful brown spots on the back and wings. We kept him a spell and let him go.

My Husband has returned. He could not get ashore on account of the breakers. He saw some of the Men on the beach and some beautiful dogs with them. They went away without bait and could not fish.

There is a squall coming. My Husband has set the signal to have the other boats come. It began to rain just before they got here, but did not get bad. They got a nice lot of fish in what little time they were gone, of different kinds; about 150 in all. There were three or four crawfish, a good deal like a lobster. We had a nice lot for supper and I think I never tasted any fish so good as those were. Now the Ship is going along through the water at a great rate. The Island will soon be far behind.

November 21st. It is the Sabbath and a very rugged one, too. Nothing but a jar of noises all day; the Sea breaking over the Ship, things rolling about on deck, and the wind whistling through the rigging. The dishes can with difficulty be kept on the table while we are eating.

November 22nd. It continues quite rugged. I don't like it at all. I can't go around like the Sailors, as I can in a smooth day. I have been on deck a few minutes, but was glad to come down again. The air is raw and cold and nothing is to be seen of importance. In about a week we shall be at the Cape of Good Hope.

INTO THE INDIAN OCEAN

November 28th. It continues rugged. A Ship in sight. She looks beautiful with her canvass all set. She has more sails than our Ship but she doesn't gain on us. We are off the Cape of Good Hope; 'tis not in sight. We are this afternoon in the Indian Ocean.

November 29th. Quite rugged; going 10 knot. The Ship has gone 220 miles in the last 24 hours. Two Ships in sight today — one that we saw yesterday. Caught a porpoise this morning. Thanksgiving, that day of all others that we take so much comfort in at home with Friends, is over now; we knew nothing about it here. It is the first one I ever spent and did not know when it took place. No-one spoke of it here except when I did. They said that they were used to it.

December 3rd. Not quite as good a breeze today. It was squally in the morning but came off quite pleasant about noon. At half past three, the welcome cry of a spout was heard from aloft, and the cry was but just made when the boats — four — were lowered. I went on deck and when I got up, there the whale was, close by the Ship. It lay there, playing about, as if all unconscious of the near danger. It was so near us that I had a fine chance of seeing all that was done. I saw them when they threw the two irons into it. Then he thrashed about in the water and took the boat along with him at a rate that I should not fancy going. I could see him as he went along, throwing first his flukes and then his head out of water, then spouting a stream of blood into the air. But still he kept on and on. I did not know where he would take them, but they did not go out of sight. I could see that the whale was getting weaker, as its motions were less frequent and fainter. It was soon dead and the two boats were not long in towing it to the Ship. The other two boats had returned before and everything was got in readiness on board the Ship to make the whale fast when it came alongside.

It is truly wonderful to me, the whole process, from the taking of the great, and truly wonderful monster of the deep till the oil is in the casks. It is curious to see them towing it to the Ship, the boats attached by a long line, the whale drifting along behind, a monster indeed, the hurry of the Men to make it fast, first getting the end of the line from the boat, the Men all pulling away at it as hard as ever they can, till it is all hauled in and made fast by large heavy chains. All is confusion till it is fast.

When it was over, I went to the side of the ship to see the whale for this is a right whale and I had not seen one before. It is quite different from the sperm whale, being a great deal larger, though this one is not more than half as large as some of them. They have been known to make over 200 bbls. This will make from 80 to 100 bbls. they think. This kind is more round and full than the sperm whale, having a very different shaped head, too. The flukes look the same to me as I can see them in the water, but the fins are a great deal thicker. They are not going to cut him in till morning when I shall have a better chance to see the monster and can give a better description. They are cutting off his lips and hoisting them aboard. I could see the inside of the mouth with the slabs of bone set in rows like teeth and covered with hair on the inside. The Albatross are around the whale as thick as they can be after the bits of blubber that they may chance to catch from cutting in. It is real fun to see them swimming about like geese and fighting for the pieces. I saw five fighting for one piece and gabbling as hard as they could. They would take great junks and swallow it down at one mouthful. The Steward caught several with a hook and line and took them on deck. They are very handsome, a good deal larger than the largest goose I ever saw. Some of them are all brown and some of them a pure white with the tips of the wings beautifully spotted with black.

December 4th. This morning the Men were up as soon as they could see to work, cutting in the whale. It has rained very hard all night and all the morning it has come down in torrents. The poor Men had a bad time, all of them wet to their skins. I went up on

deck when they were hoisting the head up. It certainly is a great
curiosity. How can I describe it? It seems to me I should want to
examine it for a week to give a correct opinion of it.

I could not stay up but a few minutes, it rained so very hard. My
Husband wanted me to walk into the whale's mouth. He pushed
me in a little ways, so I think I can say that I have been inside of a
whale's mouth. Six or eight people could easily go in and sit down
at one time. I would not hesitate about going in and sitting down
if it was clean, but it was very wet and dirty from the rain. One
cannot imagine without seeing it, how the mouth looks. Those long
slabs of bone, set as thick together in the jaw as they can be — two
rows of them — are like two rows of teeth though nothing like them
in looks. I should say that the longest of these slabs was about six
feet, but they tell me it is not at all uncommon to see them 15 or 20
feet long. These grow gradually shorter all the way from the back
of the head to the entrance of the mouth, being quite short there
— not more than two or three inches — and the hair very thick and
white. All the rest, the whole length of the slabs, have hair on the
edge, making the whole of the mouth lined with hair. It is black,
the color of the bone, only that close to the roof or where the bone
sets into the jaw. I could not imagine for what purpose this hair
was, till my Husband explained to me. It seems that their food
floats in masses, literally covering the water in spots. It is a fine substance, about as big as mustard seed, and surrounded by a gluey
substance. This food floats on the top of the water. The whale
moves along with his mouth open and draws in large quantities of
it and it is strained through this hair. It seems singular that such
fine food should have been formed for so large a fish. These fish
are truly one of the wonderful works of God and well may we think
that everything in the deep is wonderful.

It cleared off fine about eleven o'clock so I could sit up on deck
a spell and see them when they took out the bone from the jaw. It
was really curious to see it when there was nothing but the jaw
and slabs. The Men had taken all the flesh and blubber away and
were cutting around what I should call the gums, with axes; then
they jerked it by the ends till it came out by the roots. They would

take out three slabs at a time, the largest I should think was a quarter of a yard wide where it was set in the jaw. The outside edge is a good deal thicker than the inside where the hair is — that being quite keen. The slabs seem to graduate in size, in length and in width, tapering off at the ends, almost sharp. The jaw is somewhat curved in shape, so the mouth is shaped something like an arch. We can conceive something of the size of the mouth when the tongue, though it fills that large cavity, will make eight bbls. of oil. That is what they think this one will make.

I expect I have not given a very accurate description of the right whale, but perhaps I may tell more about it when I see another. The men are now cutting up the blubber, and getting ready to try it out. These whales were taken in Lat. 40,30 — Lon. 36,29.

December 5th. It is a pleasant day with a good breeze. The Men did not quite finish the oil yesterday, so they will have to finish it today, though it is the Sabbath. It doesn't seem like it to me, but all, except the work, is as quiet and orderly as it can be. It is quite repugnant to my feelings, but I know that it is necessary to do it, or it will spoil, and I well know that they can't afford to lose it as it is so hard to get a cargo of oil.

Those Friends that are this day enjoying all the great and blessed privileges of the Sabbath on the land, little know the privations and sufferings of the Sailors' life — not only being deprived of Society and Friends, they suffer the hardships of heat, cold and wet, besides the great dangers they encounter which make the Sailors' life a hard one.

December 6th. It is a very fine day, with a good breeze. The oil is all in casks now. It is not far from 100 bbls. All hands seem to be much pleased with the good success they have had so far, and are now ready to see another whale. It seems dull on board, now the excitement is all over. One sail seen this morning from aloft.

December 13th. It is very unpleasant today. The sky is clouded over thick, and the wind is blowing a gale. We shall reach the Island of St. Paul's by the day after tomorrow. It is a desolate Island, I am told. There is but one family on it. A French family that makes a business of packing fish which are caught there in great quantities, and very nice kinds. The Men are making great reckon on going there to catch some if it is not too rugged.

December 15th. It remains rugged. Has been quite so all night. The Ship going 10 knot, passed the Island of St. Paul's in the night. The Men feel disappointed about their not having their good time afishing. We spoke a Brig this morning. Her name was Test. She was an English Brig. It is the only time we have spoken a Ship since we left home. She is bound to Sidney, Australia.

December 20th. It was pleasant this morning, with a good breeze, and before I was up, the cry of whales was given from aloft. They proved to be Sperm whales, two of them, and the boats were lowered for them but did not succeed in taking one. They returned and had just seated themselves at the breakfast table, when the cry of whales was again given, and this time there seemed to be a good many of them. The boats were lowered again; not one minute more did the Officers stop to eat, but were off. It was not long before my Husband was fast to one. It seemed to me every minute as if his boat would be stove. The whale took them along at a great rate, and I thought that I had never seen one act so bad in the water as that one did. After a while I could see that it stopped and spouted blood very fast. The water was red with blood for some ways. While I was looking at them through the glass, one of the other boats got fast to a whale. They were a good way off. It was not long before my Husband came on board. He had taken a large one. He thought it would make about 70 bbls. He looks like a monster, sure enough, as he lies alongside. There are deep lines or furrows all over his back, as if he was an old customer. He is the largest one that I have ever seen of the sperm kind.

Now the First Mate has returned. He struck a whale and it capsized his boat. The Men and everything were in the water, but the courageous Men righted the boat and took the same whale. They were so much disabled that the Second Mate took it to the Ship. It is a very large one. The Men say it is larger than the other. They are all highly elated with their morning's fortune and are now preparing to cut them in. One of the Men caught a porpoise this morning. That seems to be great fun for them. All hands are very fond of the meat also. I cannot say that I am.

December 21st. It is quite pleasant today, but very bad for the Men to cut in the whales. They did not finish cutting one yesterday. It was quite rugged by the time the Men got ready to work on them, and they had to leave them or they would have lost a good deal. It has not been much better today. There has been only a little wind, but a heavy swell which kept the Ship rolling very heavily. That almost prevented the work going on.

It is now almost sundown and they are not quite done. They have had a tedious time, but will save all the blubber. The monstrous heads that were hoisted on deck are enough to astonish one, and they are not the entire heads, for the immense jaws were taken up separately. The Men think the heads alone will make 30 bbls. of oil each. Some part of the staging gave way today, and Mr. Morgan, the First Mate, and the Cooper were precipitated into the water. It appears that the Cooper ran a very narrow chance of being drowned. In falling, he struck the whale, which hurt his head some and stunned him a little, so that he had not command of himself and he went partly under the whale. His clothes got full of water and his boots, which were thick rubber, made him clumsy so that he could not help himself and had to be helped on board. The Mate got along himself quite well. I felt sorry for the poor Men, to see them work so hard and have such a bad time to work. They can't all cut to advantage; some few are on the staging at work — those that understand it — while a good many are cutting the blubber into pieces suitable for the machine; some are trying it out.

December 22nd. Another busy day. Did not finish cutting in last night, but have finished now and will soon have done trying out. The real spermacetti is in casks on deck. It looks beautiful — as

white, clear and transparent, as can be. That is what they boil out
of the case, one part of the head. These two were very fat whales.

I went up on deck to look at the heads after they had been hoisted
up. I thought that I could give a better description than of the others. I think that I have spoken of the spout before, but did not understand quite where it was. It is on the extreme end of the head of
the Sperm whale, and rises in a bushy form, but the Right whale's
spout is about 15 feet farther back and throws the water higher, and
in the form of two curves. One of the heads had quite a number of
white spots on it, varying in size, from very small ones to some as
large as the palm of my hand. I have a piece of skin taken off from
one of those white spots. It is quite thin and transparent and yet
very tough. It can all be peeled off in the same way, but is a mouse
color, with the exception of these white spots.

December 24th. We have a nice breeze today and are going right
along. The Men finish the oil tonight. I think they will not be
sorry. There is a good deal of hard work about it, from beginning
to end, but they don't seem to mind it much. As soon as it is over,
they are impatient to take more. I never saw Men so elated with
their prospects as these are. There is nothing else talked about; in
fact, there is not much else to talk about on board a Whale Ship.
Some are betting on how much oil these will make and wishing for
more before they get to New Zealand. They took these two in Lat.
41,10, So. Lon. 96,00, East.

December 26th. The Sabbath has once more come around. All is
quiet again on board. It really is pleasant to have it so after so
much confusion as has been the last week — the constant noise of
heavy chains on deck; the driving of the hoops; the turning over of
the casks of oil till it seemed as if the Ship shook; and the loud orders of the Officers — all together, would make a nervous Person go
distracted, I think, but it cannot be avoided on board a whale Ship.
Oil is what they came after and there is a great deal of hard work
and noise, attending it.

December 27th. It is not as rugged as yesterday, but a good breeze. We are off New Holland today, though we cannot see the place. The next place will be South Australia.

December 31st. Not as rugged as it has been. Unpleasant and foggy. There appear some signs of fish today. There are a good many Sperm Whale Birds about, and a peculiar smell about the air, which indicates that we are in the vicinity of Whales.

January 1st, 1859

It was quite foggy this morning. It has been very rainy the rest of the day, till towards sundown it cleared away. About this time there was seen not far off a large flock of birds that appeared to have been attracted there by some object. The Men thought that some Ship had taken a Whale not far off and the birds were around the carcass, but we had not seen any.

January 2nd. Today is the first Sabbath of the new year, and it has been a beautiful day and a very quiet one.

January 4th. Van Diemens Land [Tasmania] was seen from aloft about 7 o'clock this morning. About 10 o'clock I went on deck and could see it quite plainly. It must be a large island. There seems to be a good deal of land and some very bold looking rocks out from the main Island. We were about 10 miles from those. The breakers were dashing against them, fearfully to behold. We could see the white foam go quite over the top of one of the very high ones. It looked grand, but I thought that we were full as near as I should like to be.

We were not near enough to the Island to see anything but the bare hills.

It has been a splendid day, quite mild, and I have been on the house to sit a spell with my Husband, viewing the land through the glass. Then I came down and spent some time watching Mr. Morgan fishing over the stern of the Ship. He caught one with the hook

and line. He called it a Baracooter. It was a very handsome fish,
long and slim.

It is now about a month since I have written any in my Journal and
many things have transpired since then.

The 10th of January we had a gale of wind that lasted till the
12th, the heaviest gale we have had since we left home. On the 11th,
the fore sail was carried away. We spoke the Whale Ship Rodman,
Capt. Babcock, on the 11th, bound home. Did not exchange many
words, it was blowing so hard. They had Pigeons on board and four
of them flew on board of us. They are very pretty and my Husband
has had a nice house made for them. We have a fine healthy Boy,
born on the 12th, five days before we got into Port.

We arrived in the harbor of Monganua [Mangonui, at the northern end of New Zealand] on the 17th. I had to stay on board the
Ship two weeks. Captain Butler, the Harbor Master, came on board
as soon as we were in. He came below to see me, and told me that
he would send for his Wife and she very soon came on board to see
me and came every day and washed and dressed the Baby. She did
everything she could for me, till I was able to go to her house. I
had every attention paid me, both on the Ship and at Mrs. Butler's.

The Men, when they went on shore, often brought me Fruit
and Flowers, and the Captains of the Ships came on board to see me
and brought me something nice. Captain Dehart of the Ship Roman 2nd, came to see me several times, and brought me Oranges,
Lemons, several kinds of Preserved Fruits, some Arrowroot, a nice
Fan made on one of the Islands that he had stopped at, and a bottle
of currant wine.

There were eight Ships in the Harbor when we arrived. One of
the Captains — Capt. Charry, of the Ship Harvest — had his Wife
with him. She had been stopping with Capt. Butler's family ten
months. She came to see me with Mrs. Butler. She had a fine boy
born at their house.

Capt. Childs had his Wife and two Children with him. They left
the day after we arrived. Captain Dehart had left his Wife at the

Sandwich Islands. Captain Soule was in Port, of the William C. Nye. I was some acquainted with him. I had seen him and his Wife in New Bedford.

There was all kinds of work going on, on the Ship, it seemed to me, before I went on shore. They were taking on board, Potatoes, Onions, and Water from Monganua; the Cooper was setting up casks for the water; the Carpenter and Blacksmith were also at work, and all hands were busy about something.

My Husband had some trouble with two of his Men; the Blacksmith sold bread from the Ship to the Natives for honey. He did not go on shore next time that his watch went. Then he got saucy and refused to go to work, and was put in irons till he said he would go to work, which was the next day. I was glad when he had them off, but I am afraid that he is inclined to be a bad Man, for the first time my Husband gave him liberty on shore, he ran away and one more with him. The Natives caught them and brought them back. My Husband did not keep the Ship in harbor much longer after that. He went to the Bay of Islands to discharge his oil and send it home, and then came back to Monganua for me. He did not go into the harbor, so he did not lose any more Men. I stopped not quite two weeks on shore, but I enjoyed myself very much while I was there. They are a nice Family, extremely kind and affectionate, and every one of them seemed to try to see which could pay me the most attention. They have a large Family — eight Children, three of them grown up Daughters, quite accomplished and pretty Looking. They all sing, dance, and play on the piano. They are quite a lively Family and one of the young Boys plays on the violin.

The Captains meet often there, to spend the evening, and the time passes very pleasantly, in the Shipping Season, but it must be a dull place when there are no Ships in the harbor. There is nothing but the Hills to be seen. There are three houses besides Capt. Butler's, and a Store, with plenty of Native huts along the beach. The harbor is beautiful and is landlocked, so that I could hardly tell where we went in when I first came on deck. There is a point that hides even the harbor and Ships from Capt. Butler's house, so that it looks like a beautiful pond in front, and one would scarsely think it led out to the vast ocean.

The water come within three yards of the gate when the tide is in. It is a beautiful spot where their house stands. They have splendid flowers and handsome wild ones grow in profusion. There are nice trees — they have some Apples and Peaches, but they have some nicer ones on other parts of the Island. Mr. Fletcher, a neighbor of Capt. Butler's, brought me from the Bay of Islands, a basket of as nice Pears and Peaches as I ever saw. They were quite large.

Capt. Butler came to Monganua to live 19 years ago. The Natives were then in an uncivilized state. The Maoris, as they are called, were at war together, and in some parts they ate human flesh. The first house he went in after he landed, was a place where the Queen held counsel with her Subjects. She was pacing up and down the room, with her long black hair streaming over her shoulders, and talking as fast as she could. She was saying that no good had come to them since they left off eating human flesh, and they must commence again. She then raised her arm to her mouth and bit out a piece.

His interpreter communicated to him what she had said and he said it made his flesh crawl on his bones. He had a good deal of trouble with them for a long time and came near losing his life several times, but finally the Queen (she has been dead some time) and all her Subjects were great Friends to him. They now call him and his Wife their Father and Mother. I think they are extremely kind to them.

There is no Church at that place, but there are in other parts of the Island where Missionaries are stationed. Capt. Butler is his own Minister. He has Episcopal services in his house. He has Family prayers morning and night, and at every meal asks a blessing and returns thanks.

The Natives are quite dark and make themselves look homely by tattooing themselves so much. A great number of them — Men Women and Children — can be seen sitting on the beach all day in the burning sun, with nothing on their heads or feet. They are mostly indolent, but raise beautiful potatoes and onions.

I think I have said more than will interest.

I was much pleased with my visit there, but had to return to the Ship. We soon reached her, the Baby and I were hoisted on deck, and we were soon off.

SHIP *FLORIDA* BOUND TO THE JAPAN SEA

February 5th.   A beautiful day, and quite calm. The land was in sight this morning. We have not come far since we left New Zealand. It has been quite calm and I have been walking on deck a little while. Our Boy is well, and grows finely.

The Men have been busy picking over the potatoes that came from Monganua and the Mate has been trying paints to see what color to have the little boats.

We have a little dog on board. His name is Blucher. The Mate brought him from Monganua.

February 6th.   It is the Sabbath, and a beautiful day with a fine breeze. Everything is as quiet as a Sunday at home.

February 7th.   It has been a beautiful and mild day. Not much wind but a heavy swell. All hands have been at work mending sails.

My Husband has been painting his boat — blue bottom, then a narrow white stripe, then a broader black one, then a white one. It is real handsome.

February 10th.   A beautiful day with a fine breeze. Made the land this morning, called Sunday Island. I saw a Ship not quite near enough to make out her name.

Got near enough to the Island this afternoon to go on shore and my Husband with his boat's crew went. They have not yet returned. They have gone to get some chickens and cabbages.

February 13th. It is the Sabbath day, and a very gloomy one here. It is foggy and damp on deck, and dark and unpleasant below. The swell makes the Ship roll and that is not very pleasant, though I have got very well used to it now, except when I start for some place in a hurry and get there quicker than I want to. But I think I shall practice caution now for the Baby's sake.

Today is Stancel's birthday. Oh, how I wish I could see him! Words are too feeble to express the great desire of my heart to once more set eyes on those Dear Children, that Dear Home, Parents and Friends, but long and patiently have I got to wait, and as time is ever on the wing, the next three years will fly away like the past, and if God is willing, we will arrive safely at home.

February 15th. Suffocating and warm. All hands are mending old sails today and making a new lug sail for the Mate's boat. I took a few stitches on it.

February 20th. The Sabbath has come around again. A very quiet one and some of the time very unpleasant. Frequent showers. This afternoon we had one bad one, a good deal of rain with the wind. My Husband called me on deck to see a waterspout. It was a fine sight. It seemed but a short distance from the Ship. The shower had passed over us and seemed to be moving off with the spout. There was what appeared to be a cloud close to the water, causing a great commotion in the water, and there was a thin, small spire-like cloud, that went straight up to the clouds from the one in the water. It was quite singular and it soon passed away.

February 24th. It continues warm and squally. It makes it very unpleasant some of the time. The sun comes out as hot as fire, then the next we know, it rains and sometimes very heavy wind with it. One of our Pigeons flew overboard and was drowned today.

The Baby is well and healthy and sleeps a good deal. He is a very pleasant Baby. We call him William after his Grandfather Williams.

February 28th. A beautiful day and fair wind, what there is of it; extremely warm.

My Husband has been making a lug sail for his boat. Mr. Morgan had made one for his and towards night they lowered their boats to try them. My Husband's boat beat.

While they were down, spouts were seen from aloft. Immediately they took their line in and went off. The other boats lowered too in a few moments. Sperm Whales were seen all about, a large school of them. I was a long time looking at them over the Stern of the Ship. I thought I hardly ever saw a prettier sight — those five little boats with their blue and white sails on the vast water, the Whales all around them. But they did not succeed in taking any. They were running away from danger as fast as they could.

March 1st. A pleasant day, fair wind, but not much of it. It seems as if we should never get anywhere out of these warm latitudes. My Husband is most discouraged and I think all hands must be.

March 2nd. We had quite a shower this morning. It then cleared off hot enough to melt one. The wind is fair, but not enough of it to make hardly a ripple in the water.

March 3rd. A pleasant day, but very warm. A very little more wind.

The Men are all sweating away at their work; some in the rigging, some turning. The Cooper and the Blacksmith are at work, and a variety of other kinds of work are going on, as usual.

March 4th. A cry of Whales was given from aloft this morning before I was up. It proved to be a Sperm Whale, and it seemed to be the opinion that it was a large one. The Men lowered their boats, but did not succeed in taking him. He was going very fast. My Husband thought that he saw the Ship. There has not been much wind today.

March 5th. There has been a very good breeze today. It looked rather squally all the forenoon and this afternoon about three o'clock we got it in good earnest. The wind blew and the rain came down in torrents. My Husband lowered his boat today to try his Whaling gun. The gun is quite different from any other kind. They fire an iron from it into the Whale. I suppose they can fire it a good deal farther than they could throw it. I went up on deck to see my Husband fire it. He threw a keg into the water for a mark. The iron shot under the water, but I could not see how far.

March 7th. It has been not very pleasant today. Rather squally. We have had bad weather most all the time. We almost despair of ever getting to the Japan Sea in season.

March 8th. A very unpleasant day. It has been squally all day and all night. I have just been on deck picking out my pair of Whale's teeth from the lot. I very soon had to come below for an awful squall is close upon us.

March 11th. We spoke a Ship this morning before I was up — the Young Hector, from New Bedford, Capt. Hager. He is a Sperm Whaler. He has been out eighteen months and has 400 bbls. of Oil on board. He came on board of us. He seems a very nice man. Our Mate has gone to spend the day with his Mate, to have a gam as the Sailors say.

A few minutes after we spoke the Ship, land was seen from aloft. We had the Captain to take breakfast with us, and then I dressed the Baby and got him to sleep and went on deck. Ocean Island was all in sight.

It is a pretty Island to look at, quite a small one, but all covered with green trees. The most of them, I should think, are Cocoanut trees. The houses are queer looking, very low, the doorway just high enough for them to crawl in on their hands and knees. They are made mostly from the leaves and other parts of the Cocoanut tree, but they never cut them down while they bear. I did not see the Natives, except through the glass. My Husband and the Captain have gone on shore.

March 12th. A fine day and a strong breeze. The Ship rolls some — considerable today. We have left Ocean Island far behind.

We have about one hundred Chickens running about the deck, that my Husband got from the Island yesterday. We didn't get but a few Cocoanuts. They do not like to part with them. It appears that they live almost entirely on them. They are a very indolent People and do not cultivate their land any of any account. I could not learn that they raise anything except a few squashes. Their wants are few as they do not care for anything but their tobacco and pipes. They trade their Chickens to the Ships for these.

The Natives usually come off to the Ships, but they did not this time in consequence of the taboo of the King, which is practiced certain times of the year. These Natives do not wear any clothing.

March 15th. A very pleasant day and a good breeze. Passed Strong's Island today [Køusaie in the Caroline Islands].

March 16th. We are having fine weather. The wind is fair for us, a strong breeze, going over 200 miles a day.

March 18th. A very fine day and a good breeze, but very warm. I take the Baby on deck every fine day to take the air. I think he begins to understand when he is going on deck for he looks so well pleased when I am getting him ready.

March 28th. A very pleasant day, not fair wind. We do not make much headway. My Husband wanted to be in the Japan Sea by the first of April, but we shall not.

April 1st. A beautiful day. We have had company all day. Before I was up this morning, there was a Sail seen from aloft, and when I went on deck we could see her quite plainly from the deck. We looked at her through the glass a spell. She gained on us, and my Husband thought he would wait until they came up to us, to see who they were. It was the Arctic, Captain Philips. He had been to the Sandwich Islands and his Ship is half Clipper. My Husband was acquainted with him, but as to that — the Captains are all acquainted when they meet.

He came on board of us and stayed all day. Our Mate, with a boat's crew, went on board of them and stopped all day. Captain Philips is a very pleasant, agreeable Man, to all appearance. He is bound to the Japan Sea with us. I suppose he will get there first. He has gone on board of his Ship this evening. He brought us some papers from the Islands, some of them New Bedford papers, later news than any we have had since we left home. I had some nice oranges given me. He had his Wife and four Children with him the last voyage.

April 4th.   The wind has been blowing quite fresh the fore part of the day, but this afternoon it has been quite moderate and has been very pleasant while I was on deck. The Boat Steerer from aloft sang out a spout. It was not far from the Ship and could be seen quite plainly from the deck. The Men had quite an argument as to what kind of a Whale it was. They finally concluded it was what they call a Sulphur Bottom. My Husband lowered for it and fired at it with the Bomb lance gun, but did not hit it. It went down and that was the last we saw of it. It made quite a loud noise and looked large in the water.

April 7th.   The wind is blowing quite strong today. The Arctic came up with us this afternoon and came across our stern, near enough for us to speak her. Then she came alongside. She looked splendid indeed. The Captain told us that he came very near going ashore the day before, on the little Island we saw. There was a strong current setting in from the land, and it was with difficulty he kept her off.

While I was looking at the Ship, there was a Killer playing about in the water and keeping along with the Ship, all the time throwing itself out of water. It was a fine looking fish and it was sport for me to see him. They are about as large as black fish and are called the killer, because they kill the Whale such a monster as it is. It seems they worry the Whale while under water, and when he comes up to breathe, they get on him and cover up his spout hole so that he can't breathe. Then when he opens his mouth they dart in. This seems a novel way of killing, but that is the way they tell me it is done.

April 8th. A very fine day and a good breeze. We are in the Yellow Sea now, and will soon be in the Japan Sea. This is a small sea and my Husband tells me that he thinks there are soundings anywhere in it. The land is in sight, not very plainly to be seen. The Arctic is pretty near.

The Carpenter has been making a beautiful little chair for the Baby.

April 9th. A very fine day, and a good breeze. The wind blew a gale in the night. My Husband was up most all night. Such a noise there was on deck all night that I could not sleep. This afternoon we are in the Japan Sea, with a good deal of land in sight but not near enough to see how it looks. A great many Porpoises are about and a few Finback Whales. The Mate fired at one but did not hit it. There are three Ships in sight and I suppose that there are a good many more cruising about in this Sea. We spoke one this afternoon, the Jireh Perry, Capt. Cannon. He came on board and took tea with us. The Ships exchanged boat's crews, as is the custom when Ships speak one another, to have a gam, as they call it. They stayed aboard till twelve o'clock. Capt. Cannon and my Husband found enough to talk about where they had seen Whales and had been for them, and where they should go, and looking on their Charts to find the places. Capt. Cannon brought me some nice oranges, but they have gone on board their Ship now and I have nothing more to write about.

April 10th.   It is a beautiful day, and a nice little breeze, quite
enough on whaling ground. It is quite cold on deck, but we have
a fire below.

There are a great many Birds about here. The Men have been
singing out, "There blows" all the morning. There were a good
many Whales about; several Right Whales, but the most of them
Finbacks. Four boats were lowered for them, but they did not succeed in taking one. They saw the boats, I suppose, for they went
down and when they came up again, they were a good deal farther
off and going fast. The Arctic and Jireh Perry are in sight, but not
very near.

April 11th.   It has been a beautiful day with a nice breeze, but no
Whales. Capt. Cannon of the Jireh Perry was on board here last
night. He spent the evening with us and brought me a nice lot of
Cocoanuts.

April 12th.   We have had a very nice day and a good breeze.
There is a good deal of land in sight. The mountains are all covered with snow.

The water has been dotted, here and there, with little Japanese
Junks. The Men were fishing, but as soon as they saw our Ship
heading towards them, they began to hoist their sails and made off
as fast as they could. Mr. Morgan took one of them by surprise and
overtook him. They seemed to be so busy fishing that they did not
observe him, till he got close alongside of them. They appeared
frightened almost to death when they saw him. They went to the
farthest part of their boat and motioned our Men to be off. They
tried to make them understand they were friendly, but it was no
use. One of them was so frightened that he frothed at the mouth.

They had on board a dish of boiled rice and some little fish that
they had caught. Mr. Morgan made motion to the Fish and one of
them took up a little Fish and ate it right down raw. They
thought he was after the Fish, and commenced throwing them into
our boat. The Mate motioned to them that he did not want them.
They then stopped.

The Men are large, stout looking people and there was a Woman on board, who, the Mate said he should think would weight nearly two hundred. Their boats are rude looking, but strong.

The Mate brought me the strangest looking Fish I ever saw; it is light brown with black spots on it, but the most curious part is that it has four little horns, as sharp as needles, two sticking up straight on its back, and one on each side. Its back is as hard as the shell of a turtle.

April 15th. Not very pleasant. It has been hazy all day. We have a good breeze. No Whales yet.

April 16th. It has been foggy and rainy all day and the wind is blowing a gale. It is a cold rain, and all that can are glad to be around the stove.

April 17th. It has cleared off beautiful with a good breeze. Right Whales are in sight. Two boats have gone down to see if they can take any. No Ships in sight. Did not succeed. Saw them again this afternoon, but did not take any.

April 18th. It has been a fine day and a good breeze the fore part of the day. This afternoon it has been quite calm. My Husband called me on deck this forenoon, to see a Japanese Junk. It was a good deal larger than the ones we saw yesterday. It was a rude looking, flat bottomed vessel, with one mast and one sail. It had some kind of open lattice work on the sides.

We do not see Whales yet; only now and then a Ship, and a very few Birds. Ships are generally surrounded with them when Whales are around.

April 19th. A very fine, mild day and a good breeze. I went on deck right after breakfast to take the air and walk a little. The Baby was asleep. While up there the first and third Mates were talking about a Ship that was in sight and not far off. The third Mate thought it was the Splendid from Cold Spring; but the first Mate thought it was the William C. Nye, and so it proved to be — our old friend, Capt. Soule. We spoke him and he came on board and spent the day with us. We saw him in Manganua. He left the week before we did. He has not taken any oil in this Sea.

April 23rd. It is another find day and quite mild. We spoke the Abraham Barker, this afternoon. [The Captain] came on board, but did not stop long. He had but just come on board when the Man at masthead sang out "There blows!" Both Ships lowered boats but did not take any.

April 24th. A very fine day. No Ships in sight. A Junk in sight, but not very near. Lowered a boat for a Siberian Whale, but did not get him.

April 25th. It was a fine morning and the Abraham Barker was in sight about three miles off, cutting in a Whale. It seems that they have been lucky, and I am very glad of it. About 9 o'clock a thick fog came on. We have a good breeze.

April 26th. I have been on deck about an hour today with the Baby, walking. Mr. Morgan carried him for me. It has been a splendid day and quite warm. A Ship in sight. Spoke her this afternoon. She is the Cicero, Capt. Courtland, of New Bedford. He has been out 30 months and has 800 bbls. He took tea with us. He struck a Whale the other day, but did not save him.

April 28th. It has been quite foggy all the morning, but cleared off fine before noon. Right after dinner there was a Right Whale in sight. The boats were all lowered for him and the first Mate's boat got fast to him. He fired three Bomb lances into him and got near enough to him to cut him with the spade several times, besides the Boat Steerer darting two irons into him. They afterward lost him. One iron proved to be worthless and broke short off. Then the other, after holding him a spell, broke and away he went. They tried to find him again but could not. At night he was seen again and several others with him. Took in sail and hoped to see them again in the morning.

April 29th. It is quite pleasant now. No Whales in sight. They were heard through the night several times, but it was such thick fog this morning that we could not see but a very short distance from the Ship. I saw a lot of Cow fish this afternoon. They are a curious looking fish. It is real fun to see them throwing themselves out of the water. I wish that I could describe them but they are so quick in their movements, that I am afraid I cannot give a good one, if I try.

April 30th. A rainy, unpleasant morning. It has rained all night. There is a great noise on deck among the Men. There is a Finback in sight. The first Mate has just fired at him, but missed him. Saw more Whales towards night. My Husband lowered for them, but they proved to be Hump Backs. Spoke the Ship Washington, Capt. Purrington, of New Bedford. He has one thousand bbls. of Oil on board. He has been out two seasons. Took a Whale the other day that made him 120 bbls. Also spoke the Ripple, Capt. Chadwick. The Cicero was quite near at the time; her Captain was on board the Ripple.

HAKODADI

May 5th. A very pleasant day. Quite a little breeze. A plenty of land in sight. We are about 30 miles from Hakodadi [Hakodate]. It is now two o'clock and we are going there to get water. We will not get there tonight, I think. A sail in sight. There seems to be quite a town on this land, close down to the water. I can see through the glass that the brown houses look as thick as they can stand, and now and then a white one. The mountains are covered with snow, but down by the water the green grass looks beautiful.

May 6th. We arrived in the Harbor of Hakodadi last night and anchored about dark. This place is quite large. There is no great show about it — the houses are all rather small, and all with the exception of a very few are brown. This is a splendid Harbor and a large one. There are several Whale Ships and a Russian Man of War in here besides any number of Junks and two or three Schooners in which the Japanese go out after Whales.

A Japanese Pilot came aboard of us, but left to go aboard of the Roman 2nd, Capt. Dehart, that was then coming in. Capt. Tabor came aboard of us and piloted us in; he is Master of the Adeline.

A good many Japanese came aboard of us; they were all over the ship, looking at her. Finally they came to the wheel and were looking at the compass when they caught sight of the Baby and me. They looked at us a long time with a great deal of curiosity, it seemed. I am going on shore tomorrow and can tell more about the place then.

May 8th. A very nice day and quite smooth. I arose very early this morning, to have everything in readiness to go on shore.

Quite a number of the Japanese Officers came aboard early to transact Ship business with my Husband. They were dressed nicely though quite singularly, to me. Their dress is quite loose and slouching, very loose pants if they can be called such, and a kind of loose cloak with very large sleeves. Their shoes are quite odd. The big Folks wear very handsome ones ornamented with cord; the common People wear wooden ones, making a good deal of noise as they walk.

These Officers carried two sheaths in their belts and my Husband wanted to see them. They did not like to have him even touch them, but after some coaxing, they took them out. One was a sword and one a long, sharp dirk knife, very nice and bright.

They had an interpreter with them and he raised the knives to show how they used them and how the Americans used them. He said they struck with the sword and we ran it into the body — and they cut off the head with the knife, which it seems they do for a small offence.

They were highly pleased with the Baby. They crowded around him, feeling of him, and talking and laughing with him. It appears that they take their offices as soon as they are born, for little fellows that can just walk are dressed like Officers, with their swords by their sides.

Very soon after breakfast Capt. Tabor, with his Wife and two little Boys, came aboard of us. They intended to have sailed today, but decided to stop one more day with us. They are old Friends of my Husband's. We went on shore with them and spent the day there. There was a funeral procession just going to the Temple as we landed. We landed among Junks as thick as they could lie in the water, it seemed. We stepped out of the boat onto the stairs. There are several long steps where the boats land.

There was a crowd of People and we thought we would like to go and see the ceremony, so we followed right along in the procession to the Temple. Four Men were bearing the litter, a frame of some kind, on which was placed a barrel containing the Corpse. It is pressed down in a sitting posture and the barrel covered all over with white cloth and quite a fancy little house over it. When we reached the Temple, it was set down just inside of the door and the house taken off, but the cloth was not removed.

There was a railing all around the room (which was not large) forming a large space in the center and a good deal of room outside of it. There was a stand within the enclosure where stood a row of Men dressed somewhat differently from the rest, chanting or singing over something. The Priest once or twice struck a bell near him. The Doctor also was there. They were all muttering over something. On a stand near them was burning incense in a small saucer. The Japanese were sitting around the floor in the center of the room and the mourners on the floor outside of the railing, with white cloths on their heads. There was no appearance of sorrow among any of them. The Minister made a long prayer, and they all jumped up and hurried away. The Corpse was carried to the mountain, where they are burned and the ashes buried.

After the crowd had gone, we went around the room to look at the curious things they have. All one side of the room was sliding doors. One of the attendants slid one after another to show us what was in the room beyond, but would not let us go in. We could stand and look in. There were arranged on tables most beautiful ornaments of the most exquisite workmanship. There were Images, Candlesticks with Candles in them, splendid Flowers, and ornaments too numerous to mention, some of them of solid gold. Whether they worship those things or not, I could not learn. All around the ceiling of the room was the most beautiful carved work that I ever saw, and all about the floor were bits of money about as large as our ten cent piece with a hole in the middle. The People had thrown them down for the Priest. It takes forty-nine of them to make one of our pennies.

One end of this large room is used for making rope, which is made from grass. Just outside the building is a little house on a rising bit of ground, with steps leading up to the door. We could not go in, but we could look through the grating, and there, on a stand, was a beautiful Image of the Emperor. On one side of him was a small Image of a Child and on the other side was a splendid flowerpot with a tall plant in it. I thought it was to represent some kind of lily. They said it was all solid gold. I presume they worship the Image of the Emperor, but could not find out. There was a box just inside the grate, with a lot of pieces of money that the Japanese had put in.

From there we went to the Bazaar, where is exhibited for sale the most splendid Lacquer Ware I ever saw, Work Boxes, Glove Boxes, and a great variety of other ornaments, quite cheap, too. The Japanese in attendance are extremely polite, never seeming to get tired of the numberous questions that are put to them by Strangers. There were several Interpreters there.

The very large ware room, with all the nice ornaments really looked beautiful.

After looking around as much as we wanted to, we walked up and down the streets, past stores, looking at the different articles for sale, and occasionally calling in to price some article. The Doctor accompanied us and could talk with the Japanese in their own language.

We went back to the office and took dinner with the Doctor. He is a young, single man. There are no Women there from foreign Countries, except that the Russian Consuls and Russian Doctors have their Wives and Servants. There are very few Foreigners there. The Consul, or rather he is a commercial Agent, is sent there to do business for the government, for which he receives a salary.

We intend to visit Hakodadi in the fall when I can say more about the place and People. We had some fruit, but not very nice. Pears and Oranges are poor. They have a kind of Fig that is very good.

OKHOTSK SEA

May 10th. Ship Florida on her way to the Okhotsk.

A very beautiful day, quite smooth, no wind. The Ship Roman, quite near us. I have been on deck some time, walking with the Baby. I saw a Seal in the water, close to the Ship, and another kind of Fish. This afternoon have been reading quite an interesting account of Nagasacka, another Japanese Port. It has a fine Harbor and is a much larger place than Hakodadi, having 70,000 inhabitants. We may go there before we go home. The Lacquer ware is made there quite extensively.

May 11th. A very fine day with a little breeze. Whales in sight, but not Right Whales. The Roman is in sight yet.

May 15th. It is the Sabbath, and a very gloomy, unpleasant day. It has been foggy and rainy all day. O, how I wish that we could be at home now, and enjoy the beautiful May weather. I know it must be beautiful there now.

May 20th. A very unpleasant day. Lowered for Whales twice to-day. Late last evening heard spouts from the ship; about 4 o'clock this morning saw 3 Right Whales and lowered for them. Came near striking one, but think they saw the boat. Did not see them again till towards night. We went back to the place where we saw them, and lowered the boats, but it shut right down thicker fog than ever, and they had to come back — could not see anything.

May 21st. A clear, nice day, very little wind. About noon saw a Ship coming the same way we were and there were all manner of surmises among the Men what Ship she could be. Some thought she was the Junior; my Husband and the Mate said it was the South Boston. Waited for her to come up and when near enough to tell, sure enough, here was the South Boston, Capt. Randolph. I had not dared hope it was she, I wanted to see her so much, for she was out from home a month later than we, and we expected some news from home. I went on deck to look at her and she came quite near us. The Captain lowered his boat, after we spoke him, and came on board. Mr. Morgan's Brother was with him. We were happy to meet them, old Friends, too. The Boy, our Neighbor's Son, and Capt. Randolph had been with my Husband two voyages in that same Ship. I have been aboard of her once.

He brought us a letter and a package of papers from Mr. Fish, one of the owners of this Ship; and from Mother, her picture and a nice Rigolette [scarf] for me. It was a great pleasure to know that they were all well at that time.

Capt. Randolph left his wife at Hilo, Sandwich Islands. She was quite seasick on her way there. I shall expect to see her next year. We did not get our Dog that we lost in New Bedford before we sailed. We are very sorry for we were in hopes that they would find him and send him to us by Capt. R.

May 22nd. A beautiful day. The South Boston quite near. Capt. Randolph came aboard, and stopped till dark. It was so foggy then that he had to go aboard his own Ship. He is going to the Okhotsk.

He has discouraged our going to the Arctic as we intended. He is just from the Islands and says there will be a great number in the Arctic, so we have tacked Ship and are bound now to the Okhotsk hoping that we will be fortunate there.

Have spent a very pleasant day with Capt. R., though the Baby has been rather cross; he is not quite well — nothing serious, I think. It is quite cold weather now.

May 23rd. A cold, raw day with a very strong breeze. A plenty of land in sight all covered with snow. It looks gloomy enough. They tell me there are no People living there except a few Hunters and Fishermen. We are now passing through what they call the 50th passage [Amphitrite Strait]. At 12 o'clock today we will be in the Okhotsk Sea. The South Boston and one other Ship are in sight; don't know who she is yet.

May 24th. A find day with a light breeze but very cold. The South Boston still in sight but astern. Have spoke the other Ship. She is the Orazimba, Capt. Pease. My Husband has gone on board of her.

A fine afternoon. My Husband did not stop long on board the Orazimba for they were both anxious to be getting along to whaling ground. He has been out one season and got 600 bbls.

May 25th. A very find day and almost calm. Sung out for Whales this noon. They proved to be 2 Right Whales. Lowered for them but could not get near them. They were going quite fast.

One Ship in sight. I have been walking with the Baby on deck and he liked it much.

May 28th. In the night the fog made so much water and froze, that this morning the rigging and sails are loaded with ice. A part of the day it has been fine, with the sun shining quite warm, so that it thawed the ice which fell down constantly, especially when the ropes were pulled, when it would come down in great masses, endangering the Skylight not a little. The Men have been pretty busily engaged sweeping it from the deck. A very thick fog towards night.

May 29th. The fog cleared up last evening and about ten o'clock the land was seen about 20 miles ahead. It is called Jonas Island. It is a very small Island. It is a very fine day, the Sun shining beautifully.

The Mate called my attention, while I was on deck, to the water which does not look as clear as it has done. It has a thick, dirty appearance, which he says is occasioned by the Whales' food, he having seen it sometimes almost as red as blood, indicating that there are Whales about.

We expected to have seen ice about this time, but have seen none yet. It is quite mild now and my Husband thinks that he may not encounter as much ice as formerly. We are now where we expected to see Whales every day.

May 30th. It is a splendid day indeed. A great deal of land in sight — one quite large town called Aian. We are not near enough to see how the place looks, but there are Barracks there and a Hospital. The English sent a Fleet there and frightened all the Russians. All this land about here is inhabited by the Russians.

The mountains are covered with snow.

Saw a Bowhead Whale today and lowered for him, but he was going very fast and could not get up to him. All is anxiety now to see Whales. It appears that it must be a very early spring here or else it has been an open winter and not much ice, for we have not reached any yet and all the Men say they never saw it like this before. In former seasons Ships could not get near this land for ice.

May 31st. A very beautiful day. It is as warm as spring at home. It is quite calm today and I have been on deck with the Baby to walk. The Carpenter is making a wagon for him.

Saw a Bowhead and lowered two boats but could not see him again. Saw some floating ice towards night, some large cakes. The land is all about and the Islands ahead of us are called Shantarski Islands, big and little. There seems to be considerable ice near shore. We want to go into Southwest Bay if we can get in. My Husband thinks the ice is blocked in the passage yet.

June 1st.   A very fine day but quite calm. Do not get along much. Two Barks in sight; spoke one, the Ontario of New Bedford, Capt. Foster. He came aboard and spent the afternoon with us, and seems to be a very pleasant, sociable Man. He is out only 7 months from home and has taken no oil. His Cooper came aboard to see us. He was with my Husband last voyage.

There is some floating ice and I can hear one of the junks bump against the Ship occasionally.

June 2nd.   A fine day. There was a very little fog this morning and it was quite calm until afternoon when a fresh breeze sprung up. Southwest Bay right ahead. There are great quantities of ice around the land; it is not solid but seems jammed together. It has been brought into the passage by the current and lies right across it I can see, as we near it, from one point of land to the other. I cannot see how we can get through, but my Husband says he is going through. It is clear water beyond and there are 4 or 5 Ships there. I have been on deck, standing a long time and looking about. It is a rugged country and awfully grand, one bluff after another rising to view, interspersed here and there with a valley; the hills covered with snow; the ice jammed up in large masses in the water; the Ships and all together make it an interesting sight.

This afternoon, we and the two Barks have got safely through the ice and are anchored with the other Ships in the Southwest Bay. Spoke the Harrison in here and my Husband has gone aboard of her.

June 3rd.   We are having very beautiful weather — almost calm a good part of the time and quite warm and comfortable. A good deal of ice is coming along all the time; so much of it and such large pieces came against the Ship all last night, it frightened me so that I could not sleep. My Husband was up about all night.

We, with some of the other Ships, have sent boats up to the head of the Bay, as far as they can get, to see what the prospects are for whaling up there. We can't get any farther on account of the ice. We don't expect the boats back for 3 or 4 days.

Have spoken today the Thomas Dickason, Capt. Plasket. My Husband went aboard of her. He sent me a jar of preserves. I have received a good many presents of nice things from the Captains; they are all very kind to me.

June 4th. Still fine. A good deal of floating ice. We have gotten through it a little farther. I counted 10 Ships today when I was on deck. It looks pleasant to see them lying about at anchor. Spoke the George Howland, Capt. Pomroy. He has been aboard here. He is quite a fleshy, good-looking Man. He is just from the Islands and almost two years from home. He had his Wife and two Children with him last voyage.

June 5th. A fine day, but rather cold. Ice still coming all the time. Went through some way, as far as north head, but came back to our old anchoring place at night. Did not like to stop and have the Ship jammed about with the ice. Some pieces of copper are knocked off now.

Have just spoken the Bark Florence, Capt. Spencer.* He came aboard and stopped a spell. He said that he did not know but he had letters for us. My Husband went aboard of his Ship, and brought me a letter from my Brother Albert. It truly is a great privilege to hear from Friends. I feel it so. And it came so unexpected, too. It was as late as the 30th of January. All were well at home then. My Husband has gone aboard of the Northern Light, to tea.

June 6th. It is not very pleasant today. The wind is blowing a gale. Some ice floating about in the night. My Husband was up a good part of the night.

* Fifteen years later my grandmother was in these same waters in the bark *Florence* and Capt. Joe Spencer was also there in an English ship. H. W.

We have taken up the anchor. I hardly know where we are now. I know that the Ship is heading north by west. Have tacked Ship several times; have been steering for the ice and away from it; saw a boat in the ice, the other side, this morning but do not know whether it is ours or another Ship's. Are quite anxious to find out. I hope in mercy that they will not suffer. The wind and ice will keep us apart a spell I am afraid. I saw several ships from off deck. Some were steering this way and some the way we are; the land all in sight. This is the fourth day since we sent the boats off.

June 7th. The wind is still blowing a gale; did not blow quite as hard this morning. About half past six saw boats through the ice. They seemed to have a hard time getting along. They had to get out on the ice and drag their boats over it. About 8 o'clock I went on deck and they were very near us. I counted 12, but there were 15 in company. We took aboard 5 boat's crews besides our own. We had 10 boats on the cranes at one time. We gave them all their breakfast and in a short time spoke the Ships that they belonged to and they went aboard. There was another Ship near us that took boats also. They did not come far this morning. They stopped over night just around a point of land ahead of where we took them aboard. We saw the smoke last night and concluded they would stop there.

This is the 5th day since they left the Ship. They could not get very far the first day on account of the ice. The next day they got to the head of the Bay which is 40 miles. They found there a Russian fishing company. There were about 20 houses but only two of them occupied at that time, all the Men but one being off fishing up the river. They call the place Dobarry Town. There is a large settlement not far from them where they trade. They seemed to be quite comfortable and had plenty of dried salmon and milk. There was quite a number of Women and Children — one crazy one. She was very noisy.

Some of the boats belonged to a Russian Bark. Those Men could talk very good English, so they could interpret to our Men what those Russians said. They invited the Officers to stop with them over night, which they did, and the Sailors slept in the unoccupied ones. They had benches around the room which they sat on and also slept on, covering themselves with skins. They seem to know all about the Whales. They say it is not time for them to come in the Bay yet; they come in their regular season with other fish — first, White Fish which are plenty now, then Salmon Trout (they are catching a few of those now), then Salmon, and last Bowheads. They say the Salmon will come in 7 days and the Bowheads in 15 days, when the Bay will be full of them.

There is the wreck of the Whale Ship Phoenix laying up there [Elbow Island]. She was lost late last fall in a gale. The Ships had all left the Bay. Our Men did not go to the wreck, but the Russian showed the Mate a letter that the Captain of that Ship left with him to give any of the crew of the wrecked Ship if he fell in with any of them, telling them where they would find him. They must have been all lost but the boat's crew.

June 8th. The wind is blowing a gale and we are tacking about once in a while, keeping off from the land and away from the ice. It is quite unpleasant but clear. The wind is from the northeast.

June 9th. The wind has ceased to blow. It has been, since 10 o'clock this morning, quite foggy. When the wind ceased the fog came on.

We, with 6 other Ships, made for a little harbor there is just around a point of land that was ahead of us, towards the head of the Bay, and we have all anchored. It is a snug, safe spot. The view is rather picturesque and romantic, one high cliff rising above another, the high ledges of rocks, and for miles, standing as thick as they can stand to all appearance, are a kind of Cedar trees. They look to me through the glass like our cedars, but my Husband tells me they are a little different. I have not been ashore yet, but am going when it is a nice day for the Baby. In the middle of the day it is quite warm on deck, and it looks pleasant and neighborly to see

the Ships lying about. About every day now we have some of the
Captains aboard and my Husband goes aboard of them occasionally.
None of the Ships has seen anything of the Ocean Wave.* Nothing has been heard from her, they tell me, since the fleet left here
last fall. Some left as late as October and she was seen then near
Shanter Bay. The Captains were in hopes that her crew had been
saved and had wintered at one of these settlements, but not hearing anything about her here, fears are entertained that all hands
were lost.

It is sad to hear such news from the Ships. It is only the other day
that we heard of Capt. Palmer being killed by a Whale, or rather he
got fast in the line and was taken down by the Whale and never
seen again. His poor Wife and three Children are at Hilo, and
will not hear about it till fall. It is very sad news for them to hear.

June 10th. A very beautiful, warm day. I have been on deck with
the Baby. There are Ships now coming in here. We have shifted
our place of anchoring, for the ice began to come along in large
quantities and we were all afraid of its damaging the Ships. My
Husband was on board of the Ship George Howland with a number
of Captains gamming. He came aboard and the Ships have all now
anchored in a good harbor around another point.

June 11th. A fine day. I have been on deck looking around. I
took the glass to look at the Masters of the Ships on the beach. My
Husband and a number of others were snowballing, having some
fun.

The Bark Wavelet has come in. Capt. Swain of her has been
aboard of us with others. I had a very handsome bouquet of wild
flowers they gathered for me.

It looks pleasant to see the Ships lying about here — within
hailing distance of each other some of them are — and see the boats
going from one to the other to have a gam, and some going ashore
to have sport.

* The *Ocean Wave* was lost on Elbow Island, October 12, 1858.

June 12th. It is not as pleasant today as it was yesterday. The wind blew quite fresh this morning, but began to blow harder till it blew quite strong. Several Captains came aboard about 8 O'clock, but went away just before dinner was ready. It blew so strong that they were afraid something might go wrong with their anchors. We have let go another anchor.

We did expect our boats today, but shall not look for them now as long as the wind blows so hard. They all think that the head of the Bay is open to Ships, and as soon as it comes fine, I expect we will all move as far as we can get. The Baby is 5 months old today.

June 13th. Not very pleasant early this morning, but the wind had ceased blowing in the night. It began to rain in the night and rained quite hard till about 7 O'clock this morning when it came on a thick fog. About 10 O'clock we, with several other Ships, took up anchor and went farther up the Bay. Plenty of ice ahead. About 12 O'clock, two of our boats came back. They brought 6 of the wrecked crew [of the *Phoenix*] back with them — the Captain, Boatsteerer and 4 others. They have been living up to the City. 17 others have been living on Elbow Island, where the Ship went ashore. They have suffered a good deal in going over the mountains to the City in the snow. After they left the Ship, they suffered intensely with the cold. Some of them had their feet and ears frozen. They were fortunate in saving things from the wreck. They stayed by her as long as they could save anything — that was, most all the provisions, clothing, 5 boats. Two of these were badly stoven, but they fixed them up quite well while stopping at the Island. They did not save the oil or bone. They did not have much.

Captain Handy told us a good many of his adventures after losing his Ship and living among the Russians. I have not time now to write it all. They were kind to him and his Men. They were with them almost 9 months. The head man is the Priest. They have a Captain over them but the Priest has the most power. The Captain is very much afraid of offending him. When he meets any of his people, he kisses their hand, which they consider quite a favor.

They use Dogs with Sledges instead of Horses. They do a good deal of work for them and run quite fast for miles across the snow. Bears are quite plenty in the mountains and are quite savage if attacked. Not long ago a Sailor was killed and carried off by one before his companions could rescue him.

They have splendid Sable furs among these People to sell and a good deal cheaper than they can be bought at home. They have nice fox and other kinds of skins, to sell.

June 14th. A very beautiful day. Have been on deck twice, with the Baby. Sent off a boat to the Massachusetts with Captain Handy. He is a Brother-in-law to the Captain of that Ship, Captain Chatfield. We wanted him to stop longer with us, but he felt anxious to go, thinking to receive letters from his family at home.

Yesterday the Ship was right in the midst of the ice a spell. Worked out after a while. A boat a little way from us was fast in the ice, but got ashore after the ice worked off a little. I don't know what Ship she belonged to. Have gone still farther up the Bay. Have put down the anchor again.

June 16th. I think that I never worried so much in my life in one night as I did last night. The wind began to blow strong and my Husband said that he would not go to bed. He wanted to be up when the tide turned, and did not know but the ice would bother him; and it did give him trouble enough in the night. The wind ceased blowing about 12 O'clock and the tide set the ice against us. We had down 4700 [pounds] of anchor and with all that we dragged four hours, sounded a good many times till we got to 4 fathoms, and then fortunately the tide set us off a little in deeper water.

June 17th. A very pleasant day. It has been raining all day very hard and has been foggy a part of the day. We are laying at anchor now, but we have to take up the anchor once in a while and have a Man at the wheel to keep clear of ice that is drifting about. Our boats are ashore yet. Two of the Cossacks' boats came alongside of us this morning. We took the Men on board and they will stop with us till their Ship comes along.

June 18th. A very unpleasant morning. Rained quite hard, but came off beautiful after dinner. We have been fast in the ice all day, a complete Sea of ice. It doesn't look much like catching Whales. Past the middle of June and surrounded by ice.

Last night I got somewhat frightened again. It rained very hard all the evening. About 9 O'clock it began to blow quite fresh and the ice came along in very large cakes. The current was setting it on us and the anchors dragged some time by spells. My Husband was up most all night, but we came off nicely. I am so afraid of being dragged ashore by the ice. When the current sets in shore, the ice goes in and then out with it. We have one thing in our favor. There is scarcely any night here. It is dark less than three hours as the sun does not set till about 9 O'clock and it is light before three in the morning. It is full moon just now, too.

The wind has blown from the northeast ever since we have been in here, with the exception of a few hours the other day when it blew from the southwest. If we could have the wind from that quarter a day or two, it would drive the ice all out of the Bay, but the wind from the northeast keeps the ice in only as the current sets it out a little way, when it comes back with the next tide.

June 19th. The prospect looks rather gloomy today. It is foggy but that is not all. We are jammed fast in the ice. I have been on deck but I was glad to come down. The deck is wet from the fog and it is cold and uncomfortable enough — besides the looks are enough to freeze one, to see nothing but ice around, not a spot of water big enough to float the Ship in. The cakes, I should think, would cover an acre of ground. The fog is so thick that we can't see a Ship or the land. Our boats have not yet returned. We think that they are aboard of some Ship. The Cossack's Men are with us yet. This afternoon, one of them, a Portuguese, had his hand badly hurt. The Mate had been firing off his gun and this Man was in the act of drawing in the line when the iron came against his hand, cutting a deep gash clear across the thick of the thumb. It bled very badly. We had him down in the Cabin to dress it. My Husband sewed it up. He has two Brothers with him. They felt very bad about it.

Have worked out of the ice. Some floating cakes about. Made sail and have reached the fleet and anchored. The Cossack's Men have left for their Ship. My Husband has gone on board the Ontario this evening.

June 21st. A very fine day, though it was quite foggy this morning. The Captains were here to dinner today. After dinner we all went on shore. I took the Baby, and it was very warm and pleasant on the beach. We went just around a point. Up in the valley and on the hills the trees are just putting out their leaves. I found some very pretty wild flowers and some nice mosses. All the trees that I saw were Hackmatack, Spruce, and Fir. We found a nice little brook and drank some water; it was delightful roaming around on shore a little while after being aboard of the Ship so long.

I could not find any curiosities but there was a plenty of muscle shells. I sat down on the skull of a whale on the beach and saw a hut that some of the Whalemen had built to stop in for the night. We stopped a spell on shore and it began to get a little cooler. We came back to the Ship on account of the Baby. My Husband had gone aboard of Capt. Swain to tea. I have been on Siberian land.

The Midas, Capt. Tallman, came in this afternoon and anchored close by us, quite a near neighbor. The Florence carried away her foretopmast yesterday. The Java and the Wavelet have got, each of them, a Whale, the Wavelet a large one.

June 24th. It has been quite a pleasant day, and almost calm. The Wavelet is in the distance, boiling. We saw one bowhead today but there was no chance to get him. We took up our anchor about

9 o'clock this morning and got under way. It was not much use, though. There was scarcely any wind. We let go the anchor again. About noon, the Ships (all but two) that were laying near us, got under way. It is quite warm weather now.

Saw two boats coming towards us about 4 o'clock. We thought they were ours and ran up the flag, but they seemed to run off towards shore. My Husband thought that they did not see the flag, and fired the gun. They were our boats and had been to the head of the Bay. They came aboard about 6 o'clock. They have been chasing Whales all day, but could not get near enough to strike. The Massachusetts boat fired two or three times at one and got him, and that frightened the rest. The wind is northeast today.

June 25th. A very fine day. The wind blowing northeast. Hove up the anchor 7 o'clock this morning to go farther up the Bay, but the tide was not fair. When the tide turned we went a little ways, but it has been almost calm all day, so could not get far. Let go the anchor again 5 o'clock this afternoon. We are now about up with some of the Ships. A very large cake of ice passed quite near us after dinner. A good deal of small ice floating.

Saw a bowhead. My Husband lowered for him, but did not see him again. Sent two boats away this morning.

June 26th. It is the Sabbath, and it has been a very quiet day. Have seen a number of boats — one near enough to hail. They said that there was a plenty of Whales up to the head of the Bay, but shy. Boats from two ships got each a Whale yesterday. We saw one today, but going very fast. The Wavelet's Whale made about 140 bbls.

June 27th. It has been a pleasant day, quite calm the fore part of the day. A breeze sprung up about one o'clock. Saw a plenty of boats about. We thought that some of them might be ours, and so they proved. Three of ours and two of the Thomas Dickerson's came aboard about 4 o'clock. Their Ship is at Shantarr Bay, they think. They will stop with us. We are now going there when the tide is right, for we have heard unpleasant news from there. Two Men, one from each of our boats up there, have run away, the one from Mr. Morgan's boat taking the Boomlance Gun with him. They also took a bag of bread with them. They have got no Whale yet. The Wavelet's boats got one up there; our second Mate got a White Fish at the head of the Bay, but left it there. It appears from what our Men learned, that some of the Florence's Men have had some difficulty with some of the Russians, one of them having fired a ball at one of the Russians. It seems he had been drinking and had some words with the Russian. The Man may die. The ball was in him yesterday. I am afraid that it will cause the Florence some trouble.

June 28th. A foggy morning. Sent off two boats to Shantarr Bay at 12 O'clock last night. Took up the anchor at that time and are now bound there too. Went as far as we could with that tide and let go the anchor at 8 O'clock. Took it up again at ½ past 12. Have had quite a breeze. Not as foggy as it was this morning. We can see for some miles now. Came up with the Callao, Capt. Fuller. Thought we would speak her, but it did not come right, and in a short time it came on a thick fog so that we could not see her or the Ship's length. We knew that Elbow Island was not far ahead, but could not tell exactly where. We struck the bell and blew the horn, to be answered from the Ship. We soon saw the Midas and spoke her — said we were about 8 miles from the Island; said the Calloa had taken a Whale two days in succession, making them about 150 bbls. of Oil. We saw them boiling. Have let go the anchor now at ¼ past 5. Some floating cakes of ice about.

June 29th. It has been quite foggy all day, and some parts of it so thick that you could not see the Ship's length. My Husband has been aboard of the Russian Brig. He heard from them that the Daniel Wood, the Thomas Dickerson, and other Ships are near us. According to their bearings, we are about three miles from the

Island. Have been laying at anchor all day. Some large cakes of ice floating about. There has been no wind today. The Ships have been answering each other all the afternoon with guns, horns, and ringing bells. In the night late, we heard a fog horn blow from some boat. Then we heard them holla. We answered them, but in a little while they stopped; I suppse that they found their Ship or some one.

June 30th. As foggy as ever. We know that we have neighbors, but can't see one, and only a trifle beyond our own Ship. It has breezed up today. My Husband has been aboard of the Russian Brig. No news of importance from there. The Thomas Dickerson's boat left us today to find their Ship which is not far from us. The Ships keep some run of each other by firing guns, ringing bells, and blowing horns. I do wish the fog would clear away, but I don't know when it will be. They have it foggy here a month at a time. We have been laying at anchor all day.

July 1st. A very unpleasant, foggy day. It is just like rain. In the night we had very heavy ice come on us. It made the Ship tremble as if she would go to pieces. There was a heavy swell also that made her roll some. I thought it a very disagreeable night. I could not sleep.

We had a nice breeze this morning, and we, with the Brig, took up anchors, and got under way at 7 O'clock. In a short time, Elbow Island was in sight.

July 2nd. It has been quite an unpleasant day again; not quite as foggy as it has been. Can plainly see the land and the Brig. It has been raining quite hard all night and day so far. My Husband has gone this morning in the boat to sound in the passage between the main land and the Island, to see where he can have water enough to go through. There is a sandspit that makes out from the Island, and the water is quite shoal over it in some places. We are at anchor now till the tide is right to go on. My Husband has returned and found aplenty of water for our Ship to go over. In the shoalest place it is a little over 4 fathoms. Our Ship draws 16 feet; the Brig, only eleven. It has come on a thicker fog and there is no wind at all. The Russian Captain has come aboard to tea. They have made up their minds to wait till tomorrow before they start.

July 3rd. A very unpleasant morning, foggy and raining quite hard. In the fore part of the night, when the tide was going out and was about on a turn, Mr. Shepard came down and told us that there was less than three fathoms of water and the tide still going out. That frightened me, but the tide soon turned and we had a plenty of water. This morning we have changed our place for deeper water.

A 11 O'clock the fog cleared away and it stopped raining. I have been on deck. It is very wet up there and the clouds are still heavy, but the land is quite near and also the Brig. A little breeze has sprung up. The Brig and we have sent off boats to sound the spit again. Saw two boats pulling for us when I was on deck. They are now aboard of us. Have been 5 days trying to find their Ship, the Daniel Wood. It has been blowing so hard where they have been, some of the time, that they did not dare venture from the beach. One of them had his boat stove, taking a Whale. They have been with our boats at Shantarr Bay, and left to find their Ship. They have had a hard time. They had to mend their boat with a piece of old canvass; then their provision gave out, and they have been living on mussels for the last three or four days. They were wet, cold and hungry when they found us. They saw our Ship as soon as the fog cleared away and pulled for her. They will stay with us till they find their Ship.

The Whaling Schooner has lost a boat's crew at Shantarr Bay. They were fast to a Whale, and had their boat stove. The Men got on the bottom of the broken boat, but it was very cold and they one after another got numb with cold and fell off and perished; but the boatsteerer held out a little longer and was taken off by the other boat that got there just in time to save him.

My Husband has been aboard of the Brig to see what he could

learn of our boats at Shantarr Bay. Two boats have come back from there. Aboard of the Brig they saw two of our boats just around the point ahead of us today. They did not know where to find us. We have sent a boat to them. We took up our anchor at 2 O'clock and came over the sandspit without any trouble. Have anchored again.

About 7 O'clock we heard a gun, then a bell. It was too thick then for us to see much more than the Ship's length. The next moment we heard a chain; then a Ship came out of the fog close to us and was getting ready to drop her anchor. It was the Daniel Wood, the very one we all wanted to see. I went on deck to see her. She looked beautiful coming out of the fog. The Captain came aboard. He was glad to find his Men — he had worried about them a good deal. We had their stove boat on deck ready to mend tomorrow.

July 4th. It was thick this morning and all night. About 12 O'clock the Cooper told us that there were boats around. He could hear their horns. We waited a spell and heard them nearer. We expected our boats but we did not know when to look for them. My Husband went on deck, had the gun fired, and struck the bell. Very soon they came alongside. They were ours. They came aboard and told us of their adventures in Shantarr Bay. They did not get any Whales. Saw some but not very plenty and could not get near them for they made for the ice right away. Some of the boats, it seems, see aplenty of Whales, and once in a while are lucky enough to take one, but not often. I have heard of one or two Ships in here that have got from 500 to 600 bbls. Our boats lost two of their Men and that was not all. They took with them a bomb lance gun, a large bag of bread and clothes and everything that they could take with them. It doesn't seem much like the Fourth of July, up here.

July 5th. It is as foggy as ever. Captain Morrison [of the Daniel Wood] has been aboard of us. He has taken his boat home. We have got a Whale between us; their boats mated with ours. Capt. Morrison's Mate got him. Mr. Morgan is going ashore after him in the morning. We are going to cut it and boil it and have half. We are now anchored off Eagle Point.

July 6th.   It is not quite as foggy as it has been this morning. I have been on deck to see the boat towing the blubber to the Ship. They took it off on the beach. It has lain some days and lost some Oil, but it is pretty fat now. The land and Ships are in sight. Mr. Morgan fetched me a beautiful boquet of flowers. They are the handsomest wild flowers I ever saw; quite a variety, too.

July 8th.   A very rainy, foggy, unpleasant day. The first and third Mates' boats came back about noon. The Men were wet through and cold. I do pity them; it is enough to kill them. Did not see many Whales, could not get at them for ice.

This morning early, saw from off deck a boat adrift just off the point and two Men on the rocks on shore. We sent after the boat and got it and towed it to the Ship. It appears that the Men had stolen the boat and evidently were taken by surprise by their pushing off the boat and running when they saw our boat. It lifted a little in the morning and disclosed our Ship close by them and frightened them. There was no name on the boat, but the irons in her were marked Superior. They had taken everything out but those, which were useless to them. A short time after, a boat came alongside from the Ship Superior. It seems they had stolen her from the Ship. They started off around the point to find them. They did not get the Men, but in their fright they had left all they had on the beach, 4 bags of bread, a box of meat, coffee, and a gun, even their breakfast they were preparing, their coffee all made and their bread toasted. The Men made way with it and took off the rest, leaving the poor Men on the beach to roam about without anything to eat.

July 9th.   It was not foggy this morning, and in a little while the sun came out beautiful. Quite a treat. We have not seen it before for nearly two weeks. It has continued fine all day.

Took our anchor this morning and have come almost to the ice in the head of the Bay. I have been on deck with the Baby. I counted 15 Ships and any number of boats along the ice looking for Whales. Have heard several bomb lance guns go off. Captain Little is laying not far off. He has his Wife with him. I shall see her soon. Capt. Morrison and Capt. Austin are here this afternoon. Our two boats, the second and fourth Mates, have come back. Did not get anything. Sent off the others this morning. About dark they came back. Saw a plenty of Whales but all in the ice. Four were struck by different boats and lost their lines, Whales and all. One Man ran a good ways and fired a bomb lance into one, but did not get him. We can judge of the ice a little when a Man can run on it like that.

July 11th. It has been a splendid day. Sent off two boats this morning. Capt. Morrison and Bussell of the Lancaster, have been aboard of us to dinner. Took up our anchor at ½ past three and are going to the ice. Some of the other ships are under way for there too. There are 19 Ships I can count. All the boats came back tonight and one from the Bark Endeavor. The Mate was with my Husband last voyage.

The boats have seen some of the wreck of the Ocean Wave that was lost up here last October. It is thought that all the crew perished, as nothing has been [heard] of any of them. Capt. Baker was Master. I think it is dreadful.

July 12th. A very foggy, rainy, and unpleasant day. We did not get clear to the ice last night. We anchored about 8 o'clock and sent off the boats this morning, but they did not stop long, it rained so hard. Capt. Morrison and my Husband went off to see what they could see, but they did not go far. They went aboard of the Endeavor to dinner.

We have seen whales from the ship today several times. My Husband lowered for one towards night but did not get near him. Saw a large Bear in the water, close to the Ship early this morning. Suppose he must have got off from the ice, but they do swim some ways from land. The Men saw one on the ice and thought it was someone.

The Baby is 6 months old today. He is a large Boy for his age, I think, and a good Boy, too.

July 14th. The ice came afoul of us in the night, causing the Ship to drag for some time. There was a large field of heavy ice that came across her bow, and we had to take our anchor up before we could get clear.

July 15th. It was foggy and rainy this morning, but came off beautiful before noon. The finest day we have had for three weeks. While I was on deck, I saw a boat towing a whale — one they had picked up — what the Whalemen call a "stinker" — one that has been dead some little time. We could tell that it was such by its being so much out of the water and swelled up.

We have mated with Capt. Morrison for a spell. He has gone to the head of the Bay and we stop here and see what we can get. Two of our boats have gone with him. Two others went to the ice this morning. It looks beautiful now on deck. It makes one forget the trials of whaling in a measure. The land is most all around us and a large number of Ships in sight. Some of them are within hailing distance. I can distinctly hear what is said aboard the Thomas Dickerson. The Captain of her, Capt. Plasket, took dinner with us today — also, Capt. Williams of the Gideon Howland, Capt. Crowell of the Minerva, and Capt. Wilson of the Endeavor.

July 16th. It was quite foggy this morning, so that I could not see the nearest Ship, but it cleared up before noon. Three of the Captains have been aboard and stopped to dinner. While they were here, and just before we sat down to eat, the Boy came down and told us that they thought on deck that one of our boats was coming with their waif set. That is to let us know when they have got a whale. We all went on deck and with the glass made out that it was our second Mate's boat. Soon he came alongside and told us that they had struck and killed a cow and a calf — a good-sized one the old one is. They are now towing them to the Ship. The other three boats we have got under way to meet them.

We are quite near the ice now. I can see it plainly, but it is melting away fast. I think it will all be gone in a few days.

About 5 o'clock they came alongside. The calf is a little fellow beside his mother, but I should think it a monster of a fish if I had not seen a larger. They think it is about a month old. The cow looks fat. They are a great deal handsomer than any other whale, I think. They are more tapering down to the flukes and have a large head. They had a great deal of trouble to get them. They chased them 3 hours and would not have got them likely, had it not been for the calf. The Mother was so anxious about it that she would turn back to look for it. They have got everything ready, had tea at 6 o'clock, and are now hard at work cutting in, trying to complete the job by dark.

July 17th. It is a pleasant day. The sun is shining beautifully, yet the fog is thick off a little ways, so that the Ships look as if their hulls were all under water, their masts only seen and some only the tops of the masts.

The Men did not quite finish cutting last night. They worked till ½ past 10, and all hands were called at 2 o'clock to work, my Husband with the rest. I have been on deck to see them. It certainly is the greatest sight that I ever saw in my life. I would like to explain it so that anyone could imagine how the Whale looks, but I have not language at will. I think it is impossible to give anyone an adequate idea how they look in every part; they must see to believe. The head is monstrous. I saw it one half at a time, as it was taken up on deck, one half with the monster tongue hanging out and the other with the bone 12 feet long and some thousands of pounds — at that, I do not know how much yet. The flukes are 20 ft. long and the blubber, I should judge by the looks, was half a yard thick. It is very fat. The little Calf is in the water yet.

This afternoon the Men have cut in the Calf. It did not take long. They have cut some of the nicest of it out to eat. Some of it is hanging up on deck. It looks like nice beef. We have had some of it for supper. It is very nice and no mistake.

They have started the try works. The bone is lying in a pile — and a large pile, too.

July 20th. It was quite thick and rainy this morning, but got quite fine about noon. I took the Baby on deck a few moments, but such a dirty place as it is! The Men, some of them, are cutting in the whales, and some are heaving at the windlass. They seem to be happy, for they are singing as hard as they work. I believe they are happier than the two that ran away from us. The last we heard of them, some of the boats had seen them on the beach. They said that they were hungry and wanted to come back. I think we shall find them yet.

The deck is covered with casks and blubber and a large pile of bone. The Men are just as greasy and smutty as they can be, not excepting the Captain, who manages to get into all the dirty work he can.

The Alice has just come and anchored alongside of us. The Master, Captain Bebee, has been aboard. He brought us papers from the Islands. I was disappointed that I had no letters.

July 21st. A very unpleasant morning and I have passed a very unhappy night. My Husband was away all night. He has been broken of his rest a good deal since we have got whales, so he went to bed early and was sound asleep when the third Mate came and called him, telling him that there were a plenty of Whales all around the Ship. He got up, went on deck, and he was so excited hearing so many (for see them he could not, it was very thick fog), that he could not stay aboard, for he felt so sure of getting one. He had his boat lowered, and started. The Officers wanted him to let them go in their boats with him, but he said "No" — he just as well could go alone. He thought they ought to have rest. It was half past nine when he was called and about ten when he got away. [We] had the bell rung a little while, as long as we could get an answer from him, but he soon got out of hearing. I was frightened when I heard them lower the boat, for I did not suppose he would go at all — or anyone go alone in such a foggy night. I worried all night long and did not sleep at all. The time seemed very, very long, every minute thinking, and hoping that he would come back, until I was very much afraid his boat had been stoven and no one to assist him. The Men in his boat could not help him, I knew. They would have to look out for themselves. The thought was awful to me and the night a long one. As soon as there was a ray of light I went on deck. I tried in vain to penetrate the thick fog with the glass, to see if I could see a boat; but no, I could hear them all around, and some near enough to hear the Men saying, "Whose boats are those?" The fog was so thick that when two boats shot out of it, they were close to our stern. We hailed them and asked them aboard, when lo! they were the South Boston's boats, and who should be in one of them but Stephen Morgan. He had not seen my Husband. They had just left their Ship to see if they could strike a Whale (it seems that fog and night are the best times to strike, if you can see them; they do not see the boats as quickly). I asked him below, gave him some mulled wine, as he seemed wet and cold. It was raining hard. I asked him how he liked going in a boat. He said, "First rate." They went off and it cleared up a very little. I went on deck to look around again. I was much worried. The Officer said that he was sure he was fast to a Whale and as he had no anchor in the boat, had to lay by him. It proved to be so. We had sent two boats off to look for him quite early. They found him and towed the Whale to the Ship. I saw him coming about 8 o'clock. He had had good luck in taking the Whale, but the unpleasant job of laying by him all night. He will make about 60 bbls.

I was overjoyed to see my Husband coming. I was much afraid that something had happened to him.

July 22nd.   It has been very pleasant, most of the day, and warm. The Daniel Wood has come from the head of the Bay and anchored close by us. He got two whales up there, making about 130 bbls. Mr. Morgan took them. There were not as many up there as here, but about as many Ships. Capt. Morrison, Mr. Morgan and my Husband have been aboard of Capt. Randolph. They have just come aboard. He has been sick some time with a bad cold. He is better now. He sent me a good many nice things. The Captains all bring me something. I have had letters and papers from home to-day. Mr. Morgan got them and letters for himself. My news is no later than what I had from Albert. It was written at the same time, but it is very acceptable.

We have not got through boiling yet. The cow whale that we first got will stow down 180 bbls. It is the best one that has been taken in the Bay this season.

July 23rd. It has been a splendid day. I have been on deck with the Baby.

They have not got through boiling and the forward part of the deck is very dirty yet, but that doesn't trouble me for I never walk there.

July 27th. We are quite near the land on both sides. The Island on one side of us the Whalemen call "Stinker Island" on account of the dead Whales drifting along there from the ice. The last bit of ice that we saw was about two weeks ago. It went a good deal sooner this year than it did last year.

July 28th. It has been very foggy all day. Sent off two boats this morning. They have not come back tonight. Have not seen nor heard any Whales from the Ship. We have been at anchor all day.

We picked up a mast tonight, belonging to the Ocean Wave. It came close alongside of us. It is a nice large mast and must have been the main mast. It was all whole except where it was broken off at the end that was set in the Ship.

July 29th. It was quite foggy in the morning but came off fine about 9 o'clock. When it lifted, here were Ships all around us, that had come and anchored yesterday. Among them was the Daniel

Wood. My Husband has been aboard of her. Capt. M. is aboard of us now.

Our second Mate has come back and Mr. Carter has got a Whale. They are going to take it aboard the Daniel Wood to boil.

Captain Williams sent me some books today.

We got under way about one o'clock to go through what they call the "Gut", a passage between the land to Taylor's Bay. We want to see if there are Whales there. We came to anchor this evening.

July 30th. A very splendid day. We are anchored quite near the land, with the Daniel Wood. Quite a number of Ships are laying off a short distance. Capt. M. has been aboard of us all day. They have been taking their oil aboard, that we had.

We saw a large Cow Whale and Calf this morning and lowered a boat, but there were other boats around. Our boat got pretty near, but another got near enough to get fast to the cow. We don't know who got it, but they are towing now, two boats of them.

This afternoon we saw another large one. My Husband is off now to try and get him. Capt. M. has gone to steer for him. I can see his boat some ways off. I think they see the Whale now.

The Bay is dotted with boats; it looks pretty to see them with their white and blue sails set. There are a good many birds around, called Gulls. The land looks beautiful. As far as the eye can extend all around us, is land, excepting the passage out to Sea. The land is mostly high — one bluff after another, but it is interspersed with valleys here and there. Some parts of the beach are nice to go ashore on. There everything is green and nice. There are flowers and several kinds of berries in season. Two small Islands are in sight. On a nice, clear day, these Bays are beautiful and no mistake. There are several. There names are Big and Little Shantarr, Taylor's, Mercury and Southwest Bays. When the Whales are molested in one place, they generally leave in droves for another place, and after a while they will be back again. The Bays are full of their feed, so much so that the water is dirty in appearance.

The Captains have given up the chase after the Whale and have come aboard. It came on foggy before they reached the Ship. I never saw fog come on as quickly as it does here. It will be beautiful and fine and all of a sudden the fog will come on.

August 1st. A very beautiful day. We have anchored close to the land and it looks very pleasant here. The mainland is on one side of us and an Island on the other side, with another Island a short distance off. Ahead of us is what they call Mercury Head. I have been on the beach this afternoon and think it the handsomest one I ever saw. It is covered with beautiful round flat stones for a good ways from the water and any quantity of drift wood back of that, showing what a distance the water throws it up. There are some large trees that have been torn up by the roots and carried along by the ice and then thrown up there. The woods on the shore show what awful tempests they have here sometimes, for there are immense quantities of trees thrown down, strewn in all directions and a great many leaning — nothing but the bare, dead bodies. Everything must grow very fast here, for the seasons are quite short and everything seems at its perfection almost. The grass was up to my shoulders, and only a very short time ago the snow and ice was all about here. It is extremely warm ashore now, and there are any number of large troublesome flies. There are no shells on the beach here.

August 2nd. A very fine day. Got under way early this morning and have had a good breeze all day. (It seems odd to have the Ship in so much motion after being still so long.) We have passed all the Bays, left Mercury Bay just behind, and are on our way to Saghalin Gulf, to see if we can find Whales. Ships can't stop there long this time of the year, they have such winds, but plenty of Whales are often found there in this month and September. The Daniel Wood is ahead of us.

August 3rd. We are now tonight in Saghalin Gulf. It has been foggy all day, some; quite thick in the morning. We can see the land. It is not more than 10 miles off now and it is not nearly so foggy as it has been all day.

We have an opportunity to send home. The Daniel Wood is going home when this season is over, and the Mate, Mr. Howland, says that he will go to Wethersfield and see our folks and take anything that we would like to send. I feel very much pleased and very thankful for such an opportunity.

August 4th. Just at night the fog cleared away, and we can see land quite plainly. Saw a Ship also. My Husband has been aboard of her. She is the Eliza F. Mason of New Bedford. My Husband tells me that she is a beautiful Clipper Ship. She is a Lady Ship, too; Capt. Smith has his Wife and Child, a young Lady Companion, and a little Girl that they brought from the Bay of Islands, New Zealand.

August 5th. It was quite foggy this morning but came off fine before noon. This afternoon I have been with my Husband and Baby on board the Eliza F. Mason and have had a nice gam with the Ladies. This is their second season out from home. They are going to Honolulu after they leave here. Mrs. Smith likes the Sea much. She has been going on the water now 10 years and has been at home a little over one year out of that, in all. She is in a fine Ship now. She has a beautiful cabin, a plenty of room, and all nice, pleasant and convenient. They have a very fine Boy Baby about 15 months old. It seemed very pleasant to me to see a Lady. They were quite sociable and seemed quite pleased to see me. We stopped there till evening and then came home. We would have stopped all the evening, had it not breezed up so strong that it was getting quite rugged. Mrs. Smith tried to coax my Husband to let me stop all night, but he wanted to get under way in the morning.

August 6th. A splendid day. It was some foggy this morning. The Ship is in sight and we are both under way. No other Ships are in sight. We are not very near the land but can see it. Have not seen any Whales yet. We are getting tired of this place and afraid we shall not get any Oil here, though Captain Smith has taken one Whale in here that made him 200 bbls. of Oil. It was a very large one and the bone is large and beautiful. He only saw three. They were all large ones.

August 7th. A fine morning and a strong breeze. We are under way and the Eliza F. Mason is in sight under way. The Captain was aboard of us last evening. We have seen a plenty Devil Fish and a Muscle Digger, a small kind of Whale. Did not lower for them. They were going too fast and it is quite rugged. The water is quite muddy. On top it is fresh, a little brackish. This is caused by the water from the Amore River.

August 8th. We are on our way to Southwest Bay, to see if we can find Whales.

August 9th. I have a sad event to record on this page today. The day was propitious of good. The night before, I wished that the first sound that greeted our ears would be the cry of "Whales!" and true, the first sound that I heard, and which awoke me for it was quite early, was the third Mate calling my Husband and telling him that there was a large Whale in sight. He went on deck and had the boats lowered. In the meantime I slept a little, and when I had been dressed a few moments, I heard Mr. Morgan's voice on deck, talking with my Husband. I knew that something had happened, for I had been just told that his boat was fast to the Whale, and thought he must have lost it by his being back so quickly, but what was my consternation, when he came below, to see that he was wet to the skin.

He told me that Tim was gone. It happened in this way. They hauled up to the Whale, after making fast to him, to kill him with the lance, and he came up under the boat, tipping it to one side until it filled half full of water. It righted again, but three of the Men out of fear jumped into the water and then immediately turned and caught hold of the boat, capsizing her. The other boat was near and picked up the Men, but poor Tim got foul in the line and went down with the Whale. A short time after, they saw the Whale and got him, and they found poor Tim fast in the line, it being wound two or three times around his arms and once around his body. They buried him in the deep. He was bruised a good deal by being dragged on the bottom. It is a dreadful thing — and to think it happened aboard our Ship! He was the best boatsteerer they had and they all say there is no better to be found. He has taken more Whales for us than any other Man aboard of the Ship, and never missed one. But it is not his services alone that I think of; it was such an awful death to die. He was a colored Man. He was a very pleasant Man. I never went on deck and met him but what he had a smile on his face.

August 10th. A very fine day. The Men have finished cutting in the Whale, and are boiling. He is a noble, large Whale, as large as any taken up here this season, if not larger. He was about 80 feet long. His flukes, across from one tip to the other, measure 22 ft. His blubber is about half a yard thick in some places and so fat that when they cut it the fat would run out. The bone is large, nice bone. We think that he will make 200 bbls. But at what an awful sacrifice we got him — or her. It was a cow and had a little calf with her, about as long as a black fish. They did not get that. There are any number of birds about the Ship. Her wake is thick with them. They are called Haglets. They keep about the Ship to catch the bits from the carcass.

We are now under way and in Southwest Bay.

Captain Pomroy has been aboard of us all day and we have had a very pleasant time below. He has a young Man with him that he can psychologize. He asked him below and put him to sleep. He then asked him questions. It was amusing and interesting to hear his answers. Captain Pomroy believes in the spiritual doctrine.

In the evening, Captain Cannon of the Jireh Perry came aboard.

We spoke him just after tea and I went up to see his Ship. She lay close beside us and is a beautiful Clipper Ship. We saw him in the Japan Sea.

August 12th. A very unpleasant, rainy day. Captain Chatfield of the Massachusetts, and Captain Handy of the wrecked Ship Phoenix, his brother-in-law, have been aboard of us today; also, Capt. Morrison. Captain Handy is stopping with his Brother till this season is up. Then he is going home across land. He has a Wife and Child at home.

There are about 10 Ships around here. The rest have left. We got here a little too late. The Ships that were here a few days ago got a nice cut of Oil — some of them 600 bbls. The Whales were plenty. They have left now.

We are under way, but there is not much wind. Feklistoff, Big and Little Shantarr, and Sugar Loaf Islands are in sight.

August 15th. A very fine day. I have been on deck with the Baby. He loves dearly to go up.

August 16th. A very beautiful day and a good breeze. The Reindeer is quite near and my Husband is aboard of her, gamming. The land is in sight; several Islands.

My Husband has now returned and Capt. Ashley sent me some geranium leaves off one he has aboard. It was quite a treat to me. He sent me a jar of figs and a new boiler for my Stove. I had none.

August 17th. A splendid day. Only the Reindeer in sight. We are now in Mercury Bay; land quite near. Capt. Ashley has been aboard. Our boats have been off to look for Whales. Saw two or three but could not get near them. Capt. A. has done well this season. He has about 1000 bbls. This is his last season. His Wife and little Boy are at Hilo, so he is going there and home.

August 18th. A fine day. We are today in Shantarr Bay. There are about 30 Ships. A good many of them are boiling.

August 19th. A splendid day. Have had the Baby on deck. He grows very fast, is very heavy and is all the time quite well and healthy. Capt. Ashley says that he is larger than his Boy was at a year old.

We have taken up our anchor and are going to see if we can't find Whales somewhere. We are almost discouraged. We have not got 400 yet and don't know as we'll get any more.

August 21st. It is not very pleasant today. Two Ships in sight. My Husband went aboard of the Bark Warren, last evening. Capt. Miller has not taken a drop of Oil this season.

We were waked up in the night, about 11 o'clock, by the raging of a terrible thunderstorm. It frightened me some, waking out of a sound sleep to hear such a confusion of noises — the roaring of the heavy thunder and the no less heavy wind, with the rattling of sails, rigging and blocks, mingled with the loud orders of the Officers, made it all a scene of confusion for a short time. It did not last long.

Prokofieffs Island is in sight. That is all the land there is in sight today. We are under way, bound for Whales, I don't know where.

August 25th. It has cleared off and is a very fine day and the land is all in sight as well as 3 or 4 Ships, but no Whales. Just at night we spoke the Midas. Poor Capt. Tallman is dead. He has been sick some time. I should think that he had consumption. The Mate took the Ship to Aian for the Captain to be under the Doctor's care. He died a day or two after he got there, quite suddenly. The Ship is now commanded by the Mate, now Captain Tuttle. He has been formerly a Master of two or three Ships. He lost the last one on a reef in Wawo; then he shipped as Mate to the Midas. He came aboard of us and spent a little while this evening.

August 26th. A fine day. We have been making a real Sailor's Cot for the Baby to sleep in. The motion of the Ship keeps it in motion all the time. The Baby is delighted with it.

August 27th. This is a very bad day. The wind is blowing a gale and it is raining very hard, the Ship is jumping about, all is confusion, and I am almost seasick. I am sitting on the bed writing.

August 29th. The wind ceased to blow just at night and this morning is a beautiful one. Indeed, we are quite near the land. There is no Ship in sight for we have outsailed them.

August 30th. A very fine morning, almost calm. Just after dinner, saw Okhotsk City from aloft and not long after, my Husband called me on deck to see it. I took the Baby up on the house and could see it quite plainly — through the glasses, very plainly — Churches, houses, trees and all.

August 31st. A very beautiful day. Just at night one boat came with the waif set to let us know that we had a Whale. The Man at masthead saw it when it was a long ways off and when it came near, they told us that Mr. Morgan had struck a large Cow Whale. The other boats have come aboard. They were not with these two. Sent one back to Mr. Morgan. He was 15 miles from the Ship and we had no wind to go to him with the Ship. Have all seen a plenty of Whales today. They will not get the Whale here until most morning.

September 1st. Have got the Whale all cut in. The boats brought it alongside about 4 o'clock this morning. They were towing it all night. They had a very unpleasant time as it rained quite hard, and hailed, and was very dark. It is a nice large Whale with the longest head we have had. There are 600 slabs of bone in its mouth, and it is 12 feet long. It was a very handsome Whale. The flukes and fins were all white, and the throat. She had a very young Calf with her. She was quite fat.

September 3rd. We have had a nice day. The Capt. of the Midas has been aboard. He and my Husband have been to the City this afternoon. The head Man of the place took them to his house and treated them very kindly. We had one of our Men in the boat that lived with the Russians last winter and could talk with them. They wanted me and the Baby to go and see them. The Gentleman's Wife sent me a dress such as they wear in cold weather. It is made of Fawnskin, long to the ground almost, trimmed with fur, I don't know what kind, though it looks nice around the bottom of the sleeves and the bottom of the dress, with velvet about a quarter deep embroidered with silks and worsted in colors, very nicely. There is no opening, but it is put on right over the head and a hood of the same comes close over the head with a piece to come up to the face to keep off the wind. With one of those dresses on, I should think they would never be troubled with cold. I think it a nice present and a curiosity.

September 4th. A very fine day. Mr. Morgan brought me a Salmon. He got it from one of the Russians.

The Baby has one tooth. We have just found it.

September 5th. We have had Company all day. Last evening a boatload of Russians came aboard, two of them Officers. One of them could talk a very little English. One of our Men that stopped with the Russians last winter, could talk first rate with them. He came down in the cabin and interpreted for us. They seem a very social People and quite free-hearted. They brought me a dress similar to the one that I had sent me, but I did not think it right to take it. One of them gave me a nice pair of gloves made of skin, the fur inside, worked with silk outside.

They stopped all night with us. They have just left. I have been on deck and it was fun to see one of them go down the Ship's side. They all went down well enough but him. He was afraid to go down by the Man ropes. Our Men were full of fun but did not like to show it much until they had left. Then they did laugh. He ought to see our poor Sailors scrambling up and down the Ship's side without any Man ropes, and in a hurry at that — but the fun was, that he would not go until they made him fast by a rope and let him down. I don't think that he ever was aboard of a large Ship before.

September 8th. It has been a beautiful day. I have just come from the City. It is most dark. The Baby and I stayed all night at the biggest Man's house in the place. Some of them are merchants, two Priests — Catholics — and there is one Church. It is a small place. The Natives are all Surfs. They call the Governor, the "Supranic." They appear to be a very nice, kind People and did everything for us that they could. They would take all the care of the Baby, hardly giving me time to nurse him. They took me to all the biggest Families and they all wanted me to stop all night, but the first Family claimed the privilege of keeping us. They were anxious to have us stay a long time. They had everything nice that could be obtained — most of the kinds of vegetables that we have at home, but meat, nice butter, and milk. They make very good tarts but no cake; sweetmeats, and confectionery. They have very nice berries of several kinds. They treated us to wine, tea, and coffee which they make very nicely. What troubled me the most was that I could not talk with them and they wanted to talk with me all the time. There was a Native Woman that had learned a few words of English somewhere. I could talk with her a little. One of our Men could talk with them quite well, but he could not be with me but a short time as he had to go back to the Ship. I liked them very much.

The houses are quite plain looking outside but furnished nicely. I stayed there until late in the afternoon, and when we came away the Lady where I stopped put up a lot of milk and vegetables for us. She is the Lady that sent me the dress. We then stopped at the Supranic's house to bid them good-by, and they wanted to give us lots of things. They gave us a beautiful Bearskin, a nice little fur coat for the Baby — it is embroidered very prettily around the bottom. His Wife gave me a handsome pair of worked boots. We could buy but one Sable skin. They are quite small.

All the folks came down to the boat to see us off.

September 9th. It is a very bad day. The wind is blowing quite hard. I am very glad that we are back on board the Ship. No boats off today. We have taken up the anchor and are under way, going farther off shore.

September 13th. A very nice day. The boats have all been off. Have seen a plenty of Whales. My Husband went off this morning and before noon he came back with his waif set. He had shot a large Whale.

September 14th. The wind is blowing a gale and everything is confusion on board the Ship. My Husband, Mr. Morgan, and myself are a little seasick — I don't know how many more. It was lucky for us that we got the Whale cut in last night or we would have lost him. We can't try the Oil out until the gale is over. They finished cutting in about 12 o'clock last night.

September 15th. An awful day indeed. The wind is still raging, and the Sea looks awful. It is a great deal the worst gale that we have had. The Baby and I have been on the bed all day, for it is not safe for us to be up. I was up for a few moments this morning. I could with difficulty keep my feet. The wind sounds dreadfully. I pity the poor Sailors who have to go up in the rigging today. We have but little sail out.

September 16th. The gale is over but there is an awful swell on. We have started the try works at 5 O'clock this morning. One Ship in sight. We are making for the land again to look for more Whales. We think that they will be in shore now after this gale.

September 17th. It is quite pleasant today. Some swell yet. We are quite near the land but not back where we were before the gale and where we want to go now. Two Ships and a Bark in sight. The tops of the mountains are all covered with snow. The Manuel Ortez has lost her fore top gallant mast in the gale. We came near losing one of our boats. The davy or one of them that holds the starboard bow boat broke down by having such heavy seas break over her. We had to turn the boat up and lash her to the rigging. She was damaged some, not much. It was an awful gale.

September 18th. A very bad day again. I am afraid that we are going to have another gale. There is a strong breeze and a very heavy swell. The Ship is rolling so badly that it is hard work to write. The clouds look angry.

September 19th. It is very unpleasant and there is a heavy swell. We have not got back to Okhotsk City yet, where we started from before the gale. We are a long time getting back, but we have not fair wind. We drifted one hundred miles in the gale — almost back to Aian.

September 20th. We have another gale of wind. It commenced in the night to blow, and has increased to a gale. I don't think that it is going to be as hard as the other.

September 21st. The wind is still blowing a gale, but no harder than yesterday. One Ship has lost her fore topsail. We have had our jib torn very badly. There is an awful swell on and everything is rolling about the Ship. It seems as if she is going under sometimes. The chests and trunks that are not made fast go across the Cabin. The Sea looks awful.

September 22nd. It has cleared off and is very fine, except that there is a swell. The land is all in sight, Okhotsk City about 30 miles off. The wind is not fair to get there. One Ship in sight — the Cambria.

September 23rd. A very fine day with a gentle breeze. We are now very near Okhotsk City. We have been over a week away from there, beating about in two heavy gales of wind and trying to get back again. It is going to make our season for whaling short, for in less than two months it is all ice here.

The Cambria is just in sight astern. The rest are out of sight.

September 25th. It is quite pleasant today. Two of our boats stopped ashore last night. They have just come back — the first and second Mates. Mr. Morgan tells me that the folks there are quite anxious to have me go there again. They say that they wish the Captain would anchor nearer and leave me there while he stops here. The Governor sent us some vegetables. They sent lots of love to me. Mr. Morgan caught a Seal and brought it aboard. He said that I might have it for a pet. We kept it a little while and let it go in its native element.

September 26th. It is a very nice day. The boats all went off early this morning. The Men on deck have been scraping and drying the bone. The Boats have returned and saw but one Whale all day. Three or four Ships have done extra well in these Bays — one got over 2000 bbls. The Gratitude, the Ship that Lewis is in, we heard has one thousand bbls.

September 27th. It is a very fine day, but we had a bad night. The wind commenced blowing fresh in the evening, and increased until it blew quite a gale. I woke up about 11 O'clock and the Ship was dragging her anchor. The Mate called my Husband up, and then all hands were called to take the anchor and we stood away from the land. By daylight the wind had abated a good deal and we stood in to the land again. It is very fine on deck now. We have come to anchor close to the City, with the land all about and the water almost calm.

I have been on deck with the Boy. It looks quite lonely up there with all five boats off. My Husband has gone to the City. There is no one on deck, except the Carpenter, Cook, Steward and two Boys.

The boats have now returned, and Mr. Morgan had his boat capsized from a sudden squall of wind that he did not expect, from the land. He said he did not expect it for it was nice and smooth until then. They were in great danger of losing their lives, for they had the sail set and could not right their boat, and there the poor Fellows had to hang onto the boat the best way they could for over an hour. They were over two miles from the beach and could not swim so far. The water was freezing cold and they were every minute perishing. It makes me tremble to think of it. They began to think they would not be saved for the other boats were a good ways off. The third Mate's boat was the nearest to them and they were not near enough to understand what was the matter. They saw the sail go out of sight and thought that Mr. Morgan had taken it in and stood away from them. The poor Men had a little hope when they saw the boat stood towards them, but when they saw it standing off, they began to give up. One Man got very uneasy and wanted to let go. Mr. Morgan had all he could do to quiet him and make him keep hold, but fortunately for them, the third Mate was afraid something was wrong and sent to their relief. He took them all off, and the Boatsteerer was almost lifeless. They righted their boat and came back to the Ship, thankful to God, I trust, for the preservation of their lives.

September 28th. The wind is blowing a gale. It commenced in the night from the southwest. We had to take the anchor about 11 O'clock and get under way.

September 29th. The wind is still blowing a gale and harder, if anything, than yesterday. Everything is knocking and rolling about the Ship and I can't write.

September 30th. The wind has abated a great deal, but there is an awful swell on. The Ship rolls very badly. I could not sleep last night, there were so many noises of all sorts, and we could hear the casks down in the lower hold. Some of them had got loose.

October 6th. It has been a fine day but very cold. The water freezes on deck now. I am sorry for the poor Men who have to go off in the boats after Whales these cold days and return day after day with no success but cold feet and fingers. It must be very discouraging to them.

Since I commenced writing this, the Men have sung out that my Husband's boat is fast to a Whale. I have been on deck a minute to look at him. It is some time after he struck him and I thought he must be dead, but he was running fast. He had taken them clear in shore. He ran three hours before he died. They could not get near enough to lance him for some time. They have brought him alongside now. It is after 8 O'clock, but fortunately for them, it is quite light on account of the moon. He is a large Whale.

October 8th. It has been a very fine day, but cold. I have had the Baby on deck a few moments, but it makes his nose and cheeks rosy.

October 9th. It has been a beautiful day, but very cold. This morning the pump was frozen up. It is growing cold fast. We only want one more Whale and we will be content to leave this place for a better one. I am afraid that we will not be fortunate enough to get that one, though.

October 10th. It has been a very pleasant day. The boats have all been off, but saw only one Bowhead and he was going very fast.

Spoke the Northern Light — Capt. Austin. My Husband has been aboard. He has taken two Whales up here. He has 900 bbls. in all and wants one more Whale before he leaves, but says he shall start the first gale we have. He says there have been heavy gales in the Bays and he came near going ashore there in one. He says that only one or two of the Ships have done well.

October 11th. It has been blowing a gale all day, but not a bad one. About three O'clock in the night the wind commenced blowing from the northeast and it snowed hard, continuing till this afternoon when it changed to rain. As we get away from the land it is a good deal warmer. We have got the Oil all stowed down. The last

Whale made 120 bbls. The Northern Light is in sight but is putting off as fast as she can, and we also.

October 12th. It has been a very unpleasant day — not much wind, but a heavy sea and raining hard. It is gloomy enough. The Northern Light still in sight, but she will soon beat us for she is a Clipper.

BOUND SOUTH

October 14th. The wind is blowing a gale from the northwest and it is snowing. The Ship has been rolling very hard all day. My rocking chair was made fast at one end of the cabin, and one heavy roll tore it away and sent it, with Baby and me, to the other end. It did not hurt us, but broke my poor chair's back. The Baby looked wonderstruck and wanted to cry but changed his mind. Nobody is safe today.

October 15th. The wind began to get less towards morning, but the weather looks bad yet. Just after dinner, they sung out, "Right Whales in sight!" Lowered all the boats for them. They had not been gone long, when a very bad squall came up. I was much worried about them, but they all came safely back, much to my joy. Mr. Morgan got near enough to one to hit him with the iron, but not near enough to get a good hold. The squall is all over now.

October 16th. It is Sunday, and a very pleasant, quiet day. We have a good breeze and fair, and if it lasts three or four days, we will be in Hakodadi. Not one Ship in sight. We saw a beautiful Swan swimming close to the Ship this afternoon. No land in sight.

October 17th. It has been a very pleasant day. All hands are improving the time, washing up their oily clothes and making a general cleaning time before reaching Hakodadi. We have a good breeze and are going right along.

October 18th. The wind has been blowing a gale all day, but it doesn't seem to increase and I don't think it will be a bad one. It is fair for us and the Ship is going 10 knots an hour.

October 21st. We are not through the Straits yet. The wind is ahead and here we are, beating about, and can't go along.

I saw the most splendid sunset tonight that I ever saw in my life. The sky was a perfect sea of gold and red around the Sun, and I saw the last ray as it disappeared in the water. It was a beautiful sight.

October 29th. We are now in Port. A Japanese Pilot came aboard and we let go the anchor about 7 O'clock in the evening. This morning, the Officials came aboard with their papers, on business, and the American Consul and several Gentlemen. My Husband went ashore with them.

The Consul is a jolly Man. He amused the Baby for me while I was getting my Husband ready. I expected to go ashore this afternoon, but it has been raining all the time.

November 10th. This will be our last day in Port. We have had a very pleasant time. I have been on shore the most of the time, stopping with Capt. Fletcher's Family. Have been around considerably and have seen and learned a little of the Japanese, their manners and customs. I am afraid that I have not formed adequate ideas of them, for they are a peculiar people. They know a great deal, and have a great variety of different articles of their own manufacture, both useful and ornamental. The laboring class, which is by far the most numerous, seems a tough, hardy, and hard-working People, but slow, I think.

It is cold here now, for they are in about the same latitude that we are at home — and yet, they go very thinly clad; in fact, some of them are almost divested of clothing. One morning I noticed some of the Boatmen with so little clothing on that I thought they must perish, for the snow and hail was coming down on them; but they appeared not to notice it at all. They kept on singing, as happy as larks.

I think that the poorer class of Japanese are quite poor, yet they seem more comfortable than the poor of some countries, for their wants are few. They live principally on fish and rice, and they like a little Sake, which is a kind of spirits distilled from rice. It is intoxicating, too.

There seems to be a great many Officers among them, of different ranks which they inherit. I have seen little Boys, just beginning to walk, their swords by their sides and knives in their belts.

They are very strict in their law. While we were there, one man was beheaded for stealing, and one was sentenced to be burned alive for setting fire to some building. All criminals are made Priests and have their heads shaved like the other Priests, which is singular, I think. I supposed that their Priests had a great deal of sway, but it is not so. They are of small account. I saw one of the principal Officers — Ohoss, they call him — and one of the interpreters with him. They were doing some business at Captain Fletcher's house, where I was stopping, and they sent for a Priest. As soon as he entered the door, he bent his body almost to the floor, till he reached him, and then went on his knees to talk with him. They seem to be of small account among the People, but there seems to be a good many of them. There are quite a number of Temples and I think every morning a great number of People come out of them. They go there very early in the morning to mass, or something of the kind.

November 11th. We got under way this morning and have left the Port of Hakodadi behind. We had a very pleasant time while we were there and now we are going South, in hopes of falling in with Sperm Whales and getting some Oil.

November 12th. I have to record a bad accident today, but we are in hopes that it will not prove a serious one.

This morning, just as we were arising, a Man fell from the main top gallant yard. The halyards parted and jerked him off from the yard. He caught somewhere, coming down, which broke the fall, but he came down again and struck on the waist boat across the oars which was well for him, because the oars yielded to him and made his fall a good deal lighter. If he had fallen on the deck or had struck most anything else in coming down, I am sure it would have killed him. As it is, it hurt him badly, but we hope not seriously. We think there are no bones broken, only bruised. It frightened me much. He is a Portuguese and belongs to Brava.

November 14th. It has been quite pleasant and warm. The Men have been mending sails on deck, and I have had the Baby up there. He has been down on the sail, playing with the ball of twine and getting in the Men's way all he could. He climbs up by everything and will soon walk.

November 15th. The wind is blowing a gale from the Northwest. The Ship is rolling and I cannot write. The Baby wants very much to be down on the deck playing, and I suppose he wonders why he can't today, as well as any day.

November 16th. The wind is still blowing a gale, and is increasing, if anything; at least, it blows harder by spells. It has been raining quite hard all night and day, so far. All the moveables that are not made fast stand a good chance of getting jammed some, today.

November 26th. It has been a very fine day. The Men have finished washing bone. It makes a great show on deck. I suppose that there is about 10,000 lbs. of it.

November 27th. It is the Sabbath and it has been a very quiet day. Almost calm this morning, but a nice breeze this afternoon. We expect to see Wellington's Island in the morning. We will stop one day. It is so very warm that we can't take much comfort. For my part, I liked the cold weather in the Okhotsk Sea a good deal better than this.

November 28th. It has been a very fine day, and I have been on shore, at Wellington's Island, and spent the afternoon. I liked it quite well. My Husband took the Baby, and we had a nice walk among the cocoanut trees and along the Beach. We got a few shells, but not a variety. The Island, or rather, Islands — for there are three of them, but joined together by a coral reef — are surrounded for, I should think, a quarter of a mile, with a beautiful coral bottom as white as can be. The water has a blue cast. Our Boat could just float, but the rowers got out and waded. It is a nice Beach to get out on. The People all flocked to the Boat to see us, and the Women had a chair in readiness to carry me to the house but I preferred walking. It was only a step to the house where we went. It belongs to a white Man. He is the King of the Island. The Natives are 150 in number. They have no head from their own People and think a good deal of their King. He has been there 5 years. In the first place, he was left there sick. [At that time] there was a white Man there as King, but he left. They did not like him. This one has a Native Wife and two Children.

The People are quite dark, with black curly hair and very dark eyes. They are not very bad looking and are kind. They wear very little clothing; the Men, nothing about their shoulders and waist; the Women, a simple sack and short skirt, nothing on their heads, any of them. They are fond of ornaments and make wreaths of flowers for the head, beads about the neck and flowers in their ears. Some of them have stretched the lower part of the ear till the hole is very large, and they roll up strips of bark and leaves as large around as an egg and put it in the hole. It appeared strange to me how the ear could be stretched to such a size. They begin to stretch it when they are infants.

They all seemed very pleased to see me, particularly the Women. They decked my head with flowers. They were very fond of the Baby and said that they would steal him. They talk but very little English. I think this Man has not taught them to speak English much or to read, but he seems very kind to them and they look up to him as being superior to them. I think that a missionary might do a great deal of good there; but they are so few in numbers, I suppose that is the reason that no one has been sent there. There are but few huts. They are divided off into familys. Several may be living in one House. They are made very simple, open at the sides and thatched with coconut leaves. This nut is very abundant and constitutes the most of their living. There are not many kinds of fruit on the Island. It is a small one. There are a few bananas and mummy apples. The ground is not cultivated. They raise a few Hogs. They live on the nuts. We bought those and a few ducks of the white Man. Arrowroot is found there. It is singular how many useful articles are made from the Cocoanut tree. The Natives make a kind of spirits from the tree. The roots are very strong, and they make a strong cord from them and the bark of the body. The leaves are used for mats, of which they make some very pretty ones — and baskets they make with some ingenuity and taste. They tell me that there is not a part of the tree, from the leaves to the roots, but what is useful.

It looks beautiful to see such a green Island, covered with Cocoanuts as thick as they can stand with their straight tall bodies and handsome leaves coming out in a bunch on the top, with the large nuts in a cluster among the leaves. At Home we don't have the luxury of a nice, fresh picked Cocoanut right from the tree. It is delicious indeed to drink the milk out of the shell. We have a plenty of them on board now.

I believe I have written all that is of interest about Wellington's Island. The white Man, Mr. Higgins, is going with us to New Zealand, and from there he thinks to go Home to his Friends in the States. He takes his oldest Boy with him. He is a bright looking Boy. His Mother did not show much feeling on parting with her Boy, but they tell me that is the Native's way.

November 29th. We have a fair wind and expect to see the Island of Ascension before night. It is very warm and it is not quite as pleasant on deck as it has been, for we have a great many hogs and ducks, also 5 large turtles up there running about, that we bought at the Wellington's Island. The Men try to keep them forward but they will get aft sometimes, and when they do they make the deck quite dirty, though the Officers soon have the Men clean it off nice. We have a great many Cocoanuts on board to keep the hogs on, and some nice fresh ones for ourselves.

November 30th.   Our Ship is anchored in the Harbor of Ascension [Ponape, formerly Asuncion Island, in the Caroline Islands]. The Pilot came off and took the Ship in. It is a nice Harbor when we get in, but somewhat dangerous it looks to me to be; they tell me that it is perfectly safe with a Pilot. They understand the Harbor well and the way in. It is all coral bottom except where we anchor, and coral reefs extending from one Island to another, for there are several of them, all belonging to Ascension. Beautiful green Islets of the Sea they may truly be called, covered with verdure all the year around.

I was truly delighted with the Island. I spent a week very pleasantly with the Missionary Family, the Rev. Mr. Sturges. They are a very good People. I like Mrs. Sturges very much. They have two very pretty little Girls and they were very fond of the Baby and he of them. I enjoyed myself so well there that I hated to leave them. It was pleasant to me to be in such a good Family, where God is worshipped and goodness reigns supreme; where God's blessing is asked on the food they eat, and prayers offered at High throne, morning and night, His praises sung, His holy word read and studied, and also taught to the Heathen. They have services every Sunday morning for the Natives in their own language and Sabbath School for all that will attend. They have taught some of them to read pretty well. There are always some to attend the evening prayer meeting and they appear quite devotional. It is very surprising to see such a heathen People go on their knees to a God that they once knew nothing about. Mr. Sturges says that his work is very slow among them, as it appears it is hard to get them interested. He says that he has tried hard to get Nanakin, the Chief or King, interested in the cause of religion, and he thinks that he has

succeeded in a measure. I think that will be a great step towards interesting the People, for they look up to him as their head Chief.
There is one great hindrance to Mr. Sturges' doing much good to
them right away; there are a few Foreigners on the Island and they
are a bad class of Men and their influence is very bad among the
People. They brought bad habits with them, drinking and smoking.
The Natives are very fond of their tobacco and pipes. They distill
a kind of Spirits from the root of a tree that grows on the Island. It
is intoxicating. They call it Kava. They prefer foreign liquor to
their own if they can get it.

They seem a quiet People but there has been a time when they
warred together. They are a very indolent People. Their food
grows for them in abundance and all they have to do is to pick and
eat. They do not raise anything of consequence and the land can be
made to raise fine potatoes, corn, pumpkins, and most everything.
Mr. Sturges has had a nice garden.

I saw a great curiosity in a tree. One day Mr. Sturges took us all
to sail up the river in his Canoe. After we got up a short distance,
we all got out and took a short walk among the trees, where we saw
a wonderful tree, very large and tall, with the roots standing out of
the ground all around the tree for some distance, like boards, about
3 inches thick in places and 3 feet high, some of them growing in
odd shapes; one of them very much like an armchair, and one place
formed around like a well with a deep cavity in it. We put a stick
a good way down. It must be quite deep. It is the most singular
tree that I ever saw. All about it were the most luxuriant vines
growing from the ground to the top and hanging down in clusters
all about the tree. Way up the body are large plants growing,
where a little dirt and moisture or moss has collected enough to
nourish it. It is delightful up that river with the Cocoanuts, Palms,
and other trees growing along the sides, some in the water, loaded
with fruit, and a nice little green Island in the middle of the River.
I drank of the nice cool water, picked flowers from the surface,
drank the milk of Cocoanuts, and enjoyed it all very much. The
Baby was delighted, but bothered Pa continually to put his feet and
hands in the water.

They have some very pretty plants and flowers, mostly foreign ones, and there are quite a variety of wildflowers growing on the Island, some very pretty ones. The Natives are fond of dressing their heads with them. There is one kind that is very fragrant — a bright yellow flower, rather coarse. They string them and put them around their heads. If there are a number of the natives in the room, the room will be filled with the fragrance.

The Natives wear but little clothing. The Men mostly wear a belt about the waist with a heavy fringe about a half yard deep hanging from it, and no other clothing. The fringe is made from the Cocoanut, a kind of thin bark fringed out narrow. The Chief, and now and then [a Man] I saw with a pair of pants, shirt, or hat on — seldom more than one article on one. They seem to think they are well-dressed if they have on one thing. The Climate will not admit of one's wearing much clothing at any time of the year. Mr. Sturges' Family all go thinly clad. They have induced the Women to dress more than they used to and many of them put a little slip on their Babies. The Women simply wear a piece of cloth, not more than a yard of it I should say, pinned about the hips [and] a handkerchief with a place cut in the center, for the head.

December 11th. We left Assention this morning. The Pilot came aboard yesterday to take us out, but he was intoxicated and my Husband did not think it safe to have him. Today he got out without a Pilot. We sent boats ashore to a small Island belonging to Assention, and got them full of Cocoanuts. The King told us to go there and get all that we had a mind to. We are now going direct to New Zealand and are in hopes to get some Sperm Oil on the way there.

December 13th. We have had a pleasant day but no wind, and the heat is intense. My Husband has been very busy, with the Men's help, for two or three days, making more room for us. He has let another Stateroom into ours and now we have a nice large one. He has made another large one for the Officers.

Today I found that the Baby has two upper teeth just pricking through. He was 11 months old yesterday and he has not had but two teeth till now, and those he had at 8 months old. He goes all around by holding onto things, but doesn't quite walk. He stands alone but seems afraid to step.

December 19th. It has been a very pleasant day but very warm. We are most on the line and must expect warm weather. We can hardly keep comfortable.

December 24th. We had a heavy squall of wind and rain towards morning, and it continued to rain powerful till about 8 O'clock when it cleared off very fine and the wind about all died away leaving it very warm indeed. A Finback came close alongside of the Ship and spouted several times. My Husband shot at it but missed. The Men have all been busy mending sails and (doing) other things too numerous to mention. Tonight is Christmas Eve. I would like to be at home.

December 25th. It is the Sabbath and Christmas Day. It has been very pleasant and everything quiet. It has been unusually warm today. No wind to speak of.

December 31st. This is the last day of the year. Another year has rolled swiftly away, another year is taken from our allotted time here on earth, and well may we look back and reflect how we have spent that time that is passed never to be recalled. It is a serious thought.

January 1st, 1860

This first day of the year is a very beautiful day indeed, the Sun shining in all its splendor, a nice little breeze cooling the hot air of this latitude, and everything quiet like the Sabbath — for such is the day — a fitting day for meditation, as the past year has just rolled away, and this is the first day of the new year and the holy Sabbath, too. Oh, may we all aboard of this Ship be enabled to keep God ever before our eyes this year in all we do and say, and live as becometh Christian People, though we can't enjoy the privileges of religion as the People do at home.

The Men are all reading about the deck excepting those on duty. The Cabin Boys have been learning their lessons from the primer and reciting it to me. It really appears to me that the hogs, hens and ducks do not make as much noise as usual — the reason, I suppose, that they do not get driven about as much as on a week day.

Have seen nothing today but a few tropic birds which are very handsome, being perfectly white with a few black spots on the wing and tail. Saw a school of Porpoises a distance off, but they did not come near the Ship. The Ship is heading southsoutheast, and we are in Latitude 9, 52, south, Longitude 172, 7, east.

January 2nd. It has been a very nice day. We have had a good breeze a part of the time, and a part of the time it has been quite calm. Have seen nothing but a school of Porpoises and a few Birds. The Men have been busy about something all day, mending sails, painting about the Ship, and butchering Hogs, which last is done about every other day. We have a plenty of fresh [meat] now, and it is no treat. Though we could not have the pleasure of partaking of the Christmas and new year's dinners with our Friends at home, I think that we had very much such dinners here, for we have a plenty of Ducks and Chickens, and another luxury we have had of late [is] milk without the trouble of milking the Cow. But I suppose the Boy thinks it full as much trouble, as he has to scrape the Cocoanuts and strain the milk out, morning and night. It is very nice in tea and coffee.

January 4th. It has been a very pleasant day, and we have had a fine breeze, all sail out and going right along. I am glad to have a breeze, it is so much more comfortable. The Baby likes to be on deck most all day. He goes all about the deck by taking hold of things but does not go alone yet. He seems afraid to venture. He will climb a good deal for such a little fellow. He doesn't mind if the Ship does roll. He goes to the top of the stairs alone, and we have to watch him quite narrow. He is a year old the 12th and has 5 teeth.

January 5th.   It has been a very nice day and a strong breeze. Have been 140 miles the last 24 hours. We shall get to New Zealand, we think, in about a week. We do not see any Whales yet.

January 10th.   We have had a very fine day and a good breeze a part of the day. We had quite an excitement this morning before breakfast, trying to get a Black fish. There were several about, one quite large one. All the boats were in pursuit, but did not get one. This is Henry's birthday. He is 5 years old. I hope the little fellow has enjoyed himself today with his Grand Pa, Grand Ma, and Brother Stancel.

January 11th.   It has been a fine day. We have had a good breeze. It is getting cooler and that makes it pleasanter. Some of the Men have been painting about the Ship, and the rest have been busy about various other kinds of work. Mr. Morgan caught a Skipjack this morning. They are a good kind of fish to eat. They are rather dry [but] are quite a good sized fish. I like to see them playing about in the water.

January 12th.   It has been a very fine day and a good breeze. We saw a school of Sperm Whales this afternoon. The Man aloft raised them about 3 O'clock. Soon lowered all the boats for them. We watched them from the Ship with a good deal of anxiety. Two boats soon got fast — my Husband's, which unluckily soon got loose again for some reason, the irons both drawn, and Mr. Morgan's. They succeeded in saving theirs. No other boat got fast. We were very sorry not to get any more out of the school. It is a small one that Mr. Morgan has — a calf — but we think it will make about 10 bbls. They soon got it alongside of the Ship. It looked quite natural though it is some time since we have seen a Sperm Whale.
   The Baby is a year old today and has 5 teeth.

January 13th. It rained quite hard all night and most all day. It is almost calm. The Men have been cutting in the Whale. It is pretty fat. There are a plenty of Sharks about. They have gnawed great pieces out of the Whale. The Men killed several of them and Mr. Morgan showed me one of the Jaws. The teeth are very sharp. I should not like to get near one of them.

January 19th. It has been fair today and a strong breeze. We are going right along; shall see land tomorrow. The Men have been painting the Cabin and Stateroom. The Baby has been very busy helping me, *the backward way*.

NEW ZEALAND

January 21st. It has been a very fine day. The land in sight is the land just before we get to New Zealand, called the Three Kings. It is pretty high land. There are three [Islands] that look quite round in the cluster; one part runs off long.

January 22nd. It has been a beautiful day. Had a fine breeze all night but it died away calm about 5 O'clock in the morning. The Land all in sight; Monganua about 10 miles off. We wanted to go in there in the boat and spend the day but don't think that we shall have wind to get in. We are going to the Bay of Islands to anchor and shall stop about a week. Have seen plenty of Porpoises, sun fish and Birds about today. The Men caught a very large tiger Shark this afternoon. It is very handsome, white on the belly, the sides a light drab, the back Jet black and shiny. It has a fin on the top of the back and three rows of very sharp teeth. They are saving them and the skin to use as sand paper. It is very rough. The Natives of New Zealand wear the teeth in their ears as ornaments.

January 23rd. A very fine day. We are now in Port. We came to anchor about 7 O'clock last night. It is a beautiful Harbour and rightly named the Bay of Islands, for there are several small Islands in the Bay. There are a good many buildings here, mostly right along the beach. It looks like any little Village. There are 6 Ships in the Harbour besides us — the Desdemona, Capt. Smith; the Mt. Wollasten, Capt. Coffin; the Oneida, Capt. Vincent; the Japan, Capt. Grant; the Naragansett, Capt. Gardiner; and the Harvest, Capt. Manchester. He has his Wife with him. They came in about 2 hours ahead of us. Capt. M. is an old Friend of my Husband's and as soon as we anchored, he came aboard. I was very glad to hear that he had his Wife with him. He brought her aboard this morning to spend the day with me. I like her much and have had a nice visit from her; heard her experience of sea life, etc. They are out 8 months. It is her first voyage as well as mine. She has no Child with her but one at home, a Daughter, 11 years old. Tonight we are going on shore to stop while we are in Port. They are just gone to get ready and I must leave this and get ready and write more when I return to the Ship.

February 2nd. It is not a very pleasant morning. It looks rainy and bids fair for strong winds outside. We are now about to take our anchor. Have been on shore 9 days and enjoyed it very much. Have just returned to the Ship, bright and early, to take an early start. Capt. M. and his Wife have just gone aboard their Ship. There is quite a swell in the Bay, indicating a heavy blow outside. The Ship is rolling some now and I must leave writing to put my things to rights before she rolls worse.

After 3 or 4 days of tardiness I have sat down to write a short description of Russell Bay of Islands and my visit there.

We went on shore the next day after we got into Port and stopped with Doctor Ford's Family 9 days. We had a very pleasant time. The Doctor and his Wife are very kind and social and take a great deal of pains to make it all pleasant for the captains and their wives stopping with them. They have a little Son, 8 years old, a very pleasant Boy and their only Child out of eleven. They have lost 10, 4 of scarlet fever.

The house was full of Ship Masters when we got there: Capt. Gardiner, of the Naragansett; Capt. Coffin of the Mt. Wollasten; Capt. Worth of the Swift, Capt. Marsh of the [?] Jenny; Capt. Grant of the Japan; Capt. Vincent of the Oneida; Capt. Smith, of the Desdemona; and Capt. Manchester, of the Harvest, and his Wife. They arrived in Port about two hours ahead of us. They were all lively and pleasant and we enjoyed it much. Mrs. Manchester is a very pleasant lady and I enjoyed her company a great deal.

It is quite a pretty little place. There are a good many high buildings, some quite pretty, two Churches, one on each side of the Bay — the Episcopal, of course, as it is an English Port. There are several Stores, one quite handsome, and a very good assortment of goods. Mrs. M. and myself bought each a flat or hat, as they call them, to be in fashion with the Ladies there, as they all wear them. They are much cooler than bonnets.

There is now and then a Native hut about the beach, but the most of the Natives live back in the Country. They are to be seen all about the beach, Men, Women and Children, any and all times of the day. They bring their produce and fruit from the back Country to sell to the Ships — potatoes, onions, cabbage, apples, peaches and gooseberries. They all dress like our People with the exception of the head. They mostly go without any covering for that part, though a good many wear hats.

There is a great state of immorality among the Natives, particularly among the Women, like all other Natives, I believe. But I think, from what I learned, that they are worse than the Natives of Assencion though I was pleased to learn that those in the back Country of New Zealand were a good deal better than those about the beach and that Missionaries had done a good deal of good with the mass and that quite a good many had been admitted to the Church. I am inclined to think that both the People there and the Government are somewhat afraid of the Natives. They must be powerful for there are great numbers of them. They have arisen once, not many years ago, and burned the place. It was much larger then than it has been since. There were not many killed but they cut down the English flagstaff; it is lying on the hill where it was cut down. The English had a standing army at the place for a good while.

I went with the rest of our company to walk, and we visited among other spots, the hill where the English flag is now waving. It is a beautiful, sightly spot, overlooking the back Country and the vast hills, the valleys, and the beautiful Bay, at that time quite smooth, the Ships lying quietly as if the winds and waves could never affect them. It is a very handsome sight to stand on that hill and look around — a Native hut here and there, the cows and sheep feeding on the hills. Among the bushes everything looked very dry. There had been no rain for three months and but very little for six months. I do not think they have many forest trees; I did not see many, but there are a great many evergreens and ferns, the handsomest I ever saw.

The climate of New Zealand is fine, not extremely hot any of the time, and cool and comfortable mornings and evenings. There are some beautiful rivers there. One fine day we went up one for a sail, all of us. There was quite a company of us — three boat loads. We went to visit a Friend of Mrs. Ford's, Capt. Right's Family. It is a beautiful place where they live. They have a large farm and a very good one. We could not see the house till we got close by. It is nestled away in the bushes and fruit trees. We landed on a beautiful beach, covered with coral, stones and shells, right in front of the house. [There were] beautiful rose bushes and geraniums like ours at home but growing so large and luxuriant as to look like bushes compared to ours. Everything was in full bloom.

Mrs. Right met us at the gate and welcomed us very cordially to her house. Most of the Captains were well acquainted with them, having been there before. She is a jolly old Lady, over 70 years old and as smart and lively as a cricket. She chatted all the time. Her house is the picture of neatness, everything in and about it. They have a fine orchard. I think that I never saw such thrifty fruit trees, take them as a lot — Apples, Pears, Peaches and Figs, loaded with Fruit, large and fair and very delicious and no blight on the trees whatever. Mrs. Manchester and myself spent a very pleasant afternoon with the company. The old Lady had a granddaughter, a young Lady. She was very social and agreeable. We walked on the Beach, gathered shells, and among the bushes and gathered ferns and wild flowers, then returned to the house and spent the time chatting with the old People and eating Fruit till tea time. The old Lady had everything nice on the table that the house afforded — tea, coffee, nice wheat bread, cake, pies, honey, and different kinds of preserves from their own fruit. They gave us fruit to take away with us. They have a great deal to sell, and I believe all the Captains bought of them. After tea we returned in our boats to Mrs. Ford's, having the old Lady's good wishes and a pressing invitation to visit them again if we ever came to New Zealand.

NORTH THROUGH THE ISLANDS

February 3rd.   The wind has been blowing a gale all day. As soon as we got outside yesterday it was blowing strong and increased to a gale. After we got out a little ways we spoke the Harvest; Capt. Manchester was then standing along with us. We were steering northeast and we agreed to keep in company if we could, as we are going to the same place. I have been seasick all day. I would like to know how Mrs. M. gets along.

February 4th.   The gale is as bad as it was yesterday. The Harvest is in sight but some ways astern. There is another Ship in sight. We think that she is bound into the Bay of Islands.

February 5th.   The wind is still blowing a gale. The Harvest is not in sight. She is astern. We have had less sail out to have her keep up, and she could not.

February 6th.   It has been quite pleasant. Have had a strong breeze all day. Have been 190 miles the last 24 hours. The Men have been busy picking over potatoes and onions. Some have been blacksmithing and some have been getting their boats and craft ready for whaling. The Harvest is not in sight yet.

February 12th. It has been a beautiful day, with a fair breeze. It is Sunday, and everything is very quiet aboard. Today for dinner we had duck, nice New Zealand potatoes, and duff (which is always a part of our Sunday fare for dinner), with honey for sauce today — which we also got from New Zealand. It is quite plentiful there. We are having, also, Peaches and Apples to eat raw or cooked in pies, and preserves, and we have a few eggs every day.

February 15th. It has been a beautiful day, quite squally in the night but we have had a fine breeze all day. This morning raised a Whale from aloft. It spouted a number of times and all hands thought to be sure it was a Sperm Whale, but concluded after a while that it was not. I was in hopes that it was and that we might get him. I want something new to write about. I have nothing now but the same thing over and over, unless I give a description of our hog stock, which I might do if I felt much interested, for it is not to be sneezed at. We have about 40 little pigs since we left Ascension, and nice ones, too.

February 20th. It has been a very fine day with a good breeze. Have had all sail out. The latitude is 2, 14 today. We are almost to Pleasant Island but don't think that we shall fetch it. There is a strong current here, heading us off, and the wind not quite fair. The Men have been breaking out the after hold for Molasses, and stowing off again.

February 21st. It has been a beautiful day and a strong breeze. We will not see Pleasant Island this morning. It was 30 miles to windward.

February 23rd. It has been a very fine day and a strong breeze. The Men have been busy breaking out the after hold for meat, making rope which they do as well as at home in the rope walk. If they want any small rope for any purpose, they take new large rope and part the strands and lay them up by hand and the reel. It is nice and smooth. They made me a nice, long clothesline in the same way.

We expect to sight Strong's Island tomorrow morning.

February 24th. We have had a fine day. Quite early in the morning, Strong's Island was in sight, and we got ready as soon as we could, to go on shore. There was a strong breeze and it was quite rugged. I was afraid that I could not go, but my Husband came down and told me that he thought it would do for the Baby and me, so we went and we enjoyed it very much. It is a beautiful, green Island, about as large as Assencion, some parts very high indeed. It has one of the handsomest Harbours in the world, a nice harbour for Ships to go in and lay to make repairs, but very bad to get out, some parts of the year. The wind blows right in and it is dangerous getting out. Ships go in sometimes to make little repairs and think of stopping a week or so and are detained a month or two. My Husband, last voyage, put in there to stop a leak in the Ship and could not get out for nearly two months. There is a reef on both sides of the Bay, that makes out a good way, so that the passage for Ships is rather narrow.

When we went on shore, the breakers looked fearful indeed. We went to the Missionary's House and spent the day, Mr. Snow's. It is on a small Island, a little separated from the larger one. His house is on a point close to the water, a beautiful white sand beach to land on perfectly dry, the water as smooth as a pond. I think it a very pleasant spot where they live. They have a good substantial Native house, much larger and better than the Natives live in, very well furnished, the rooms large and airy. I liked it all very much. The Baby enjoyed it full as much as I did. He wanted to be running all about the house and on the grassplat with the little Children, a little Girl between three and four, and the Boy, two. I liked Mr. Snow and his Wife very much. She is as lively as a cricket, and both are very social and pleasant. They seem as happy in their distant Island home as it is possible for anyone to be anywhere. Mrs. Snow says she sometimes thinks that her Husband may be taken away first and she left among those half savages for a long time before an opportunity would offer to get away, but she says she doesn't allow herself to think of it often. The Natives are very kind to them; it appears to me, they are much kinder than they are on Assencion.

We went out in the lot to see their Cattle. I think they have as fine looking Cattle as I ever saw. Mrs. Snow makes nice butter — and such beautiful milk as she gave us to drink! It was a real treat. They have a good many nice fowl and lots of eggs. She told me she thought she had sent a hundred pounds of butter and she could not tell how many eggs, to the Missionaries on the nearest Islands to them. She gave me all the fresh eggs she could find in the house and in the nests to fetch on board. They gave us books and papers — some quite late ones — which we were pleased to have. We told them that we were going to Assencion, and Mrs. Snow sent a letter and a book to Mrs. Sturgis.

A great many of the Natives came about the house to see us. They seem to think a good deal of Children. We called on the King, and he seemed much pleased to see us. Mr. Snow went with us. The King has a nice new house, much better than the houses of the other Natives but made after the same style. Some of the canes were painted red, giving it a showy appearance; also, the twine was red, or some of it, and woven in handsomely. On the ground were canes woven together for a covering, and some seats made from the same material — also the same for a foot path through the yard to the house. He has hung all about the walls of the house, war clubs, hatchets, and curiosities that he has gathered together, and overhead, fancy Canoes all decorated. They look quite pretty. It made me think of a museum. The whole house, I think, must be in one room. In the center of the house was a large frame, suspended from the beam, where they kept their food. In the centre of the ground was the place for fire — a square spot about five feet, with stones around it, the fire in the centre. They cook in ovens made in the ground, outside.

When we went in, the King was lounging on a frame with a mat on it — I think it is used for a bed. He had on what was once a white shirt, very dingy then, bound around with red. They are all dirty and slovenly in their appearance. His Wife, or rather one of them, was there — for he has two. One of them was in another house. They had a little Boy with them, perfectly nude.

He has a large feast house close by, which looks very much like the one I went in on Assencion.

We only stopped a few moments. They treated us to Cocoanuts, which was the best they had to offer, and some to take away with us. We bade them all goodby and left for our boat. It was getting towards night, and we were in a hurry to come on board. It was quite rugged, and I was glad to get aboard. The breakers looked fearful indeed. It must be a dangerous place for Ships. Several have been lost on the reef — one last May. In trying to get out, she went onto the reef and went to pieces. No one was lost. She was the Lexington. I saw the timbers and parts of the wreck on the beach.

We were not long in getting to our Ship. Our boat danced over the waves, and the great rollers came tumbling by us, not forgetting to throw a good deal of water over us. But we are safe on board, and our good Ship is again under way. With this breeze we shall soon reach Wellington Island.

February 25th. We have had a very fine day, though it was very showery early this morning. About 9 O'clock the Island called MacAskill was in sight. It is a pretty sight to see the breakers and the reefs making out so far into the Sea — the Ship lying near enough to the Island in plenty of water, to have a good sight of it, and with the aid of the glass to see the huts back in among the trees, the Natives running about the beach, their canoes all along the beach — the Natives in a perfect state of nudity, their heads the most prominent objects, being as black as Jet.

My Husband has been conversing with Mr. Higgins whether it was safe to go on shore. Some years ago a Ship called there, the Captain went on shore to trade with the Natives, and they took some offense at what they thought to be unfairness on his part. When he next touched at the Island, he went ashore in his boat, and as soon as he landed they fell upon him and his Men and killed them all. Mr. Higgins seemed to think it perfectly safe for anyone to go among them that would treat them kindly and trade honorably with them. He thinks them an inoffensive People. There has never been much intercourse with them; but very few Ships have ever stopped here.

However, our boat went on shore, and we watched them and the Natives on the beach with some anxiety, with the glass. We could see when the boat had got nearly to the beach, the Men lay on their oars and were somewhat afraid to land. The Natives seemed equally afraid, for they started back from the beach. The boat immediately landed on seeing them so much afraid, and as soon as the Men stepped on shore, the Natives surrounded them. It made me some anxious, I must confess, to see my Husband in the midst of such a crowd of what appeared to me to be Savages, but we could see that it was all right in a very short time.

Among the attractions of the day was a sail in sight, soon after our boat left. They sung out from aloft, "Sail ho!" and soon I could see over the tops of the trees (for they are the highest objects on the Island) her masts. Soon she came around the point. She looked handsome. She is a clipper, or half, the Josphine, Captain Chapman, of New Bedford.

Our boat has just come off to the Ship, with Cocoanuts, Bananas, Mummy Apples, Turtles, Chickens, and Yarrow root. Some of the Native Men came, too. I ran below when I saw that they were in the boat, and they came along to the skylight to look down to see me. They are large, powerfully made Men, all tattooed, which makes them look hideous.

My Husband has just come on board and it is most tea time. We expect Capt. Chapman on board right away, and I must stop writing for now . . .

Captain C. has taken tea with us and left for his Ship, for the weather looks squally. It is almost dark and I can scarcely see to write.

My Husband says that the Natives are very peacable. Mr. Higgins could talk with them, and they wanted him to stop and be the head, but he thought he had rather live on Wellington Island. We shall be there in the morning. It is only 60 miles off.

February 26th. It has been an awful day, indeed. It commenced to be squally in the night, and we ran about 40 miles and then lay back until morning. Saw the land quite early. Had very heavy squalls of wind and rain all the fore part of the day, — one awful one that frightened me very much. Mr. Higgins says that he has never known one so hard since he came on the Island. There was no danger of our going ashore, for the wind was blowing off shore.

Then there was an occurrence that made the day most unpleasant. In Mr. Higgins' absence there had a Man come on the Island and laid claim. He came off in a boat to the Ship and had some hard words with Mr. Higgins, forbidding him to go on shore and stating that he had the first right and best, as he was first on the Island. My Husband would not allow them to have a quarrel on board and hurried them on shore. He then went to attend to his own business. I understand that the two men had a quarrel on the beach and then made it up, or partly so, during the day. Mr. Higgins' Native Woman came off to see the Baby. It rained powerfully and she was very wet, but those People don't mind being wet a bit. They are very fond of Children.

I gave them a few articles, such as would please them, but they think more of pipes and tobacco than they did of anything that I gave them. The Women are immoderate smokers, as well as the Men.

Mr. Higgins has been getting his things on shore from the Ship, and we have been getting Cocoanuts and Bananas from there. My Husband and all hands are wet through from going back and forth. They have now come back for good and we are getting under way.

The Island looks beautiful and greener than ever after the rain on the trees and shrubs.

The Josephine is laying off and on shore; she has not got under way yet.

Mr. Higgins' little Boy cried very hard to come back to the Ship and ran to get into the boat when it came off last. The Dog wanted to come back, too.

February 27th. It has been an unpleasant day — squally with wind and rain. The fore topsail split and parted the foot rope, and they had to take it down to repair and put up another. We expected to have gone to Assencion this morning and spent the day with Mr. Sturgis' Family, but it was so thick this morning that we could not see land far off, and when we did see it, we were some few miles to the windward of it, and very bad weather, so we had to give up the idea of going there this time. We have letters for Mr. Sturgis from Mr. and Mrs. Snow.

February 28th. Another unpleasant day — frequent squalls of wind and rain, not heavy though. Have not seen the Josephine since we left Wellington Island. It is quite unpleasant below. Just at this time, the warm weather has caused the Ship to bilge, and our nice new white paint is about as black as if it had been painted that color. It also causes a very disagreeable smell, and to make the matter worse, it is such bad weather on deck that we must stay below — and worse still, have the skylight on.

The Men on deck have been opening Cocoanuts all day for the hogs.

March 3rd. It has been a beautiful day. Guam is in sight. It is a large Island. We are now getting ready to go on shore and spend the night. We want to get some Men from there if we can.

March 6th. It has been a beautiful day. We have been on shore at Guam and spent two nights and a part of two days. Had a very pleasant time and returned towards night yesterday. My Husband shipped 4 Men and has the Second Mate of a Brig that was condemned here not long ago. He is going North with us, to see if he can't get a chance on board of some Ship up there.

When we came down to come off, one of the Men had not got there, and my Husband stopped to get him and came in the other boat. I came right off with the Second Mate and Capt. Whalon came with me (of the Ship Omega). She has been laying off and on with us. We did not go into the Harbour to anchor. There were a number of Ships laying there at once. They all stopped at the same house that we did.

Now for a short description of Guam. It is the only Spanish Port that I have been in, and I felt somewhat interested as well as amused. Though the People are under Spanish government, there are only two or three real Spaniards on the Island. They are all half [breeds]. The Natives are called Chemoras [Chamorros]. The Governor is a true blood from Spain. There are two families besides that, who are of the quality, and they feel themselves such. We visited them. They called on us as soon as we got to our boarding house, and invited us to come. One is the Commissary's Family (Chief Magistrate); the other they call the Mayor's Family. There are about a dozen young Ladies in the two Families, and they are very dressy and gay. They do no work but a little embroidery and play the piano and dance, which they are exceedingly fond of.

We were invited to take dinner with all the Ship Masters at the Commissary's house, and they made a grand dinner. I could not begin to tell the different dishes that were set before us — roast pig, duck, chickens, beef, venison, cooked in all ways, wines and licquers in abundance. At last, coffee and dessert. There were three Priests at dinner — Padres (that is Father with them). At home we would call them hardly Priests, for they look on sins lightly and partake as freely of sins as any of them. As I look at it, Sunday is a holiday with them. They all go to church, or mass, in the morning early, and stop a spell. The rest of the day is spent in music, dancing, drinking, and worst of all, cock fighting. The Priests go and make bets. They are great card players.

I did not go to Church. My Husband went, but it was so early that I could not leave the Baby — but their performances are just like all the rest of the Catholics. I had a chance to see some of them in the street, as it was Lent.

I was sitting in the piazza looking around, and right in front of the house the People belonging there were erecting a little house, a few feet square. They stuck 4 poles into the ground and covered them over the top and sides with matting made from the Cocoanut leaf, and the same on the ground. On the inside was pinned up all around gay calico, and there was a small table in the centre, covered with a bright red cover and a white curtain around it. When this preparation was all over, I saw the Women come to the house and take two images, one of Christ and the other the Virgin Mary. They then placed them on the table and put wax candles in them. I looked on, wondering what that meant, when I cast my eyes around and saw a number of the same had gone up within a few minutes all along the road. I asked the Woman of the house what was going on, and as near as I could understand her Spanish and poor English mixed up, it was to honor Jesus Christ, as it was Lent. Shortly the Military came in sight with their band; then a long procession of Men and Women, mostly Women, dressed in their best — the Women with gay skirts, and a good many of the younger ones with white waists and handkerchiefs over their heads — some quite handsome ones, embroidered.

They were following an image, set up in a frame carried by 4 Men, that they called Jesus Christ. It was as large as a Man, with long flowing hair, a crown of thorns on the head, a cross on the shoulders, bright red garments on — and black like themselves. In front of all these little houses with the images, they halted and turned the large one face to the small ones. Then the People knelt down on the ground and chanted over something, got up and crossed themselves, and passed on to the next.

But of the Island. It is beautiful and green, and quite large. There must be a good many inhabitants, for this little town is thickly settled, with quite regular streets and houses quite near on

both sides of the way; the houses are low, homely and rather poor
— mostly of wood and thatched the same as those at the other Islands. The best houses are of stone, large and airy, but all low.
They have heavy shocks of earthquakes there. The People all
throw themselves on their knees till the shock is over.

On the Island they raise yams, sweet potatoes, pumpkins, corn.
They have nice sweet Oranges, Limes, Bananas, Mummy Apples
and Bread fruit. Of the Animals, the principal ones seem to be the
Bullocks. They look queer drawing a load, one yoked to each
team, a queer looking little team. The Buffalo, too, they use in the
same way. The carts make me think of the emigrant wagons I
have seen at home. I saw a few horses about.

It is quite dangerous going on shore in a rough time, when the
wind is blowing strong outside. There is a long reef that makes
across by the town, and about a quarter of a mile from the beach.
The breakers look grand but fearful. The great body of water
rushes wildly over the rocks. It was quite rugged when we went in,
but my Husband used a great deal of caution, and I did not know
the danger until it was all over. There were a great many People
on the beach, and among them Capt. Whalon. He had watched us
with a good deal of anxiety, when he saw that there was a Lady and
a Baby in the boat, for he had just had a boat capsize there, and
some came near being drowned. It broke the boat a good deal.

March 8th. It has been quite pleasant with a good breeze. Have
lost sight of the Omega; have not seen her since the day that the
Captain was aboard of us. She is a dull sailor, and this Ship sails
first rate.

Saw a school of Black fish this morning, and lowered 3 boats for
them. Got quite near, but did not get any.

March 10th. It has been a fine day. There is a heavy swell on,
and once in a while a Sea comes over. I was this morning sitting
on the Booby hatch with the Baby, and a Sea came over in that
place and covered us all over, wetting us to the skin. It is the first

time I ever got served so since I have been on board the Ship. I
had to take off everything from us both and wash the salt water
out of them.

March 11th. I am anxious to see the South Boston. I expect that
Captain Randolph has letters for us, as he is right from the Islands.
He has brought his Wife with him, too, and I shall have the pleas-
ure of seeing her and that little Boy Baby. We heard from them at
Guam. Capt. Whalon has been in company some weeks at Sypan
and Assencion with them.

I have just been on deck to see a fine sight. There are quite a
number of Dolphins swimming about the Ship. They are the handsomest fish that I ever saw. They turn quite a good many beautiful
colors under the water — gold, green, and a splendid blue. They
are quite a large fish. Some of the Men tried to catch one. They
got a hook in one, but it tore out and they lost it.

OFF JAPAN

March 14th. It has been a fine day with a good breeze. A plenty
of Chinese land in sight. There is a large, long Island, called on
the chart, Loo Choo [Okinawa]. Then there are a number of
smaller ones around it. Some of the land is pretty high. We are not
near enough to see much how it looks.

March 15th. It has been a very unpleasant day, indeed. It has
been quite rugged all day and is now raining quite hard. The land
is out of sight, and we are now in the Yellow Sea. We expect tomorrow to be on Whale ground. Whether we see any Whales or
not, all hands are preparing for it, getting boats and Whaling gear
in trim. Have finished picking over potatoes for the present and
mended the last sail today.

For my part I dread it, much as we want the Oil. I am so fearful
that something may happen, but I will hope for the best.

March 16th. It has been a very unpleasant day. It has been rain-ing very hard. I have been below all day, but William would not be pleasant below, so his Father took him up three or four times when it did not rain so hard, for a few minutes.

Mr. Morgan shot a Pigeon this afternoon. I am going to have it for my supper. There are Pigeons in the Japan Sea. There has no work been going on today, but the usual work.

March 17th. It has been a very unpleasant day, the wind blowing half a gale and the Ship rolling pretty bad. It has been quite cloudy the most of the day but not raining. We are now on Whaling ground but have not seen any of the fish yet that we want. There are a few birds about.

March 18th. It has been a very fine day. Saw a sail this morning from masthead. We thought likely it was a Whaler and were in hopes it was the South Boston, but soon we saw her from off deck and made her out to be a Merchantman, probably bound for Shang-hai or some other Chinese Port. She looked nice. She had more sail than we had.

March 19th. It has not been a very pleasant day. It has been rain-ing some of the time, and some of the time there has been a strong breeze with a heavy swell. This afternoon the Man aloft sung out "Right Whales." Then there was plenty of excitement. They were quite near and the boats were lowered to go in pursuit. In a very short time the Second Mate was fast to one, and in a much shorter time his boat was all stove to pieces, and the Men and everything were in the Water, the boat bottom up. The Men got on her, and we immediately lowered another boat, picked up the Men — or rather took them off — and brought them aboard. Another picked up the stoven boat and the oars and all the loose things, and in that time Mr. Morgan got fast to the same Whale. He is an ugly cus-tomer, I know. I hope he won't serve them a mean caper. He is taking that boat along as fast as he knows how. When I was on deck Mr. Morgan was lancing him, and he was spouting blood. They have sent another boat to him.

It is coming night and setting in foggy. There is a heavy swell (which is quite natural to this Country). The Whale is not dead, but is still running, throwing his flukes about and acting as bad as he can. The Ship is going for them but doesn't make much headway, there is such a swell on. Now we have lost sight of the boats in the fog, and they are preparing lights for the rigging and are going to fire the big gun. I have got to make cartridge bags for the powder and must stop writing for the present. We are very much worried about the boats, are afraid that they will have to be out all night. Have just sent another to look for them. It may blow a gale and they will be lost.

I have sat down this evening to note the good news. One boat returned and said they had seen the other boats, and they were lying near the Whale but a good way from the Ship. Soon after, the other boat came and said they could not get to the Ship, there was such a heavy swell. It took them a long time to get here; some of the time they would lose sight of the Ship entirely but heard the guns, and sometimes saw the lights. We saw their light once in a while, but finally lost it entirely. Mr. Morgan has now come and I am so thankful that they are all here at last. I had rather lose the Whale than have them off in such a time, but I think that we shall have it in the morning. They attached a boat to him and set a waif in him, so if it is not foggy in the morning, we shall be quite likely to find him. We shall [be] about here all night.

Mr. Morgan has had a very unpleasant time — off till about 10 O'clock — dark some of the time, foggy some of the time, could not see the Ship and did not know where to find her, could hear the echo from the report of the gun but could not steer by that, a heavy swell, not near any land, and with the gloomy prospect of stopping out all night on the broad deep, fast to a Whale. There was but one consolation, and that was that they would have enough to eat as long as the Whale was with them. They cut adrift and started once to find the Ship, but Mr. M. thought he would go back, for he did not know as he would find the Ship, and they would be sure, if it came to the worst, of having something to eat. When they got back to the Whale, they saw the Ship, but it was no use to stop there for us to get to them, so they started for us once more. Their candle had burned out, and the matches were damp so that they could not get another light. Some of his men were getting discontented, but they rowed like good fellows when he started to come back — and now I think that we will all retire to rest and hope to find the Whale in the morning. It has been a day of adventure. The Second Mate had his boat stove most all to pieces, and all hands were in the water till they were chilled through. I think it was very providential that the poor Fellows met with no worse fate. One — a Portuguese — was so chilled and frightened that he would have been lost, had not the Officer assisted him. They all got dry clothes on and were soon comfortable again.

March 20th. It is not very pleasant today; cloudy, raw and cold. But we have had the good luck to find our Whale; not long after daylight they raised him. The waif was plainly to be seen, and he was not far off. They have brought him alongside and made him fast, now, and now that we know we have him, I never before saw a handsomer sight. I never had so plain a view of one. He is right side up, just as he was when they struck him — a rare occurrence, my Husband says. They generally turn on their backs before they die. There is such a swell on and it heaves the Whale all out of the water so much that I can see the whole shape of him to good advantage. The swell is so bad that they can't cut him in today.

There was a brig in sight just after dinner and she ran off to us about three or four miles, thinking we were in distress, but when she saw that we had a whale alongside, she luffed to and stood off. I sat down and wrote part of a letter, all to no purpose, thinking that she was going into some Port and could send it home.

March 21st. It was a rainy morning but came off tolerably fine before noon. All hands were up by light and had the Whale all cut in by 10 o'clock.

About 8 o'clock saw a boat on the water ahead and thought it to be a stoven whaleboat at a distance, but soon made it out to be a Junk. Could not see anyone on board, but as we got nearer we could see that she was at anchor. The folks were in the Cabin — for they had one. It was a good sized boat. All hands came on deck, and they were much frightened when they saw a Ship bearing down on them and so near. They began to wave their hands and shout to us. We set the foresail and passed them nicely. I suppose they were glad. It was a fishing craft, and they were about one hundred miles from any land.

March 25th. It has been pleasant a part of the day — rather unpleasant in the morning, hazy and a little rainy. Have a good breeze. There are two or three Ships in sight, the same that we saw yesterday, and we have raised two or three other Sails. Have seen Whales several times, lowered for them twice, but did not succeed in getting near.

March 28th. It has been a fine day with a strong breeze, the pleasantest day we have had since we came to this Sea.

March 30th. Have lowered for Whales twice, but did not get any. There were quite a number around this morning, but we could not get near. They were going very fast.

March 31st. This morning there was a Merchant Brig in sight. The Mate went aboard of her before breakfast. He was in hopes to get some late papers, but when he got on board, he found her to be a Dutch Brig, so we did not get any papers. She is right from Canegor. We learned from them that the Japanese there had killed two Dutch Captains and some Sailors and horridly mutilated them. We did not learn what the cause was. This Ship is bound to Shanghai. She will be there, with a fair wind, by the day after tomorrow.

April 1st. It has been a very unpleasant day, blowing a gale all day and the Ship rolling very badly. I can't keep the Baby in one place, and he gets a good many bumps.

April 3rd. We have had a very beautiful day and a pretty strong breeze this morning, early. Before I was up this morning they sung out from masthead, Sail ho! When I went on deck after breakfast, she was right ahead and about one mile and a half off. My Husband and the Mate thought she was the South Boston at first, but as we got nearer, we found her to be the Washington, Capt. Purrington. We saw him at Guam. My Husband went aboard and found him well. He has not been here long, sailing from Guam the day after we did. Has not taken any Oil since.

Saw a Merchantman in the gale, with his fore topmast over the side.

April 4th. It has been a very fine day with very little wind, the most of the day. There was a good breeze this morning. About 9 O'Clock saw a Right Whale and lowered three boats. It was a cow, and she had a small calf with her. My Husband got pretty near and thought that the next moment he would be sure of her, but she went down. The boats came aboard, and we thought we would see them again, but have not. The Washington is pretty near and has a Whale alongside.

April 7th. It has been a very fine day with a strong breeze. It is a fair wind for us to go into the Japan Sea, and we are almost to the Straits. The rocks are now in sight. They are just this side of the Straits. There are quite a number of them and a small Island, called Hococo. The Bark Dromo is in sight.

April 8th. It has been a very fine day; a strong breeze all day but not fair — almost ahead. We are now in the Straits, the land all around us, and the wind is getting fierce. We shall get through by morning, I think.

We raised a Ship this morning, and when she was a long way off, they knew her to be the Omega. We soon came up with her, and Capt. Whalon came aboard and spent the afternoon and evening with us. He has seen no Whales since we saw him before; he has had very bad weather.

April 9th. We have left the Straits behind out of sight, also the
Omega. She is a dull sailor. We are now in the Japan Sea, and I
hope that we shall be fortunate enough to get some Oil. The
weather looks very bad tonight, dark, heavy clouds all around and
a very strong breeze.

April 12th. It has been very pleasant a part of the day. It is
cloudy now. Saw two Ships early this morning. We ran for them to
see who they were. When I went on deck they were quite near, one
right ahead, the nearest one, and one to the leeward pretty near.
We spoke the one ahead. She is the Oregon, Capt. Toby. We saw
him at Guam. He was aboard of the other Ship, the Gideon Howland, Capt. Williams. He was on board of us in the Bays, last season.
Capt. Toby came across our stern when he went to his Ship and
spoke with my Husband. Said he had been in this Sea two or three
days. Had seen a plenty of Whales, but they were so wild he
could not get near them. He has not taken any oil since he left
Guam.

My Husband has been aboard of the Gideon Howland to see
Capt. W. He has taken 140 bbls. of Sperm Oil, on the line, since he
left the Islands and two Whales in the Yellow Sea, making him
120 bbls.

We have seen a number of Whales today and have lowered for
them, as have the other Ships, but they were going so fast, could
not get near.

April 13th. It has been a very fine day and not much wind. We
take in sail every night, for we do not want to go much so as to run
by the Whales, and make sail in the morning to look for them.

Capt. Williams spent the evening with us. It came on quite
squally while he was here but did not last long. This is his last
season. He gave me some nice Oranges and some late papers, as
late as Jan. 5th.

We have seen a number of Whales today. Got pretty near to
one, but not near enough to strike. They are very wild.

April 14th. It has been a beautiful day and quite wild.

I believe that the Gideon Howland is the only Ship in sight now. She has her boats down. They see Whales. There has been a French Ship in sight once today. She is a Whaler. We see Junks every day — one is quite near now.

April 15th. We have had a beautiful day. It is almost warm enough to walk the deck without a shawl. It is the Sabbath and everything is very quiet. I would like much to be at home today, to go to Church.

April 16th. We have had a very fine day, and I have had a very pleasant gam with Mrs. Dehart, this afternoon. We spoke them early this morning, before I was up. I heard my Husband enquiring of Capt. Dehart how his Wife did, and quite readily concluded that she was the South Boston and that it was Mrs. Randolph I was going to see, but in a few moments I found out to the contrary, that she was the Roman. We have met with Capt. D. several times, but I had never had the pleasure of seeing his Wife. I was much pleased with her visit. My Husband went on board of them in the morning, and rightaway after, we saw Right Whales. Both Ships were whaling till afternoon. There were quite a number about but they were rather wild. My Husband got pretty near one, but neither Ships got any. They all went off to the windward and we did not see them again.

Then Capt. D. came aboard with his Wife and little Boy. He is a big Boy of his age. He is 2 years old. The Children were very much pleased with each other. Mrs. D. has been stopping at Hilo a year.

April 17th. It has been a very fine day and quite warm, almost calm. Have seen a few Finbacks and two Ships — one of them the Omega, Capt. Whalon, and the other, the Winslow, of Havre, a Frenchman. I do not remember the Captain's name. Both Captains came aboard. The French Ship is a large and beautiful one. Mr. Morgan went aboard of her. He says that she is a fine Ship and carries 5000 bbls. of Oil. He has been out one season and got 500 bbls. He will be a long time filling her at that rate, but he says that he will not stop but one season more, whether he fills her or not. He has about 60 Men and has a Doctor on board. He has been in this Sea two months and has seen a plenty of Whales but has not taken one.

April 23rd. This morning it rained quite hard and was rather foggy. As soon as I was up, I heard that there was a Ship ahead, and I was in hopes that it was the South Boston, for we thought we might see her about here. To my Joy it proved to be. My Husband came to the skylight and told me that I might expect to see Mrs. Randolph, for he was going to speak the Ship in a few moments. Very soon he came down and told me to hurry and get ready to go on board. I was not long getting Willie and myself ready. We went aboard before breakfast and stayed till evening. We had a nice gam and spent the day very pleasantly.

Mrs. Randolph is not at all well. She was very much pleased to see me and said that this is the first day she has sat up all day for some time. She has not been on deck for 6 weeks. She has been seasick ever since they left the Islands — 5 months. Calm or blow it is all the same. She is getting over it some, she thinks, since they came into this Sea. They have a little Son, 9 months old. He is the most pleasant, quiet Child, I think, I ever saw, and well for her it is, for she has not been able to take care of it. She has an excellent Cabin Boy. He does everything for the Child, washes, irons, and even sews for it. He washes and dresses it, feeds it, and puts it to sleep. I don't see what she would do without him. He is an American Boy.

We got our letters — one of them from home — and feel very thankful to hear that our Dear little Boys, Father, Mother and all were well at that time, which was in June. I regret much not getting more letters but feel grateful for what we did get. We think we will stop about here a day or two, as we have seen several Whales today, and I shall see Mrs. Randolph again, I hope.

April 24th. It was a delightful morning and has continued so through the day. I went to washing this morning and thought to hurry and get through early to go gamming with Mrs. Randolph. I was about half way through when my Husband came and told me that there was a Ship in sight that he took to be the Harvest and I would likely see Mrs. Manchester. She was soon near enough to speak, and it was the Harvest.

I put by my washing and prepared to meet Mrs. Manchester on the Florida, but it was agreed that the Ladies should meet on board the Harvest, and so we did. I got aboard but a few minutes before Mrs. R. She looked smarter than the day before and said that she felt a good deal better. She thought it did her good to see company.

I found my friend, Mrs. M., quite well, but they were all feeling bad about a death they had had on board. They had a foremast hand, sick with some throat disease for some time. They did everything they could for him, but he kept getting worse and died. He was buried in the deep Sunday. He belonged in the same place that Mrs. M. did. It cast a gloom over them all.

We spent the day very pleasantly and left for our Ocean Homes about dark.

It is a delightful evening.

Capt. M. has taken 75 bbls. of Sperm Oil since he left the Bay of Islands. He got a nice Right Whale in the Eastern Sea and got it to the Ship but had the misfortune to sink it alongside. Capt. Randolph has got no Oil since he left the Islands.

April 27th. It was quite an unpleasant morning, quite foggy, but cleared up beautifully before 9 O'clock. Before I was up my Husband came down and told me that the South Boston was no more than a quarter of a mile off. My Husband invited them to come aboard, and they did before breakfast, and spent the day with us. We enjoyed it very much. I think we Ladies have beautiful weather to gam. I wish that Mrs. Manchester was here with us, but their Ship is not in sight. We have been all the morning chasing two

Whales. Finally they lost one and chased the other, and the Captains agreed to mate. If either one got him, to divide. About ½ past two, the Second Mate of the South Boston got fast to him; about ½ past three he was spouting thin blood, and about four he was spouting thick blood. Before 5 he was dead. Mrs. Randolph, the Children and myself were on deck and had a good view of him. He was not far off. It looked nice to see the string of boats fast to him, 6 of them. They were not long in fetching him alongside of the Florida. He is a very large Whale, quite a large spot of white on his belly, the rest all black. Mrs. Manchester had never seen one alongside before. She thinks he is a monster. Before dark they had the head on deck. The bone is not quite as long as some we have got, but it is a large head.

The Men from both Ships worked hard. The Whale was not bad to get. He was on feeding ground. They put 6 irons into him and bomb lanced him. He is an old warrior. His Jaw is broken on one side and he has many scars. He is large enough to make 150 bbls. They have taken his lip in, the Men heaving at the windlass and singing as hard as they could. They will finish cutting him in in the morning. There has been very little wind today — not enough to reach a Whale if he is going fast.

April 28th. A beautiful day. Finished cutting in the Whale this morning. He is very poor. Will not make as much as they thought for.

Mrs. Randolph stayed with me all night. Capt. R. and my Husband thought it best to separate, as they might see Whales, so Mrs. Randolph and the Boy have gone aboard of their Ship. I was some disappointed, as well as herself, for we had reckoned upon a nice gam today, but it is whaling times now, and the Ladies must submit. Have seen Whales once today. It has been a nice day.

April 29th. Have had a nice day and a strong breeze. There were this morning 7 Ships in sight — the South Boston, the Winslow, the Harvest, and the Graffenburge, Capt. Enburge, a Russian. The other[s] we did not know.

Spoke the South Boston this afternoon. Capt. R. came aboard and stayed a short time. He said that his Wife has been some sea-sick today. The Baby is quite smart. They have seen Whales today and came very near striking one. We have started the try works.

April 30th. Have seen no Whales. We went aboard of the South Boston just at night and took tea with them and returned about dark. We keep run of each other. Till Capt. R. gets his Oil we look for Whales through the day and meet at night. Mrs. R. has been quite smart today.

May 1st. Have had a pretty good day. Three Ships in sight. Saw Whales and lowered for them about 9 O'clock. There were plenty of them. The Ships all had their boats down at the same time. The Whales were not as shy as they have been. Mr. Morgan went on to one and got fast to him, and he took his line — all of it — about 300 fathoms. He was spouting blood at the time. They were in hopes to get him again but did not succeed. The boats all gave up the chase and no one got a fish for all there were so many about. We were all disappointed.

May 2nd. It has been a fine day. Have finished boiling. The Whale made 140 bbls. Capt. Randolph has sent for his part of the Oil and got it on board, and now we shall separate again.

May 3rd. Have seen 3 Ships but no Whales — a few Finbacks. Have our Oil all stowed down. Willie is very cross today. He has two large double teeth coming. They come quite hard, and to make the matter worse, he has burnt his wrist, though not very badly.

May 4th. It has been a very fine day, with a strong breeze. There are two Ships in sight — one of them, the Chandler Price, has been cutting in a Whale. We have seen Finbacks today but no Right Whales. We have had beautiful weather the most of the time since we came into the Japan Sea.

May 5th. The Men at masthead sung for Whales this morning before we were up. They proved to be Right Whales. It was quite smooth, so my Husband went down with his Greener gun. The other boats lowered, Mr. Rennard in Mr. Christy's boat. He is off duty. He has been laid up with the rheumatism ever since we left the Bay of Islands. After the boats lowered, they found out that the Whales were Humpbacks and one Sulphur bottom. Mr. Rennard got fast to the last named, and he took the line. That makes two lines that we have lost this week and got no Whale.

May 6th. It has been a lovely Sabbath day. Have seen one Ship from aloft. Have seen Whales twice and lowered for them. The first time did not get near them. The next time it was after tea and getting late — about 6 O'clock. There were 3 Whales, a cow and a calf and the male. They were quite near and playing about as happy as could be, throwing their fins and flukes out of the water. They were up all the time that the boats were going to them. Mr. Morgan went right on and struck one, it seemed without any trouble, and I thought surely that Whale was for us, when I saw all four boats fast to him. I came down below with Willie, for it was getting late, and I had but just got down when Mr. Rennard came aboard, all wet through. He had been up to the Whale to lance him, when he stove the boat all to pieces. Then Mr. Morgan had to cut from him to pick up the Men, and we lost him altogether. The other irons came out, and away he went. Mr. Morgan says that he fired three bomb lances into him. They think that he must die. It is not very likely that we shall get him, though. We have very bad luck lately. This is the first Whale that we have struck on Sunday, the voyage.

May 7th. It has been a beautiful day and smooth. I have been washing. My Husband, with the Cooper and some of the Men, have been repairing the broken boat. It looked so badly stoven to me, when I went on deck this morning, that I thought it almost useless to try to repair it, but it looks a good deal better now. They have considerable done on it but it will take several days to finish repairing it, I think.

We were greatly in hopes of seeing the Whale we struck last night, some time today, but have not and probably will not now. We saw Finbacks this morning but no Right Whales.

May 8th. We have had a nice day and a good Breeze. There are 7 Ships in sight. Have been whaling — two or three of them, the nearest to us. We could see their boats down. Four of our boats lowered for a Whale right after dinner, and in a very short time Mr. Morgan went on and fastened to him. He was quite near the Ship, and I had a good view of him. He did not run at first, but rolled and threw his flukes into the air, fighting all the time, but after all they lost him. The Iron broke. We have very bad luck.

May 9th. White Rock is in sight. A good many Whales have been taken about there, in seasons past.

May 10th. It has been a beautiful day, quite calm. There are 3 ships in sight. The land is all about us. It is the Coast of Tartary. We want to go into Broughton Bay. A good many Whales have been seen in there about this time of the year. It is some miles ahead and we have no wind to go in. We have seen a few Finbacks today.

May 11th. It has been a beautiful day, calm and warm — the land quite near. Have been to the head of Broughton Bay. Did not see any Right Whales — a plenty of Humpbacks. We are having splendid weather but don't get any Oil.

May 12th. It has been a very beautiful day, quite warm, perfectly calm. We are quite near the land. It looks fine to see land. I can plainly see, through the glass, fields of grain and the Fishermen's houses. It is a fine sight to me and full of interest. The land is beautifully varied by mountain, hill and vale — the fine white sand beach, the water as smooth as glass and covered with fishermen's boats. Our Ship has been surrounded by them all day. Some of them came aboard. They view every part of the Ship with eager curiosity and are very noisy with their talk, but we can't understand a word they say. My Husband tried to find out by them if they knew where the Whales were. They motioned that there were plenty in shore.

These People look a good deal like the Japanese and must, I think, be one race of People. They dress a good deal like them. They must keep warm, for their clothes are a mass of heavy, quilted cloth. Some of them are dressed in skins and skin shoes. A good many of them are very ragged, and all of them are very dirty. They seemed to have nothing to eat on board but rice and a few little fish. They gave us some fish, and we gave them some bread.

About noon there were some Humpbacks in sight — one quite near. My Husband lowered his boat and chased him, striking him, himself. He had but little trouble with him. He was soon spouting blood and before 2 o'clock was dead and alongside the Ship. Before dark he was all cut in. He was large for a Humpback — the blubber thin, as is the case always with that kind of Whale. They are seldom caught, for they are hard to get, always run bad and are very apt to sink after they are dead. They are more curious than any kind I have yet seen. They are full and round, the head straighter than that of any other kind, the bone very short — about 2 feet long. They are quite black, the fins not at all like those of the other kind, being long and narrow. These measured 17 feet from the tip to where they joined the body. They were spotted black and white very handsomely. The belly was all deep ridges, the ends of the fins covered with barnacles. I have one that they saved for me.

The Tartars seemed quite amused and astonished to see the capture of the Whale. They crowded about the Ship to see them cut it in; some went on shore and fetched others off; one Junk came off with what we supposed to be the big Folks, for they were dressed a good deal better than the rest. Some had very queer looking hats on, very high with small round crowns and broad brims, made of a kind of very fine wire. It seemed to me like woven open work. They were dressed in nice white linen — coats and pants — and had their tobacco cases attached to their belts with silk cord. They had on sandals like the Japanese.

These People came aboard just at dinner time. They came down into the Cabin, which seemed to be a curiosity to them, and were interested to see the manner in which we partook of our meals. We offered them something to eat, which all but one took in their hands. I thought that he used the plate, knife and fork as if he had used them before. It amused me very much to see them. They wanted to look at everything, and they were very curious to know all about everything; but they all wanted watching, for they would steal everything that they could lay their hands on. For my part, I was glad when they left, for I began to be tired of them long before they went. They carried away boatloads of Whale meat. They eat it. I saw a number of them eating great Junks of the Blubber. It made me sick to see the fat running out of their mouths. They were very much pleased with the Baby. William is 16 months old today.

May 13th. We raised a Ship just before noon, right ahead, and just before night we saw another. We ran off and spoke one — the Chandler Price, Capt. Holcomb. The other Ship is the Levi Starbuck, Capt. Jernegan. The two Captains were gamming together. My Husband has been aboard of the Chandler Price to have a gam with them. They have not done very well this season. Capt. H. has taken two Whales. He had the bad luck to sink two the other day. The other Ship has but one Whale. Capt. H. has been to Nangasaki. He likes the place much better than Hakodadi. He says that the Vesper, Capt. Bailey, and the Russian Bark Amore, Capt. Finton, came in collision in the night a short time ago, doing a great deal of damage to the Amore, and she had to put back into Nangasaki for repairs. Capt. Finton jumped overboard that night and was drowned. We did not learn the reason. I think that it is very sad.

May 14th. It has been a fine day, with a strong breeze. We have been standing in towards the land in the morning and are now running down along the land. Have seen a number of Humpbacks and lowered for them but did not get any. Mr. Morgan was quite near one once or twice, but they saw him.

There are four Ships in sight, doing nothing the same as ourselves.

May 25th. Between 6 and 7 O'clock we saw Humpbacks, and my Husband lowered. He had not been gone over an hour before he struck and killed one. They have now brought him alongside. The George and Susan has taken one alongside today.

May 26th. We have had another beautiful day — a good breeze but quite warm. We are pretty near the land — no Ships in sight — a plenty of Birds, Porpoises and Humpbacks around.

All hands were called at daylight and soon had the Whale cut in.

About 9 O'clock we lowered the boats. Mr. Morgan got fast to one, and soon after, Mr. Montross got fast to another. They were quite near the Ship, and I had a good view of the whole. It was a pleasant sight to see 5 boats, all after the Whales, and they playing about, so happy in their native element, all unconscious, it seemed, of danger; but it made me feel very bad to see them spouting blood as thick as it could be, and the last struggles of death after they had run and sounded and the boats had pulled up and lanced them and fired bomb lances into them — then to see them lie tumbling and rolling about in the water, dying. I could not bear the sight, but it was soon over.

It is worth seeing — all the boats towing them to the Ship. It looks like hard work, the Whales so deep in the water that I could but just see the hump. It is hard to keep them from sinking sometimes, and the boats have to hold them up.

We spoke the Charles W. Morgan tonight, Capt. Hamilton.* He came on board and took tea with us. He is only 7 months from

* This is the famous whaleship which has been preserved at the Mystic Seaport Museum in Connecticut.

home and only 30 days from the Islands. He brought us some late papers and told us that he had taken 800 bbls of Right Whale Oil before he got to the Islands.

May 27th.   It has been quite an unpleasant day — the sun over-clouded all day and rain a part of the day.

We have seen a number of Humpbacks and lowered the boats. The Mate got fast to one with the Greener gun. The Whale ran very badly and finally drew the iron out. It must have killed him, I think.

May 29th.   The wind has increased, till it is now almost a gale. The Charles W. Morgan has taken a Whale today. We think he must have picked up a dead one, for it has been very bad to lower for any other, and then he did not change his course or take in sail.

May 30th.   We have had a warm, pleasant day. Have started the try works. There are a plenty of Humpbacks and Porpoises about. The Men caught a Porpoise.

We have stood in close to the land and so near White Rock that I had a nice view of it. It is a bare rock, not a spear of vegetation on it, and is white. It has been washed by the Sea and bleached by the Sun for centuries — a large rock with a number of small ones around it. There are thousands of Birds on it, and Capt. Whalon went on shore there a short time ago and got about 40 dozen birds eggs. They are very good.

I had a little start in the night about the rock. The Second Mate came down about 12 O'clock and told us that the Rock was quite near. My Husband went on deck, and they wore around, but when he came down he said that there was no danger. It was not quite so near as Mr. Montros had thought at first.

June 4th.   We have had a very pleasant day. There are quite a number of Ships in sight, among them the Omega — Capt. Whalon. He has been aboard and took dinner with us.

Saw two Right Whales just before dinner, and soon after, our boats went down. Capt. W. went in one of ours to try and strike one, for our Mate had gone in his boat aboard of his Ship. The boats chased the Whales for some time, and Capt. W. got pretty near one, but they all had to come aboard at last without any fish. Capt. W. stayed to tea and has now gone on board of his own Ship. He was kind enough to fetch me some fresh laid hen's eggs for the Baby who is very fond of them.

June 14th. We have had a splendid day, quite mild with a gentle breeze. Willie and I have been on shore and had a nice ramble. There are two Islands in sight — one very high and nearly round, called on the Chart, Risiri. The top is covered with snow, but all up the side it looks green and nice. The other one is long and not so high. It is called Refunsiri [Rishiri and Rebun, off Hokkaido]. It was this one that we went on. Where we went in the rocks it was pretty bold. I could hear the cawing of the Birds in the crevices. There was a little spot of nice beach where we landed. The ground back was all steep. I climbed up and gathered some very pretty wild flowers. On the beach were plenty of shells, but they had all lost their beauty by being washed by the water and bleached by the sun. There were the remains of some Japanese huts — fishermen's, I presume.

Willie enjoyed it as much as I did. He sat right down in the sand and would fill the shells with it.

About sixty miles from this one is another small Island, called Monneron. There we are going to stop tomorrow to get water. I am going ashore if it is fine.

June 15th. We are laying off and on the Island of Monneron. It has been a very unpleasant day, quite rainy and foggy off shore.

Quite early this morning the Men saw on shore among the rocks a great number of Animals that some of them call Sea Elephants. They afterwards concluded that they were Seals. I went on deck and took the glass to look at them. It was quite a curiosity. They make a great noise. They say that on shore the noise was most deafening, there were such a great number of them. They are hair Seals, very large, some of them as large as a young Creature. My Husband went on shore before breakfast and took his gun thinking to shoot some, but could not get very near them. They were frightened at the Men, took their young in their mouths and left.

It is further down where the watering place is and a pleasant spot, a nice beach and easy to get water. We have about one hundred bbls. and are now leaving the Island behind.

June 16th. Have had a very unpleasant day, thick fog all day, very little wind. It is quite discouraging. We can't get anywhere that we want to to look for Whales, and the season is fast wearing away.

INTO THE OKHOTSK SEA

June 17th. It has been quite foggy all day, occasionally clearing away so that we could see about two Ship's lengths and then shutting again thicker than ever, and as wet as if it was raining. We are in the Straits, going through into the Okhotsk Sea. We can't see the land although it is on both sides of us and there is a rock in the centre. There are about twenty miles each side of it. I think it needs some caution in going through in a thick fog. On one side is Saghalien Island, and on the other is Yezo [Hokkaido], all Japanese land.

June 18th. It has been a beautiful day, mild with but little wind. We have got through the Straits and are now in the Okhotsk Sea. Saghalien Island is in sight, or rather, one end of it — the broadest end. It is a large Island, about 500 miles long. It runs off narrow at one end. Have seen a number of small Whales, called Muscle diggers, also a few Seals and Birds. Just before dark we saw a large

Humpback — a Cow with a small Calf. The Men got ready to clear away the boats, but when the Whale came up again, she was going very fast, and my Husband didn't think it best to go down for them, as it was getting late too.

June 19th. It was quite pleasant this morning. Before noon the Sun became overclouded and it has since rained and snowed a little. It has been calm all night and today, so that we get along slowly. The land is still in sight. It is very dull on deck. The usual work is going on, the Cooper is setting up Casks, and as for me, I have been ironing for one thing and doing other little things too numerous to mention. Thomas has been reading a good part of the day, and Willie has been through his usual course of mischief.

June 25th. It has been a very fine day and mild, the wind from the South, what there has been, but it has been almost calm all day. I have been washing, the fore part of the day, and on deck with the Baby a good deal this afternoon. He enjoyed it much, being drawn in his little wagon and running about the deck. Have seen some kind of Whales from aloft once or twice a good way off. The Men have been breaking out the run for Sugar and other things.

June 26th. It has been quite pleasant, but cold and almost calm. Have not seen a Whale and scarcely a Bird. It is dull — very dull. We have not seen a Ship since we were in the Straits.

June 30th. We shall not stop about here any longer, but think of going into Yausk Bay [probably Tausk Bay].

July 3rd. It has been foggy more or less all day until almost night, when it cleared up quite fine and we could see the land, an Island called Olskei. It is in the passage to Yausk Bay. We are going in there. The mainland is about 30 miles off but not in sight yet. It is the Russian Continent.

Have had a little shower of rain since the fog cleared away. On deck they have been mending the Fly Jib and setting a Main T Gallant Stay Sail. The Second Mate has been making a Gaff Top Sail for his boat. The Third Mate has been enlarging his boat sail. They are getting everything ready for whaling in the Bays.

July 4th. Have had a beautiful day. It was calm most all night, so that we did not get into the Bay as far up as we wanted to till just at night. All the fore part of the day it was calm. We had a good breeze after dinner till just before night. We then let go the anchor. It is now quite calm and beautiful, the land all around. It is a large Bay, a new place to me as we did not come here last season.

July 5th. It has been a very fine day. There is a Brig in sight ahead. We expected to see a number of Ships in here but think that they have been here and found no Whales and left. We shall leave right away if we do not see Whales. Today we sent off four boats at three O'Clock this morning, in pursuit of some in shore. Have seen a little floating ice in here. This afternoon my Husband has been on board of the Brig — a Dutchman. He says there are 15 or 20 Ships farther up the Bay. Some have taken one, some three, and others not any Whales. He hasn't any.

Our boats have returned. The first two reported that they had seen nothing. The Mate and third Mate had seen three or four small Bowheads. We are going to try one day more here.

July 6th. It has been a warm, pleasant day with a nice little breeze most of the time — rather hazy around the land. Four boats went off at three O'clock this morning. About 10 O'clock a boatload of Russians came off to see us and to trade. They came from a little town about 8 miles off, called Yausk [Tausk?]. The Priest came in the boat. He is the head man of the place. He came down in the Cabin and one with him that could talk a little English. He was very well dressed, but the rest poorly, mostly in skins. They were quite dirty. Their trade consisted in Bear Skins, some Deer Skin coats for Ladies, trimmed with fur and embroidered quite pretty, Ladies' and Men's Boots and Gloves made of Skin and embroidered. They brought off some nice milk and a few nice Salmon. They haven't caught many yet as it is rather early for them. We traded a little with them, mostly for milk and fish. They wanted molasses, tea, soap, and other things.

Our boats have returned without success. They saw one or two Whales. We shall leave here as soon as we have a fair wind.

July 9th. It has been a very fine day and a nice breeze. We are now running along the North Shore and have come to the Three Brothers' Bay. Right ahead is Horse Shoe Bay and not far off is Okhotsk City. We intend to look for Whales along here.

July 10th. Have had a beautiful day, quite mild, a light breeze. We are now going into Horse Shoe Bay. The Europea is here and a Dutch Brig. She came down and spoke us. The Captain's name is Williams and the Brig's name is the Comet. In shore at anchor is the Harvest, Capt. Manchester. We have spoken him, and the Captain and his Wife have been aboard to take tea. Capt. Manter and Capt. Williams have been aboard, too. Tomorrow we are going on board the Harvest to spend the day. Capt. Manchester picked up a dead Whale the other day, that made 60 bbls. of Oil. That is all he has got this season. We are now at anchor.

July 11th. We have been aboard the Harvest and spent the day, having just returned. We have enjoyed it very much. Willie was much pleased with everything, particularly the Birds. Mrs. M. has two Canaries, and they sing a good deal.

While we were aboard there, we saw a Bowhead in shore, and the two Captains lowered for the Whale, chasing it for some time and then losing sight of it entirely. The boats have returned and report seeing three or four. Another Ship has come in and anchored. She is the Maria Theresa, Capt. Cook. We saw him at Guam.

July 12th. It has been a splendid day. The boats have gone off. Capt. Manchester and his Wife and Captain Cook have been aboard. Capt. Manchester and his Wife spent the day. My Husband's and Capt. Manchester's boats have been getting a raft of water for us. We were all going on shore a little while and waited till they got the water, to have the boat, and then a black cloud came on and with it a sprinkling, so we had to postpone it. We have spent the day pleasantly. Willie is a year and a half old today.

The boats have returned with poor success. They have not seen a Whale today.

July 18th. It has been quite calm all day, with the exception of a few minutes at a time, just long enough for us to take the anchor and get under way. Then we would have to let it go again. We have done so several times today. It is slow headway towards Okhotsk City. I suppose that the boats have got there before this. Sent one in shore this forenoon to see what they could see. Saw nothing but Muscle diggers and Seals.

July 20th. It has been foggy a good part of the day, calm and mild. We had a good breeze last night a short time, so that we went along a few miles. I don't know how we shall get anywhere with this weather but hope to have some wind soon. We don't know where our boats are. Sent the fourth Mate off yesterday to see if he could find them and tell them where the Ship is. Have fired off the big gun several times, when it was foggy, that they might know where we are if they should be near enough to hear it.

Our boats returned about 5 o'clock. They brought back a nice lot of Salmon. Mr. Morgan saw the Governor and one of the Merchants and their Families, the same that I stopped with when there last season. They want me to visit them again.

July 21st. We are now going to the Bays as soon as we get a fair wind.

July 24th. It has been cloudy most all day and some foggy around the land this morning. We made the land last night just before dark and thought it to be Aian, by the make of it, but it was a poor horizon all day and we could not get a good Longitude. We did not think we were as far along till this morning we made this land and raised several Ships at anchor about here. We spoke the John P. West, Capt. Tinker, and he told us that we were in Mercury Bay. The strong tide had set us some off our course, and the Ship has been going faster than we thought for. We have now come to anchor.

This Bay is next to, and close to Shant[ar] Bay. This afternoon have been on board the John P. West and spent the afternoon very pleasantly with Mrs. Tinker. She came out across land to meet her Husband last fall. She brought their little Boy. He is about 2 years old and a fat little fellow. They have not been fortunate in taking Oil this season. The ice has been out of this Bay 3 or 4 days.

July 26th. It has been a splendid day, quite warm. The land looks beautiful, covered with green. It makes me think that I should like to go among the green on shore. Capt. Tinker's Wife and little Boy have been on board and spent the afternoon. We enjoyed it much — the Children in particular.

We have sent the boats into a small Bay, called Potter's, to look for Whales. We have just learned that Capt. Allen, of the Onward has about one thousand bbls. of Oil this season. He is a lucky Man.

July 27th. It has been quite foggy all the morning, but is now very fine. The boats are all off. Two of them came back last evening with poor success. They saw 3 or 4 small Whales. The Mate of the Charles W. Morgan came aboard with them. He is looking for his Ship. He has struck a large Whale and thinks it will make 150 bbls. of Oil.

July 28th. It has been a fine day, and Mr. Shephard, our fourth Mate, came off about 9 O'clock to tell us that we have a Whale. He and the second Mate have been off towards Shanta Gut and found this dead Whale. It had washed ashore. It was a large one. They think about 125 bbls. We think we may save about 30 bbls, but the bone is nice; about as nice and as large a head as we took last season. My Husband had just gone to look for Whales, and they called him back. We have now taken the anchor to go for the bone and what we can save of the blubber.

July 29th. It has been a very fine day. It was almost calm yesterday, after we took the anchor, and we could not get along. We could not fetch by the point of land ahead, for the wind was almost ahead, so we let go the anchor about 8 O'clock. It was then head tide. At 12 O'clock at night the tide changed, and we took the anchor but did not go any more than the tide took us, for there was no wind. About 7 O'clock this morning, my Husband went off to the Whale to see what he could do — then about ten miles off, the Ship getting along slowly. About 5 O'clock this afternoon, we came within a mile or so of the Whale and let go the anchor. The two boats came off loaded with bone. It is splendid bone. My Husband has seen Whales and chased them, with poor success though, and has now returned to the Ship.

July 30th. It has been a fine, warm day. The land looks nice and green. I can see the Whale quite plainly through the glass. One boat has been ashore and got all the blubber they could save from the Whale, and all the bone. There are over 500 slabs of it.

The Bears come down from the mountains every night for Whale meat. Mr. Morgan and a boat's crew went on shore to try and shoot one. He shot at one, and he fell over but got up and ran away as fast as he could.

August 1st. It has been foggy all day. Have been firing guns and ringing the bell all the morning. We had one boat off alone and wanted them to know where to find the Ship, if they were near enough to hear the sound. They did hear and came aboard before noon. We want to go through the passage, into Shantarski Bay, but the tide is not fair, and the fog so thick tonight that we can scarcely see the end of the Flying Jib Boom plainly.

August 3rd. It has been quite foggy all day and is now raining very hard. Our two boats that left Monday to go to the Bay ahead of us, have returned tonight. Have seen a number of Ships. They, with but one exception, have done very poorly. One ship was in the ice 70 days. Have all been in it more or less. There is a good deal of heavy ice there now at the head of the Bay. They did not see any Whales, but heard them. We are now at anchor very near the place that we lay last season, when I went on shore in Shantarski Bay. We had a bad time getting through the passage. It was thick fog. We had not much wind and could only go a little way with the tide. At one time there was a heavy swell setting us all the time on the land, and we had to let go the anchor. At another time we came near getting ashore on Bear Island. We saw the point just in time to wear around and had to send the boats ahead to find the land, that we might run in safety.

August 4th. It has been very foggy all day and quite rainy a good part of the time. We have gotten two boats off and don't know where they have gone. We have taken the anchor once or twice today and gone a little way with the tide, farther up the Bay. My Husband and Mr. Morgan went on the beach a little while this morning. They took hooks and line to get some trout, but they were glad to come back without any. It rained very hard and they were wet through. The mosquitoes were so thick that they could not stop. Mr. Morgan fetched me a handsome bunch of flowers, so I thought that I was well enough off.

August 5th. Have had another very unpleasant day, foggy and rainy. Saw a great quantity of floating ice this morning. The tide took it past us. There were some cakes that came against the Ship with great force, but the most of it was tender, breaking into small pieces all about us. This weather will soon carry it all off. Tonight we are surrounded by ice. A good deal of it is quite heavy. We can plainly hear the Whales and saw a Cow and Calf quite near. My Husband went down to see if he could strike one but came back unsuccessful. The other boats have been around the large body of ice, and returned. The Second Mate struck, or rather shot one. The Whale took the line, and they lost him.

August 8th.   Have had another rainy and foggy day. Had quite a strong breeze all night, and this morning have got under way and gone a little ways. We don't know where we are going, only what we guess at. We have to use judgment that we do not go too near land, and there are Ships all about. They have to fire guns and ring bells quite often when under way, that they don't run afoul of each other. It makes it very unpleasant. Tonight, just before we came to anchor, we heard an anchor from some other Ship close by. We spoke the Ship, the L. C. Richmond, Capt. Hathaway. He says there are quite a number of Ships about here. The Hillman is one.

August 9th.   It has been a rainy and foggy day. We have gone a little further out of the Bay. It let up a spell tonight, so that we could see several Ships. Mr. Morgan has been aboard of the Bark Oscar, Capt. Landers. He sent us a late New Bedford paper. He says that a great number of Whales have been seen around the Rocks, for the last two or three days. The place called the Rocks is about 3 miles from here.

August 18th.   Came in sight of Okhotsk City this afternoon and came to anchor just before dark, about 4 miles off. It is a splendid evening. Willie and I have been on deck till we came to anchor, since tea.

September 5th.   We are having fine, mild weather the most of the time, with an occasional blow. We got our first Whale Monday. It was small but very fat and will make about 100 bbls. of Oil. Willie and I have been stopping on shore at Okhotsk City, over two weeks, and spent the time very pleasantly until Willie got sick, which happened only 3 or 4 days before we left. He took a violent cold that settled on his lungs, and I was afraid he was going to have the Croup. I had considerable trouble to make the people understand what I wanted to give him, but I got along very well and doctored him up, and he got better. We have just brought him aboard; the People did everything they could for him and showed us all the hospitality and kindness that we could ask for while we were there. They seemed much pleased with our visit and were quite sorry to have us come away.

We visited with several of the best Families in the place — the Supranic and Merchants — and went all about the place, though there is nothing of note there. There are a good many buildings, the most of them of a poor class, two stores and one Church, Catholic. I attended Church twice. It is a plain but substantial building. Inside, about the altar, is some very nice carved work and a good many beautiful paintings, a great many nice candlesticks and the candles burning in them. The ceremonies are similar to the Catholic ceremonies at home. There are two Priests in attendance, and they wear very rich looking surplices. One Priest is higher than the other. They are very pleasant, social Men and seem to enjoy life as well as any of them.

The season for cultivating the ground is very short. They raise a good many of the kinds of vegetables that we do at home, but they grow so fast and the frost nips them so early, that they don't arrive at the same perfection that they do at home. They have no means of getting any luxuries, except those few Families that receive supplies from the Government. A small vessel comes there once or twice a year to fetch them. They have some nice things from Irkutsk, a large City inland about 800 miles from there, where several of the Families came from. The poorer People live mostly on fish and are very poor.

There are beautiful rivers about the place, and they abound in fish of various kinds, of which the most numerous are Salmon. They have some very fine Trout.

While we were there, we had several sled rides, drawn by dogs. They had 14 harnessed to a very light sled, the same kind as they use on the snow. They must go very fast, for I took the swiftest ride that I ever took over the ground. I liked it very much. The dogs are large and strong. They have a great many of them and use them as Beasts of burden altogether. They have Cows, but I saw no Oxen used. Further back they have great numbers of Reindeer.

They kill great numbers of Bears and other Animals for their furs and skins, the best of which is the Sable. They are beautiful indeed.

We had while there, all the milk we wanted and nice beef, fine berries, of which they get several kinds from the mountains. They had the best of tea that comes from China, but very little coffee. That seems a great luxury. They have as nice, white sugar as I ever saw. They raise a very poor kind of wheat which makes very black bread, though sweet. They are much pleased to get wheat flour from the Ships.

September 6th. We have had a fine day with a good breeze. The boats all went off this morning and just before noon the Fourth Mate struck a Whale. My Husband went right down in his boat, and they soon had it dead and alongside. Tonight it is all cut in. It is larger than the last one they got and very fat. The bone is a foot longer. It is 11 foot and the other 10 foot.

September 7th. It has been a fine day. Three boats have been off and returned tonight. They saw but one or two Whales. We have started the try works and have been stowing down the Oil from the other Whale. He stowed down about 90 bbls.

September 9th. About three O'clock we saw two of our boats coming, towing something that we supposed to be a Whale. We got under way to go and meet them, and we saw that they came along very fast. When they got alongside, lo, it was a White Fish. They had skinned it, so that it looked small. They hoisted it right in on deck with a small tackle. I never saw one before. It is quite a sight. It is just as white as snow, not a spot on it, about as large as a Black Fish — short teeth like them, a small head and small flukes and fins. He is just as fat as butter. Have not seen a Whale today.

September 10th. It has been a pleasant day. The boats have been off, but have returned without seeing any Whales. We spoke the Lancaster, Capt. Russell, today. He has been aboard to see us. He has his Wife and little Boy with him. He did not fetch them aboard with him, for his Wife is not well. Her lungs are very much affected, and she is careful about going in the air. They have not done well this season. Have taken about 300 bbls. of Oil.

September 11th. Have had a very fine day. I have been washing this forenoon. The Men on deck have finished stowing the Oil. Our last Whale made a little over one hundred bbls. of Oil, so that the two made about 200. This afternoon my Husband, Willie and I have been aboard of the Lancaster to see Mrs. Russell. We spent the afternoon very pleasantly. The two children enjoyed it much. Two boats have been off. Have seen no Whales. Two of our boats have been to Okhotsk City since Monday. We are some miles from there and it is not in sight. We are going there as soon as we can get there. We have no wind.

September 13th. Have sent the fourth Mate to Okhotsk City, with provisions for the other two boats, till they can get aboard.

We spoke the Brig Constantine, Capt. Lignum. He came aboard to see us. He belongs to Finland. He has taken 700 bbls. of Oil this season.

September 17th. We have had a fine day with a strong breeze most all day. Last evening we came to anchor within 3 miles of

Okhotsk City. Our two boats came from there last night. Mr. Morgan brought a nice fat Goose with him. His boatsteerer shot it flying. They had not seen any Whales. Today the boats have been off, but we called them aboard before noon to help partake of the Goose we had stuffed and baked for dinner.

One of the Ladies in Okhotsk sent me 3 Ducks, nice ones, and some milk. Mr. Morgan brought a little black Dog for Willie. The Mate of the Cambria gave her to Mr. Morgan. Willie is much pleased. They call her Mink.

September 18th.   Have had a very fine day, and my Husband, Willie and myself have been to the City to spend the day. We had a very pleasant time, but it was quite cold in the morning — fine coming back. We got to the Ship about Sundown, and to our great joy found a nice Whale alongside. We knew that we had one just after we left the river, for we saw that the Ship was under way, and she would not have been unless they had one. The third Mate got it. The Mate got a nice Goose and several Ducks today.

September 27th.   It has been a clear, cold day. The ground, as far as we can see, is covered with snow, and the mountain tops have been covered for over a month. It won't be very long now before this water will be one sheet of ice. It is very cold on deck. One wants a greatcoat and mittens to stop up there to walk long now. The ice was falling to the deck all night from the rigging. For a day or two we have had a great many small Birds about the Ship. They were blown off from the land. We have seen 3 or 4 Bowheads from the Ship, but it was most night and we did not succeed in getting one.

September 28th.   It has been a beautiful day but very cold. We are laying quite near the Town. We came to anchor yesterday afternoon. There are three Ships in sight and not far off.

The boats have just returned to the Ship. My Husband went to the beach to get a load of wood. They did not see Whales until just at night when they saw one, and my Husband came near striking him. Mr. Morgan got some nice fat Ducks and one Partridge, while off.

October 2nd. It has been a fine day. The Bark Maria Theresa and the Othello are in sight. My Husband went aboard the Maria Theresa, and when he got on board, he found out that she was the Othello, Capt. Hillmer. Lewis [Capt. Williams' brother] is aboard of her, and he went to see him. In the evening, they all came aboard to see me. They cheated me some. They did not fetch Lewis down in the Cabin but kept him back a few minutes. He then came down, and at first sight I did not know him. He has changed a good deal. We spent the evening very pleasantly. Tomorrow they will come aboard again.

October 3rd. It has been a pleasant day, and Capt. Hillmer and Lewis have been aboard to see us. Have had a very pleasant visit. I have been getting some letters ready to send to the Islands by them, as it is not likely we shall go there this fall, and they will not be long going, as they have a Clipper Ship and a fast sailor. I do not think we will stop here much longer, as we do not see any Whales and there is some prospect of bad weather.

October 4th. Have had a very unpleasant day, the wind blowing a gale from the Northeast. It commenced blowing in the night. To-day the Ship is pitching so badly that it has made me quite sick all day. We are now some ways from Okhotsk City, and if the gale continues it is not likely that we shall get back. We shall get so far off that it will take some time to go back, and it is getting so late in the season that it will not be worth while.

October 5th. The gale has not abated much. We spoke the Othello this morning. The Captain is not going back to look for Whales but is going direct to the Islands. We shall not go back, but go to Hakodadi. The Othello is in sight tonight.

October 6th.   The gale has now abated and we have had some of the time a good breeze and some of the time calm, some fog, some sunshine. We spoke the Othello about noon. The Capt. and Lewis came aboard a few minutes. They are in a hurry to go along as well as we. My Husband and Mr. Morgan finished their letters to send by them. They are still in sight. We have bent a new sail today, one that we have not used the voyage — the Crotchet Sail.

October 7th.   It has been quite a pleasant day with a good breeze. The Othello is still in sight, so that she has not beat us very badly for a Clipper Ship.

October 8th.   It has been an unpleasant day, cloudy, and a part of the time, rainy. The Othello is out of sight. We shall be in Hakodadi in about 10 days, with a good breeze.

October 14th.   It has been a beautiful day, and we have had a good breeze. We are now in the Japan Sea, and if the wind holds good, will be in Hakodadi in two days. The [place] where I visited a short time when we were here last July is in sight. We were quite alarmed in the night. The Officer came down and called my Husband up, telling him that there was land on the larboard side, quite near; but they had plenty of room to wear around though we were close and very soon she would have gone ashore, for she was going 10 knots an hour. I think it was quite providential that we saw it as quickly as we did. It was a clear night which was in our favor.

October 15th.   It has been a nice day, but the wind is contrary and we are not making much progress towards Hakodadi.

October 16th.   It has been a pleasant day and quite smooth. We are getting along slowly. The wind is not fair. On deck the Men are getting everything ready to go into Port and I am trying to get ready, that I may not have anything to do when we get in.

October 17th. It has been clear and pleasant. Hakodadi is in sight, but we will not get into the Harbour today, I fear, for it is quite calm.

October 18th. It has been a nice clear, warm day, quite calm this morning, but it breezed up a little soon after, and at 7 O'clock tonight, we let go the anchor. The Officials will be off soon, I suppose, and I must leave writing. I think I shall go on shore tomorrow.

BOUND TO THE COAST OF CALIFORNIA

November 1st. It has not been a very pleasant day — quite windy and cold with some rain; for 2 or 3 days the weather has looked threatening from the Northeast. We have been busy all day, getting ready to leave, putting all the things on board that were not already on.

We have a Passenger that we are going to take with us. We are now going direct to the Coast of California to cruise for Whales and are going to see that Mr. Morsland gets to San Francisco. He is going home to his Family in the States. He has been for the past 3 years a Chief Engineer in the Russian Service, on board the Russian Man-of-War Steamer, Japanese. He seems a very smart and nice young Man.

I have not been on shore today but have spent the time that we have been here very pleasantly on shore. We had nice, mild weather the most of the time, and I have been around a good deal to see what was to be seen and shopping. The Japanese have made a great many improvements about their streets, so that it is nice walking. It was very muddy when we were here before. In the stores they had a very large and good assortment of goods such as Malacca and lacquered Ware, Porcelain, and Silks.

November 3rd. The wind has been very strong all day, with some rain; but it is fair wind, and we are going right along. Tonight we are about 400 miles from Hakodadi. Last night was a very bad night, quite squally. The water came on deck a good deal — once over the stern in large quantity, coming below and covering the Cabin floor.

November 4th. It has been a very pleasant day — a strong breeze but not nearly so rugged as yesterday. I have been on deck to walk a short time. Willie and I both enjoyed the nice, cold bracing air, for we had been cooped up below for two days. I have some new Pets to take care of now. Mr. Bradford gave me two Canaries; one of them is a fine singer. Willie is much pleased with them.

November 9th. It has been a pleasant sunshiny day, but the wind blowing almost a gale and the Ship rolling very badly. I have been trying to iron a little, but cannot keep my iron on the stove, so have given it up for today. Willie is not very well. He has taken a bad cold.

November 10th. It has been a very unpleasant day, quite squally, with rain and hail. Tonight the wind has increased to a gale. It looks fearful on deck. The clouds are dark and heavy, the Seas running high and every little while coming over the side. The Men are now taking in sail. I dread a gale in the night.

November 11th. A very bad day indeed. The wind blew fearfully all night and all day today, the water coming over onto the deck quite badly and some of the time below a little. All is confusion; everything that can get loose is sliding about the Ship. It is a head wind, which is worse than all, and it is still increasing.

November 12th. It is still blowing a gale, but has abated a good deal. It blew so fearfully in the night that it frightened me very much. I did not know what might happen to us. The Ship was going 10 knots under close-reefed Main Topsail, the Water coming over constantly, over the stern, breaking the skylight, tearing away a hen coop that was built up on the stern soon after we came out from home. The Sea never has affected it till now. The Water came down into the Cabins and Staterooms, so that they dipped it up by pailfuls, wetting the carpets through. All was confusion and with all the rest of the trouble, one heavy roll of the Ship lifted our bedstead out of the place it ran in and tore it down altogether. That frightened me again, and Willie was much frightened. I have been on deck a few minutes, but it is quite unpleasant to walk there is such a bad swell and the deck is not dry yet.

November 12th. We have gained this day by crossing the meridian — and a very unpleasant one it is, too. It has been wet and cold, raining and hailing — a strong breeze most of the time, and among the rest of our trials we lost a Man overboard this afternoon. He was standing on the rail, doing something or other, and fell overboard. The Ship was going very fast, but not so fast as she had been going a half hour before. I do not think we could have saved him then. They threw an Oar over for him to catch while they were lowering a boat. He swam well, but could not have stood it more than a minute longer. I knew that something was wrong when I heard the confusion on deck, getting the Ship around and lowering away the boat in such a time. I was afraid they would not get to him before he was gone and was relieved and thankful that he was saved. He was a forward hand and a Portuguese.

November 13th. It has been blowing a gale all day and is still increasing. I think that we have the worst part of the gales in the night. It is a fair wind and we are going right along.

November 14th. It is still blowing very hard, but has moderated a good deal. Last night was a very bad one — some awful Seas came over and any quantity of Water below. We have more or less rain and hail about every day.

November 15th. It has not been a very bad day. Have had some rain and a little hail in squalls, but some of the day quite pleasant and almost calm.

November 17th. The weather has been very changeable today — some of the time, fine sunshine and quite mild; then a strong breeze and cold; then almost calm with occasional squalls of wind and rain — and in one of these, after dinner, it carried away the Fore Topsail Yard; the wind is fair now.

November 25th. We have had a nice day, a good breeze most all day. We have about 500 miles more to go and think that with this breeze we will accomplish it in about 4 days.

November 29th. It was foggy all night and till three O'clock in the morning when it cleared away very fine and has remained so all day. Just at night yesterday, we raised the land. We are now running along the Coast to San Francisco. It has been nearly calm all day, and we have gained but little. We are now about 20 miles from the Harbour. Have seen quite a number of small Crafts today.

November 30th. It has been very foggy all day. We are now going away from San Francisco. We have not been there, as we expected. The wind was not fair — and the greatest thing was that my Husband found out that some of the Men would run away. Then he gave up the idea of going at all. Mr. Morsland left us last evening. We put him on board a Pilot boat. My Husband went aboard with him and took our letters and got some late papers. We shall miss Mr. M. much. He is going to see our Folks when he gets home. I hope that nothing will happen to prevent. I reckoned upon going to San Francisco to spend one day with my

Husband and Mr. Morsland, but am disappointed and must make the best of it now. We are going direct to Turtle Bay to cruise for a kind of Whale, called a Devil Fish or California Grey. We have about 1000 miles to go. It will not take long if we have good winds. It is now about calm.

December 3rd. It has been the finest day that we have had for over a month. It has been really beautiful, and Willie and I enjoy it much. I think that I can fully appreciate it after having so much unpleasant weather. On deck the Men are mending Sails.

December 4th. We have had another very fine day, a gentle breeze. Saw from aloft some kind of Whale, I don't know what. A plenty of Porpoises. Caught two. Have been having the skylight in the House enlarged, which makes it much lighter and pleasanter below.

December 6th. It has been a very fine day. An Island in sight, called Guadaloupe. We are now about 140 miles from Turtle Bay.

December 8th. Another beautiful day. This morning we passed some of the most barren land that I ever saw in my life. It was a portion of the mainland, and there was nothing but rocks and dirt — not a vestige of vegetation could be seen; but this is not a fair representation of California. I know that there is a plenty of beautiful land in this Country. This is only the barren Coast. This is Lower California.

At 10 O'clock we came to anchor in Turtle Bay. It is a fine Harbour but not a fine landscape as far as the Country is concerned. It has an unpleasant aspect — the land, uneven and rocky with scarcely any sign of vegetation. From the Ship I cannot see a tree or even a shrub. It is beautiful weather here, the water smooth, a plenty of Birds, and it looks pleasant after all.

There are four Ships besides us — the Congress, Capt. Stranburg; the Jeanette, Capt. Winslow; the Coral, Capt. Sisson; and the Florida, Capt. Fish came in and anchored this afternoon. Mrs. Fish is on board, so I have a Lady for a Neighbor.

December 9th. It has been a splendid day, and my Husband, Willie and I have been aboard of the Florida, to see Capt. Fish and Wife, and spent the day very pleasantly. They have a little Son with them, 6 years old. We all went on shore a short time for a walk and to see some graves. There are 8 Men buried on a rise of ground a few minutes' walk from the Water. One is an English Captain's grave. He was buried in the year 1819. The graves have all simple boards at the heads with the names, ages, and years. There are four buried in one grave. They were killed by a Whale last season. The spot is very barren. I saw not a spear of grass — one or two simple weeds of some kind, but with rather pretty flowers on them, a striking contrast with the desolation around. I thought that I would not like to be buried in such a barren spot, far from Friends and home — but would, I think, prefer even that spot to the deep.

December 10th. It has been a very fine day, and I have been washing. Mrs. Fish has been washing, too, so she has not been aboard to see me but will probably come tomorrow. The Captain and his little Boy were aboard a few minutes this morning.

The Bark Isabelle came to anchor last night, Capt. Tucker. A French Ship passed the Bay about the same time. She was coming in, but seeing several here, kept on her course.

December 12th. We are having beautiful weather in here. Capt. Fish and his Wife have been aboard and spent the day with us. I have enjoyed it very much. Their little Boy was so much taken up with the fishing that he did not come. The Milo, Capt. Fordham, has come in and anchored close by. He, with the other Captains have been aboard a short time.

December 13th. Another fine day. We had quite a little shower in the night. The Onward, Capt. Allen, is outside. He has been in with his boat and has been aboard to see us. He says that he doesn't know whether he will come in with his Ship or not, there are so many of us here now. I believe all the Captains have been aboard today.

December 14th. Have had a very fine day. I have been on shore a little while this afternoon with my Husband and Willie. We enjoyed it very much. It was a nice place where we landed, a good dry Beach. We have a nice run on the Beach. It is like all the rest — very barren. This Bay abounds in Fish of various kinds — very nice Turtle, Clams and Oysters. We had a nice sail and returned to the Ship, Willie quite tired with his run and glad to go to sleep. Captain Winslow was ashore and gathered some nice moss for me.

December 15th. It has been a splendid day, and we have enjoyed it very much, going a sailing, trying to catch Turtle, and visiting the Beach. We did not succeed in getting any Turtle, but saw several and a plenty of Seal and Porpoises — Birds in abundance. When they alight, they remind me of an Army of Soldiers. There were a great many boats out fishing. Captain Fish, Wife and little Boy were on shore. There were more signs of vegetation there than I have yet seen. I got a very pretty bunch of red flowers from a thorn bush, but there was hardly a green leaf on the bush. There were three graves near by with boards to mark the names and ages. The Beach was strewn with bones of Whales captured in seasons past. We have had a nice walk and returned to the Ship this afternoon.

The Clipper Ship, Speedwell, Capt. Gibbs, and the Bark Cleone, Capt. Simons, have come in and anchored. My Husband has gone this evening aboard of the Speedwell to see Capt. G. and his Wife.

December 16th. It has been a beautiful day. My Husband, Willie and I have been aboard of the Speedwell to see Capt. G. and Wife. All the Captains were there a short time. They have been in the same Ship one voyage before. They have no Children. They have a fine Ship, a nice Cabin and a nice quarterdeck. We spent the day with them, and enjoyed it very much indeed. Their Ship is now under way. They are going home and are going to cruise on their way.

December 19th.   It has been a very fine day with splendid sunshine. It is the same about every day with scarse any rain. The Callao has come in today and anchored, Capt. Fuller. My Husband has been aboard of her — also the Europa, Capt. Manter. He got Sandwich papers as late as November.

December 20th.   The Ship Ontario, Capt. Foster, has come in and anchored. There are now 12 of us. Most every day one or more passes by or comes in.

December 22nd.   A Steamer passed by on her way to San Francisco. With the glass I thought I saw her Passengers on the deck.

December 23rd.   It has been a very fine day. My Husband, Willie and I have been aboard of the Florida and spent the day very pleassantly with Capt. Fish and his Wife. Captaing Hempstead and his Wife were there. I liked them very much. Mrs. H. is a little, small Woman and quite pretty. Capt. Sisson was there also. In the afternoon, we all went on shore a short time for a walk, and enjoyed it much. We came near having an accident. When we got to the Ship they were hoisting us up in the boat when the brace to the after davy gave way. Luckily it held till we got out of the boat and saved us from a ducking in the Water. After tea several of the Officers from other Ships were here. Mr. Dunham, First Officer of the Isabelle had a very nice Accordian which he played finely. He also is a very good Singer. We enjoyed it very much, not having the privilege of hearing music very often.

December 25th.   It has been a very fine day. We have a plenty of company and beautiful weather but no Whaling yet. The boats see 3 or 4 some days and one or two have been fast, but the Whales run so badly that they have to cut from them. There are now 15 Ships in here. Last evening the Cabin was full of Captains. One Ship has gone out — the Callao.

December 27th. Capt. Smith, of the Fabious, has got a Whale this afternoon. It is the first one that has been got this season and Capt. Smith was the last one in the Bay.

December 29th. Willie enjoys this place and weather much, I know. He almost lives on deck, and he is generally full of mischief when he is up there, throwing his Shoes and Cap, or something, overboard.

December 31st. The Steamer, Golden Age, passed this forenoon, on her way to San Francisco. When our boats returned at night, they brought a large package of papers that they had thrown from the Steamer to them. The other boats got a lot also. They were, with the exception of 2 or 3 New York papers, all late San Francisco ones so that I suppose they must have passed the other Steamer on her way to New York and exchanged papers.

January 1st, 1861
   It has been a very fine day. Last night the Fabious got another Whale. No other Ship has one yet.
   This is the first day of the new year. Oh, how I wish I could be at home today and participate in the kind wishes of a happy new year, with all our Friends.

January 4th. Another beautiful day. The boats have all been gone again today. It seems very lonesome indeed. My Husband shot at a Whale but was not quite near enough. The Fourth Mate got a nice large Turtle today.

January 5th. We have such beautiful weather every day — not one whole unpleasant day. It is foggy, or rather, hazy, once in a while.

Early in the morning, generally. We have all the time heavy dews at night. A Person would die of thirst on shore now, for there is not a drop of fresh Water to be had. Two Men attempted to run away from the Congress the other day, but were glad to come back again.

January 8th. This morning we took our anchor and left Turtle Bay, as did the little Florida. The other day the Congress and the Europa left. It will be much better for those that are in the Bay now, for there were too many Ships in there to do well. We are now bound to Banderas Bay or Humpback Bay, as the Whalemen term it, on the Coast of Mexico, about 700 miles from Bartholomew's Bay.

January 12th. It has been a fine day and a good breeze. We made the Cape called Cape S. Lucas, about noon. After dinner we went ashore and spent 3 or 4 hours very pleasantly with Capt. Fish, Wife and little Boy. It is not much of a place. There are quite a number of grass houses — or Mexican houses — and two frame ones, one of them a very large one, owned and occupied by an Englishman. He has a Mexican Wife and several rather pretty Children. We went to his house. An American lives in the small house. They treated us very kindly. It is quite warm on shore, though it is the winter season. It is also the dry season and everything looked like it. It is very sandy, and it was with difficulty we could walk to the house — only a short distance from the boat.

They ride mostly; horses are plentiful. There are thousands of head of Cattle in the place, but at this time of the year they suffer for the want of water and food. Consequently they look very poor. They told us that a great many die every year in the dry season.

There is very little sign of vegetation about the Bay where these People live, but they live near the Water in order to be convenient to the Ships, as they do a good deal of business with them. They exchange their products for anything that the Ships may have to spare. Their farms are back among the mountains, and they raise plenty of Sweet Potatoes, Oranges, Grapes and Figs. We could get all the new Cheese that we wanted, though it is not very nice, I think. The Raisins are very nice and fresh, and the Figs are very good. I saw a good many Cactus growing right on the sand banks, very thriftily, but not in blossom. I saw nothing that would tempt me to live there.

We came aboard early and are now under way again, with a good fair wind.

This is Willie's birthday. He is two years old today.

January 14th. We got into the Bay and came to anchor about 4 O'clock this afternoon. The Bark Callao is in here, Capt. Fuller. He came aboard and took tea with us — has taken one Humpback in here, but the Sharks ate him almost up before they got him to the Ship. They saved about 20 bbls. The Sharks are very numerous here. They have seen a good many Whales since they came in, which is about a week, but they are very wild so that they cannot get near them. It is a nice looking place in this Bay — everything looks green and beautiful on shore, as far as we can see. There are settlements here, and fresh water rivers.

The Mexicans have been aboard to see Capt. Fuller and to trade. They have Beef, Chickens, Corn, Cheese, Eggs, that they offer in exchange for anything they may want. Cloth they seem anxious to get. There are a plenty of Oranges, Lemons, and Mummy Apples, growing on shore. It seems to be a good place for Men to run away. Capt. Fuller sent a boat in shore today to have the Men cut some wood and the Boy stole the victuals and ran away. Some of the Men got poisoned with running ivy.

There is nice wood growing here — Mahogany and Ebony. There has been some shipped from here to New York. I want to go on shore here, to have a run and look around a little. I suppose I shall some day while we stop.

The Florida came in and anchored soon after we did.

This afternoon we have been on shore for a little run. Capt. Fish and his Wife and Capt. Fuller were on shore also. We had a pleasant time — we Ladies gathering small shells on the Beach, while the Gentlemen were gunning. Then we sat down a spell under the shade of a large spreading green tree.

Everything looks green and nice on shore. There are a variety of trees, but none familiar to us except the Palm Tree and the Cabbage Tree. There is some kind of Apple growing on one kind of tree — very small and quite poisonous. On one kind of tree there is growing Fruit in Bunches. I do not remember the name. It is quite soft inside and tart — tastes a little like the Pineapple. They are very good. Several Natives were gathering them. One was a Woman. She was very kind and pleasant looking. Capt. Fish had a Man who could talk with them. These People lived across the Bay and were going all around, gathering this Fruit. The Woman had a horse that she rode. Some of the Men had Mules and some came in a Canoe. The Woman wanted to have Mrs. Fish and me ride, but we did not. She rode on a side saddle. She was dressed quite neatly — also the Men.

We saw but one kind of wild flower on shore, and that a kind of wild Morning Glory.

January 19th. We had a nice day today and spent it very pleasantly. Capt. Fish and his Wife and Capt. Fuller have been aboard and spent the day and evening, though we have not had the Gentlemen's company all day. They have been up to one of the rivers, to a small settlement. When they came back, they quite amused us with their description of the place and People. There were only a few People, who live in a kind of grass house. They were dressed quite well. One Man was teaching some four or five Children, under a tree, and at the same time cooking his breakfast. One Man, they said, was very sad. He had been obliged to flee to this place from where he lived, on account of the revolution, and leave all his Family and property behind. His life had been threatened. These People kept all their valuables hid in the woods for fear of their enemies' stealing them from them. Our Folks liked the looks of the place. There were a plenty of Lime trees, loaded with Fruit, a plenty of Game, some handsome Birds — but the river is full of Sharks and Alligators — a great many out running on the Beach. They said they looked awful, with their mouths open, but did not offer to touch anyone. They were so well pleased with their jaunt that they have promised to take us Ladies some day.

January 20th. Another fine day. We have spent this Sabbath very pleasantly and quietly, on board the little Florida. Capt. Fuller was there. Willie enjoyed it much and was as mischievous as usual. He threw his Hat and Willie Fish's overboard and one Shoe, but we got them.

January 21st. The Men are today cleaning the Ship outside, to paint her.

January 22nd. We have had a beautiful day, cool and refreshing after the rain. We have commenced painting the Ship today. One boat has been ashore to get some sand to cooper with.

January 23rd. There have been a good many Whales in the Bay, and the Ships have had all their boats off this morning. The little Florida's boat got a Whale and soon killed him. It was not far from the Ship and did not run badly, so that they soon had her alongside of the Callao and cut in. The three Ships are mated so that they will cut in sometimes on one Ship and then on another, if we are fortunate enough to get any more. This afternoon one of the Florida's boats got fast to another Whale and lost him, he ran so and so far out of the Bay. When it came night they were obliged to cut from him.

January 24th. It has been a very fine day, and we have all been on an excursion to the Town. Capt. Fish, his Wife and little Boy, Capt. Fuller, my Husband, Willie and myself. We had a delightful time. We started as soon as we had had breakfast — had a fair wind, and it was not very long before we got to the River, thought it is about 10 miles to the Town. It is a nice River and the Country beautiful and green. Along the river bank was a plenty of game, such as Ducks, Snipe, and several other kinds — Pelicans and Cranes innumerable. The Captains had their guns with them and killed a number. The river is full of Alligators and Sharks. In some places on the beach, the Alligators were lying as thick as they could, sunning, with their mouths open. They are a dirty, bad-looking creature. The Men shot at several, and one Captain Fish killed and cut off his head and saved it to carry aboard with him.

January 25th. We have had a splendid day — a plenty of Whales in the Bay, and the Callao's boat has got one. They brought it to our Ship and have now got it cut in. It is necessary to work quickly when they get one in this Bay, for the Sharks are so numerous that in a short time they would eat the whole Whale. What short time they were cutting, they ate a good deal of the blubber. They are quite large and they take great mouthfuls.

The Florida's boat has a Whale, and it ran very badly, so that it took them a long way out of the Bay. The Ship has got under way and gone after it.

January 26th. The Florida has come back into the Bay. The Captain has been aboard. All hands feel disappointed about the Whale. It was a large one, but they did not save much of him. It was very rugged outside and some time before they could cut him in, so that the Sharks got about all. I think it is quite provoking to be so bothered with Sharks.

January 27th. We have had a splendid day. The boats went off this morning, and soon after, Mr. Morgan got fast to a Whale. They took him alongside the Florida about noon. I went on deck when they were close by. It was a pretty sight to see the boats, 12 of them, towing the Whale.

January 28th. All three of the Ships are boiling today. We are also calking decks, and consequently are dirty enough. Willie has a good time with it all, and between the Oil and Tar, I can't keep him clean an hour.

January 29th. We heard tonight, by way of the boats, that the People had been obliged to leave the Town. The Men from the boats saw them this morning on the beach — Men, Women and Children. They told them that a gang of Men, calling themselves Liberals, came there to rob them and they left everything, not having time to go into their houses to save anything. Those that could, took their horses, but these Liberals go around the Country plundering such small places and driving the People off till they are obliged to settle in some other secluded spot. There was one old Gentleman among these few, cut in the forehead and wrist pretty badly.

February 2nd. The boats brought in word that one of the Florida's boats had another Whale, in shore a good ways from the Ships. It was late for them to tow him so far, so we got under way and our company went aboard of their own Ships. They got the Whale alongside about three O'clock this afternoon. It was a large Cow Whale and fat. They think she will make about 50 bbls of Oil. There were plenty of Sharks about but they ate but a little. It is a nice green spot here by the river.

Mr. Morgan fired at another Whale today but lost him by the line becoming fouled. The Florida's boats got a California Grey today, also a Killer.

February 6th. It has been a very fine day but almost calm and very warm. We have been stowing down Oil. The Whale only made 55 bbls. Capt. Horn spent the night with us and went to the Town this morning. He is quite social and told us a good many interesting things about this Country. He belongs to San Blas but was obliged to leave there for the present on account of political affairs. He is a Military Officer. There is a great deal of trouble at the present time in Mexico. The political affairs are very unsettled and bands of Robbers go about the Country to the great fear of all the People of the small, quiet places. The Country is so thickly wooded — for the most part impenetrable — that the People know nothing of their approach till they are upon them, and they rob them of everything.

February 7th.   Towards night I saw a large Leopard Shark. He came close to the stern of the Ship, so that I could look right down upon him. He looked awful and yet was handsome, the beautiful, bright, round spots on him all over, showing many colors under the water. He had a fin on his back and went through the water very fast. He was as long as a Whale boat, had a large flat head and was for a long time playing about the Ship with his mouth wide open to catch fish, till Mr. Morgan came alongside and chased him a little way and hove a spade into him, but he did not fasten to him. They say this kind of Shark is the worst kind.

February 9th.   It has been a very fine day and a good breeze, making it cool and comfortable out of the Sun. We have been up the river this afternoon, gunning, but did not get much game. Saw a plenty of all kinds of Birds, Alligators and Sharks — saw the Pelicans catching fish. They dive down into the water, catch a large Fish, which swells the large bag under and attached to their very long bills, to its full size. Sometimes they get one so large that it is with difficulty that they swallow it, and sometimes the bag is broken by the Fish. Tonight Capt. Horn came aboard and took tea with us. He says that the People at the Town have been having a jolly time over some weddings. Four couples have been married. He says their good time consists in the Men getting drunk and the Women dancing.

February 10th.   A very beautiful day, everything very quiet. Some of the time I have been amusing Willie by letting him fish over the stern with a stick tied to a string, and he would haul it in and say that he had a fish.

February 12th.   We are having such beautiful weather in this Bay all the time, and if we only had a plenty of whaling business, all the time or even a part of the time, we would be perfectly satisfied with our quarters for the present, but on the contrary, the boats go off day after day and bring nothing back. Today the fourth Mate struck a Whale and from some cause did not get fast, so we lost him. He stove the boat a little.

February 15th.   This morning early, my Husband went to the Pond to see if he could get some Ducks and took Willie with him. When they returned, he said that he met Capt. Fish and Capt. Fuller there. They were gunning also. They all were quite lucky. My Husband got about twenty in all — Ducks (some of them quite large), Curlews, Snipe, and Pheasants. They enjoyed the sport much. Willie seemed as fresh as when he left in the morning, though he had been gone all day. His little shoes were wet and full of sand, so that he limped when he walked, but he did not seem to mind it. All he could say was "Papa, bang go the Ducks."

February 17th.   The third Mate of the Florida says that they saw about 20 Whales yesterday afternoon, all coming into the Bay — two small Calves with them. The second Mate of the Callao struck one but they had to cut from him. This afternoon Mr. Morgan struck a Cow Whale. She had a young Calf with her. They succeeded in getting the Whale and towed it to the Ship before Night. They think her a good sized one and very fat. Mr. Morgan told me that she took her Calf on her fin and ran with it after she was struck. When they killed the Calf, she stopped and fought the boat. She stove two but not very badly.

February 18th.   Have had a very fine day. Have the Whale cut in and commenced to boil. It is very fat blubber. While they were cutting in, the Sharks were very thick about. I saw the Men cutting them with their spades. If they cut them in the back of the neck, they will die instantly. I saw them cut a number in that way.

They spun around and around, turned on their backs and sunk out of sight. They did not get much of the Whale, for the Men kept fighting them off.

February 20th.   The Callao has come over and anchored close by. My Husband and Willie have been aboard. While they were there, they saw a gam of Whales not far off. My Husband sent Willie home and then Capt. Fuller and he went down to try and strike a Whale. My Husband struck one and the Whale brought his flukes down on the head of the boat and stove it quite badly, so that they had to come right aboard and had to bail all the time. The iron broke, and the Whale went off. One of the Callao's boats was stove a little by coming in contact with the first boat.

February 26th.   A Ship came in and anchored close by us about noon. She is the Cambria, Capt. Pease. The Captains have all been aboard of her to get the news. She is right from the Coast of California.

Capt. Pease says that in Turtle Bay some of the Ships have done very well. Capt. Foster, of the Ontario, has done the best, having got 7 Whales — but Capt. Allen of the Onward, at Maria Island, has done the best of anyone, having taken 900 bbls. of Oil since we last saw him in Turtle Bay, which was sometime in December. The Monmouth, that we saw in Turtle Bay, has been ashore and was damaged so much that she will be condemned. The Delaware is a total loss.

We got some papers of Capt. Pease. One was as late as February the 8th.

Capt. Pease has his Wife and little Boy on board. He is going to send them home from Acapulco, on account of Mrs. Pease's poor health. She will get home in about a week from the time she leaves there. They are going there direct and will soon be there. We will send some letters by her to our Friends. I am going on board to see Mrs. Pease this evening.

ACROSS THE PACIFIC

March 26th. A good breeze and fair. We are now bound to the Islands. This is the first time that I have taken my pen to write in my Journal, since we left.

An event worthy of recording in these pages has transpired since then. We have had an addition to the Florida's Crew in the form of a little Daughter, born on the 27th of February in Banderas Bay on the Coast of Mexico. She weighed 6-¾ pounds, is now one month old and weighs 9 pounds. She seems very healthy and is also very quiet. We are, as may be supposed, well pleased with her. Willie is much pleased with his little Sister.

Since we left Banderas Bay nothing else worthy of notice has transpired. We stopped at Maria Island, about 60 miles from the Bay, two days and got quite a quantity of wood. A variety of wood grows there — Lignumvita, Yellow Ebony, Ironwood, and a kind of Cedar are the principal kinds. There are a plenty of Birds, beautiful Parrots, and also a plenty of very large Snakes or Serpents.

March 31st. I have been on deck to walk. I was looking at a piece of Iron Wood. I hefted it, and it is rightly named, for it is very heavy, and when thrown overboard immediately sinks.

April 1st. We have had a pleasant day and a good breeze. We expect to see the Island of Hawaii one of the Sandwich Islands group in the morning. It is very high land, and one of the highest Mountains in the world is on it. It is seen a long way off. It is the largest Island of the group. I want much to see them, as I have not been there the voyage.

April 3rd. I have been on deck to look at the land. It looks beautiful and green, but I could not see the top of the Mountain. There is a mist hanging over it. This is the season of the year that they have a good deal of rain, sometimes for weeks together. We have a fine breeze now and are going right into the Harbour. We are not far off and will get in by noon, so I much stop writing and get ready to go ashore.

April 9th. I have sat down to write a very little about my visit to Hilo, on the Island of Hawaii. We returned on board the Ship last evening and immediately got under way. We are now bound to Honolulu, the Island of Oahu, and expect to arrive there tomorrow.

April 20th. We have just returned from Honolulu, or I mean to say it is one week since we returned, and this is the first opportunity that I have had to write one word in my book. We have not been very well, any of us. My Husband has had a very bad cold, accompanied with a cough and a severe headache. Willie has been quite unwell with a summer complaint. He was sick one day in Honolulu, but we enjoyed ourselves very well generally. We rode out and had a good view of the place. We went up in what is called the Plains. It is a fine spot and much pleasanter to look at than right in the heart of the City. It is beautiful and green with nice flowers and patches of Yarrow and Bananas growing. It is quite cool up there, but is extremely warm in Honolulu in the middle of the day. It is a pretty place, though, and reminds me much of home. I went out shopping two or three times and thought it a good deal like shopping at home.

I did not have the opportunity of attending Church, as we were not there on the Sabbath. Mr. Damon, the Missionary, and his Wife called on me. I liked them much. They gave me a very handsome, bound Friend.*

There are some handsome buildings in Honolulu. The Sailors'

---

* The Reverend Samuel C. Damon was a missionary of the American Seamen's Friend Society and minister of the Bethel Union Church. He was also editor of the weekly newspaper, *The Friend,* which carried a great deal of whaling news.

Home is a nice one.* The King's Palace is spacious but no great beauty outside. I did not have the pleasure of seeing their Majesties, the King and Queen.

Honolulu has an excellent Harbour — perfectly safe. There were quite a number of Ships there and a good many smaller Craft. In years past, there have been great numbers of Ships in there, so many that anyone could walk from one to the other. Then there was a good deal of business done at that place, and it was a very noisy place, too, in the Shipping Season, compared to what it is now — so many Sailors congregating together from the different Ships. After being so long a time on Ship, they would be noisy on shore. Now a good many Ships go to San Francisco. I do not know that I have anything interesting to say more, so will stop scribbling. [Captain Williams became a mason in Honolulu in November 1852. A photograph of him taken while wearing his masonic apron was Mrs. Williams' favorite.

Mrs. Williams noted in a letter that the people in Honolulu were anxious about the situation in the States and were awaiting the newspaper printing of the inaugural address of President Lincoln to learn the policy of the new administration. They thought the fate of the Republic would hang on this.]

April 22nd. We have had good winds ever since leaving the Islands and are quite thankful for them, as we are in a hurry to get along. Have had beautiful weather but very warm. According to our reckoning, we have to throw away this day. We are today in East Longitude. Consequently, today is Monday, though we keep it as Sunday.

April 23rd. We have had a very fine day, but the heat is almost intolerable. It is very dull just now, though in the way of work

---

* This Sailors' Home was a three-story building with a veranda on two sides at each floor, built by the Honolulu Sailors' Home Society for the officers and seamen of ships spending a few weeks in port or one single night or one meal. It was advertised at that time in the newspaper, "officer's table with lodging per week $6.- and seamen's ditto $5.-"

there is always something going on on Shipboard. The Men are very busy making Spun Yarn, small rope, out of large, repairing and painting boats, making and mending sails, besides the usual duties of scrubbing decks, etc.

May 8th. It has been cloudy and some rainy all day, and there is a head wind now. The Island of Niphon is now in sight. We will soon be in Hakodadi, if this head wind does not last.

May 10th. Tonight we are off Cape Siriga Laki, about 60 miles from Hakodadi.

May 11th. We are now in the Straits of Matsumae. This morning we came very near getting aground on a reef in going around a small Island. The reef made out, though it was not to be seen. We found ourselves in 3 fathoms of water and immediately let go the Anchor. It did not catch on the reef but slipped over, and we were in 11 fathoms right off and all safe. Still, we think we had a narrow escape.

May 13th. We have at last got into Hakodadi. We came to anchor about 9 O'clock. We anchored last night some miles from here. It was quite calm. About three O'clock a breeze sprang up, we took our anchor and got under way. Then we had a head wind and had to beat all the way in. The Pilot came aboard, and before we anchored, Capt. Randolph came aboard. There are quite a number of small Craft in here — about 400 Junks, and the two Whalers — the South Boston and the Gratitude. There is one Steamer.

The rain has been pouring down all day, so that I have not been ashore, but will go tomorrow. Several of the Foreign Residents have been on board to see us. Capt. Fletcher, Mr. Wilke, Mr. Bradford, and the Japanese Officials have been aboard.

May 14th. We have spent the day quite pleasantly, running about and looking at and admiring all the pretty things — making quite a number of purchases, also. It does appear to me that we can get about anything we want in the way of fancy things, here. The Japanese People pay a good deal of attention to Foreign Children that come here. They notice Willie a good deal and get around him in crowds wherever he goes. He is quite lively, and that suits them much. He enjoys the sport a great deal and will go to any of them.

We have enjoyed ourselves very much today and took tea with Mr. Pits at his house. He takes Mr. Rice's place (the Consul) while he is gone to the States. They expect that he is now in Washington and will be back in about three months.

May 15th. The sun shone finely today, but the wind has been blowing a gale, and the Children and I have had to stop on board. There is a very heavy swell right here in the Harbour. The Junks are rolling and pitching and swinging around. On shore the sand is blowing in clouds about, and shingles are whirling in all directions. The Japanese are beginning to put on shingles like ours, I see, on some of the new buildings. Formerly they put them on and covered the roofs with large round stones to keep them on. Almost every Japanese building in Hakodadi is built in that way.

May 18th. We got under way about three O'clock last night — the South Boston at the same time.

THE LAST SUMMER

May 19th. It has been a fine day and a very quiet one. Have not seen any Whales. We have got through the Straits and are now in the Japan Sea, with a good breeze. There is a Merchant Ship close by, bound, I suppose, to the Amoor River. We have not seen the South Boston since we have been through the Straits.

May 20th.   It has not been a very fine day — a part of the time foggy and some of it, rainy. It has been clear this afternoon, and we say two Whales — a Cow and a Calf. Lowered three boats, and the first Mate got near enough to prick the Cow with the Iron from the Greener Gun, but it drew out.

May 25th.   It has been foggy a good deal of today and some rainy. The Land is in sight today. My Husband has been down to try his new boat sail that he has been making.

We are now off Victoria Bay. The Land all about is high and there is snow on the tops.

May 26th.   White Rock is in sight from aloft. This has once been a noted Whaling place; it is not of much note nowadays.

May 27th.   It has been a very foggy day and not much wind till tonight. We have now a strong breeze. It is not fair to go to Broughton Bay where we are now trying to go. Little Mary is three months to day.

May 28th.   A head wind. Broughton Bay is about 30 miles off. The Cooper has been making me a Washing Machine today. I am afraid that I shall not use it very much.

May 29th.   We are now in Broughton Bay. Have been quite near the land. Have seen no Whales except a few Humpbacks. Shall leave tonight.

May 30th.   We have a fair wind and are leaving the Japan Sea as fast as we can.

May 31st.   My Husband has been turning me a rolling Pin of yellow Ebony. It is very pretty. Tonight we are off what is called the Wood Lands.

June 1st. Before breakfast the Man aloft raised a Right Whale. My Husband and the Fourth Mate lowered their boats and went to try to catch him. My Husband got quite near and the Boatsteerer darted his Iron but missed. It was an excellent chance, they all admit. How he came to miss him, no one knows. We all were very sorry to lose the Whale.

June 2nd. We are now bound to the Okhotsk and are in a hurry to get there to see if we can't find some Whales there.

June 3rd. Between 4 and 5 O'clock this afternoon the Man from aloft raised Right Whales. Mr. Morgan's boat was lowered with my Husband at the head and Mr. Morgan as boatsteerer. It was late, but they thought they would go down and try their luck. Mr. Morgan's boatsteerer is sick.

The Whale showed a very good chance to strike and they struck him soon after they lowered, putting two Irons into him. He ran badly some of the time and fought a good deal. They could not get near enough to lance him, and it was fast getting night. I got the Baby to sleep and went on deck to see the fun. While up there, the Whale came quite near the Ship and I had a nice chance to see him. I could see almost his whole back breaching, turning flukes. Then off he would go, giving the boat's crew a nice ride. While I was on deck I could see that it was setting in a thick fog, and I began to wish they would come aboard. Since I came below, my Husband came aboard with the Second Mate. He has gone back to the other boats. They are still hanging on to the Whale, but I don't think they will save him, for he is spouting clear yet and it is most dark and a thick fog. The Ship is keeping along after them.

June 4th. It has been foggy all the fore part of the day. It cleared up about noon. They had to cut from the Whale, and came aboard last night about 9 O'clock. Have seen no Whales today except Finbacks.

June 5th. It has been foggy most all day but cleared up about 4 O'clock. About that time we raised Right Whales — three. My Husband and the first Mate lowered first. Soon after, the other boats lowered. My Husband was in the first Mate's boat and got a chance to shoot at the Whale under water. The Iron did not go into him, so no Whale today. The boats have come aboard.

June 7th. Willie has met with a bad accident this afternoon. He was playing in one of the Staterooms and fell off from a Chest and cut his lip open very badly — with his teeth, we suppose. It bled a good deal. His Pa sewed it up. The poor little Fellow bore it better than I thought he would. We are in hopes that it will not leave a bad scar.

June 8th. Willie by some means got the stitch out of his lip today and had to have it sewed again. He did not like to have it done very well, but bore it well.

June 9th. More or less foggy all day. We are pretty near the Straits, we think. Can't tell exactly, not having the opportunity to take an exact observation for some days. Have not seen land.

June 10th. Quite foggy the most of the day. The greatest distance we could see at any time today has been about 4 miles. Have tacked about, not knowing exactly where we are. The land can't be far off. We want to get through the Straits but think it not safe to try in the fog.

June 11th. Was quite foggy this morning but has cleared away so that we can see several miles. Have had a good breeze and are about through the Straits — through the most dangerous part. The name of this Strait is La Perouse — Saghalin Island on one side and Yezo on the other. We passed quite a large Japanese Tower on Saghalin Island. There is a Russian Settlement near by, on the same Island.

June 12th. We are now in the Okhotsk Sea, bound to what the Whalemen call the Weed G[r]ound — a place where Whales have been seen plentifully.

June 14th. It has been a fine day, and a good fair wind. There is not anything going on worth mentioning. On deck, they have been butchering a hog. The cooper has been making me a bathing tub to bathe the baby in; it is a very nice one. He has taken a great deal of pains with it; it has got eighty pieces in it, made of African cedar, and narrow strips of boat board between the staves.

June 17th. We are just on the edge of the whaling ground. Have had light winds all day. We shall stop about here a spell to see if we can get some oil.

June 18th. It has been a fine day. We have not seen a ship yet, nor one whale. Have been going some over the ground, tacking about, have not had much wind though.

June 19th. It was foggy this morning a spell, but came off quite fine. Last evening, saw and spoke the Bark Pacific, Captain Howland. My husband went aboard and got the news. Capt. H. has seen several ships about here. None of them have seen any whales on this ground yet. He has seen the South Boston, the Florence, the Camilla and others. The whales are here though; this afternoon, the first mate's boat got near enough to one to dart, but missed. My husband struck a large one and lost him.

June 20th. We have had a fine day but have not seen any whales. Have been looking for them all day. Have seen a bark some ways off and a ship that we call the South Boston. We have heard that the ship Superior, Capt. [Wood], had been taken by the natives [in the Solomon Islands] and burnt, the Capt. and all the crew, with the exception of 6 in number, murdered in cold blood. The Capt. of a trader went there and took off three, all he could get.

June 21st.   It has been a fine day with the exception of early this morning, when it was quite foggy. When the fog lit up, the bark Florence was close by. We spoke her and Captain Spencer came aboard to breakfast. He has just gone this evening. We had potatoes for him from the Islands. He brought us some fine oranges. He has got about 1200 bbls. of oil in the Japan Sea. He has seen and been aboard the Othelo and the South Boston lately.

June 22nd.   The fore part of the day has been fine but a strong breeze, about nine o'clock, the very welcome sound of there blows was heard from aloft. There were three or four Right Whales in sight. The boat was lowered, a large cow with a calf showed a good chance, and the fourth mate soon went on and struck her. She ran very bad and the Capt. kept up all the time. It was very rugged, and after holding on some time, they lost the whale, line, and all. So goes our luck. It set in thick fog not long after.

June 26th.   Spoke the ship Rousseau this afternoon, Capt. Green; he came aboard and stopped a short time. He has taken one whale that made 125 bbls. of oil, this season. There are two other ships in sight and a bark. There are a great many small land birds aboard the ship. I suppose they must have been blown off for the land is some ways off. There are several kinds, one little wren has been aboard several days. It is quite at home, flying about the cabin and lighting on the bird cage.

June 28th.   This morning it was blowing a gale. Quite early, they raised a whale but it was too rugged to lower for him. We kept run of him all day, tacking whenever he altered his course. He did not go far either way. Toward night, the wind seemed to lull a little and the water seemed a little smoother. My husband thought there might be a chance of getting him and lowered his boat, taking the mate with him. The second mate then lowered. I felt uneasy and went on deck to see how the weather was; I found that the wind was blowing bad and the sea very rough. The frail boats looked like specks as they rose on the top of a large wave and then disappeared behind another large one. The boats got quite handy to the whale but soon returned to the ship, for it was of no use to strike him when it was so rugged and the wind had begun to increase. The whale is still in sight and we shall try to keep run of him till dark, and we are in hopes of seeing him tomorrow.

June 29th. It has been a very fine day. We saw this morning the bark Ontario and spoke her. Capt. Foster came aboard and spent the day; he has not gone aboard this evening. He has lately got a whale and is not boiling. It was a large one but poor. He thinks it will stow down 50 bbls. We have had quite a pleasant gam; Capt. Foster is quite a social man. He has seen several ships; California, Othel[l]o and others. They have not any of them got much oil. There is a ship in sight now on the starboard quarter but some ways off; don't know who she is yet.

July 2nd. It has been a fine day and a good breeze. Raised a right whale and lowered for him. Before noon, three boats were after him but could not get near enough to strike and came aboard. After dinner, he was quite near again, and the boats went down again but could not get near him. He seemed to know that there were boats about and dodged them well. We are now going to leave this ground and think of going to the Northeast Gulf to look for bowheads.

July 3rd. It has been a very foggy day and a strong breeze. Tonight, the wind is increasing and we have just taken in sail and will lay back tonight, not thinking it safe to run as the land is not very far off.

July 4th. Today is Independence. Oh how I would like to be at home and enjoy this day with family and friends. We cannot celebrate it here with any degree of pleasure. It has been quite a fine day. Just after dinner, we spoke the bark Monmouth, Capt. Ormsby.

He came aboard and stopped a short time. He has not got any oil this season. He reported the loss of the clipper ship Polar Star, Capt. Wood Master. He has seen Capt. W and has got some of his men aboard. The ship went ashore on the West coast of Kamehalka, in latitude 56:50 longitude 156:10 East on the 24th of May. It was night, a dense fog and the wind blowing a gale. He was between the land and ice. They saw the high land and before they could wear around struck solid. They could not get her off; all hands were saved. There were two other ships astern, the Alice and Oliver Crocker, and so near that the Oliver Crocker struck several times, but lightly. The Capt. and crew left the wrecked ship, saving all that they could, from her, and went aboard the other ships. Capt. Wood will have to stop up here till the Oliver Crocker goes to the Islands, in the fall, when he will join his wife in Hilo. We saw them both when we were there. I think it was very fortunate that Mrs. Wood did not come with her husband up here this season. Capt. Ormsby also told us that the Alice Frazier is lost. Capt. Walker under took to winter in the Okhosht Sea; he had his ship in Horseshoe Bay, on the North Shore. His object was to be there when the ice broke up in the spring, hoping to get a large quantity of oil. As early as November, the ice came so heavy about her that it parted her chain. Then came a heavy blow and carried her out to sea. Capt. W and crew wintered with the Russians.

July 6th. About 9 O'clock, we raised muscle diggers or, as the whalemen often call them, devil fish, so called because they run so bad. There were a great many about today. We lowered two boats for them right away, after we first saw them. The fourth mate struck one and brought him to the ship before noon. He did not act bad, the fourth mate got overboard but nothing bad happened. The whale is a small one. I went up a few moments to look at him alongside. It was raining quite hard when I got up there. They had just begun to cut in. Have seen a few scattering cakes of ice tonight. I suppose that there is a body of ice not far off; it is later this season than some.

July 7th.　This morning, early, we had a breeze and came into the Bay. We found three ships in here, the California, Capt. West, the Jeannette, Capt. Winslow and the South Boston, Capt. Randolph. We sent a boat aboard for him before breakfast. He has spent the day with us. We have enjoyed it very much. He has received a box of books, and papers, and some letters from his wife. He brought me some papers. These ships have not done much yet; the Jeannette has one whale, Capt. R one muscle digger. The Othelo, Capt. Killmer, is up in the Gulf. There are no whales here now. We have not come to anchor and think of going a few miles further for water.

July 8th.　It has been quite an unpleasant day, a strong breeze and quite rainy. Early this morning, it was quite pleasant and sent boats ashore to look for water, but found the place a bad one to get the water and will not get it yet.

July 9th.　It has been a lovely day, quite mild. I have had a nice walk on deck with the children. Have been trying out the whale that we got before we came in here. We have had two boats off looking for whales. They returned tonight, have seen one bowhead, going very fast. There is a Russian settlement a few miles from where we are laying. They are the Tongoormen. A good many of them have been aboard of us, a priest among them. On deck, they have been eating blubber. They will cut great junks with their knives and eat it down like so much cake, the grease running out of the corners of their mouths. They have not brought any fish aboard yet. They have not come in plentiful yet; the ice has been gone only a few days. When the first ships came along the coast, there was a large body of ice and this bay was full. The natives were going about on the ice on sledges drawn by dogs. There are a plenty of reindeer here. They have got some aboard of the California, and the Jeannette. Capt. Randolph and my husband are going to get some. Our little whale will make us about 15 bbls. of oil.

July 10th. We let go the anchor last night in 16 fathoms of water, and about 15 miles from the other ships. It has been a fine day. The boats have been off looking for whales. Jamskaia Bay, I think, is very well in fine weather, like today, but I should not like to spend my days here. There is a town by the same name, some miles off; they say it is quite a place.

July 11th. We have had a very bad day. Last night, they came down and called my husband. It was breezing up and a good deal of swell coming in, and the ship was dragging her anchor. When I woke, she was going right along with it. They took it up not far from one o'clock and got under way and not long after, it was blowing a gale from the Northeast and has continued so through the day. The ship rolling pretty bad and the water coming over some. Tonight, it is about over but a very bad swell. The other ships are at anchor yet. We have passed quite near the Jeannette once, and within hailing distance of the South Boston. They seemed to be riding at anchor quite easy then, but had been throwing the water well a few minutes before. We will not anchor till morning. I have been seasick most all day. We have not much sail out now and she is much easier, and I have got about over being sick.

July 12th. This morning was very fine and mild, the water was quite smooth. We let go the anchor. Then my husband came down and told me that we would go aboard the South Boston a little while. I had just put the baby down to sleep and thought I would leave her. I gave the steward charge of her if she awoke before we got back and went aboard taking Willie along. We were not long going, we stopped aboard a short time and Capt. Randolph showed us all the nice things that he has been collecting together for his wife. He has got a very nice set of porcelain ware that he sent to Nagasacka for and two pair of birds, Parakeets, that he got of a gentleman that got them from the Maley Islands. They are very handsome, being all bright colors, green, yellow, red and black. They do not sing but make a loud shrill noise. He has a pair of stuffed birds of paradise, very beautiful. He showed us a knife box and work box that he has been making; they are very pretty. Capt. Randolph came back with us and has spent the day with us. I found the baby all right.

July 13th. It has been a rainy, unpleasant day. Capt. Winslow of the Jeannette has been aboard a little while. He wanted to get some boat boards to mend his boats. His boats were stove in the gale, also the California had one or two of hers stove and lost one entirely. They were on shore; the crews had anchored their boats the night the gale commenced, and went to sleep on shore. They had been looking for whales for two or three days and had not been to their ships, they being some ways off. They stopped nights on the beach, making tents for themselves and cooking their own victuals. When they awoke and saw that the wind was blowing a gale and their boats going to pieces, they went to the water to try and save what they could of them as they came ashore. Such awful swell and surf forbade them entering the water at all; they came near losing two or three of them in the surf. They saved all the boats but one; that went off but in a wrecked condition. The South Boston's boats were inshore, two of them, but in a safer place. We had none ashore, lucky for us. Capt. Randolph has been aboard, and a Russian man, his wife and little boy. They seem quite poor; I made tea for them and got them something to eat. I gave the woman some little notions, such as tea, needles and some victuals, to take home with her. It did me as much good as it did her, she seemed so thankful to me.

July 15th. I have been washing and my husband has been off gunning but did not succeed in getting any game. He saw plenty of ducks but they were very wild. After he came back, a Russian boat came alongside. One of the men was a merchant from the town. He came to trade; he had some very pretty skin coats, two very nice sable skins, that we bought. They charge a high price for these, 20 dollars, but we paid in trade. They want most everything they can get on board the ships. The salmon have not come in plentifully yet. We have had one nice salmon trout this season; it was a real treat. I have been on deck this afternoon to walk with the boy. It is beautiful, the fog banks was hanging over some parts of the land but the Bay looks very pleasant, smooth and nice. It looks cold in places on shore; there is a good deal of snow yet in many places, quite down to the water. Then there are spots where it looks quite green. I suppose the flowers are in bloom on shore. I would like to go and see.

July 16th. It has been a splendid day, warm and the Bay smooth and nice. Early this morning, Capt. Randolph and my husband went to the town; they have not returned yet. I expect them soon; do not know why they do not get along. It is now past 7 o'clock but it is a long ways where they have gone.

July 17th. We have had a very unpleasant day. Since morning, the wind has increased to a gale, and is still increasing tonight. The ship is pitching very bad and the great waves come dashing against the ship furiously, now and then one coming over the bows. The wind roars and altogether it is dismal enough. The other ships are pitching very bad. Our boats are all off and have had to take to the beach long before this. It is very lucky that Capt. R and my husband got back early this morning; they came back about three o'clock. I had a very unpleasant night of it; I was much worried. I stayed up all night, except a few moments two or three times I layed down to still the children and keep them to sleep. It was a splendid night and broad daylight till 12 o'clock and quite light till one. There is hardly any night in this country. I was on deck a number of times through the night to look for the boats. I could not think what had become of them but they came back all safe. They were in the river waiting for the tide to turn. It had gone out and left them on the flats. They built a large fire, killed some ducks and Capt. Randolph cooked them; so they made themselves quite comfortable. They could not trade with the natives who did not want to sell their nice fat deer, though they had a great many. They offered for sale the poor ones that they or any one else would not want. They made out to buy one young one, Capt. Randolph had half.

July 18th. In the morning, two of our boats came off. Mr. Morgan says they had a very unpleasant night. He did not sleep a wink. They were obliged to take to the beach, they could not look for a good place. It was dangerous being in their boats. There was no shelter where they landed nor any chance to build a shelter. It was raining very hard, they were obliged to turn their boats up on the stones, then they covered their sails over them, and that was their shelter. Some of them slept soundly. They had company from other ships and enough to eat. The water came very near to them.

July 21st. Another splendid day. We have got under way now and are going to the Northeast Gulf.

July 24th. We have had another foggy, wet unpleasant day. Calm most all day, we have to feel our way along for we know that the land is not very far off. Tonight, a man was sent aloft to see if he could see anything from there. He saw the tops of the mountains over the fog, some miles off. This morning, we had a thunder shower. I thought then, it would clear up and we would have a fine day, but not so.

July 26th. We have had the good fortune to get a whale. Last night, about eight o'clock, we raised one bowhead; they lowered one boat. Very soon there was a plenty of whales about; they thought that some of them was devil fish. The boats had not been down over twenty minutes when Mr. Morgan struck one. The rest then left and it was so late it was of no use to chase them. Before 12 o'clock, Mr. Morgan had his whale alongside. All hands then had some hot coffee and something to eat, then commenced cutting in. They had him all cut in before 6 o'clock this morning and it was lucky they did commence in the night for it begun to breeze up this morning and increased to a gale before noon.

July 27th.   Mr. Morgan has found a first rate place to get water in here and we are going to stop and get some tonight. Have just let go the anchor; I should not think the beach was over a quarter of a mile off. It is a bold shore; the water quite deep close in. I have been on deck to look at the land, the mountains are very high, a great deal of snow on them and, now and then, a beautiful green spot. I could plainly see where they are going to get water, a deep gully in the mountain and it looks as if a powerful stream run all the way from the top down and a plenty of snow along the sides. We have commenced boiling out the whale.

July 28th.   Last night, we got the raft of water off about 12 o'clock. They said that they could fill a cask in a few moments. It is as nice as any ice water I ever drank at home. Mr. Morgan brought me a bucket full of flowers, the handsomest and largest variety of wild flowers I think I ever saw. To stand on the deck and look at the land, one would not think they could be found there.

July 29th.   Before 4 o'clock, we raised whales and lowered the boats but they could not get near enough to strike, and then called them aboard to breakfast. Soon after, they was around again, the boats went down, but it was breezing up, then strong, and then it set in thick fog. Two of them came aboard and all the time till noon we was firing guns and striking the bell for the boats that was off to find us. It cleared up a little about noon and the boats came aboard this afternoon. It has been blowing what we call a whale-men's gale, too strong a breeze to lower for whales. The whales have been all about us, one came under the bow almost near enough to strike; a large one too. It made all hands feel bad to see them all around and could not lower for them. We are going to the head of the Gulf now. There is a narrow straight that we go through to get to the head. We think there are whales up there.

July 30th. We came through the straight in the night and came to anchor this morning. Have sent two boats in shore farther up to look for whales. It is quite clear, only about the land it has been smooth and nice all day. We are stowing down our oil today. Our whale will make about 90 bbls. of oil.

July 31st. It has been a very nice day and smooth but we have not seen any whales. There are no ships in here. There is a Russian settlement not more than 15 miles from where we are laying. A boat load of them came off today. They call themselves Oeoots. They brought fish, and some skin boots and shoes to trade. They seemed to want tobacco most; they would give 5 salmon for two plugs of tobacco. They are fine salmon and we had some for supper. These men were a stout, hardy and healthy looking lot, smarter looking than the Tongvose. I think they say there are a plenty of whales in here.

August 2nd. It has been a lovely day and quite mild although we are in 61 and over latitude. That is farther north than I have ever been. This morning, we had two boats go up the Bay to see if they could find whales. Mr. Morgan [went] out for whales as soon as he got down, so we had two other boats go down. One of them had a boat stearer for a boat header, and one to strike the whale for our third officer is sick with a bad cold. In fact, most every one on board have got bad colds. Willie and the baby have been most sick with hard colds. The last named boat struck a whale soon after they lowered and soon killed it, but the tide was running so fast and against them that they could not bring the whale alongside till the tide changed. So we got the ship under way and went after it and soon had it alongside, for it was not far off. A boatload of Russians came alongside and it was amusing to see them when we cut the whale in. They laid in a boatload of meat and ate all they wanted. They are a dirty looking set; they dont look as if water ever touched them. They are dressed in dirty looking skins. Our whale is very small and wont make but about 10 bbls.

August 3rd.   My husband has been off and got a whale. He had a poor crew, all Kanakas, but Antoin, the steerage boy, was boat steerer. I was on deck and saw my husband strike the whale. He made the white water fly for a moment and then run very fast, but they soon killed him and brought him to the ship as soon as the tide turned in their favor. It is a small whale but larger than the other. There seem to be a plenty of them here but all small. They are easy to strike but, if we do not find larger ones, we will leave and go outside where we came from. There have been a great many Russians aboard all day. Five boats came alongside at one time. Their boats are large and made of skins with just a light framework inside to stiffen them. They are rude looking but strong. They catch whales in them. I have one of their irons, a rude imitation of ours. They are made of bone and pointed with stone, and made fast to a pole with raw hide straps. They are successful in getting a whale sometimes. They also get white fish and other large fish. I should think that they live in their boats a good part of the time for I saw fires in them with large pots over the fire with ladels in them as if they were cooking in them. In one boat, I saw two women. I could only tell them by their faces for they were dressed just like the men and helped pull the boat. They had small hands but so dirty, if there could be any difference, they were more dirty than the men. They smiled to me when I looked over the rail but they would not come up the side as they were afraid. We gave them something to eat. One boat went to help my husband when he got fast to the whale. They are all hands now on deck cleaning the bone to save the gum. They eat it and think it a great treat. Some of them will dip the pieces in dirty oil and suck it off and repeat it till they eat all they want. They will sell anything they have about them for tobacco.

August 4th.   About noon, it commenced to rain hard and the clouds looked bad and like a blow. We called the boats aboard. At three o'clock, the boats from up the Bay came aboard. They reported no whales up there. The Russians have been aboard all day. They slept in their boats last night, the boats made fast to the ship.

To night, we have got under way and are going out. It is fine weather now.

August 5th. We have had a fine day, and are now about on the spot where we got our first whale. About eight o'clock tonight, we raised a great number of bowheads. All the boats lowered and very soon the second mate got fast to one. My husband went up and lanced and killed him. They have just brought him alongside and are going to cut him in tonight. It is a small one and they were all small that they saw. We think they are the small whales that we saw in the Bay.

August 6th. The land is not far off and the man aloft has raised a ship, in shore about 10 miles off. We think it is the Othelo; she is boiling. I do not think we will speak her this afternoon. We are stowing down and boiling.

August 7th. We raised the ship again in shore and stood in and spoke her. She is the Othelo. My husband did not stop but a few moments but came back most disheartened for they have taken in here 800 bbls. of oil. They have got all large whales. The Ontario is in sight and Capt. Kilmer says that he has taken 7 whales. Now the Othelo's boats are towing another whale; so much for good luck.

August 8th. We have had a very fine day. Early this morning, they raised whales from aloft. My husband and all boats went down. The fourth mate struck a large cow whale. They had to tow it against a strong head tide and we went to meet them with the ship and took the whale alongside. About 4 o'clock, I went up to see her, she is a monster; I should think a third longer than the ship. I could not begin to tell how large in circumference, might take a little walk on her. She was very wide across the throat. They commenced cutting right away and are still cutting this evening. They have just hove the head in and I have been up to see it. It is a monster head and splendid bone. It looks inside the mouth like a good sized room.

August 9th.   They finished cutting in the whale about 12 o'clock last night. The boats have all been off today but my husband's. About noon, Mr. Morgan brought a large whale alongside. It was a little foggy all morning in shore and when it lit up about ten o'clock, here was Mr. Morgan and the fourth mate, Mr. Braly, with a whale almost to the ship. The tide was against them and they could not bring it alongside, so we took the anchor and went to meet them. They have now gone to try and get another as they saw plenty more. The Othelo and the Ontario have been very lucky in here having each of them taken over one thousand bbls. of oil in a very short time. We have now come to anchor in a bite in the land, or a very small Bay. When we got in here, we found at anchor a large whale with a pretty little American ensign stuck in it. It looks very nice from deck, we are close to the land and it looks green and pretty, but there is some snow yet.

August 10th.   It has been a fine day. While we were cutting in this whale, the boy sung out that the boats were towing another and we soon had it alongside. It is a nice large one and the boats have left for they saw a plenty more when they struck this one. Mr. Morgan got this one. We are now going to stow down to make room for more. Then we will cut in this whale. The Othelo's boats have come for their whale and they came aboard to see us.

August 11th.   This morning, it was fine and a good breeze but the breeze has increased to a gentle gale and tonight it is not very pleassant. We have taken our anchor and are under way again. We have got our whale cut in. Our boats have not returned since yesterday.

August 12th.   This morning the wind was still blowing quite hard and a heavy swell. The clouds looked threatening but about noon we came in sight of the Othelo and Ontario laying at anchor in a bite and all smooth and nice. We came along close to the Othelo and spoke her. My husband, after passing the usual compliments, asked Capt. Killmer if he had seen our boats. He replied "yes, they are right in here" or one of them with two whales for you. The other boat with Mr. Morgan has gone to look for his ship.["] "Good" said my husband, "two whales" and he threw down his old cap on the house saying "I am all right now." We then came in close enough to anchor and our boat came off to us. We cannot take the whales off today for the tide is not right. Capt. Killmer has a large whale laying at anchor close by. Both of ours are large ones. They got them both before ten o'clock yesterday morning which makes 5 in four days. That is doing well and will make us 900 bbls.

August 13th. It has been a fine day and a good breeze this morning. We got one whale off as soon as we could in the morning; had to wait for the tide. We have got him cut in now. It was a bad and long job for the whale was bloated so bad by laying so long. There is quite an offensive odor to that I don't fancy much. That odor with the smoke that comes below from the try works is quite unpleasant, but I can bear it all first rate when I consider that it is filling our ship all the time and by and by it will all be over and we will go home. We have lost some of the head, not heaving it in on deck, and the gum that holds the bone was loose and tender and the heft of the bone caused it to give way and it went overboard and sunk. It is a very fat whale, the oil is running out in streams.

August 14th. It has been quite an unpleasant day. It has been raining hard and a strong breeze but for all that we have got the other whale alongside and have cut it in. It was a very bad job as it has lain longer than the other and the oil was running right out of the blubber. We lost more than one half the head and it was a nice one. They saw that they would lose it, they took all the precaution they could, they made the bone fast with ropes, but for all that, the largest half sunk. The other half went overboard but it did not sink, the ropes holding it. We sent a boat down and they secured it and towed it ashore; then took it on the beach and cut the bone apart and loaded their boats with it and brought it on board. We have lost about one whole head in all and will lose a good deal of the oil too. It is a rainy bad time to cut the whale in and we have a dirty looking ship. We are a dirty looking people altogether, not excepting the baby, the dirt has got all over the ship. Our neighbors are the same and a good many other ships, if they are lucky enough to get oil. I for one can put up with it first rate if we can only get a good season's catch and then go home. We have got a very convenient ship to take a good deal of oil on. She is large and we have a plenty of room but not quite as much help as we could do with, nor all as good, but they all have to work hard now, and early and late, my husband as hard as any of them and broke off his rest and sleep quite as much as any one. Little Siss and I are deprived of our nice promenades on deck for they are so lumbered up with casks and bone, and so dirty, that it is quite impossible to walk at all. Willie goes up once in a while and tumbles around in the dirt.

August 18th. At three o'clock this morning, the second mate came down and called my husband, telling him that the ship was dragging her anchor. It was breezing up quite strong from the Northeast and the prospect was of a bad blow. She soon began to drag worse and we had not much room to spare. My husband did not like to call all hands to heave up the anchor, they had been broke of their rest so much, so he slipped it and got under way, and came out.

August 19th. It has been quite unpleasant all day, the fore part of the day it was blowing hard, then the wind lulled a good deal and it rained powerful. Toward night, it became quite calm and a haze, or fog, in shore. We were running along the land and the wind left us and the first we knew the rocks were close by. The large rocks were not far off but not more than a quarter of a mile off were some sunken ones and the breakers breaking over them. We narrowly escaped the danger. We have been looking for our boats; we are afraid they are suffering with cold and hunger.

August 20th. We have been running along the land looking for the boats. We raised the Ontario towards night and soon had the pleasure of seeing our boats coming from that ship. They are now on board and two of the Othelo's boats. She has not yet hove in sight. The men have had a very wet and unpleasant time and have not seen any whales.

August 21st. We got under way and this morning, about 9 o'clock, we spoke the Othelo; her boats have gone aboard. Both the Othelo and we stood in the bite to take our anchors that we slipped in the last gale but we did not either of us find them. We could not see the buoy that was attached; it was pretty rugged and we did not look long but left. The Ontario got hers the other day, yesterday I think. Capt. Killmer has seen whales since he has been gone and he told my husband that he would tell him where. I suppose that he intended to come on board but the breeze kept getting stronger till it has increased to a gale. It is from the Southwest and is blowing hard tonight. We are steering the same course with the Othelo and she is not far off.

August 27th. Last evening, Capt. Foster came on board and spent the evening. His ship was quite near. He has not seen any whales, he thinks of leaving and going right whaling. He has got about 900 bbls. of oil. We have both of us come out on the West Arm to-day. We are quite near the land, there is an island close by. I have taken the baby on deck for a little walk; she enjoyed it much, she is 6 months old today.

September 5th. It has been a fine day but almost calm a good part of the day. This morning, we were off Jamskaia [Yamsk], we are now off the Cape called Piaghin. We will not be long in going to Horse Shoe Bay, if we have good winds, We have seen a few muscle diggers off this Cape.

September 8th. It has been a fine day. a strong breeze but not fair. We have given up going to Horse Shoe Bay for the present but are going in to Taovisty to get some water and see if there are any whales. We are almost in the Bay now at four o'clock. We can see a ship in the Bay from aloft. I have been on deck to walk for the first time for a week. Green Island and Fog Island were close by then.

September 9th. It has been a fine day. We came in the Bay just before night yesterday. We found the South Boston in here. Capt. Randolph came aboard and spent the evening, also Stephen Morgan. Capt. R feels almost discouraged, he has not got but one whale since we saw them last, that was in here. He was about leaving here when we came in. We raised whales just as we got in last night, one large bowhead close to the ship. We lowered for them and Mr. Morgan got handy to one but not near enough to dart. This is a large Bay and there is one quite large settlement in here. Capt. R has been on shore and got a good many furs, fresh butter, very nice after it is salted. The Russians do not salt their butter. There has been quite a snow storm, the land is covered with snow, though the gardens are in their perfection on shore, green and nice. They are about erecting a church at the settlement. Capt. Randolph brought lumber, glass, etc. from the Islands for them. I saw the priest last season that preaches here.

September 10th. It has been a fine day and a few whales in sight but they are very uneasy and it seems quite difficult to get near them so that we will not stop but leave and try to get to Horse Shoe Bay. Capt. Randolph has been aboard a short time and bid us good by, and has gone right whaling. He brought me some butter and some nice turnips, they were a real treat.

September 11th. It has been quite a pleasant day, a strong breeze but nearly ahead, we having tacked about all day to gain a little. Some of the time, the land has been quite near, it is deep water close in shore. I suppose that the jib boom might touch the rocks and not be aground. It is very high bold land and quite barren looking. It is quite dull with us now, nothing going on except mending sails, picking over potatoes or something of the kind. It is 4 weeks since we got a whale and I am very much afraid that we will not get another this season, for the season is most up.

September 12th. It has been a pleasant day, some fog around the land. We were in great danger last night and this morning of going ashore. Before night yesterday, we had a strong breeze and we were close in shore, when the wind of a sudden left us. It was deep water and the bold ragged rocks astern looked as if they were too near by a good deal. The tide was setting in and the ship had sternway on and it seemed to me must go ashore. They tried to get her off and to the wind but it was of no use, they could do nothing with her and it came on night and dark. They let the small anchor; soon after they thought she was dragging and took up the anchor but it proved to be the tide acting on the ship. She was not dragging and they let it go again. There was not wind enough to get her under way. We were in hopes to have a breeze this morning but there is no wind. So they have been warping the ship out by sending a boat out ahead with a kedge, or small anchor, and letting it go. Then with a line haul the ship up to it and keep doing so until we got as far out as we wanted to. There was a light breeze a little out of the bight beyond the point. I am thankful that we are out, the land is near now but we can't see and hear the breakers quite as plain as we could this morning.

September 20th. We are now bound right whaling the rest of the season. We will look on the ground that we were on in June and, if we do not find anything, will go farther South off Aloid Island, and stop a few days, and then steer for our port, San Francisco as fast as we can go. We will most likely have strong winds as they generally do this time of the year in those latitudes. This is our last season, I suppose, and I would like much to get some more oil before going into port.

September 21st. It has been a pleasant day and a strong breeze. We have been going right along, we are preparing to take the benefit of all the wind we can get between this and our port. We have been reaving new rigging and bending new sails. I expect we will go right along when we get once started for Port and will not be long going.

September 22nd. It has been a fine day and we have made a good deal of headway. Have had a strong breeze all day and have been over our old whale ground, saw nothing and kept on our course. At three o'clock this afternoon we raised a sail. We passed near enough to read her name; she is the Oliver Crocker. We did not speak her, we think that she has been taking a whale lately, by her looks. We will stop about here one day to see if there are any whales here.

September 23rd. It has been a nice day and a good breeze. This morning, about 10 o'clock, we raised a lone right whale. We lowered two boats and in a few minutes after, Mr. Morgan was fast to him. He did not run but a very short distance and did not act bad at all. They soon had him spouting thick blood and shortly after dinner had him alongside. He is a large whale but they think not very fat. They have commenced to cut in, they say the whale is large enough to make 170 bbls. of oil but is so poor they are much afraid he will not make one hundred. I went on deck a little while the boats were fast to him. I stood looking over the stern at him, the poor fellow was too much exhausted to run but was laying still the most of the time, rolling and spouting thick blood. I was astonished on looking through the glass at him to see how thick he threw the blood out of his spout holes. They were quite near to the ship and I could see plain all the movements of the boats. The whale went down and stopped some minutes and when he came up it seemed as if he threw the blood thicker than before. He came up near the boats and threw the blood all in the boats and all over some of the men. I did not like to look at the poor whale in his misery any longer and so came down below to write a few words about it. Saw the Oliver Crocker today, she is boiling.

September 25th. The wind has commenced to blow in good earnest as if we were going to have a good Okhotsk Sea gale, and I think that we will. We have commenced to try out but can't try out much today, it is too bad weather.

September 28th. It has been a good deal more pleasant today, the wind has abated a good deal and the sea gone down considerable. We are now off Aloid Island. It is a very high island and nearly round. The top is covered with snow and looks white enough. There has been a volcano on the island. We have not seen any whales except finbacks today.

September 29th. Saw whales early this morning and sent the boats down but could not get near them. They are very wild and act as if they had been chased of late.

September 30th. We have not seen any whales today. This afternoon we spoke the Ontario. Capt. Foster has been aboard this afternoon. He and my husband have been doing business most all the time, they having exchanged some men. We had some Kanakas that we had got to see that they were returned to Hilo and Capt. Foster had some that would like to go to San Francisco, so they exchanged. Capt. Foster has not got any more oil since he left North East Gulf, 900 bbls. He was in hopes to get one right whale that would make him 1000 bbls.

HOMEWARD BOUND

October 1st. We took in sail last night and lay back in hopes of seeing whales today. We have seen a number but it has been too rugged to lower for them. Tonight, we have got under way and are going direct to the port of San Francisco as fast as we can go. We will not be sorry to leave this country, any of us. I don't think it will be likely the last port we shall visit before we go to our own home port. The Ontario has got under way and is bound to the

Sandwich Islands. We have not seen the South Boston, we think she has left for port.

October 3rd. We have had a gale of wind all day and have gone 200 miles the last 24 hours. The ship has been rolling very bad and this morning she shipped a sea when Willie was on deck. He was standing in a good place to catch it all, it knocked him down and the poor little fellow was rolling in the scuppers all drenched through with salt water. The boy brought him down, he looked as if he had been overboard. He made a great noise about it, I had to change him and wash him, clothes and all.

October 4th. We have had a pretty fair day with light winds the latter part of the night and fore part of the day, but a bad swell. On deck, they have been stowing down the remainder of the oil. We have taken in all this season 740 bbls. I have been starching and ironing for fear that we shall not have even as good a day as this before we get to San Francisco. Tonight, we have a strong breeze.

October 8th. We have had a fine day and a good breeze. We are going right along again. I have been working. On deck, they have been breaking out the bone to scrape, dry and clean for market.

October 8th. We have crossed the meridian today, and have gained one day. We have butchered a nice pig today, quite fat and very nice leafs of lard; she weighed 200 lbs. It shows what can be done in the pork line on ship board; she was raised on board this ship and is of the Wellington Island breed.

October 12th. This morning, we had a very strong breeze; the wind increased in the night and was squally, and carried away the main top sail yard. The wind has been increasing all day and now is blowing a pretty bad gale. Have shortened sail all day till we have got down to the mizen top sail. The ship is rolling very bad, much worse not having the main top sail set. They have been to work all day getting a yard ready to send up.

October 13th. The weather is much better today but still blowing a strong breeze and a bad swell. This morning sent up the main top sail yard and the ship goes along much easier since the sail was set. It is 12 days tonight since we came through the Straits and we have come some 2000 miles and expect, if the wind holds good, to get in port next Sunday.

[The *Florida* anchored safely in San Francisco Bay on the afternoon of October 26, 1861.]

CREW LIST OF THE SHIP *Florida*
1858–1861

THIS Crew List of the ship *Florida* is taken from the "Whalemen's Shipping List" of the sailing on September 7th, 1858, from the port of Fairhaven, Mass., as furnished by the Whaling Museum and Old Dartmouth Historical Society of New Bedford, Mass., and from the account book and the journal of this voyage.

NAME	ADDRESS	LAY
Thomas W. Williams: Captain	Wethersfield, Conn.	1/12
Samuel B. Morgan: First Mate	Wethersfield, Conn.	1/22
George Silvia: Second Mate	New Bedford, Mass.	1/35
Horace Montross: Third Mate	Peekskill, N. Y.	
	(up to 1/35)	1/50
Antone Christie: Fourth Mate		1/55
Dennard Shephard: Fourth Mate, 1860		
Braly: Fourth Mate, 1861		
John Bachus: Boatsteerer	New Bedford, Mass.	1/95
Vincent Manuel: Boatsteerer		1/95
Timothy Reed: Boatsteerer		
killed 8/9/'59	New Bedford, Mass.	1/95
James Currey: Cooper	New London, Conn.	1/50
James Edwards: Carpenter deserted	Greenburg, N. Y.	1/180
John Bont: Blacksmith deserted	New York, N. Y.	1/180

Charles Baptiste: Ordinary Seaman			1/190
Charles Fontaine: " "			1/190
Andrew Fratus " " deserted			1/190
Charles Murphey " "		Jefferson, N. Y.	1/190
Borden Black: Greenhand deserted		New York, N. Y.	1/200
Robert M. Blair "		Peacham, Vermont	1/200
George Burwell "		(3rd season 1/180)	1/200
Michael Carroll "		Ireland	1/200
Joseph Casseles "	deserted	Haverstraw, N. Y.	1/200
Joseph Gibson "			1/200
George W. Johnson "		Mansfield, Conn.	1/200
John Marshall "		Enfield, Conn.	1/200
Merritt Marston "	deserted		1/200
Henry McFadden "		Wiscasset, Maine	1/200
James B. Osgood "	deserted	Rochester, N. H.	1/200
Thos. Punsele "			1/200
Randolph Snyder "		Lancaster, Penn.	1/200
Edward Alfred Teixeira "		Rutland, Vermont	1/250
Alanson M. Wardwell "	deserted	Green, Maine	1/200
Silvanus Wilcox "		Fairhaven, Mass.	1/200
James S. Wyman "		Flagstaff, Maine	1/200
James D. F. Dennett: Steward	deserted	Hollis, Maine	1/135
John Williams: Cook		Charlestown, Mass.	1/140
Antone C. Silva: Boy		New Bedford, Mass.	1/250

Six men were shipped at Brava, Cape Verde Islands, Oct. 13, 1858. Some Kanakas were shipped at South Pacific Islands and from Hilo. Four men were shipped at Guam, March 6, 1860. These men all got 1/200.

Outfitting the *Florida*
1858

THE OUTFITTING of a whaleship for a three- to four-year voyage was quite a long job and a costly one. The hull of the ship was carefully checked by heaving the ship on her beam-ends alongside the wharf, first one side and then the other. The copper sheathing was repaired and the outside planking calked with tarred oakum. The spars and sails were put in good condition and all poor wood about the ship and her whaleboats was replaced. Everything was painted except the decks, which were holystoned to a natural wood finish.

The ship was equipped with supplies for the long voyage which consisted of food in barrels, tubs and cans, extra sails, cordage, knocked-down casks for oil and all the materials needed for making repairs during the voyage.

There was the slop chest of clothes for the crew from which their needs were supplied and these costs were deducted from the man's lay, or share in the profits of the voyage.

There were materials to be used in trading with the natives of the foreign places where the ship would put into port for fresh food supplies.

There follows a listing of the items carried on the ship *Florida* when she sailed from Fairhaven in September 1858 as recorded in the account books of that voyage.

PROVISIONS AND STORES

120	Bbls.	Flour in casks	800	lbs.	Dried apples
132	"	Baked into Bread — 20 of which is in 6 casks for cabin use Marked Bread	1	bbl.	Pickles
			1	box	" 12½ gal. jars
			1450	gals.	Molasses
3	"	Kiln dried Meal	15	bushels	Beans
126	"	Extra & Prime Mess Beef	2	boxes	Mustard
			50	lbs.	Pepper
135	"	Prime Pork	1	bottle	Cayenne
15	"	Rumps	1	pail	Ginger
2	"	Tongues & Sounds	12	lbs.	Allspice
800	lbs.	Codfish	4	"	Nutmeg
500	"	Hams	3	"	Cloves
1500	"	Butter	1	mat	Cinnamon
600	"	Cheese 10 in tins	4	jugs	Saleratus
		2 packed in alcohol use first	1	package	Hops
			2	cans	Sage
			2	"	Summer Savory
1400	"	Sugar	1	box	Pepper Sauce
1	bbl.	crushed sugar	1	bag	Salt
10	"	Vinegar	10	gals.	Lamp Oil
1200	lbs.	Coffee	1	jug	Cream Tartar
250	"	Souchong Tea	1	"	Soda
20	"	Hyou " 2 chests	2	bottles	Sweet Oil
2	boxes	Chocolate	1	box	Lemon Syrup
2	casks	Raisins (1 Box)	3	bottles	Essence Spruce
1200	lbs.	Rice	1	bbl.	Sperm Oil Soap

PRESERVED MEATS

7	doz. 1 lb. cans Boiled Beef	2	doz. 2 lb. cans Boiled Chicken
1½	" 2 " " " Chicken	1	" 1 " " Beef Soup
5	doz. 1 lb. cans Boiled Mutton	3	" 1 " " Green Peas
3	" 2 " " Oysters		

3 doz. ½ pint cans Milk   1 cask old Bread
2   "   2 lb.   "   Roast Beef   1 bbl. "   Beef
1   "   1   "   "   "   Turkey   1   "   "   Pork

MISCELLANEOUS

2 casks Saw dust   100 Lances
2   "   Sea coal   2 casks Powder
10 "   Hard Coal 8½ Tons   5 lbs.   Fine Powder
20 bushels Charcoal   Powder in cannisters with guns
10 bbls. Tar   2 bags Shot
1   "   Rosin   2 Bomb Lance Guns
200 Iron Poles   1 Greener Gun 20 irons

NEW SAILS	OLD SAILS
3 Jibs	1 Fly Jib
2 Fly Jib	1 Foresail — ¾ worn
2 Foresails	1 Fore-topsail
2 Fore-topsails	1 Fore-royal
1 Fore-royal	1 Fore-topgallant sail
1 Fore-staysail	1 Foretop studingsail
2 Fore-topmast studingsails	1 Mainsail
2 Mainsails	1 Main-topsail
2 Main-topsails	1 Main-royal
1 Main-royal	1 Main-topgallant sail
2 Main-topgallant sails	1 Main staysail
1 Maintop staysail	1 Lower studingsail
1 Lower studingsail	1 Topmast studingsail
1 Topmast studingsail	1 Main spencer
1 Main spencer	1 Mizzen-royal
1 Mizzen course	1 Mizzen-topgallant sail
1 Close mizzen	1 Mizzen topsail
1 Mizzen topsail	2 Topgallant studingsail
1 Topgallant studingsail	1 Spanker

SAILS IN CASKS

No. 1 Light Mainsail & Fore-staysail
2 Mizzen Topsail & Main-royal
3 Main-topsail
4 Mainsail & Fore-royal
5 Main-topsail
6 Fore-topsail
7 Foresail & Fly Jib
8 Foresail & Lower Studingsail
9 Main-topgallant Sail & Fore-topmast Staysail
10 Main-topgallant Sail, Fore-topgallant Sail & Topmast
Studingsail
11 Jib with Bonnet, Main Spencer & Close Mizzen
12 50 Yards No. 3 duck
55 " " 4 "
39 " " 6 "
106 " Cotton Ravens duck
80″ Sail Twine
10′ Bees Wax
1 Set Leach Ropes for Topsails & Courses
Lot Light parsling and old Lower Studingsail

OARS

20 — 16 feet oars   10 — 18 feet oars
20 — 17 " "   11 — Steering "

BOATS

6 New Boats   1000 feet Boat Boards
2 Old "   1500 " White Pine Boards
1 Part Boat, stern timbers, stern   800 " Yellow Pine Heading
boards, etc.

CORDAGE

1	Coil	4½	inch	Manila	1	Coil	3¾	inch Tarred
1	"	3¾	"	"	1	"	3½	" "
1	"	3½	"	"	½	"	3¼	" "
3	"	3	"	"	1	"	3	" "
5	"	2¾	"	"	1	"	2¾	" "
7	"	2½	"	"	1	"	2½	" "
3	"	2¼	"	"	1	"	2¼	" "
3	"	2	"	"	½	"	2	" "
2	"	1¾	"	"	1	"	1¾	" "
2	"	1½	"	"	23	Fathoms	5	inch "

2½ Coils 18 Thread Ratline   33 " 4¾ " "

3	"	15	"	"	3 Coils Fine Seizing
1½	"	12	"	"	6 " Spun Yarn
2	"	9	"	"	1 " Bone Yarn
½	"	6	"	"	Several pieces from 3 to 5 inch

NOTE: 100 fathoms = 600 feet in a coil
size is the circumference in inches.

OLD APPARATUS

B# 1 @ 30 = 2 casks   Heads & Hoops   142 Bbls.
A# 1 @ 35 = 2   "   old   "   177   "
BX 1 @ 17 = 1   "   new   "   95   "
            1   "   Round Hoops   500 lbs.
            1   "   Hoops been 1 voyage ⎫
          10   Bundles Heavy 5°   ⎬ 24 Bundles
          10   "   Light   5°   ⎭
           4   "   Heavy 4°

NEW SHOOKS

1 Cask B 1 @ 16-   32 @ 40 inches   92 Bbls.
1   "   N 1 " 18-   "   "   "   "   119   "

1	Cask	O	1	@	18-	32	@	40	inches	119	Bbls.
1	"	Q	1	"	18-	30	"	38	"	103	"
1	"	O	1	"	22-	32	"	40	"	131	"
1	"	K	1	"	18-	32	"	38	"	107	"
1	"	A	1	"	18-	"	"	"	"	109	"
1	"	R	1	"	16-	32	"	36	"	88	"
1	"		17	"	33-	32	"	40	"	104	"
1	"		34	"	49-	"	"	"	"	107	"
1	"	Y	1	"	18-	24	"	32	"	71	"
1	"	H	1	"	16-	32	"	38	"	102	"
1	" No.	1		"	17-	32	"	38	"	101	"
1	"	T	1	"	18-	32	"	36	"	100	"

IRON HOOPS

100″	2°	Hoops	4500″ L 5°	Hoops
1000″	3°	"	3250″ H 5°	"
2500″ H 4°		"	500″ assorted	"

NOTE: ° designates the width of iron
hoop in inches.

NEW SLOPS

Cask No. 1	10 ex. Heavy Bay State Jackets	$ 3.—
	10 " " " "	2.75
	30 pair Cass. Trousers	1.50
	30 " heavy Sattinett Trousers	1.12
	15 Red Flannel Shirts	1.00
	60 St. Kersey "	.80
	75 " " under "	.58
	3 doz Blue Mixed Socks (Falmouth)	5.00
	3 " Nova Scotia "	3.00
	4 " Mittens	2.50
	1 " heavy Gurnsey Frocks	11.00
	55 pair St. Kersey drawers	.58

Above: Captain Thomas W.
Williams and his wife Eliza
Azelia Williams. *At right:*
Eliza Azelia Williams as a
great grandmother.

"Right Whaling in Behering Straits and Arctic Ocean with Its Varieties."
Lithograph of a drawing by Benjamin Russell. *Courtesy of the Whaling Museum, New Bedford, Massachusetts. At left,* Cape East; *left center,* the Diamedes; *right center,* Fairway Rock; *right,* Cape Prince of Wales. The following activities are represented: ship abandoned, crushed by ice;

Scrimshaw: this scene of a whale being towed to the ship is carved on a whale's tooth. *Courtesy of the Whaling Museum, New Bedford, Massachusetts.*

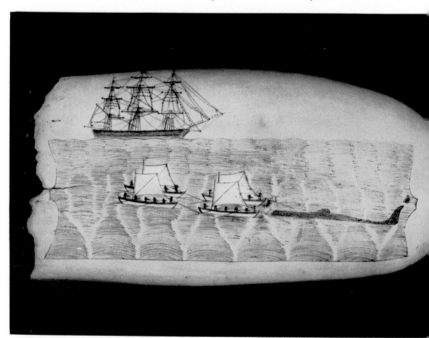

towing blasted whale to ship; trying out at anchor; blubber logged; bowhead whales pursued; full ship bound home; boat in full chase; lancing a
bowhead; taking in the head with whalebone; ship boiling her last whale;
walrus on the ice.

Cutting blubber from a whale. From a painting by C. S. Raleigh. *Courtesy
of the Whaling Museum, New Bedford, Massachusetts.*

This view of New Bedford harbor in 1845 is a lithograph by F. H. Lane from a sketch by A. Conant. *From the Forbes Collection, Hart Nautical Museum, M. I. T.*

The bark *Platina* at a New Bedford dock. She has her whaleboats in the water to keep them tight; riggers are bending sail on her. Port of Fairhaven in the background. *Courtesy of the Whaling Museum, New Bedford, Massachusetts.*

	20 pair dark Kersey drawers	.67
	2 doz Neck Comforters	2.75
	6 " Linen Thread	.75
	3 doz Russian Caps	8.00
	2 " Sheaths & Belts	1.25
	1 " Palms	1.25
	3 " Sheath Knives (Coca handles)	1.50
	4 " Iron Spoons	.38
Cask No. 2	6 Reefing Jackets	2.50
	8 " "	2.75
	4 Monkey "	3.—
	1 " "	3.50
	7 " "	3.75
	12 pair duck Trousers	.67
	75 " Best Denim	.62
	40 St. Cotton Shirts	.45
	1 doz Fancy Calico	8.50
	2 " "	7.50
	2 " "	7.00
	7½ doz Falmouth Stockings	7.00
	48 Denim Frocks	.45
	15 pair Blankets	1.50
	15 Bed Comforters	.88
	2 doz Rogers Knives (large)	3.50
	2 " " "	3.13
	2 " " "	2.75
	2 " " "	2.13
	500 Needles	.75
Cask No. 3	2 Cases (12 pair each) Thick Boots 6 to 11	29.00
	50 pairs Hip Brogans	1.08
	50 " ex thick Shoes	1.02
	100 " " Pegged Pumps	.95
	32 " Secord Slippers	.55

Case A	2 doz South Westers	4.—
	2 " Round Top Hats	3.50
	6 " Palm Leaf "	.12 ea
Case B	4 doz Pots and Pans	1.17

ONE BOX OLD SLOPS

1	Bundle Yarn	
26	pair Mittens	
3	Red Shirts	
4	Red drawers	
8	Gurnsey Frocks	
8	Tarred Hats	
8	pair Slippers	
6	Mounted Palms	
8	Boxes No. 1 Tobacco 800"-	.15½ cts
11	" " 2 " 1299"-	.13½ "
10	Thousand Cuba Sixes	$3.00 per M
1	" Spanish Cigars	8.00 " "

RECRUITS
(replenishing trading supplies)

No. 205 case	1	1035	Yards Denims	10	cts.
778	1	1148	" "	10½	"
596		524	" " 12 pieces	10	"
		648	" Blue Drills 15 pieces	9½	"
20	1	1846	" 4/4" Blea. Cottons	7¼	"
	1	1490³	" 7/8" " "	7¾	"
		513'	" 13 pieces Lawrence Brown	8½	"
		500³	" 11 " 4/4 " "	7	"
596 Bale		679'	" Fine Brown Cottons	8½	"
		275²	" 7 pieces Prints	9½	"
		319'	" 9 " "	8	"

		203	Yards 5 pieces Scotch Ging- hams	17	cts.
		492	" 15 " ⁴⁄₄ oil Col. Furniture	10½	"
No. 1		20	Bbls. per gallon American	32	"
No. 2		4	" " " Cognac	$1.00	"
case	4		Anchor Pipes per Box	1.62	"
	4		Smooth " " "	1.12	"
	13		Winchester Salt Water per- fume Soap	6	cts.
	20		J. H. Burgess White Perfumed Soap Expressly for Whalemen	5¾	"
	10		J.H.B. yellow soap " "	6	"
No. 1	5	60	Bars J. H. Burgess 58″ soap	5	"
	2	36	" J. H. Burgess Ext fam- ily soap	6	"
Boat Sails		4	pieces Rockport duck	16	"

DESCRIPTION OF THE *Florida*

THE *Florida* was a full-rigged ship of 522–83/95 tons, 123 feet long, 30 feet 10 inches beam, and 15 feet depth of hold. She was built in New York City in 1821, probably for freight and passenger business, as she was a large ship for that time and modeled for speed. She was considered a "fair sailer" and a good sea boat. She had an intermediate, or "between deck," which extended the entire length of the ship. Her cabin was entirely below the upper deck with the usual structure aft, called "the house," covering the galley on the starboard side and the companionway leading to the cabin on the port side. The main deck was flush fore and aft without a break and her bulwarks were high and substantial.

Below, there was a large forward cabin with roomy staterooms and a large after cabin with the usual upholstered "transom," or sofa, across the after end of this cabin. The Captain's stateroom opened off the after cabin on the starboard side and extended nearly to the end of the forward cabin. A small room and a toilet room were aft of the stateroom. A large swinging bed was in the Captain's cabin instead of the usual fixed berth. The two main cabins were well lighted by a large skylight and the staterooms by deck lights and ports.

The ship was painted black with white ports (not portholes), a style that was popular with the older shipmasters and owners, and well suited to the ships of that day, as it reduced their tendency to look "chunky" and gave them a longer and more rakish appearance.

She first sailed as a whaler in 1845 from New Bedford to the Indian Ocean and continued in the whaling business until she was sold in San Francisco in November 1861. She was a "five boat" ship which meant she carried three boats on the port side and two boats on the starboard all swung outboard resting on cranes which permitted the boats to be lowered quickly into the water.

This ship did not pay during the Civil War and she was returned to whaling in 1866, again under Captain Thomas W. Williams for the first season's voyage. She continued as a whaler until lost in the 1871 disaster in the Arctic Ocean.

The Whalers in the Civil War

THE reader may be interested to know what happened to the whaling fleet during the Civil War. The War Between the States was a surprise to the whaling industry because the lack of communications made it difficult to advise the captains. The practice of three- to four-year voyages with whaleships scattered over the oceans made it impossible for their owners to instruct the masters. If the captains learned of the war in some port of call, it was not much better to remain idle in port than to continue the pursuit of whales. The whaleships in the Pacific Ocean were not molested for some years. The ships in the Atlantic Ocean did not fare as well and three whaleships were captured and burned by a Confederate privateer in 1861. Several rebel privateers operated in the Atlantic Ocean and intercepted whaleships. Many owners did not send their ships out again after they returned safely to port. Ships were sold and transferred to foreign flags. Several ships in the Pacific were put under Hawaiian registry, if not actually sold to shipowners of that country.

The steam privateer *Shenandoah* entered the Pacific Ocean in 1865 and she captured and burned several whaleships during the latter days of June. These ships were captured in the Okhotsk Sea, Bering Sea and the North Pacific Ocean. The *Shenandoah* captured a total of 38 ships and 30 of these were whalers. Four whaleships were bonded to transport officers and crews to ports, and the others were burned.

Captain Thomas W. Williams was master of the bark *Jireh Swift* of New Bedford from September 2, 1862, until she was captured and burned by the *Shenandoah* on June 22, 1865, in the North Pacific. The ship went to the Pacific Ocean and was reported as sailing from San Francisco on December 9, 1864, with 32 men aboard to return to the whaling grounds, after discharging 1540 barrels of right whale oil and 20,950 pounds of bone. She was captured after the wind dropped late in the day when she had been sailing too fast for the *Shenandoah* to catch her. The Siberian coast was seventeen miles away but it is very doubtful that the ship would have been safe inside the three-mile limit because the *Shenandoah* entered Ascension Harbor (Ponape) and burned four whaleships, in disregard of international laws.

Other whaleships were captured that same June day and the captains tried to convince Commander Waddell of the *Shenandoah* that the war was over, telling him of Lee's surrender and the fall of Richmond, also the assassination of Lincoln which he was willing to believe but not the defeat of the Confederacy. He was shown newspapers that indicated the end of the war was imminent but nothing could deter him from his illegal acts. The *Shenandoah* was possibly one of the last pirate ships of history as Captain Waddell was a typical pirate. He robbed the men he captured of money, jewelry and other valuables and he did not pay his officers and crew more than one half the money they had been promised. The ships' papers, nautical instruments and small stores were taken by the boarding crews.

The descendants of Captain Thomas W. Williams have a photograph, taken by Bradley & Rulofson, San Francisco, of the following:

> Capt. F. C. Smith — ship Wm. Thompson
> Capt. M. Tucker — ship Sophie Thornton
> Capt. J. C. Hawes — ship Milo (bonded 1865, sold out 1872)
> Capt. Tho. B. Hathaway — ship Euphrates
> Capt. T. W. Williams — bark Jireh Swift

The following is printed under these names of captains and ships:

"Captains of the Whaleships
Captured and Burned in the North Pacific on the 21st and 22nd of
June, 1865, by the Rebel Cruiser Shenandoah: the last act of ex-
piring insolence."

There was another use of whale ships in the Civil War — the
"Stone Fleet." These ships were used to blockade the harbor of
Charleston, South Carolina, in an attempt to stop blockade runners
from using this harbor to aid the Confederacy. The ships were as-
sembled in New Bedford harbor and sailed from there on November 16, 1861. They were stripped of sails and everything useful on
arrival at their destination and were then sunk by allowing water to
enter through holes bored for this purpose after pulling out the
plugs. The ships had been loaded with stone to make it possible to
sink them quickly.

The *Florence* was reported as condemned at Honolulu in 1859
but she had a long career afterwards and Captain Thomas W. Williams made several voyages in this ship until she was lost in the
Arctic Ocean in 1878. This ship is the whaler of Part III of this
book.

The *Florida* herself was sold for a freight ship in San Francisco
in 1861, but was not successful, and Captain Williams took her
whaling again in 1866-1867. She was lost in the Arctic in 1871 under
Captain D. R. Frazer, as is told in Part II of this book.

PART II

THE DESTRUCTION OF THE WHALING FLEET IN THE ARCTIC OCEAN IN 1871

ADDRESS BY WILLIAM FISH WILLIAMS

TO THE BROOKS CLUB, NEW BEDFORD, MASSACHUSETTS,

IN 1902

THE WRECK SEASON OF '71

I T IS now many years since the fleet of 32 whaleships was abandoned in the Arctic Ocean, a lapse of time in which many of its
leading participants have cleared for their Last Voyage and in which
the event itself has become little more than a memory even in the
city of New Bedford, the home of its greatest sufferers.

What I shall tell you of this season are the recollections of the
experience and impressions of a boy, for while my father took his
family with him on a number of voyages, on this particular voyage
I was only 12 years old. My nautical surroundings extending up to
the age of 18, no doubt have enabled me to retain a clearer recol-
lection of the more important events which transpired during this
voyage than would be true of the ordinary passenger of even more
mature years. In addition my memory has been very much helped
by the further fact that I was in the Arctic the season before, and
subsequently, at the age of 15, made another voyage of a year's
duration, although not to the Arctic Ocean, during which the "loss
of '71" was as you may appreciate, a frequent theme of discussion.

We returned to Honolulu in the bark *Josephine* from the season
of 1870, and on Nov. 24, 1870, we sailed again in the bark *Monticello* of New London for a cruise in the South Pacific and the Arctic
Ocean, the first part of the voyage being commonly known as the
"between season cruise," and so arranged that we would reach the
Arctic Ocean by the time the ice had passed out, the object being

sperm whaling and the "breaking in" of the crew. The time at my disposal this evening will not permit me to go into the details of the cruise in the South Pacific, although it abounded in interesting experiences.

Our last port of entry was Yokohama, from which we sailed on the 10th of April, 1871, and laid our course direct for the Bering Sea. I do not recall ever having any lonesome or long days in my experience on a whaler, but if there were any dull days it was when "making a passage." Then more sail is carried and whales are seldom seen; but on these trips I had to devote more time to my studies, which I kept up all the time I was at sea, so that when more interesting events were taking place I could have a holiday. In the early part of May we entered the Bering Sea, well over toward the Asia side and made the ice near Cape Thaddeus. We were in this ice nearly two months, at no time was our progress fast, and some days we actually lost ground. During this time the view as far as the eye could see was one expanse of snow-covered ice, broken here and there by narrow leads and small areas of clear water. Unless blowing very fresh there were none of the usual sea motions to the ship, which was not an unpleasant relief from the ceaseless rolling and pitching which prevails while at sea.

I also recall that it marked the cessation of the daily working out of sights for latitude and longitude, which was a relief to me, as I had been obliged to learn this part of ship duty. Most of the time one or more ships was in sight and frequently close enough for visits to be made and returned across the ice. I was barred from making these trips as they were always more or less dangerous from the constant shifting of the ice opening up lanes of clear water, often requiring long detours to cover a very short distance in a direct line. Sail was kept upon the ship whenever the direction of the wind and the condition of the ice permitted of any headway whatever. A constant lookout was kept for whales, for it is the habit of the "bowhead" to leave the Arctic Ocean for the Bering Sea the last thing in the fall and to return as early in the spring as the condition of the ice will permit. Of course, it is seldom that the boat can be lowered, but bomb guns and "irons" are kept at hand,

and if a whale came up in any of the clear water spaces near the ship there would be a wild rush by everybody to get a shot at it. Sometimes when the ship was not under sail, men were kept on the ice at these openings and it was not an uncommon thing for whales to be captured in this manner, although more were lost than were saved.

I will digress at this point to state that it is a singular fact that while the bowhead is classed as the "northern right whale," he is never spoken of as a "right whale" by a whaleman. There is a similarity between the bowhead and the right whale, yet they are very different in many respects. For instance, the bowhead has only been seen in the Okhotsk Sea, Bering Sea and the Arctic Ocean, both on the Pacific and Greenland sides, never anywhere else. There is, however, a right whale which frequents the Bering Sea on the American side, but is never seen in the Arctic Ocean and this whale is different in some ways from the right whale of the Japan Sea and from the right whale of the Atlantic Ocean and the South Pacific. The right whale of the Bering Sea and of the Japan Sea is a fighter, and the female never deserts her young in the face of danger. The bowhead is not a fighting whale, rarely ever doing any injury, intentionally at least, and the females always desert their young on the first approach of danger.

While the Bering Sea [ice] is not as heavy as that met in the Arctic Ocean, it has substance enough to require considerable caution in the working of the ship through its various leads.

This particular year the ice in "the Sea" was unusually heavy, and several of the ships were injured. The bark *Oriole* was stove and became a total loss, furnishing one of the events of the season. This was in the latter part of June and we had just got through the main body of the ice at a point near St. Lawrence Island, south of Bering Straits, when the *Oriole* was seen to set her colors Union down. There were several other ships near and all sent men to assist in pumping and finding the leak. The ship was finally taken into a harbor nearby, on the Asia side, called by the whalemen Plover Bay, to be ultimately abandoned as already stated.

Shortly after this event we met the survivors of the bark *Japan* which was lost at Cape East on the Asia shore the last part of the season before. Eight of her crew had died, the rest passed the winter with the natives and had a terrible experience as they were not able to save any of the ship's provisions and were obliged to live on the native food of blubber and walrus meat cooked with the hair on. I remember how I was impressed by hearing Captain Barker tell that the last square meal he had before accepting the native diet was a few tallow candles which he picked up on the beach. I think that the experience of the crew of this ship had considerable bearing upon the decision of the captains later in the year to abandon their ships.

We entered the Arctic Ocean the latter part of June, but finding heavy ice well to the south and closely packed on the American side we went to "walrusing." Up to a few years previous the whalemen had not considered the walrus a foeman worthy of their steel, but someone had put in his spare time while waiting for the ice to move out, killing walrus and converting their blubber into oil, to discover later that it was nearly, if not quite, as valuable as whale oil. That was the doom of the walrus. At that time the walrus was captured with the regular "toggle iron" or "harpoon" (by the way, whalemen never use the word "harpoon"). The length of the shank of the iron is reduced to save it from getting twisted out of shape by the efforts of the walrus to release themselves. Nearly all of the walrus were captured in the water, and then when killed, hauled out on the ice to be skinned. In this apparently cumbersome manner our four boats killed over 500 walrus in less than a month's time, the net results of which were about 300 barrels of oil. It was no uncommon occurrence to see thousands of walrus upon the ice within an area of easy vision, and as the sun never set during this period, the hours of work were only limited by the physical capacity of the men, and that was tried to its utmost. I will add here, that in the following years the Sharpe's rifle was substituted for the iron, and the walrus was shot while on the ice. It was not an unusual record for a "good shot" to kill a hundred walrus on one block of ice without moving his position. They did not seem to mind the report of the gun, or to notice the hunter as long as he kept quiet; but it was essential that the shots be instantly fatal, as a wounded walrus would soon drive his particular colony into the water. The vital spot is the brain on the top of the back part of the head, where the bone is thin and the skin tight. Body shots are rarely fatal.

On one pleasant day I was permitted to go in the boat with the first mate, where I had my first view of a live walrus. To make matters interesting, the first walrus struck promptly drove his tusks through the side of the boat, tearing out a piece of plank large enough to have sunk us in a few minutes if the crew had not been used to such experiences. The walrus was promptly dispatched by a thrust of the lance, the boat pulled to the ice, hauled out and a canvas patch tacked over the hole in about the time it takes to tell it. After enough walrus had been killed to make a boat load they were hauled on the ice, skinned and the blubber packed in the boat, when we returned to the ship.

While an old walrus will weigh over 2000 pounds, you are not properly impressed by their size even when they are in full view on the ice, because having no legs they are always apparently lying down. In the water their size is still more deceptive, as you only see their head and a small part of their back. Their movements, too, are so clumsy, that it is extremely funny to see them on the approach of a boat get off the ice, the females fairly shoving their young overboard in their anxiety to get them out of danger, and all bellowing and barking as though bedlam had broken loose. At times the water around the boat was fairly alive with young and old walrus; but as no one else seemed alarmed I took it for granted that there was no danger, although at first my nerves got a few bad "jars," when upon hearing a terrific bellow at my back I would turn to find myself almost within arm's length of a rather vicious looking combination, of a round head, wicked black eyes and a pair of long drooping white ivory tusks, but I soon learned that he was the most frightened of the two and promptly escaped if possible, either by diving or swimming away from the boat. Now and then a female walrus separated from her young, or an old bull walrus slightly wounded, would make a rush for the boat, sometimes causing an accident to some member of the crew, although I do not recall any that were fatal. The boats, however, were frequently stove so much so that it usually took about a week after the walrusing period was over, to put them in proper repair.

During the walrusing period the ship was constantly under way, most of the time in scattering ice, which, together with the presence of a number of other ships, made navigation very trying to the nerves, requiring as it did almost constant attention to the conning of the ship. Collisions with the ice were frequent, especially when the weather was foggy, and I must confess that I could never get used to the sensation produced by the ship striking a good sized ice floe, especially when, as was often the case, it was followed by the order to "try the pumps," which always gives you a few bad moments when your breath doesn't seem to come just right and your heart wants to come up and see what the trouble is all about; but the pumps suck and with another addition to your regard for the "good old ship" you get back to your normal mental condition only to get through the same sensation the very next time the ship fetches up good and solid.

Our most startling experience that season was on an occasion when it was blowing quite fresh and the ice had suddenly shifted. We were practically cut off from open water, except for a narrow passage between two very large floes of ice. Had the passage been straight, as at first it looked to be, we would have got through without striking, but the ship was going quite fast so that when the exact situation was known, we had no alternative except to try to make it. The ship struck first a glancing blow on the weather bow, which rolled her down almost to her lee plank shear, then shearing off she ran directly into the floe on the other side, which she struck with tremendous force, bringing her to a complete stop and throwing the watch below out of their berths. After a few heavy rolls she gathered headway and went through the passage. Of course we thought she was stove. The pumps were immediately

William Fish Williams. *At right:* in San Francisco about the age of twenty-one. *Below:* In later life.

In 1876 twelve ships were lost in the ice in the same way that thirty-two had been lost in 1871. Captain Lewis Williams, in command of the *Florence* in 1871, rescued most of the crews, two hundred men in all, and brought them safely to San Francisco. Captain Thomas Williams, who had lost the *Monticello* in 1871, lost the *Clara Bell* in 1876. Captain Kelley lost the *Gay Head* in 1871 and the *Marengo* in 1876.

The three woodcuts shown here were made from sketches by Captain W. H. Kelley and were published in 1876 under the title "Arctic Perils —The Recent Disaster to the Whaling Fleet." *From the Forbes Collection, Hart Nautical Museum, M. I. T.*

Top: "The Fleet Inclosed in the Icepack."
Center: "Camp on a Grounded Iceberg."
Bottom: "Escape of the Bark *Florence*."

The *Mary and Helen* after she was bought by the Navy Department to go to the rescue of the *Jeannette* and other missing whalers. This ship, built by Captain William Lewis, was the first steam whaler in the Arctic Ocean, 1880. *Courtesy of the Mariners Museum, Newport News, Virginia.*

Sperm whale being lanced. An aquatint from "South Sea Whale Fishery" after the British marine painter William J. Huggins. *Courtesy of the Whaling Museum, New Bedford, Massachusetts.*

rigged and men sent down below into the fore peak to see if they could hear the water coming in, but they soon reported everything quiet and the pumps confirmed the report, but it was a narrow escape.

By the last of July a strong northeast wind broke up the ice which up to this time had hung close to the American shore and we began to think seriously of whaling. The ice was still heavy and well to the south all across the ocean, so that it was impossible to get to the Herald Island grounds, and as the whaling the year before had been around Point Barrow, all the ships commenced to work to the northeast, in the clear water between the ice and the American shore. The contest to be head ship was close and spirited. The right of way due to starboard tack was insisted upon fully as zealously, even to the limit of hair breadth escapes from actual collision, as ever seen in a cup race. Those old "square toes" with plenty of wind and a smooth sea, manned by crews every man of which by that time could qualify as an A.B., made a nautical picture rarely seen in even the great traveled highways of the ocean. Then again the tacking of a "square rigger" is rather an impressive evolution compared with tacking a fore and aft craft like a schooner, where you put the helm down, haul over the jib sheets and it's all done.

But the weather was fickle, the wind shifted to the west and the ice came in again, bringing the ships practically to a standstill, so that "gamming," which I need hardly tell you is the sailor's term for visiting, was frequent, greatly to my joy. You see a "gam" meant much to me, for one thing it brought a good dinner, whether I stayed at home or went aboard the other ship, as the best the ships afforded was always brought out on these occasions. It meant also seeing new faces and hearing the latest news from civilization, as many of the ships had not made the between season cruise, but had come direct from Honolulu or 'Frisco. If you have never made a long voyage you can hardly appreciate the full force of this statement; but most important of all it brought an opportunity to get new reading matter. It is the rule for the first mate of the ship that is being visited, to return to the other ship with her captain's boat, but with his own crew, and I generally went with the mate. In this way I could exchange books, and in general have more liberty. In addition our mate was good natured enough to frequently let me steer the boat and give the orders in leaving and approaching ships.

One of the incidents usually connected with "gamming" and which never lost its interesting excitement to me, although witnessed many times, was the operation of "speaking a ship" both being under sail at the time. The intention of a desire to speak was generally given by the ship in the windward position hoisting her ensign and "keeping off" for the ship she wishes to speak. The latter would then "haulaback," i.e. the helm is put hard down so as to bring the ship sharp on the wind, while the yards and sails on the mainmast are squared or "hauledaback," the yards on the foremast are "braced forward," that is with the sails full and all the fore and aft sails also full. In this position the ship is nearly motionless, forging ahead a trifle. The speaking ship when directly to windward "keeps off" and heads for about amidships of the other ship, holding her course, until to the novice, especially if on the waiting ship, it seems as though a collision were absolutely unavoidable; but just about this time the other ship shears a little, passing close by the stern of your ship and the two captains exchange the compliments of the day, usually ending by one inviting the other aboard. The conversation is also carried on without the aid of a trumpet, an omission which at first rather lowered the nautical character of the event in my estimation; but I soon became reconciled to allowing the trumpet to depart in company with a lot of other nautical fallacies which I had imbibed from the writings of Cooper, and a few others. It is quite essential that the speaking ship shall have an experienced man at the wheel during this evolution. Sometimes when it is blowing fresh, and on all ships that steer badly before the wind, two men are put at the wheel with an officer close at hand. Greenhands upon their first experience at the wheel when speaking a ship, have been known to get so badly frightened that they either run away from the wheel or become physically incapable of executing the orders.

During this time we were nearly constantly in sight of land in the vicinity of Cape Lisburne, which is a bold, strongly defined landmark, the last of the high land on the American shore. From Cape Lisburne the land slopes to the north, becoming quite low and marshy, without trees or shrubs, and of an extremely uninteresting appearance, continuing this way to the north and east with slight variations for many miles. A line of sand bars extends parallel to the shore for some distance. Uncertainty as to the exact location of these shoals made navigation close to the shore rather hazardous; the charts in use at this time were very deficient in exact information, which obliged the captains to trust largely to their personal knowledge and the lead line. It is also rather a peculiar fact that there are no regular tides on this coast, although a sudden change in the direction of the wind oftentimes produces a temporary rise and fall of the level of the sea. The compass is also very uncertain, particularly in thick weather. I have often seen the ship tack and the compass remain stationary, but by a vigorous shaking of the compass needle would finally respond to a change in direction.

The natives were frequent visitors, but with very few and rare exceptions, they were to me extremely repulsive in looks and habits. They have a disgusting fad of making a hole through the cheek near the corner of the mouth, in which they place polished pieces of ivory or stone, and sometimes empty brass cartridge shells. Then they gradually enlarge the opening by increasing the size of the ornament, until not infrequently it tears through into the corner of the mouth. You can imagine the appearance and the results, especially when they are chewing tobacco, by such an addition to an already liberal allowance for a mouth. They are confirmed beggars and not above taking things without your knowledge and consent. They are shiftless to the point of often failing, through no lack of opportunity, but from sheer laziness, to provide sufficient food for their winter consumption, entailing much suffering and often loss of life by starvation. They early took the first two degrees in civilization by learning to use tobacco and drink rum. It was their custom after making a considerable trading transaction, whereby a quantity of liquor was secured, for the entire male portion of the village to go on a spree that was only limited in time by the amount of the rum. At these times all the weapons were turned over to the women, as they had learned from bitter experience that a drunken Eskimo and a weapon was a combination that could not be trusted.

The native boats are marvels in lightness of construction, being built of the tanned skins of seals drawn over a frame of wood which is made up of small pieces of drift wood, very light and spliced together with servings of sinew. A boat that will hold ten or twelve natives will not have a piece of wood in its frame much over an inch in greatest diameter. In shape they remind one of a dory, being flat-bottomed, with flaring sides and sharp at both ends. They are propelled by paddles, usually operated by the women.

As we worked back and forth between the ice and land we did some whaling, being rather more successful than most of the ships. I will not go into the details of the taking of a whale, as that has been so thoroughly well described by Mr. Bullen in the *Cruise of the Cachalot* that I could not hope to add anything of interest in the short account which my time would permit me to give you. I have already remarked that the bowhead is not a fighter, but I do not want you to infer from this statement that there is no risk involved in their capture. For, like everything connected with the sea, you pass so quickly from comedy to tragedy, and from tragedy to comedy, that you never are safe in trying to limit the possible dangers in the capture of a whale, as a few incidents will illustrate.

One of the whales taken by our boats at this time accidentally got into close contact with the boat and proceeded literally to spank it, bringing its great flukes down on top of the boat several times. From the ship it looked very bad for the crew and the boat, but aside from a broken oar or two no real damage was done to either and the whale was killed. Of course the crew hugged the bottom of the boat pretty close, but the real secret of their escape was the fact that the whale was not vicious. If it had been a right whale or a sperm whale there would not have been enough of the boat left to pay to save, and probably some of the crew would have been killed. Another time my father's boat was fast to a whale who was running for the heavy ice, when by a sudden swerve in his course he ran the boat over a small cake of ice, capsizing the boat and running off with the line. Before we on shipboard could hardly realize what had happened, the boat's crew were all sitting astride the keel of the boat. Fortunately the line did not catch on anything, and what might have been a tragedy became a farce, and one that for some time it was not good judgment to discuss within the hearing of my father.

Now just a few words about the unwritten law of the "right of chase" as recognized by whalemen, because it may have occurred to you that a few whales among so many ships, each carrying from four to five boats, might produce a badly mixed up state of affairs. But if a lone whale was raised, the first ship to lower a boat had the right of way. Unless the ships were very close it would rarely happen that more than two or three ships would see the whale at the same time; the other ships would know a whale was in sight by seeing the boats, but they might not see the whale. Again, the boats of a few ships might be chasing different whales, discovered in separate locations, but at the same time, while the greater number of the ships would be looking on. If a number of whales were in sight and well dispersed so that all the ships could lower their boats, they would do so, but great care was used not to interfere with each other's whales as soon as that fact was established by the whale being nearer to one boat than to another.

By the latter part of August the ice had worked some distance off shore and the ships commenced again to work to the northeast. Blossom Shoals off Icy Cape were passed and it began to look as though we would reach Point Barrow, where we expected to find plenty of whales; but on the 29th the wind came strong from the southwest accompanied by snow and the ice commenced again to shut in. At this time we were off Point Belcher and my father decided to turn back. It was a beat to windward, but we hoped to get by the shoals ahead of the ice. The sea room, however, was narrow, requiring short tacks and the taking of chances in the shoal water along the shore. We had only made a few miles to the south when one of those peculiar incidents happened which make sailors believe in luck, good and bad, only in this case it was bad. We were on the "in-shore tack" trying to make every inch possible, the order was given for tacking ship, all hands were on deck, starboard watch aft, port watch forward, as was always the rule when working ship in close quarters.

The ship was almost in the wind and coming beautifully, another minute and she would be safely on the other tack. The calls of the leadsmen in the fore chains showed that we still had water under our keel, when of a sudden out of the gloom of the snow there loomed a floe of ice right under our weather bow. There was a bare possibility that the ship would swing enough to strike it on her other bow, in which event we were all right, but as the sailors said "luck was against us" she struck on her weather bow, hung "in irons" for a few moments, then slowly swung off and stopped; we were ashore. The sails were all quickly taken in and furled, an anchor laid out to windward to try to keep her from going on hard. It was not rough as the ice had made a perfect lee, and as night had then set in nothing more could be done until morning. The next day was clear and fair and showed the greater part of the fleet at anchor outside of our position. Our condition was soon known to them and all sent their crews to assist in getting our ship off. To me it was a gala day, the decks fairly swarmed with men, orders were executed with a snap and vigor that only a sailor can put into his work when he is pleased to. More anchors were laid out astern and the chains taken to the windlass and hove taut. Casks of oil were hoisted out of the hold and rolled aft, and finally she floated and was towed off to the other ships and her anchor dropped, as it later developed, for the last time.

The pack ice had swung in until it was close to the shore at Point Belcher and at Icy Cape with most of the ships lying in the clear water between the ice and the shore, which here makes a long inward curve between the two mentioned headlands. The fleet was divided into four parts; the most northern including four ships was in the pack ice off Point Belcher. About ten miles to the south and off Wainwright Inlet were 18 ships, including our ship, and all in a small area of clear water about three-quarters of a mile in width, between the pack and the shore. A few miles further south were seven ships, some in the ice and some in clear water, and just in sight from our masthead, still further south, were three more ships. At that time it was not clearly known whether the other seven ships of the fleet were in the ice or outside. At first we looked upon the situation as only a temporary hindrance, and the boats were sent off up the coast to look for whales. Our boats captured one which made us the recipients of many congratulations over our good luck. The weather was pleasant, but the wind, when there was any, was from the westward. Everybody prayed and whistled for a strong northeaster, but it did not come, instead the ice kept crowding the ships closer to the shore.

Now a word about the pack ice of the Arctic Ocean, which I will preface by stating candidly that I fear I cannot give you a comprehensive description of it as it seems to be one of those indescribable things, at least I judge so, from the fact that I have never read anything that to my mind adequately described it. The pack ice is an enormous accumulation of cakes or floes of snow-covered sea frozen ice, of all sizes and shapes, but containing very few whose highest points are more than 10 feet above the sea level, and those have been formed by the crowding of one floe on top of another. There are very few level spots of any extent, the general effect being very rough. There are no icebergs as there are no glaciers in these northernmost parts of either America or Asia. The pack is not, therefore, in its individual parts imposing, grand or beautiful, but as a whole under all the varying conditions of an Arctic sky, from brilliant sunshine to a leaden gloom, it is a magnificent spectacle; and when you stop to consider that it represents ages of accumulation and that there is beneath the surface nearly ten times more bulk than what you can see, you realize that there is something to be considered beside beautiful effects, that there is within it a power which cannot be expressed and can only be partially comprehended.

Captain Markham, an English explorer, has named the pack of ice of this, the Greenland side of the Arctic Ocean, "The Paleo-crystic Sea." I think it is an appropriate title for all the real pack ice of the Arctic Ocean. Of course the southern limit of the pack ice is not always the same. In 1871 it was unusually far south, but probably at that time there were large openings of clear water to the west and north, perhaps in the neighborhood of Wrangel Island, caused by a separation in the pack as a result of the long period of westerly winds. I do not believe that the great central ice pack of the Arctic extending from longitude 130 degrees west to longitude 160 degrees east acts often, if ever, as a unit. Here is a great frozen area which, with the exception of two small islands near its southern limit, is as far as we know, absolutely devoid of land. The little that is known of this great ice pack has been learned by the whalers, and of the many ships which have been lost in it, no wreckage has ever yet come back. It was in this great pack that the *Mount Wollaston* and the *Vigilant* were lost the year that Lieutenant De-Long entered the same pack ice, only to the westward of Wrangel Island, and again the same in which in 1876, 13 whaleships were lost to the northeast of Point Barrow. It was the central portion of the great pack that had swung south and barred our escape.

The water at the edge of the pack where we were anchored was about 24 feet deep, yet the ice was on the bottom and each day the tremendous force of the pack pressing in was driving it close to the shore.

Sept. 2nd the brig *Comet* was crushed by getting between a grounded floe of ice and the moving pack. On the 7th the bark *Roman* was crushed in a similar manner, only in this case the pack performed one of its peculiar tricks of relaxing its pressure, allowing the floe against the ship to draw back, as though gathering its energy for another attack, whereupon the ship immediately sank, giving the crew but scant time in which to save themselves. On the 8th the bark *Awashonks* was crushed and pushed partly out upon the ice. It was now apparent that the situation was serious and consultations between the captains were frequent. It was finally decided that they ought to find out if any of the ships were outside the ice. Accordingly, Captain Frasier of the ship *Florida* went down the coast in a whaleboat and reported upon his return that seven of the ships were either outside or in a position to easily get out, but that the ice extended to Icy Cape, a distance of about 70 miles from our position. He also reported that these seven ships had only just got out of a position which at one time looked serious, and that several of them had lost anchors, but the captains had promised that they would hold on as long as they could, but the most assuring message was brought from Captain Dowden of the *Progress,* who said, "Tell them all I will wait for them as long as I have an anchor left or a spar to carry a sail." And we all knew he meant just what he said. The clear water had now begun to freeze over so that the bows of the boats had to be coppered to keep them from being cut through by this thin ice. All hopes of getting out were now given up and active preparations were commenced for leaving the ships.

It was evident that the distance to Icy Cape was so great that only one trip could be made, therefore everything that was not an absolute necessity had to be left, as all the available room in the boats was required for provisions. I recall with an ever increasing regret our family sorrow at giving up the many interesting articles we had collected during our cruise among the South Sea islands and our visit to Japan.

Sept. 12th the captains held their last conference and decided to abandon the ships on the 14th, all signing a statement which briefly gave their reasons, as follows: First, there was no harbor available that the ships could be got into; second, there were not enough provisions to feed the crews for over three months; third, the country was bare of food and fuel.

My father decided that on account of my mother and sister, and perhaps also me, he would not attempt to make the trip in one day, so we started on the afternoon of the 13th and spent the night on the brig *Victoria* as the guests of Captain Redfield. I doubt if I can adequately describe the leave-taking of our ship. It was depressing enough to me, and you know a boy can always see possibilities of something novel or interesting in most any change, but to my father and mother it must have been a sad parting, and I think what made it still more so was the fact that only a short distance from our bark lay the ship *Florida*, of which my father had been master eight years and on which three of his children had been born. The usual abandonment of a ship is the result of some irreparable injury and is executed in great haste; but here we were leaving a ship that was absolutely sound, that had been our home for nearly ten months and had taken us safely through many a trying time.

The colors were set and everything below and on deck was left just as though we were intending to return the next day. All liquor was destroyed, so that the natives would not get to carousing and wantonly destroy the ships; but the medicine chests were forgotten. Later when the natives got to sampling their contents, some were killed and others made very sick, in retaliation for which they burned several of the ships. Our boat contained in addition to its regular crew, my mother, sister and me, and all of our clothing, bedding and provisions, so that we were loaded nearly to the gunwales. We got an early start on the morning of the 14th and by rowing and sailing, the water being very smooth all the way, we finally reached Icy Cape and landed on the beach just as darkness was setting in. A tent was erected for the ladies and children and great fires were built for the men and for cooking. We still had several miles to go to reach the ships, and as it was in the open ocean outside the ice, there were some fears as to our ability to make it with our boats loaded so deep. To add to our discomforts, mental and physical, it commenced to rain and blow, so that taken all in all it was a night that few of its participants will ever forget. By morning it had stopped raining and although there was a good fresh breeze blowing it was decided to start out as soon as we had eaten our breakfast. Our boat made the trip under sail and although we put in several reefs, it was a hair raising experience. My father had decided to go aboard the *Progress*. She was still at anchor and pitching into the heavy seas, that were then running in a way that would have made you wonder how we would ever get the men aboard, let alone a woman and two children; but it was all accomplished without accident, or even the wetting of a foot. As fast as the boats were unloaded they were cast adrift, to be destroyed against the ice pack a short distance under our lee where the waves were breaking masthead high.

By the next day every man of the crews of all the abandoned ships had boarded some one of the seven and sail was made for the straits. On the *Progress* there were 188 officers and men, beside three ladies and four children, one a baby in arms. Captain Dowden gave up his cabin and stateroom to the three captains with families. I have forgotten just how the three ladies and the younger children disposed of themselves in the stateroom, but in the after cabin we just managed to fit in by putting one man on the transom and two men and myself on the floor, but we were all very thankful for what we had. The other captains and officers divided quarters in the forward cabin, and rough berths were put up between decks for the sailors and boatsteerers, so that finally everybody was provided for except Captain Dowden, and I never did know where he managed to get his sleep.

We stopped at Plover Bay long enough to take in a supply of fresh water, and then laid our course for Honolulu. We had a good run and reached our destination on the 23d of October without anything taking place that was specially worthy of note.

And now with just a brief statement of the sequel which was not learned until the next year, I shall be done. In less than two weeks after we had left the ships the long-looked for northeast gale came and lasted several days. Some of the ships went off with the pack, some were sunk at their anchors, a few were burned by the natives and several went through the winter without injury. Only one, the bark *Minerva*, ever came back, and she was saved by my father the next season. Our ship was destroyed where we left her, as my father discovered a portion of her bow sticking up out of the water and recognized it by the iron plating, as she was the only ship in the fleet protected in that way. If we had waited until this gale came, without doubt the greater part of the fleet would have been saved, but this was knowledge not possessed by the captains, who made their decision after a careful consideration of the situation as it then existed, in connection with their united experience in those waters.

STATEMENT SIGNED BY WHALESHIP
MASTERS BEFORE ABANDONING THEIR SHIPS

Point Belcher, Arctic Ocean,
September 12, 1871

KNOW ALL MEN by these presents, that we, the undersigned, masters of whaleships, now lying at Point Belcher, after holding a meeting concerning our dreadful situation, have all come to the conclusion that our ships cannot be got out this year, and there being no harbor that we can get our vessels into, and not having provisions enough to feed our crews to exceed three months, and being in a barren country where there is neither food or fuel to be obtained, we feel ourselves under the painful necessity of abandoning our vessels, and trying to work our way south with our boats, and if possible to get on board of ships that are south of the ice. We think it would not be prudent to leave a single soul to look after our vessels, as the first westerly gale will crowd the ice ashore, and either crush the ships or drive them high upon the beach. Three of the fleet have already been crushed, and two are now lying hove out which have been crushed by the ice, and are leaking badly. We have now five wrecked crews distributed among us. We have barely room to swing at anchor between the pack of ice and the beach, and are lying in three fathoms of water. Should we be cast upon the beach it would be at least eleven months before we could look for assistance, and in all probability nine out of ten would die of starvation or scurvy before the opening of spring. Therefore, we have arrived at these conclusions — after the return of our expedition under command of Capt. D. R. Frazer of the *Florida,* he having with whaleboats worked to the southward as far as Blossom Shoals, and found that the ice pressed ashore the entire distance from our position to the Shoals, leaving in several places only sufficient depth of water for our boats to pass through, and this liable at any moment to be frozen over during twenty-four hours, which would cut off our retreat even by the boats, as Capt. Frazer had to work through a considerable quantity of young ice during his expedition, which cut up his boats badly.

(Signed by all masters of the whaleships
before abandoning them)

PART III

THE VOYAGE OF THE *Florence*

1873–1874

FROM A MANUSCRIPT
WRITTEN BY WILLIAM FISH WILLIAMS

PART III

THE VOYAGE OF THE *Florence*

1873–1874

FROM A MANUSCRIPT
WRITTEN BY JOHN STEPHENSON

STARTING A CRUISE

SAILING through the Golden Gate is an experience never to be forgotten. Although I had sailed through the Gate several times in my childhood, this was a special occasion as it was Christmas Day, December 25, 1873. It was a beautiful day with a clear sky and a moderate northwest wind. The whaleship *Florence* was put on a course to the southwest with the wind abeam and not enough motion to the ship to disturb the greenhorns, although some of them looked rather forlorn and apprehensive.

The procedure on the first day out of port was to muster the crew in the waist, which is the deck space just forward of the mainmast and on both sides of the main hatch — the officers and boatsteerers on the starboard side and the crew on the port side and forward of the hatch. I had been ashore two years since my last voyage and, although not a novice, the proceedings were of unusual interest to me because for the first time in my life I was not a passenger but a regular member of the crew. I had signed the "papers" as cabin boy for the 1/200th lay. It was true that my father was Captain and my mother and sister were aboard; nevertheless I was on the first round of the ladder to a regular man-size job and I was deeply impressed by the situation.

Then the first officer reported to the Captain on the quarterdeck that the crew were mustered in the waist and the Captain proceeded to the main hatch and announced that the officers would draw the men for their respective boat crews. The drawing started with the first mate selecting his man and followed in order by the second mate, the third mate and the Captain selecting their man. This process was repeated until four men had been chosen for each of the four boats. The *Florence* was known as a four-boat ship.

The boatsteerers had already been allocated but, owing to the failure of two men to report for sailing, the fourth mate was assigned as boatsteerer to the first mate and the cooper agreed to steer the Captain's boat.

The two or three men remaining were to handle the ship, with the cook and steward, when the boats were lowered. In most ships, it was not the practice of the Captain to lower for whales and he would remain in charge when all the mates' boats were away. When the Captain did lower, it was usual for the cooper, or carpenter if there was one, to take charge of the ship until the Captain or an officer returned. My father was one of the few captains who always lowered for whales unless weather conditions, or presence of land made it unwise to leave the ship shorthanded and without a fully competent man in command.

After my father had picked two men and it came his turn to choose another, he turned to me and said "I will take my boy for the stroke oar of my boat." I had no intimation of this decision but nothing could have given me more pleasure and the event will always remain as one of the proudest moments of my life. I was fifteen years old and strong and I knew how to row. I had an intense respect for my father; he has always been to me the finest type of man I have ever known. He stood six feet three inches in his stockings, was broad shouldered, straight as an arrow, blue eyes, black hair, large and fine-shaped head, and weighed over two hundred pounds with no superfluous flesh. He was a natural leader and commander of men, being utterly fearless but not reckless, and a thorough master of his profession. Like most men who follow an outdoor life, of a more or less hazardous nature, he was reserved. He was always ready to enforce an order by physical means, if necessary, but he was not a bully or a boaster.

In my long contact with men in all walks of life, I have met many boasters whose vaunted successes and accomplishments were generally imaginary. No wonder my memory goes back for relief to those men of my earlier days who could do things that required skill and courage, not occasionally but almost daily, that as personal accomplishments deserved to be handed down to posterity as the greatest heroes of those times.

As the men were chosen for the boats, those of the Captain's boat and the second mate's boat stepped to the starboard side of the ship as the starboard watch and those of the first and third mates' boats went to the port side as the port watch. The steerage boy, who had been chosen by my father for his boat, and myself belonged to neither watch as we were on duty all day and had all night in which to rest. This was also the case with the cooper, steward and cook. The foremast hands not selected for the boats were divided between the two watches.

With the completion of the drawing for the boats, the Captain made a brief but clear statement covering the fundamental rules that would govern their lives and conduct of the crew during the voyage. This simple event was the first step in the making of a whaleman and whether he became a success or a failure depended upon himself alone. The voyage had just begun and would end with the return of the ship to San Francisco.

The situation was impressive and, to most of the foremast hands, the beginning of what might be called an adventure. The officers and boatsteerers were seasoned mariners but less than half the crew had ever been in a sailing ship before. They were all young men and mostly citizens of the United States. On the whole, they were not a bad looking lot for a " 'Frisco crew." There was no one that appeared to be of outstanding character, good or bad, except the steerage boy who was a typical 'Frisco tough of the lowest type, although only eighteen years old. How he allowed himself to be shipped on a whaler was a mystery that no one ever solved. Perhaps he was double-crossed by some of his own gang in settlement of some grudge. I was to see much of him because he was quartered in the steerage as well as being a member of the crew for the Captain's boat. I was frequently ordered by my father and implored by my mother to keep away from him.

The Captain first explained that the watches were four hours long beginning with the sea day at midnight. While one watch is on deck the other watch is below, except from four to eight in the afternoon and evening which was known as the "dogwatch," when all hands were on deck. This plan changed the order of the watches so that one watch would have eight hours on deck one night and eight hours below the next night with an intervening watch of four hours in between. Every man would have to learn to steer and his "trick at the wheel" would be two hours in length, unless shortened by reason of weather conditions. He would also have to stand his lookout and masthead watches in their regular order.

They were told that orders must be executed promptly and without question as to their necessity. The safety of the ship and all their lives depended upon this one principle and every member of the crew must acquire the habit of obedience. Furthermore, all orders would be enforced no matter what the consequences were to the man who disobeyed. Discipline required that certain rules of conduct should be observed by the foremast hands. While on deck and not employed, he must stay forward of the waist, or the after end of the tryworks. If ordered aft, or when relieving the man at the wheel, or wishing to speak to an officer, he must go aft on the lee side or on the port side if the ship is sailing before the wind, and then cross to the weather side if the order requires it or he is seeking the officer of the deck. If he wants to see the Captain, he must first request permission of the officer of the deck even if the Captain is only a few feet away. Saluting was not required of the men on this ship, or as far as I can recall, it was not required on any ship that I was acquainted with.

Many men would take off their cap or touch it with their forefinger when addressing the Captain or an officer but I never saw a man reprimanded for not doing either. Of course, no sailor ever came aft with a pipe in his mouth; that is, not a second time. What happened the first time depended upon whether the officer of the deck decided it was simply ignorance or a dare. If the former, he would be told by most officers not to let it happen again, but if the latter, he would be promptly and efficiently knocked down. In all my experience on a whaleship I never saw the Captain or an officer hit a man with anything but his bare fist. I do not doubt that belaying pins and handspikes were used on some ships to enforce discipline but it did not happen on any of the five ships on which I spent my days at sea. As a matter of fact, a handspike was rarely a part of the equipment on a whaleship as very few of them had a capstan. There were other utensils lying around, such as a bung starter, which were much handier than a handspike if a weapon was needed. The captains and officers that I knew intimately were men who did not need such aids and would have looked upon their use as an admission of weakness. The sailors rarely harbored a grudge against an officer for enforcing discipline with his fists but the use of a belaying pin was rarely forgotten and never forgiven.

After the Captain had made a few remarks as to the food, he advised the men to do their best to learn the details of the ship's rigging and operation and assured them that they would have fair treatment. He said coffee would be served in the early morning watch and at breakfast with tea at supper. Bread would be served once a day of the raised white type but hard bread could be had whenever wanted; no butter or sugar but plenty of molasses at all meals and plum duff on Sundays.

The real success of the voyage depended on the "after gang," or the officers and boatsteerers. Every man whose quarters were aft of the mainmast belonged to the "after gang." In this ship it included the Captain, four mates, three boatsteerers, cooper, steward, cook, cabin boy and steerage boy, and with the exception of the two boys, every man was an expert in his position. The Captain, my father, had been following the sea almost continuously for thirty-four years. He was then fifty-four years old and had been a captain for twenty-three years and he owned the ship we were sailing. Before going to sea, he had successfully learned to be a weaver, a mule spinner and a toolmaker. He had spent little time in school and yet he was a splendid navigator and, of course, an expert whaleman.

In comparing the whaleman and the merchantman, it is quite common to overlook the fact that while the merchantman must be a navigator and a seaman the whaleman had to be both of these and a whaleman as well. In other words, he had to master two professions.

It should be said of the owners of American whaleships, either to their credit in fairness or wisdom, that they played few favorites and promotion went by merit. It was a case of the survival of the fittest and I can recall only one owner's son, my brother, who was a captain or an officer in the Pacific whaling fleet.

There were few captains at that time that had not started in the forecastle, or as the saying was "came in through the hawsepipe," and worked their way aft. That this was the rule and not the exception brought recruits from all over New England. It was common to credit New Bedford with being the home of the whaling captains but the majority came from outside that city, many of them from country towns far removed from the sea. My father went from a little village in Connecticut with no knowledge of the sea except what he may have absorbed while crossing the Atlantic Ocean in the steerage of a sailing packet with his family when he was ten years old. The family came from a little inland town in Wales so he had no early ideas about the sea.

As he was just twenty when he decided to go to sea, he had to run away, as many others did, and he knew no one in New Bedford, Massachusetts, where he shipped as a foremast hand. My grandmother told me many years later that when she received his letter telling her that he had shipped in a whaler, she fully expected him to return minus an arm or a leg as that was the condition of the sailors who came occasionally to the little town in Wales where they had lived before coming to the United States.

Young men do not do such things today and one wonders why they did it in the old days. My father's case was typical; in fact I recall the stories of the captains when gamming with our ship or calling at our home in Oakland, California, they all ran away from home to make their first voyage.

My father had a comfortable home and he had completed his apprenticeship in the toolmaker's trade which his mother had induced him to learn to get him out of the mill, as she thought it was injuring his health and held no prospects for his future. The conclusion is an obvious one, the boys had ambition and wanted adventure, so they went to sea or to the undeveloped western areas.

In view of the fact that the forecastle was the starting place of the majority of the American whaling captains, the stories of the ignorance and brutality of the crews of whaleships become little more than the imaginings of writers woefully ignorant of the actual facts. As time passed and, especially after the operations of the Pacific fleet shifted to San Francisco, the caliber of the men who shipped as sailors became very low but these men never became captains, or even boatsteerers. The business had already commenced to decline and few, if any, men of outstanding ability were added to the list of captains and officers who were in service when the whaling fleet met its great disaster in 1871. The day of the sailing ship was passing but their history is still in the making.

Many writers have been most critical of the whaleship crews while praising the merchant marine. The whalers encountered the same gales that were met by the merchantmen. It is true that the whaleships rarely made long passages under press of canvas as was the practice of the merchant ships, but when occasion required, the whaler would carry sail with the best of the merchant ships. The miles covered in the voyages of the whaleships were far in excess of those of a merchant ship and they cruised in more unknown seas and encountered the dangers of ice and land to a far greater extent than the merchant service. The voyage that I am describing of the 240-ton whaling bark *Florence* covered eleven months. During this time, the ship was at anchor a total of about four weeks and under sail the rest of the time. I admire the history of the merchant service and have no intention of discrediting its history. My interest is in establishing the whaling industry in its true position as having

made such a substantial contribution to the development of Massachusetts and developing the finest race of seamen that ever sailed
under the flag of any nation.

In my sea days, there was a tendency in all followers of the sea to
favor the branch of the service they were attached to. The Navy
looked down on every other service, including the Revenue Service,
and the merchantmen, whalers and fishermen looked down on the
Navy and the Revenue Service. A captain was an autocrat, the lord
of all he surveyed whether it was a schooner or a battleship, and the
elements knew no favorites. The captain who came in through the
hawsepipe of a square rigger never accorded absolute equality to
the man who came in through the cabin window. Life in the forecastle of a whaler, even in its best years, was an experience that only
those of the toughest fiber and strongest principles could survive.
But they did survive and gradually worked their way aft to become
captains and the greatest mariners of their day.

Much has been written about the brutality of these men who
commanded the sailors. To many people who consider themselves
refined any exercise of physical force is brutal; also profanity. To
my mind, it all depends upon the circumstances of the occurrence
and the type of man who was the victim of the brutal attack. It
should be remembered that there were two very different types of
men in the sailing ship days. Before the War Between the States,
the majority of the foremast hands were young men of ambition,
used to an outdoor life and willing to settle disputes by physical
force. This was true in whaleships and merchant ships. There
were always experienced sailors in the forecastle when the ship left
port, more in a merchant ship because the crews were smaller in
proportion to their greater tonnage and they did not have the large
and experienced after gang of the whaleship. The old sailors were
not adverse to trying physical conclusions with a young officer or
one whose courage or physical skill was in doubt. It was one of the
jokes of the old-timers to encourage a greenhorn who had pride in
his skill with his hands to take a try at the third mate at an oppor-
tune moment. It was sometimes successful as to the immediate re-

sult but it was a safe bet that the defeat of the mate would soon be repaid with interest. It might be the first mate or even the Captain, as it would never do to permit such a situation to continue. It might destroy the discipline of the ship and lead to very serious happenings. Under these conditions the use of physical force was not always brutal but there were brutal occasions. It could not be otherwise with such a range of characters and mental capacities of the men who started as sailors and later became officers. Men of brutal instincts did get promoted and they acted accordingly at every opportunity but this was just as normal procedure with thousands of men who never served on a sailing ship.

After the war, the type of men found in the forecastle of sailing ships showed a very appreciable deterioration in character, both physical and mental. The development of railroads in the West and the industrial growth that followed offered a more attractive field to the young men of the East and they stopped going to sea. As I looked over the nondescript gang of landlubbers and semi-sailors gathered in the waist of the *Florence,* and recalled the crew of the *Monticello* when we sailed from Honolulu only three years before, I wondered if they could ever be converted into real sailors. They were converted but it took a lot of energy and profanity. A new set of standards was necessary; they had to be driven because they had no ambition and no courage. They should not have been in the forecastle of a sailing ship. For some time, they obeyed orders only because their fear of the officers was greater than their fear of the dangers attached to the execution of the order. Perhaps it was brutal but they were far better men when the ship returned to San Francisco than when they sailed. They could "hand, reef and steer," if not able seamen.

Most of the foremast hands had only the clothes they stood in, so it was necessary to break out the slop chest during the first dog-watch and supply their wants. This included clothes, pots and pans, sheath knives and belts, needles and thread, blankets, soap and to-bacco. Of course, everything was charged as there was not a "plugged nickel" in the gang. There are stories of the charges for these items being greatly in excess of the cost to the shipowners but this was not true in my experience.

When a man signed the papers before a federal government official, known as a Shipping Commissioner, he received an order that was for an advance of $60 when countersigned by the first mate to show that he was aboard the ship. These orders were presented to the agent of the ship by a boardinghouse keeper, or some person who had produced the man before the Commissioner and was supposed to provide him with an outfit, including a chest and a mattress, always referred to as a "donkey's breakfast." It can be said that the outfit was never worth the amount of the advance. Generally, the man was too intoxicated when he reached the ship to know anything about the transaction. Two of our men were induced to sign the articles on the representation of the "runner" who picked them up on the street that it was a short fishing trip to the Farallon Islands that would last a few days and that they need not buy anything as everything would be furnished by the ship. They soon learned that they were booked for the biggest fishing trip they ever dreamed of. These practices by the underworld characters of San Francisco were among the list of crimes against the city.

The men were allowed to draw what they needed from the slop chest and the quality was good for the purpose. They were warned that they must not trade their clothes with the natives of the islands where the ship might touch. Tobacco was restricted to plugs of the black Navy brand and to a limited ration per month. It was a good trading currency and a highly practical substitute for poker chips when cut into small cubes. The cigarette issue of modern times is in a similar category as currency and for trading purposes.

We were rolling along on a southwesterly course with the Solomon Islands north of Australia as our most southerly objective. The weather was good, with moderate winds which gave the greenhorns a chance to find their sea legs and learn the ropes without unusual physical discomfort. The usual routine of ship life was in practice; decks were washed down in the last hour of the morning watch and again in the dogwatch while the ship was in the tropics.

Washing down on a whaleship was still conducted in the primitive way, without the use of hand pump and hose, but with water carried in buckets from a deck tub in the waist which is filled with water drawn from over the side of the ship in a bucket. The sailors sweep the water over the deck toward the scuppers using brooms made on the ship of a tough fibrous plant that grows on the South Pacific islands and is much better adapted to ship use than the house broom. Excess water remaining on the deck was swept up with absorbent mops made of the yarn of old hemp ropes. Occasionally the deck was holystoned with sand and water and the paintwork of the bulwarks washed.

Filling the deck tub with water was a more skillful job than might be gathered from the brief reference. Two men were assigned, one sitting astride the rail adjoining the deck tub, the other man standing in the main chains with his back to the bulwarks and a rope, called a life belt, across his waist to keep him from falling overboard as he had to use both hands. A rope is attached to a canvas bucket with the end made fast to some part of the rigging near the rail so the bucket will not be lost. The man holds the bucket rope in his two hands and the man on the rail drops the bucket into the water, when the man in the chains gives the rope a deft twitch which fills the bucket as the ship moves ahead and then he gives a swing with a pull and lands the bucket in the hands of the man on the rail who empties it into the tub. The repetition of this operation was as regular as the swing of the pendulum of a clock regardless of the roll of the ship. This operation looks so easy when done right but a greenhorn in either capacity could make a laughable spectacle in his first trial.

Strange to say, every movement on a ship looks so easy and simple when done by a real sailor that one only realizes the skill involved when he sees the operation performed by a novice. A sailing ship is a systematic creation in perfect orderliness. Everything has its name and its place and, with few slight changes, it is the same on every ship of similar rig. As I never knew just when I learned the ropes and all that constitutes the language of the sailing ships,

I was often amused and sometimes exasperated at the dumbness of some of the greenhorns in the crew.

For the first few days, sheets and halliards were set up and braces checked in several times a day to get the men used to the location of these ropes and the methods of executing the orders. How to pull or haul in unison, how to hold "a turn" or slack a lee brace, and how to coil the rigging after an order is executed. A rope is always coiled "right-handed," that is from left to right, which makes it run freely without kinking which is a very important matter, especially in a squall. When a coil of rope is taken off a pin and laid on deck, the inside of the coil or running part must be up and the coil must not be disarranged. For some unknown reason, a greenhorn always coils a rope left-handed and invariably capsizes the coil when he takes it off the pin.

The storms held off but one day we had quite a nasty squall and delayed taking in sail a little too long, which gave us a few anxious moments. The ship heeled down until the water spouted up through the scuppers and the watch struggled with clew lines and all the rest of the running gear, clewing up the fore- and main-topgallant sails and mainsail and clewing down the topsails. Of course, there was some excitement with many orders and much profanity as the poor greenhorns either did the wrong thing or were forcibly prevented from doing it. The poor men were terribly frightened and soaked to the skin as in a few minutes the rain came down in torrents and the wind dropped to a calm. Topsails were hoisted, topgallant sails sheeted home and mainsail reset. With running rigging coiled and hung on the pins, the event became one of the episodes in the daily life on a sailing ship that prevents monotony. Many times I have been asked "Wasn't the life terribly monotonous?" and my answer has been "No, there were never two days just alike" and never a moment that there wasn't something going on. Taking in sail, making sail, trimming the yards, setting up sheets and halliards, renewing chafing gear, setting up the standing rigging which was of hemp as this was before the use of wire rope.

One of the first duties was the fitting out of the whaleboats. The

Florence carried four boats swung outboard on davits and two spare boats on skids over the main deck just forward of the poop deck. Each boat carried whaling equipment consisting of two tubs of whale line, called "towline," made of the best Manila hemp, at least two toggle irons — the harpoon of the landsman — and there might be one or two spare irons according to the custom of the boatsteerer, two or three hand lances, a bomb gun, hatchet, sheath knife in a sheath on the forward side of the knee brace in the bow of the boat and in some boats a darting gun. This gun was to fasten to a whale at the same time that he was shot as it carried both an iron and a bomb lance. There was also a short-handled spade, a boat hook, a fresh-water keg and under the stern a long keg which contained a small boat lantern, candles, matches and a bag of hard bread for emergencies. The bomb gun was carried in a box in the bow, the irons were held in cleats on the starboard side with wood sheaths on the heads and the lances with the heads similarly protected were carried on the port side. These were the fighting weapons and they were carefully placed where they could be easily and quickly reached by the boatsteerer or officer as the occasion required.

The irons and lances were mounted on wooden poles, usually hickory for the irons and ash for the lances. If there were not a sufficient number already from the last voyage, and in good condition, each boatsteerer would make up the deficiency from the spare irons, lances and poles carried for this purpose. The irons and lances were cleaned and the edges ground to keen sharpness. The soft pine pins that keep the head of the iron from "toggling"; that is, turning at right angle to the shaft until after it has entered the whale and a strain is put on the line, were put into place. The straps, landyards and seizings are carefully inspected and renewed if there is any doubt as to their good condition. Nothing is left to chance. Every boat has a mast and a sail and these have to be looked over and new rigging furnished whenever needed. Perhaps some of the officers prefer a different kind of sail than what they find in the old equipment of their boat, whereupon a new sail will be made.

The types of sails used in boats were different, consisting of a mainsail and a jib. The mainsail had a gaff or a sprit and no boom, or a lugsail was used which hoists on a yard with no boom or jib as the sail extends forward of the mast.

My father's boat and the first mate's boat carried lugsails, the second mate's boat a gaff mainsail and jib, and the third mate's boat a spritsail and jib, which gave representation to the three types and furnished a subject for discussions as to their respective merits. I was to have an opportunity to study each type in action as at one time or another I went in each of the four boats.

The lugsail is really the distinctive sail of the three types. It reminds one of the lugsails of the Italian fishing boats of San Francisco but is not as picturesque, for the yard does not peak as high because that part forward of the mast must be kept high enough so as not to interfere with the boatsteerer when going onto a whale. The tack, or rope attached to the lower forward corner of the sail, hauls down to a cleat in the eye of the boat and fastens to another cleat on the gunwale near the boatsteerer's thwart. In tacking, this tack rope has to be released and the forward end of the yard pulled aft and around the mast so that the entire sail will be on the lee side of the mast. This is a difficult maneuver, especially in a strong breeze, and always dangerous because, if the tack gets away from the boatsteerer, the sail immediately balloons to the head of the mast and the boat capsizes. I had seen this happen to my father's boat in the Arctic Ocean on a previous voyage and had no doubts as to the importance of hanging on to the tack. If it did get away, it was usless to waste time in regrets or efforts to recover it — just climb to windward and get astride of the keel.

The lugsail, however, had advantages that more than offset its disadvantages. It was a great driving sail, especially a little off the wind, and it could be set and taken in quickly.

Filling a tub with new towline was another interesting feature of these first days of preparation. The line is received in close coiled bales 100 fathoms in length. It is uncoiled and towed overboard to take out any tendency to kink or foul as it runs out of the tub when fast to a whale. It is then coiled loosely on deck to dry after which, if it feels soft and supple, it is very carefully coiled flemish fashion in a wooden tub. There are two tubs of line in each boat, one holding 200 fathoms set on the bottom of the boat between the two after thwarts, and the other holding 100 fathoms on one side of the center-board box between the next two thwarts.

While I have mentioned only a few of the activities that must be attended to at the beginning of a voyage, it will be evident that, when added to the regular ship duties, it makes for considerable work. At least, I found it very interesting and hurried through my regular daily duties of trimming and filling the binnacle lamp, cabin lamps, side lights and such other affairs as I was told to attend to by my father, mother or steward, in order that I might not miss anything on deck.

I have already stated that each foremast hand had to learn to steer and stand his regular trick at the wheel. Steering is not such a mechanical process as one might conclude from observation only. Every ship has certain ways that must be learned and every wise sailor finds them out and profits by his knowledge. Most ships steer badly with a strong wind on the quarter or over the taffrail but, even then, much depends upon the man at the wheel. If he uses too much wheel, he will not only have a very busy time but will be roundly cussed throughout his trick by the captain or the officer of the deck. A ship is steered by watching the sails or by the compass. If the wind is favorable so that a course can be laid, it is given to the man at the wheel and he steers by the compass paying no attention to the sails. In my day, the compass card had 32 points with half and quarter points. Now, it is divided into 360 degrees. Naming the points in their order to the right from the north point is known as "boxing the compass."

If the direction of the wind does not permit steering by compass, the ship will be put on the wind with the yards braced against the rigging and the man at the wheel will be told to "keep her close to the wind." He then watches the weather leach of the upper sails to see that they are kept full with now and then a shiver to be sure that he is not getting off the wind. If the wind always blew true as to direction, a compass course could be steered on the wind as well as off the wind, but it does not blow true. Steering by the sails takes advantage of the free slants and the ship works to windward rather than to leeward. It is desirable to keep the ship moving to avoid an excessive lee drift or, if she will be nearly on her course when close hauled, the man at the wheel will be ordered to "keep her full and bye" when he will keep her sails hard full and yet she will be on the wind. Steering by the sails so as to get the maximum benefit of the wind and not get too far to leeward of the course you are steering is quite an art. It requires anticipation of the movements of the ship caused by the seas.

Of course, the weather plays an important part in the routine of ship life, although it soon becomes a matter of routine notwithstanding that it is constantly changing. The landsman naturally thinks of storms and shipwrecks, especially if he has read highly imaginary descriptions of storms at sea, but storms while never pleasant soon become just a passing event in life aboard a ship. They are never alike and never free of danger, they vary in the force of the wind and in the size and character of the sea, and in the results. My father was eight years in the ship I was born in and during that time he was in many storms but never lost a spar until the last night he spent aboard of her while hove to off San Francisco in a moderate gale. The ship dove into a sea and snapped off the jib boom right at the bowsprit cap. Nothing else happened, although it is strange that the fore-topgallant mast was not carried away at the same time.

The newspapers tell of terrible experiences where for some hours there was serious concern for the safety of these large Atlantic liners of today during a gale. I cannot take it very seriously. The largest ship that I was ever in was the full-rigged ship *Hibernia* of 556 tons. In the forty years of her life she probably encountered as heavy gales as ever blew and yet, I do not imagine, that her master or her officers were ever concerned as to her safety in so far as wind or sea was concerned. A gale on a lee shore is another matter. The *Flor-*

ence was only 244 tons, not as large as many modern coasting schooners, but she went through just as heavy gales as the largest liners encounter. Of course, whaleships were never overloaded or undermanned and it was seldom necessary to drive them. They were also splendid sea boats and some of them were good sailers for their length. The *Florence* was built on the lines of what used to be known as a Baltimore Clipper and was a very good sailer. She was rather stiff; that is to say, she did not heel easily and had in consequence a quick snappy roll to windward that could be very uncomfortable. The first mate used to say that she would carry a glass of water on the cabin table all day because the weather roll would catch it before it could capsize on the lee roll. She did not pitch badly and I prefer rolling of the two motions. I might as well confess at this time that while I was born at sea and was three years old before I really lived ashore, I was always a little "under the weather" for the first week of a voyage. I never "fed the fishes" and could enjoy the jokes played on the greenhorns while getting their sea legs. I was wise to my feelings and avoided any real trouble by staying on deck as much as possible and declining soup at meals and drinking very little water. Mark Twain hit it right when he said "you feel so bad you want to die but you know you won't," referring to seasickness.

The moss-covered advice to greenhorns to swallow a piece of raw salt pork tied to a string so that it could be pulled back would generally find a victim and I am not so sure that it was as bad as it sounds because a thorough housecleaning was what most of them needed and the sooner it was accomplished the sooner they got well. But fear was a factor with some men that time alone could eliminate. To be ordered aloft to help furl a sail, especially at night, must have been torture to the poor devils too sick to stand up on deck much less go into the rigging. Perhaps that was brutal, yet it was soon over with and I never heard it referred to except in a joking way. Going aloft for the first time at sea is an experience that will try any man's courage, especially if the sea is rough. The first real test comes when you reach the "top," which is not the topmost point of the mast but is the semicircular platform at the head of the lower mast of the mainmast and foremast of a bark; also of the mizzenmast of a full-rigged ship. This top furnishes the spread for the topmast shrouds which start from dead eyes in the upper ends of the futtock shrouds, lower shrouds, and are iron rods bolted to the mast and extending out to the rim of the top at an angle of about forty-five degrees. Ratlines are seized to these rods which are to put your foot on in going over the top and that is the proper way to do it. There is a rectangular opening in the top platform next to the mast, called the "lubber hole," which on a small vessel like the *Florence* is not large enough for a man to get through although some of the greenhorns tried it, to the great delight of the deck audience. The moment while going over the top when you are really suspended in mid air, especially if the ship makes a snappy roll to windward at that moment, is an experience no man ever forgets. This never causes any concern after the first experience but it is a pride and joy experience the first time.

A year or two after my return from this voyage I was on the waterfront of San Francisco with several of my boy associates admiring the lofty spars of the ship *Three Brothers,* at that time the largest sailing craft afloat, when one of the boys casually remarked, "Billy, you think you are a sailor, let's see you go aloft on that ship." I had a premonition that one of them would make that suggestion and perhaps I had been boasting but there was no retreat now. I took off my coat, stepped to the ship's rail and commenced to climb the ratlines of the shrouds to the foremast. When I reached the futtock shrouds I almost swallowed my heart as I realized that I could not possibly reach the rim of the top but would have to climb right out on the futtock shrouds my full length before I could reach the lanyard of the topmast shrouds and pull myself over. Well, I did it and I had to come down the same way which is, if possible, more disturbing to your nerves than going up. I had accepted the dare and met the test but I had surprised myself fully as much as my companions.

We had not been at sea but a few days when we began to see

those big birds known to sailors as "boobies." They are the original gliders as they are always sailing up and down with no perceptible movement of their wings after they get into the air. They have a very wide wingspread for the size of their bodies. They spend much time over the wake of the ship and immediately investigate anything thrown overboard that floats. In calm weather they land on the surface and paddle along in the wake picking up everything eatable. One day we caught one with a hook baited with a piece of salt pork. On deck, after the hook was removed, he proceeded to be seasick and was unable to walk without frequently falling. It was quite evident that he could not take off from the deck — which seemed strange as they breed on land — so after watching his antics for a while, someone dropped him over the side to rejoin his mates. The end of this incident was a relief to the older members of the crew who believed it would bring bad luck to the ship to kill a booby, or gooney as it may have been.

Sharks were seen every day; some were very large, and they were also looking for something to eat, trailing along in the wake of the ship with a small pilot fish swimming just over the nose of the shark. I doubt very much if they are of any assistance to the shark; in fact, they are probably the sole beneficiary of the partnership. Of course, sailors have no use for sharks, but that they believe it is a sure sign of a death or a calamity for a shark to follow a ship is a notion started by certain poorly informed writers and there is no truth in it. A shark is a scavenger, and therefore a coward. The Kanakas have no fear of sharks but they may attack a man under certain conditions. They have a remarkably keen scent for blood as shown by the speed with which they will collect around a ship when cutting in a whale. They will begin to gather as soon as the whale is brought alongside and in a short time the water will be fairly alive with them and, in spite of the terrible punishment inflicted on them by the officers on the cutting stage with their long-handled spades, the sharks will rush in and cut out pieces of blubber eighteen inches in diameter as clean as if cut with a knife and far quicker than any man could do it. A shark cannot bite out a piece by simply opening and closing his jaws, but by throwing his lower jaw down and back his mouth is practically a circle the full width of his head, with at least one row of very sharp pointed teeth, and sometimes two rows. He slides up on the body of the whale and whirls himself completely around on his head as a pivot, literally cutting out a circular piece of blubber the diameter of his mouth and several inches thick. It is done in an instant and the piece is immediately swallowed whole. I used to get into the bow of the starboard boat, fasten a piece of line to a boat spade, and practice darting it down upon the sharks as they rushed in to attack the whale. Only death could stop them, and a boat spade was too light to reach a vital point with all the strength that I could put into it. Sometimes we would catch a small shark with hook and line, but while it furnished some excitement for a few minutes, there is something so distasteful about a shark to old sailors that it had to be an unusually dull time for me to get any encouragement to try my skills at catching a shark. One day, I tried it on my own and only saved myself from going overboard by letting go the line, which the shark went off with.

We had not been at sea many days before my father informed me that I must learn how to determine the position of the ship. What he actually said was, "Boy, I am the only man aboard this ship who can work out a sight and you must learn how, so that if anything happens to me, the ship can be navigated back to San Francisco." It was a fact that not one of the officers could even work a sight for latitude, to say nothing of longitude which is a much more complicated calculation. The officers were skilled whalemen and seamen but three of them could neither read nor write and the fourth had no ambition to learn as he never expected to be a captain.

I had taken a few lessons on a voyage three years earlier and had advanced considerably in book knowledge, especially mathematics which I always liked. The *Nautical Almanac* and Bowditch's *Practical Navigator,* always referred to as the "Epitome," were brought out and I was told what to study and how to take a sight, with either a quadrant or a sextant. Taking a sight is determining the angle between the sun and the horizon. For latitude, the angle is read when the sun crosses the meridian at its zenith, which is twelve o'clock noon. At that moment, the order is given to the man at the wheel "strike eight bells." The ship's clock is corrected to agree with the sun.

Taking a sight for longitude involves taking the time at Greenwich by the chronometer at the moment of taking the angle of the sun with the horizon. My father usually took this observation between two and three o'clock in the afternoon when, the angle being less, the liability of error is less and the image of the sun is sharper. Views differ as to whether the afternoon or the forenoon is better for an observation for longitude and the weather may effect this decision. To take the time at the moment of getting the angle requires a person at the chronometer to take down the hour, minutes and seconds at the instant the observer calls "time." The correction for the gain or loss of the chronometer is then applied and the calculations made which will give the longitude of the ship at that moment. The daily error of the chronometer, or its rate, is determined by comparison with a standard chronometer at the port where the ship refits. The rate is determined over the period of arrival of the ship until departure time and a card is given with the rate of change, usually a gain of a few seconds a day as most captains prefer a gain to a loss.

I had no great difficulty mastering the mathematics of the calculations even though it involved the use of logarithms with which I was to become widely acquainted a few years later. There were a few details affecting the calculations, such as whether the sun was north or south of the line and whether the ship was north or south of the line or east or west of the meridian, that I had some difficulty in remembering. Finally came a day when my father concluded that my memory needed a bracer and, as I had the ship ashore many miles from our actual position, he casually remarked that if I had her position wrong the next day, he would give me a licking with a "rope's end." Knowing that he never made idle threats, I got very busy, found my mistakes and made no more. In fact, I became a very good navigator and regularly worked out the ship's position when a sight of the sun was possible. This led to the discovery of an error in one of the chronometers, the ship having two, that might have caused serious trouble because it was the chronometer that my father used.

With the growth in my duties, I still had time to watch the varying incidents of the day. It was interesting to note the rapid transformation of the greenhorns into sailors. There was a general mellowing effect in a growing understanding of the various members of the crew, both forward and aft.

THE OFFICERS

THE first mate was an old acquaintance although it was my first experience with him as a shipmate. He was a native of Portugal and had been following the sea ever since he was a small boy. He was a man of medium height, compactly built, wiry and quick on his feet, and he liked to tell stories. He was a good disciplinarian, kept everything shipshape and, while he had a sharp tongue, I do not recall ever seeing him strike a man. He was also a fine seaman but not a navigator.

The second mate claimed France as his native land but he went to sea so young that he could recall very little of his home life and had entirely forgotten his mother tongue. He was a rugged-looking, square type of man, with plenty of courage and physical strength. He was a good seaman but he was not a navigator. He was a splendid whaleman with the tenacity of a bulldog. He was reticent to the point of being surly at times and rarely ever joked or told stories. I was such a persistent questioner that I eventually got quite a little of his history and learned to like him. There was something about him that inspired confidence and I used to go in his boat when my father did not lower. He was typical of a good many men

then in the business and I wondered what there was in life for him
to look forward to with pleasure. He was entirely illiterate, un-
married and, as far as he knew, he did not have a relative in the
world. He received a good lay and had made quite a lot of money
but he was then owing the ship $500 and did not have a cent. He
had been ashore about two months from his previous voyage in
another ship and, during that time, he had spent his share, at least
one thousand dollars and perhaps twice that amount, together
with the advance he had received when he shipped in the *Florence.*
It had all gone to women and rum in a very cheap and sordid way.
He lived in a cheap room not far from the waterfront and it was a
continuous drunk on cheap liquor with not much food. One
might think that the absolutely normal, healthy life at sea would
enable men to shake off such utterly joyless desires and get a little
fun for their money, but they seemed to be powerless to avoid the
suckers of both sexes that were always on the lookout for them
when they returned from a voyage. The good people ashore who
were so disturbed by the brutal treatment of sailors never seemed
to realize that the greater part of this brutality lay almost entirely in
their neglect of the conditions existing along the waterfront of the
seaports of the world. The unfortunate devil who through adversity
or accident fell into the clutches of the proprietors of the boardinghouses and saloons of those regions had to be a brute to survive.

The third mate was a carpenter by trade but an uncontrollable
thirst for liquor sent him to sea, and he had become a fairly good
officer.

The fourth mate was a big Brava Portuguese, good-natured and a
good seaman, but he would probably never rise above a third mate.
In those days few black men reached the cabin of a whaleship although the whalers were the most democratic of all the sailing
craft.

There were two boatsteerers, the fourth mate and the cooper having taken that position in the first mate's and Captain's boats, and
one was a Marquesan Kanaka. He was an ideal man for this position and might well have posed for French's statue of the "Whale-

man" in front of the Public Library in New Bedford, Massachusetts. He was over six feet in height, of large frame, not fat but
not angular, straight as they ever grow, very strong, with a large
head and fine features. He was not black, perhaps brown is definite
enough, but his hair was black and straight. He had a rich, mellow
voice and it was a joy to hear him give the sailor's yodel when he
would assist in hoisting topsails, for instance. He had a fair grasp
of English; he was not loquacious but always pleasant. His brother
was a boatsteerer with us in the *Monticello* two years before and
our third mate had helped both to run away from their island and
ship on a whaler.

The cooper was quite a young man, as compared with those I
had been shipmates with before, a native of the Western Islands,
and a pronounced blond, of which he was rather proud. He was
quite a skillful "scrimshawer" and made a variety of articles, such
as tatting shuttles of tortoiseshell, crocheting needles of whalebone
with carved heads, canes of the jaw bone of the sperm whale, and
of the heart of the coconut tree, with various shaped heads made
from sperm whale's teeth, all of excellent design and beautifully
finished. His real artistic effort, on which he worked the entire voyage, was a workbox made of South Sea Island wood, beautifully in-
laid and finished. Some of the foremast hands made various articles
and the fourth mate was rather skillful in making half models with
sails set which he cut out of white pine with a jackknife, but the
cooper was the real artist and his work compared favorably with
the best I have seen. When one considers the few simple tools they
had to work with, the results showed not only great skill but high
artistic conception.

The steward was rather an old man who had evidently started
life with much higher ambitions. He had some education and
quite an experience, about which he was very reticent. I did learn
that he had been involved in one of China's earlier revolutions
when, for a brief period, he was a general and just missed a fortune,
but only saved his head by a very narrow margin. How much his
controlling taste for liquor had to do with his failure in China I

never knew, but it was without doubt the cause of his being steward on a whaler. He had been with my father before and his weakness was well understood, but it was to overcome him in spite of my father's precautions and, as I will describe later, he was on his last voyage. I liked him, partly I suppose because he expected very little of me as cabin boy, but principally because it was apparent that he should have filled a higher station in life. He was a gentleman in spite of his weakness.

The cook was an old shipmate, as he was with us on both of my previous voyages, and I had spent many hours listening to some very weird stories of his experiences. He was never too busy to entertain me and usually had something for me to eat that I liked. Of course, I had outgrown some of his earlier stories, such as for instance the purpose of the square opening in the deck to the galley directly over the front of the range, which he explained was for his convenience when frying griddle cakes. When the griddle cake was ready to be turned over, he would deftly toss it up through the scuttle and then catch it on the frying pan which he would thrust out through the small window in the side of the galley. For a long time I watched for a demonstration when griddle cakes were to be served, but the wind was either too strong or too weak, or blowing in the wrong direction, until I began to get skeptical and finally dropped the subject. The cook also had an overpowering love of liquor and, when the ships stopped their "between seasons" cruise, we had him run the kitchen in our home in Oakland under the supervision of my mother from the arrival of the ship in the fall until the departure for the Arctic in the spring. He finally sailed with Captain Ebenezer Nye in the *Mount Wollaston* on the voyage from which she never returned and all hands were lost.

FOREMAST HANDS

Looking the crew over after a few weeks at sea disclosed one old-time sailor, although it was his first voyage in a whaler. He could "hand, reef and steer" and was somewhat of a sea lawyer in his ability to keep himself out of trouble while slyly encouraging others to assert their rights and thereby get into trouble. He could spin quite a yarn from his experience and for a time dominated the forecastle but he lost caste as the others gained experience. His body was covered with tattooing from his waist up including his arms and he could do a fairly good job on others. In those days, almost every man who had been to sea for any length of time had some tattooing. I had a strong desire for the colorful badge of a sailor but my father had escaped it and he left no doubt in my mind as to what would happen to me if he ever found any tattooing on any part of my body. With his very clear description of the tattooing job he would do on me, I never was tattooed and I never regretted it.

Tattooing was an old custom with the Kanakas and followed definite designs by which natives of the different islands could be identified, but the extent of the tattooing on a particular person varied with his age and tribal position on his island. I have seen natives literally covered from head to foot but on some islands the natives had little or no tattooing. The women were also tattooed but only to a slight extent as compared to the men. Their designs were always geometrical rather than pictorial and generally well done. Lampblack was the pigment used as I never saw tattooing on a Kanaka in color. Sailors used lampblack, india ink and whatever red pigment they could get which sometimes lead to blood poisoning with awful sores and unsightly results that were permanent. The operation is extremely painful, whether performed with needles by sailors or with sharp fish bones by natives and, if the design is large, it may take weeks to complete.

Our sea lawyer was a writer of sorts and he spent considerable time on his journal of the voyage. As we had several very unusual happenings, I have often wondered what became of his stories because, if he could write as fluently as he talked, it must have been exciting reading but he never let any one see what he wrote.

Two or three men in the crew were fairly well educated and I loaned them books from my small stock. The majority spent their spare time telling lewd stories or describing their various love affairs in much detail. The few real sailors were interesting as they had experiences worth listening to but they would talk only when in the mood for it. I was not supposed to go forward of the tryworks, in fact, I was ordered not to mingle with the foremast hands as I belonged to the "after gang." Naturally the forward end of the ship became all the more attractive and I spent many of my spare moments absorbing the tales of the forecastle and I do not believe that it did me any harm. When I went aft, I was in a very different atmosphere, not much different from my home ashore, as I was with my family. No doubt it was a healthy antidote but there was my father as a living example of the fact that a young man could live in the forecastle and gradually work his way aft to the position of Captain without losing the power to enjoy and appreciate the finer things of life. My father could swear; in fact, when the occasion required he could fairly raise blisters in the air but he was never obscene, he never swore before the family and I never heard him tell a story or an experience that was off color. He did not swear for lack of words to express himself but to produce immediate and effective action, and it did because it was understood. I have heard as filthy language ashore as I ever heard at sea. Discussions on the quarterdeck were free of offensive profanity because an officer attempting to cuss out another officer would be taken to task immediately.

It so happened that my experience at sea covered a period of transition in the method of securing crews for whaleships that had a great effect on the type of men and their subsequent treatment. When the voyages started from New Bedford or other New England ports, there were always a number of youths who were ambitious to see the world and did not have to be lied to or filled with liquor to induce them to sign the ship's papers. They did not propose to live and die in the shadow of their birthplaces. These men rarely had to be driven into the rigging or taught to obey orders with a belaying pin. Naturally, there would be some old sailors and some landsmen who were tough and bad but little shanghaiing was done.

Men shipped in Honolulu were generally sailors and, although they were probably broke, they knew what they were doing. When the outfitting of whalers shifted to San Francisco, there was a radical change in the type of men who were available for foremast hands on either whalers or merchantmen. I think the merchant ships had the first call on the real sailors as their size made them more appealing, but for years 'Frisco had periods when it was full of men looking for a job. These men eventually drifted into cheap boardinghouses, and the time came when they had to be shipped on a sailing vessel since the ships were the only employers of labor who paid an advance. Under these conditions, some very poor specimens of humanity went to sea and the wonder is that there was not more brutality. One striking difference between the crew of the *Florence,* which contained few real sailors, and the crew of the *Monticello* in which we sailed from Honolulu three years before, and had no greenhorns, was that the *Monticello* crew was a singing crew and the later crew could not even yodel — the yo-heave-ho of literature. The former crew had a chantey for everything and most of them could yodel. The performance of each operation had a musical attachment and the work went with a snap that was a joy to watch. The officers never had to beg for another pull on a halliard or a brace, all they had to do was to sing out "Belay" before the crew parted some line. They were a happy crew, for you cannot sing and harbor a grudge. Reefing topsails in the darkest night, the order "haul out to windward" would be repeated by every man on the yardarm and one would wonder if it was really blowing hard. Operating the windlass, "cutting in" a whale or taking the anchor was carried on under the accompanying chanteys fitted to the rhythm of the operation.

The crew of the *Florence* were gradually taught a few chanteys but the only one ever sung with any zest was "Whiskey Johnny"; but there is a wrong time and a right time to sing that chantey if real action is expected. When this chantey is successful the first mate, after a word from the Captain, sings out "Avast heaving, lay off and splice the main brace." Then all hands file aft and pass by the steward, boatsteerers first, and each man is given a good-sized glass of neat liquor, generally whiskey. The officers get their drink in the cabin but are not restricted to one glass, although there was always a limit. As soon as the main brace is properly spliced, the windlass is again manned and the "cutting in" proceeds with a very perceptible snap to both the windlass and the chanteys. A good "chanteyman" is an improviser and carries the air with the crew joining with the chorus. He generally stands in the center of the windlass midway between the brakes and does no actual work.

The second mate of the *Monticello* had a good voice and knew quite a line of chanteys. Whenever the windlass got to dragging, he would leave the cutting stage and, climbing onto the topgallant forecastle, would infuse new life into the tired arms and backs of the men with a snappy chantey. That crew had a song for hoisting topsails that produced wonderfully efficient results and they braced the fore and main yards to a runaway song. Getting under way in port or near other ships always gave added zest and melody to the chanteys. Even the crew of a whaler may be affected by an audience.

SHIP ROUTINE

THE deck plan of the *Florence* was quite different from that of a typical New Bedford whaler with its flush deck from bow to stern and the companionway to the cabin on the port side and galley on the starboard side of the wheel. There was a poop deck aft which enclosed the cabin and was raised several feet above the main deck. There was no superstructure over this deck as in the New Bedford ships, where the space was covered by a light deck, called the house, that furnished protection from rain and spray for the man at the wheel or for the officer of the deck who chose to use it.

The companionway to the cabin was at the forward end of the poop on the starboard side. The entrance to the cabin was by a short flight of steps so that the cabin was partly below and partly above the main deck. The mizzenmast went down through the forward end of the cabin and to it was secured a swinging mercurial, or "table leg" barometer. A skylight extended from close to the mizzenmast to within about two feet of the wheel. The compass was in the after end of this skylight where it could be easily seen by the man at the wheel. The cabin was much lighter and better ventilated than a cabin entirely below the main deck as in the New Bedford type, but it was not as warm in extremely cold weather. On one occasion, it was partly flooded by a heavy sea which I do not believe would have reached the companionway of a cabin below the main deck. There was a short flight of steps to the poop deck on both the port and starboard sides and a small room on the port side at the forward end that was entered directly from the main deck. This was the quarters of the fourth mate and the cooper.

The cabin was divided into the forward cabin and the after cabin by a partition at the after end of the dining table. The table was fitted with a dish rack which was always in place when the ship was under sail. A wooden bench with a reversible back was secured to the floor, one on each side of the table. The table was always set twice for each meal. At the "first table," there was my father, mother, sister, first mate and which ever was to have the next watch on deck, second or third mate. The mate going off duty, the fourth mate, cooper, steward and I sat down at the "second table."

A good steward always served food in palatable form no matter how restricted his resources and we had such a steward. Then my mother, who was a real New England cook, would frequently make up a special dish for afternoon tea that certainly varied the monotony of the regular menu. There was always plenty to eat although, at times, it was very plain and not much different from the food served in the forecastle. Salt pork and beef were the staple items when the fresh meats were used up, which did not take long as we had no ice or other means of preserving food. We had some canned supplies and plenty of dried rice, beans, apples and peas. Too much of any one thing palls. We went into Yokohama on the *Monticello* voyage for supplies and bought a number of cases of eggs which lasted until I was so sick of eggs I never wanted to see one again and, as a matter of fact, I did not eat an egg for years after. On this voyage in the *Florence,* I was fed up with bananas and have never recovered my taste for them. We had them raw or cooked nearly every meal for weeks until I could not smell them without a feeling of nausea.

But to complete the description of the cabin, the after cabin while small was very cozy. There was the regulation sofa across the after end of the cabin with little closets at each end and the transom above with the medicine chest and chart rack and two port lights in the stern. Against the partition was a small upright piano for my sister to keep up her practice. It was a great source of pleasure besides giving a more than usual home atmosphere to the cabin. The staterooms of the family occupied the starboard side of the entire cabin, while the staterooms of the officers and the pantry took up the port side. It was rather a strain on the imagination to call my sleeping quarters a stateroom as it occupied a space over the ship's quarter that brought the berth so close to the deck that it required some skill to get in and out of it without cracking my head or elbows against the deck beams. There was no porthole and very little ventilation if the door into the after cabin was closed.

Masthead lookouts had been established very soon after sailing as sperm whales might be "raised" at any time. The lookouts consisted of a foremast hand with a boatsteerer who usually stood a two hour watch and were relieved when the man at the wheel was relieved. These men usually sat on the fore-topgallant yard, although they could stand on the cross trees, but the *Florence* did not have the hoops carried by most of the Atlantic whalers and I do not recall any Arctic whaler that did carry them. Later, when we got into colder latitudes, the regular "crow's-nest" with its canvas sides would be erected on the fore-topgallant crosstrees. Having good eyes and knowing fairly well a sperm whale's spout from that of a finback or sulphur-bottom whale, I frequently stood a trick at the masthead.

It is not always possible for an old whaleman to accurately determine from the first two or three spouts what type of whale it is, especially if some distance away and the visibility is poor. Therefore, when a lookout sees a spout it is almost instinctive to announce it, especially as there is likely to be a prize coming to the man who raises a sperm whale, and the man aloft does not want to take a chance that someone on deck may see the spout and sing out first. I never knew why most writers of whaling stories insist upon using the words "There she blows," because there is no reason for saying "she" any more than "he" and either would be a word too many. The cry was always "There blows," with the last word long drawn out and, as the spouts continued, simply the word "Blows" is cried with each spout. There is nothing so electrifying as that cry from the masthead. Instantly every man is at attention, no matter what is going on; the captain cries out "Where away" and starts for the rigging with the lanyard of his spyglass over his shoulder. For some time on this voyage, the few spouts that were seen turned out to be false alarms.

One day, however, the weather being good, all hands were called and the three port boats were lowered for a school of blackfish, largely to give the crews a little practice which they badly needed. The boats got away without accident, as was to be expected with at least two experts in each boat, the officer and the boatsteerer. A whaleship always carries her boats swung outboard, resting on the cranes, so it requires but a few minutes to throw down the falls at each davit, hoist the boat a trifle to take the weight off the cranes and swing them in against the rail, and then lower the boat into the water. The officer and boatsteerer are in their positions in the stern and bow of the boat as soon as it is ready to lower, the crew follow the boat down, unhook the falls and fend the boat off from the ship. As the ship clears the boats, masts are stepped and sails hoisted and, in this case, the boats headed in the direction of the blackfish. The wind was light and the school was moving rather fast, so the boats were recalled by setting the colors. The boats were hoisted, the yards braced forward, tacks boarded and the ship put upon her course.

One night while we were approaching the line, meaning the equator, we were treated to a demonstration of St. Elmo's fire. Suddenly and without any warning, a luminous ball of vapor appeared at the extreme end of the flying jib boom. It stayed there a few minutes and then appeared on the fore truck and, from there, it went to the main truck and then to the mizzen truck and then it disappeared. It was the subject of considerable discussion for several days. The old sailors said it was a bad omen and something very serious would happen. Later, when several terrible things did happen, the croakers referred to the incident of St. Elmo's fire as a warning that was disregarded. It was sort of spooky but what could we have done?

On a nice clear day, land was raised dead ahead which proved to be Ocean Island, a small typical South Pacific island quite near the equator and inhabited by a small colony of Kanakas. When I went forward, I saw against the sky on the horizon a collection of old frayed umbrellas apparently growing out of the water but, from my previous acquaintance with these small islands of the Pacific, I knew they were coconut trees. It was the first land we had seen since leaving 'Frisco and all hands were soon on deck speculating mostly on what we could get that could be eaten.

Ocean Island is of coral formation, quite low and surrounded by a white sand beach on which the surf never ceases. There is no outside or barrier reef and, therefore, no harbor or even anchorage as the water is very deep within a short distance of the beach.

When within about a half mile of the beach, the courses were clewed up and the ship hauled aback. A number of canoes were on their way to the ship and, soon after our headway stopped, a considerable part of the male population of the island were alongside exchanging their produce for tobacco and trade calico. The latter was printed in bright red and yellow figures and evidently made for that kind of a market. They had green coconuts, bananas, yams and a few fowl, none too well fed by our standards, to sell. However, we bought everything they had.

My father wanted to engage a couple of the natives for foremast hands and the first mate was directed to go ashore and make the arrangements with the head man of the island. My father gave me permission to go with the mate and, as it was quite smooth, my mother raised no objections other than to admonish me not to go out of sight of the beach. As we approached the beach, it was evident that the surf was much heavier than it appeared to be from the ship but the mate was an old hand at the business and a whale boat is a wonderful craft in any kind of a sea. The mate timed our approach so as to catch a breaker as it commenced its run for the beach, keeping just back of its crest until just before it started to break, when the oars were shipped and we rushed into the beach in a smother of foam but without shipping a cupful of water. The instant the keel touched the sand, the crew jumped out and ran the boat up on the beach. It was a thrilling experience for me and always was although I had landed through surf a number of times. Mishaps are easy and always dangerous. If you are just a few seconds too late or too early getting into position on the making breaker, you will have trouble; how serious will depend upon the size of the breakers.

While the mate was negotiating for our recruits, I looked over the collection of huts and their immediate surroundings. I was not favorably impressed and had no desire to explore the jungle of tropical growth that came almost to the beach. The huts were small and not very inviting, there was a persistent smell of rancid coconut oil about the natives and their huts that I did not like. The natives looked well fed and physically strong. A few had a peculiar scaling of the skin on their face and arms that was rather unsightly. It appeared to effect the men more than the women and was in evidence on other islands that we visited. The men and women were smooth limbed, of erect carriage and rather graceful in their movements. Their color was brown and their features are not Ethiopian. Their hair is black and straight and they are of medium height. The natives of Ocean Island and the other islands on the westerly side of the Pacific do not compare in size, looks or intelligence with the natives of the Sandwich Islands, Friendly Islands, Marquesas, Society Islands and Samoan Islands. As you approach the coast of

Asia, there is a perceptible change in the racial characteristics of the natives although the Kanaka, so called, predominates. I was not much impressed with the women. If I had been a few years older and had been out of sight of land for several months, they might have looked more attractive but I doubt it. I do not recall ever seeing a full-blooded native woman that I called good-looking on any of the Pacific islands and I have visited many of these islands. But if we are to include half-whites, that is another classification as some of them were handsome even to me as a boy.

The native dress is simple but adequate considering that the conditions do not require anything. The men wore either the loincloth or their native "tapa" which is a braided girdle around the waist, made of the pandanus leaf, with a fringe in front and back that hangs down partway to the knees. The women wear a "tapa" that is more like a short skirt, the fringe being continuous around the body and extending to the knees. Neither sex wore anything above their waist or below their knees except when they went aboard the ship when they would put on whatever they had secured in trade. Strange to say, it only accentuated their nudity as they looked much more dressed in their native costume. On one occasion, a chief came aboard dressed in a very dirty and rather abbreviated white man's shirt and an old beaver hat. The young children wore nothing and everybody was barefooted. Recalling the clothes worn by our women of that period and for many years before and after, one can appreciate the shocked feelings of the missionaries when they first met the Kanakas. It is not surprising that they gave their first attention to clothing these people but why they should have selected the "Mother Hubbard" for these women can never be answered. A more incongruous, unsightly dress for a Kanaka woman in her surroundings is hard to imagine. If they had been left to their own dress, they would be right in fashion with their civilized sisters.

I was much interested in learning how the natives picked the green coconuts as they grow in clusters underneath the large leaves at the very top of the tree, something over fifty feet above the ground. There are no branches or protuberances on the tree trunk, which is round and smooth and not large for its height. My wishes having been made known, a native boy who seemed to be about my age was told to go up a tree that had a number of nuts about the right ripeness. Throwing a light net made of the fiber of the husk of old coconuts over his shoulder, he stepped up to the tree and stood with the trunk between his feet. Another native passed a strip of bark from the stem of a banana leaf around both legs and the tree trunk and fastened the ends in a knot. The climber then put his arms around the tree, hitched his feet up with the soles pressed against the trunk and held there by the fiber band and then straightened his body up the tree. By a rapid repetition of this hitching movement, he was soon at the top of the tree, gathered the coconuts and put them in his net and came down. It looked very simple but I wisely declined the boy's invitation to try it.

A green coconut is easily opened with a knife and is full of a clear liquid that is cool and tasty no matter how hot the day. It is nothing like the old coconuts that you occasionally find in the markets of the eastern cities. A thin layer of a jellylike substance covers the inside of the shell which can be scraped out with a spoon and is very palatable. In time, the shell and this substance hardens and becomes a well known article of commerce under the name of copra. The natives also extract an oil from the dried meat which they rub on their hair and bodies after bathing but, as it soon becomes rancid, the odor is most penetrating and offensive.

For years, many of these islands of the Pacific were known only to the whalers but, in time, they were found by the traders and then came the missionaries. Some of the early whalers must have given the natives fowl and pigs, because most of the islands we visited were quite well stocked with them and furnished us with fresh food until we were well on our way north. Ocean Island was not well stocked and we bought one small shoat only, and it got in a panic shortly after we sailed and rushed overboard through a deck port that happened to be open.

The mate succeeded in shipping two young natives so we returned to our boat and launched her through the surf, which requires as much skill, if not more, than landing in a surf. The boat is brought down to the water's edge and turned around so as to head offshore. The mate takes his place with the steering oar and I got in and sat down in the stern sheets as much out of the way as possible. As the water from a breaker rushed up to the boat, the crew dragged the boat into the water until she was afloat. Then they jumped in and pulled hard on their oars so as to meet the next breaker before it curled and broke. For just a brief moment it was nip and tuck as to whether or not we would make it, but we did and were soon outside of the line of breakers and on our way to the ship about a mile offshore. The boat came alongside under the port quarter davits, everybody except the mate and boatsteerer climbed up the side of the ship to the deck, the boat was hoisted and settled on the cranes, after they were swung outboard, and the lashings were put on the boat. The yards were braced forward and the ship was again on her way.

The two new recruits touched the pen which attested that Joe Kanaka and Jim Kanaka had shipped for the season as landsmen, but were to be returned to Ocean Island at the end of the voyage, and thereby became members of the crew. They were rather stocky in build — good-natured young men who were good sailors before we reached San Francisco. They came aboard in native dress and it was necessary to outfit them completely from the slop chest. Although we were almost on the equator, they turned in that night dressed in everything they had.

The course was now laid for Pleasant Island, about three hundred miles west of Ocean Island, where we hoped to get more fresh provisions. We had frequent squalls with heavy showers which were soon over. At times there was a good deal of wind and sails had to be taken in, but the crew were learning the ropes and nothing was carried away. There was always the speculation as to whether the approaching white line under the intensely black clouds, that seemed to come right down to the water, was rain or wind. The nervousness of the officers rather amused me after a few experiences because they liked to kid me when my father was out of hearing by remarks to the effect that the "Old Man" did not carry sail like some of the captains they had sailed with before.

The Captain is always referred to aboard a ship as the "Old Man" but it has no reference to his age. It is an extremely expressive title and by a slight variation in the inflection of the voice covers quite a range of emotions. My reply to these insinuations was always to the effect that, if they were patient, they would get all the sail-carrying demonstrations wanted before the voyage was completed and I am quite sure they did. A tropical squall can be a terrifying affair and they are entirely different from a gale of wind which may blow fully as hard, or even harder, but comes on slower and with a much heavier sea.

The weather was so warm that I gave up my cubbyhole and slept on deck on the weather side of the skylight to keep me from rolling into the lee scuppers if it breezed on in the night. If it rained, as happened quite often, the officer of the deck would wake me and I would finish the night on the transom in the after cabin. There was a period of beautiful clear nights on the full of the moon and I was awakened several nights with the moon shining full in my face. A few days later, my eyes began to weep and were very painful when I looked out upon the water. Finally, I had to stay in the cabin with a wet cloth over my eyes until the inflammation passed off, which it did in a few days. It was a case of moon blindness which happens often; in fact, my father had a severe attack on his first voyage.

A few days after leaving Ocean Island, we raised Pleasant Island of similar formation but larger. The natives came alongside as soon as we had "hauled aback" with their canoes well stocked and a brisk trade began which provided us with a good supply of fowl, pigs, green coconuts — and some dry ones for the pigs — bananas, plantains and yams. We also acquired a stock of straw hats. Making these was an art the natives had learned readily from their experience weaving mats and tapa. Of course, the shape was poor and the hats did not vary much in size but they were a big improvement over a woolen cap, in spite of the losses from blowing overboard.

Their canoes were expertly adapted to the conditions they had to meet and extremely interesting. The islands of the Pacific were originally discovered and populated by people who came by water long before the white man knew anything about these islands. There are evidences on some of the islands of their occupation by a race who had disappeared before the present race came into existence. Where they came from or where the ancestors of the present inhabitants came from, nobody knows although there are many guesses as to their origins. They were used to the sea and undoubtedly covered long distances by water in their migrations.

The bodies of these canoes were what would be called a "dugout"; that is, it was a log pointed slightly at both ends and shaped from the bottom to produce an overhang and the sides and bottom smoothed inside and outside. In the earlier days, they used fire to hollow out the canoe and the finishing was done with sharp-edged shells. But a dugout would be a very dangerous craft to launch or land in a surf or get far on the open sea. Therefore, they added an outrigger on one side consisting of a straight piece of light wood, six to twelve inches in diameter depending on the size of the canoe, and about two-thirds the length of the canoe. The outrigger rests in the water and is attached to the canoe by a framework of wood resting on top of the sides and firmly fastened to it with sennit seizings made from coconut fiber. A small platform is fastened to this framework on which they carry everything they want to keep dry or out of the way. This outrigger gives stability to the canoe and makes it very seaworthy. A small leg-of-mutton sail is usually carried, but as the outrigger must always be kept to windward, the mast is shifted to the other end of the canoe when they tack ship.

Some of the islands preserved their ancient war canoes with their carved stem and stern posts rising several feet above the body of the canoe. They were kept in buildings erected for their protection as they were used on rare occasions only.

The canoes are propelled with paddles when not under sail, and these are rather artistically decorated in carved and colored designs which vary in the different island groups. The blade is generally long, tapering to a point with the greatest width at the upper end. The canoe of the Kanaka is not a speed craft, either under sail or paddle, and is not to be compared in any detail with the canoes of the Solomon Islands which are not equipped with outriggers but are seaworthy and fast.

A boat had been sent ashore to get supplies which could not be brought out by the canoes in sufficient quantity to satisfy our demand. When it returned, one member of the crew was missing. It appeared that he had slipped into the dense underbrush that grew close to the beach and, although a search was made by the natives, he could not be found and the boat returned without him. The headman of the island assured the mate that they would have him in a day or two, but when my father learned who the man was, he decided the man was not worth waiting for. We left him to become a "beachcomber," the meanest and lowest expression that can be found in a sailor's vocabulary. Of course, we never knew what became of him and he may have had the good luck to get away on a whaler or trader although few captains would take a white man off the beach in those days unless they were very shorthanded. The type of man who would run away on such an island was generally so lazy and worthless that the natives soon tired of his company and one day he would disappear.

The canoes had left the ship and we were on our course, rapidly leaving the island astern, when a native walked aft with a few straw hats he had been unable to sell. Although the island was several miles off, he put the hats together, stuck them on his head, walked to the taffrail and stepped off. He went down to his armpits and then struck out for the island as unconcerned as I might have been when walking down the street on a short errand. I have often thought since that if we had been more interested in finding out how this native came to be left aboard, a terrible tragedy might have been averted. But we sailed on and soon were the only visible evidence of life in a vast expanse of water.

During the dog watch, a sailor came aft with a native who had stowed away forward and who made it quite clear that he wanted to remain as a member of the crew, although this was communicated by signs as he could not speak a word of English. He was rather a likely looking native, apparently in good health, evidently older than the two men we shipped at Ocean Island and not quite so cheerful in looks and manner. He had a peculiar Malay cast to his features which was unusual in a Kanaka from the islands of that area. It seemed like a rather happy ending to our runaway affair, so the usual formalities were gone through and Sam Kanaka became a member of the crew and he was given an outfit from the slop chest. The proper record of both the desertion and the stowaway were entered in the log and the episode was closed; at least, so we thought.

The days passed rather pleasantly in relation to our personal comforts but we saw no sperm whales, although we caught six in these very waters only three years before. A prize of a twenty-pound box of tobacco was offered to the man who would raise a school of sperm whales. I spent a good many hours aloft in a vain search of the endless waste of water for that low, fluffy spout that would permit me to announce the presence of a sperm whale in a long-drawn-out "There blows — blows — blows," for which I had been training my vocal powers by calling the watch at the forecastle scuttle. This ceremony is preceded by several loud bangs on the side of the scuttle, made with the palm of the hand, and then the call "Starboard watch ahoy" or "Larboard watch ahoy" as the case may be but long drawn out with as much musical tone as the individual possesses. It is interesting to note at this time that Larboard and Port mean the same thing and Port is generally used except when calling the watch.

It is a strange thing how few days pass without a change in the direction or force of the wind that requires the yards to be trimmed and sails taken in or set. At times, the ship must be put on the other tack, a maneuver that is always interesting and generally well executed on a whaler, probably because the ship is short and minds the rudder quickly and there are enough men to handle the yards promptly. The order for tacking ship is "Stand by for stays" and the man at the wheel sees that the sails are full and not shivering, so as to insure speed enough to bring the ship into the wind. The officer of the deck may say to him, "Give her a hard full." All men are now at their stations, the cook at the foresheet, an ancient privilege that our cook never allowed any man to usurp, men at the tacks, jib sheets, mainsheet and clew lines while the boatsteerers were throwing down the braces. Then comes the order "Hard a-lee" and the man at the wheel puts it hard down and the ship swings into the wind, with the next order "Ease off" the headsails are released, to be followed immediately by "Tacks and sheets" when the courses, that is the foresail and mainsail, are clewed up. If there is a good breeze, sails are slatting and blocks banging as the ship comes up into the wind and the watch stands ready for the next order. The critical moment is approaching as the ship climbs the seas now almost head-on with all her square sails hard aback which brings her nearly to a standstill and you watch the end of the flying jib boom as it soars up and down — noting, with a feeling of relief, that it is still moving across the sky. All doubts are removed with the order "main-top-sail-haul" which is the cry of victory over the forces of wind and sea that were trying to make a joke of the good old ship by getting her "in irons" which means standing stationary until there is sufficient steerageway to swing her back to her course by shifting the wheel and hauling the jibs to windward. The wind pressing against the sails swings the yards automatically so that the men take in the slack of the braces easily with a final stiff pull on the main brace. By this time, the ship is swinging fast under the pressure of the sails on the foremast and, the last order is barely executed when it is followed by "Let go and haul," and the yards on the foremast are swung into position. Then comes the final order, "board tacks and haul aft the sheets" which takes care of the headsails and resets the courses. Nothing remains to be done except to take a pull on the weather braces and coil the rigging.

I never tired of "tacking ship" although, when beating off a lee shore, the ship and all our lives were at stake. Then, every detail of the movement had to be accurately gauged and correctly determined as an error in judgment of just a few moments could never be corrected. At such times, and there are several I shall never forget, my father was at his best. With all hands on deck, port watch forward, starboard watch aft, spray flying the whole length of the ship and scuppers underwater, he would stand on the lee side of the quarterdeck with one hand holding the mizzen shrouds, looking forward under the lee bow at the line of white foam that marked the breakers, until it seemed sometimes that we could not possibly miss going ashore. Then, as the ship started to rise to a sea, would come the order like the crack of a rifle, "Hard a-lee," and in a thunder of slatting sails and rigging, with decks covered with water, the men executing orders as they came through the roar of the wind, the good old ship swung slowly but surely to the offshore tack.

There is a limit to wind and sea that will permit tacking a square-rigger. She must be able to carry enough sail to give her steerageway until she has swung over the dead line. Therefore, you cannot tack a ship in a gale of wind, unless the water can be smoothed by standing in under the land if the wind is not blowing directly onshore. When a square-rigger has to shift tacks in heavy weather or in very light winds, she "wears ship," or swings around with the wind. This is not a pleasant operation in a gale of wind, because if you miss taking a sea over the taffrail when the ship is dead before the wind, you are quite apt to take one the whole length of the ship as she comes to the wind and you may do both, but probably will not survive to tell about it. Tacking a schooner is a very simple matter compared to tacking a square-rigger.

We had now crossed the meridian as well as the equator and had touched at several islands of the typical coral formation, without harbors and a surf constantly pounding on a beautiful white beach. They were all covered with a dark green verdure that looked very attractive at a distance, with the inevitable fringe of coconut trees. The natives came out with their trade goods, mostly bananas and coconuts, with a few seashells and pieces of tortoiseshell which we always bought, as at that time we expected to call at some port in Japan. A previous voyage had taught us that the Japanese would pay a very good price for tortoiseshell.

SOLOMON ISLANDS

WE finally arrived at New Ireland, one of the Solomon Islands which lie east of New Guinea and were about the least known, at that time, of any of the Pacific islands. We had cruised off this group in the *Monticello* three years before and, therefore, knew something about them and their inhabitants. We cruised by the islands named on our chart New Ireland, Bougainville and New Britain. They were quite large with very high land in the distance and all three heavily wooded right down to the water. The group was discovered by the Spanish navigator Mendaña de Neyra in 1567 and rediscovered by the English explorer Carteret in 1767, apparently without knowledge of their previous discovery. In 1768, two of the northern islands were discovered by Bougainville but these must have been known to Mendaña, who returned in 1596 and died there. Certainly those old Spanish and English explorers were great navigators; our charts were none too good but they had nothing. The fact that their ships must have been very slow sailers may have been their salvation, but that they survived the terrible squalls of those waters is indisputable evidence of the high quality of their seamanship. We bucked these squalls successfully in the *Monticello,* but after struggling against them for about two weeks in the *Florence,* we had to give it up and start north for a harbor as our ship was leaking badly. The islands of this group extend in a line about northwest and southeast, our contact being with their eastern shore.

The first canoe to approach us as we drew in to the land contained two natives but we were unable to entice them alongside. They were probably a scouting party to determine whether we were whalers or traders as these were their only visitors at that time. Traders were not looked upon with a friendly eye as most of them were in reality "blackbirders"; that is, they were after natives to work the Fiji Island plantations and were not too particular as to how they got them. Whalers were harmless although there had been a few attacks on boats landing from whaleships and some loss of life, but it was generally believed to have been in retaliation for natives stolen by some trader as the natives were never mistreated by the whalemen.

One rather laughable attempt to capture a whaleship happened a short time before our visit in the *Monticello.* There is a small island at the northern end of the group with a narrow passageway between it and the island to the south through which there is quite a swift current. The whaler got into this current in a very light breeze and the crew could see that the natives were gathering in considerable numbers on both shores so they did not dare anchor. They collected all the firearms in the ship, got behind the bulwarks and let the ship drift while the natives peppered them with arrows. Fortunately, the natives did not try to board and the ship soon drifted out of range but they say she was so covered with arrows that she looked like a mammoth porcupine.

Early the next day, we were close inshore and near a village when a number of canoes were coming off to the ship. As they came near, the ship was hauled aback and the canoes came alongside but only a few natives were allowed on deck. Here was a new race, in some ways the most interesting I had ever encountered and certainly they were the most primitive. They are not Kanakas and not even distantly related to that race. They belong to the Negroid type, have flat lips and noses and kinky hair which they plaster with lime or something that looks like it and build it up into a crown or pyramid on top of their head. When it is first done, it is white and later turns red, so that in either case their hair gives them a grotesque appearance that might be rather disturbing under certain conditions. They were over rather than under medium height and stood very erect. They looked lithe and strong, none of them fat, and had good teeth which excited our interest as it was claimed they were cannibals. They certainly looked like fighting men and were equipped with the finest bows and arrows, spears and war clubs that I have ever seen. The bows were quite long and made of hard wood, the arrows were made of a reed that grows very straight and round without any variation in diameter in a length of four or five feet. These do not have feathers, evidently depending on their length and balance to fly straight. The heads are of hard wood, a foot or more in length, of the same diameter as the shaft, and tapering to a sharp point. There was talk that they used poisoned arrows in their fights but I never saw any arrows with evidence of such treatment, and I examined many. The spears had bamboo shafts with hard wood heads and were finely balanced, but not one of our men could throw them any where near the distance that the natives could cover. Our men wanted to use both hands, as they would dart an iron, which caused considerable amusement in the natives who only use one hand.

No woman ever came off with the men and I know nothing as to their looks or how they dressed. The men wore absolutely nothing; perhaps the women stayed home for that very old reason of their more civilized sisters, they had nothing to wear. The absence of women with native visitors of known warlike tendencies is not supposed to be a good sign but we had no trouble with them. On one occasion, there were so many canoes about the ship, and the wind so light we could not shake them off, that a bomb gun with a good charge of powder was fired in the air. Instantly there was a wild dash for the shore and the natives on deck were over the side in a flash and did not come back for several days. After that, we knew we could clear the ship at any time by firing a gun. How long they retained that intense fear of the sound of a gun has often been a thought in my mind. They must have known at that time that a gun could kill a native and probably had seen it happen, but since they were used to killing people, there must have been something beyond its power to kill that inspired their wild fear of a gun. They were a very primitive people, as shown by the fact they had not learned to use tobacco or rum. Perhaps they had their own drugs for inducing sleep and could brew an intoxicating liquor from the sap of the coconut bud, just as the Kanakas could long before they ever saw a whaleship.

These natives were not interested in the usual trade handkerchiefs and calicoes; knives, hatchets and fishhooks must have been "taboo" as they would not touch them, but we knew what they wanted from our previous experience and were prepared with short pieces of hoop iron from which the hoops on the casks were made. We bought everything they had with these pieces of iron, three or four inches long, and there was not much to buy. We never found out what they did with the hoop iron and saw no evidence of its use. They had coconuts, bananas, alligator pears and a kind of melon found on the other islands, but the real trade items were their bows and arrows, spears, war clubs and paddles. The paddles are the best shaped and finished of any of the paddles made by the natives of the South Pacific. We obtained enough to outfit our four boats and some of the more highly carved specimens for decorative purposes.

The outstanding possession of the natives of the Solomon Islands were their canoes, which differed from those in all the other Pacific islands. They were not dugouts with outriggers but well-designed and built canoes of sufficient beam to be good sea boats, sharp at both ends with elaborately carved stem and stern pieces that rose four or five feet above the gunwales. They were of all sizes, from canoes holding twenty men to one just large enough for one person, and I wanted very much to acquire one of these. Their war canoes, which were kept in special buildings, were very much larger than any that came off to our ship. Here in these canoes was evidence of an intelligence and skill far beyond that possessed by any of the Kanakas and yet, in all other things, the natives of the Solomon Islands were far inferior to the Kanakas. We knew nothing as to how they lived, their language was unintelligible to us, and we could make very little progress with signs. The islands were attractive as we saw them, with their covering of tropical verdure, but we imagined dark and narrow footpaths through the jungles where one could be easily ambushed and this dampened any desire to land. I have read descriptions of visits to these islands but have found nothing to square with my memory or that adds anything.

We saw no whales and a spell of bad weather eventually drove us away. As I lay in my cubbyhole listening to the many complaints of the old ship as she labored in the heavy seas, I could not get out of my mind the proximity of those inhospitable islands, especially if we were on the inshore tack. No harbors and no anchorage, but if there had been either, we would not have dared to use it with those wild men so close at hand. How I longed for the open ocean with the comfortable knowledge that there was plenty of room. What if the old girl did grumble in a varying scale of sounds that you soon learned to identify with the particular spot that was under stress. She was getting a little limber but that was to be expected in a wooden ship that had had over twenty birthdays. Heavy squalls were frequent and, finally, one caught us aback and before we got straightened out a heavy sea caught the ship under the starboard counter and gave her a severe shaking up. For a moment I thought she had struck bottom. The next morning, the pumps were manned as was the custom in heavy weather and, as I lay in my berth, I automatically counted the number of strokes of the pump which passed the number of strokes I knew was normal to pump her dry. The pumps finally sucked, a sound easily recognized and a mighty pleasant sound, but not until I knew there was a bad leak somewhere. The ship had been leaking for some time, "just enough to keep her sweet" my father used to say. Later in the day, the ship was put on a northerly course as the storm continued, and Ponape was our objective. This island in the Caroline group had a good harbor in which the ship could be overhauled and wood and fresh water taken on. The weather improved and although the leak did not diminish, it did not increase — which was encouraging.

TRAGEDY

Soon after leaving New Ireland, the first mate informed my father that Sam Kanaka, who stowed away at Pleasant Island, was acting queerly and some of the men forward thought he should be put in irons. Sam was called aft and my father talked with him, but as he had learned only a few words of English, it was hard to determine what was troubling him and he was evidently distressed over something. His eyes had a rather wild and worried expression but he made no complaint against any of the men and he was evidently not being ill-treated. The Kanakas from Ocean Island were as much mystified by his actions as we were and they did not understand his language. It was finally concluded that he was homesick and that it would wear off as he became better acquainted with his shipmates.

A few days later, the wind and sea being quite moderate, the main hatch was taken off and my father with a boatsteerer and two sailors went into the lower hold to see if they could locate the leak by listening for the sound made by water entering through a seam or trickling down a timber. It was a warm day and the watch off duty were on deck except one man who sat on the forecastle steps reading a book. I went forward with the rather uncertain purpose of talking with Sam to see if I could learn the cause of his trouble. I found him seated well forward on the topgallant forecastle deck with several other members of the watch below sitting or lying down. As I climbed to the upper deck and stepped around the men, I noticed a young German lying on his side with his hat over his face to shield it from the sun. I reached the side of the Kanaka and commenced to talk to him. He soon began to get excited and talked quite fast in his own tongue. I tried to calm him but he suddenly grabbed me by the wrist and gave me such a wild look that I wrenched myself free and went aft leaving him squatting on the deck. I was probably as near a violent death as I will ever be and miss it. There was only a low rail, not over a foot high, which he could have thrown me over with ease. While I was frightened, I was quite sure that if I said anything to one of the officers on deck at the time of my experience, I would only have been laughed at.

Therefore I went into the cabin, took off the hatch to the lazaret and climbed down into the "run," or hold under the cabin, to hunt for the leak. I had no sooner dropped into the "run" when I heard an awful shriek from someone on deck; instinctively I knew that Kanaka had killed one of the men. I came up into the cabin, rushed into my father's stateroom and got his Spencer rifle, which I knew was loaded, and ran on deck. Members of the crew were running aft as I started forward and I heard my father, who had just climbed out of the hold, cry out "Don't dart." I learned later that Harry, the Kanaka boatsteerer, had reached the deck from the hold ahead of my father and had grabbed an iron that one of the other boatsteerers had been fitting and had left near the carpenter's bench just as the wild man started aft with a bloody sheath knife in his hand. Harry had drawn back to dart when he heard my father's command and held his hand, but Sam had seen him and he turned around and dropped down into the forecastle. While this action was taking place, the first mate stepped up to me and relieved me of the rifle, adding a few words that indicated in his opinion the combination might be more dangerous than the crazy Kanaka.

At that moment, the young German sailor whom I had left apparently asleep on deck walked aft, very white in the face but erect, with his arms around his abdomen. I helped him to lie down in the shade of the cabin bulkhead and then I saw that his bowels were in his shirt. Just then, my mother came on deck, and seeing the condition of the young man, she told me to go below and get some pillows and her shawl, and with these we made him as comfortable as we could. The steward had had experience with wounds and there was nothing more could be done at the moment, except to give him water and bathe his forehead, which my mother did in spite of the attempts of the mate to induce her to go below. I often marveled at my mother's courage and control of her nerves under real danger or trying conditions, because in small matters she was timid and dreaded the sight of blood. She was a little woman, weighing less than one hundred pounds, and could stand erect under my father's outstretched arm without touching it. But when a situation arose that called for the kind of courage that sweeps away all evidences of fear and leaves the mind in calm control, she was superb. Here was an awful situation; we were confined on a small craft in mid-ocean with a crazy man, but she was as cool as any man on the ship.

The third mate was in his stateroom but came on deck with his rifle when he was called. It was now known that the madman had drawn the sheath knife from the German sailor's belt and given him one terrible slash across the abdomen. He then made a slash at one of the Ocean Island Kanakas who jumped in time to save himself, although the knife cut his shirt, and he took to the forerigging. All the other men on deck at the time ran aft. The yell I heard was made by the Kanaka, I believe, who jumped for his life. When the madman dropped into the forecastle, he cut the man sitting on the steps twice as he passed him. This man sprang up the steps and fell dead on deck. The madman, not finding anyone in the forecastle, rushed on deck and started aft when he was confronted by the boatsteerer with his iron poised to dart, so the madman went back into the forecastle. My father and his officers gathered at the forecastle scuttle and my father ordered the man to come on deck, but he did not obey. He had removed all his clothes and still had the sheath knife. It would have been suicide for any man to go into the forecastle and it was decided to send some men into the forehold with rifles and tools to force an opening in the forecastle bulkhead while others guarded the scuttle, prepared to capture him if he came on deck.

While these arrangements were being made, I went below and got my old "pepper box" and loaded it. This was a muzzle-loading, self-cocking revolver about eight inches long, with six chambers, but it used caps to fire the charge which was quite apt to fire the second, and all six barrels might fire before it stopped. But I no sooner appeared on deck with my miniature Gatling gun when the second mate, who had no gun, promptly took it away from me. Evidently, I was not to be allowed to have any part in either the capture or killing of the crazy Kanaka. However, I advised the second mate as to the tricks of the weapon and he fired it once at his man but, probably for the first time in its history, only one barrel went off.

It was evident that the man could not be taken alive and the suspense was terrible. The forecastle was dark and if the man had crawled into a berth and kept quiet, he might have prolonged the situation into the night, and no one knows what might have happened then. He kept jumping in and out of the berths until finally a rifle bullet caught him and he lay sprawled on the floor of the forecastle, dead. As soon as it was certain that he was dead, men went into the forecastle and passed his body on deck. The next moment, it was slid over the rail into the ocean without shroud or ceremony. Perhaps this would be called brutal but it was an awful experience and everybody drew a breath of relief when it was all over. The body of the man killed on the forecastle steps was sewed in canvas with sufficient weight at the feet to sink it. During the dogwatch, it was brought to the waist on the starboard side and laid on the gangplank, which had been removed for the purpose, one end resting on the plank-sheer and the other on the deck tub. The ship was hauled aback with the colors set at half-mast, all hands were mustered in the waist and my father read the service for the dead. At its conclusion, two men raised the inner end of the gangplank and the body slipped into the sea. The yards were braced forward and the ship put on her course and, that most impressive of events, a burial at sea, was closed.

While all these preparations were going on, the young German's wound was carefully examined and it was evident that nothing could save him. Everything that we could do to make him comfortable was done. He lived until the next day when he passed away without a whimper. His body was committed to the deep during the dogwatch. That was the closing act of this terrible tragedy, but it was some time before we could throw off its depressing effects and get back to the normal ways of our life.

NAVIGATING THE SHIP

THE sun did not shine, although it was not stormy weather, and we were navigating by "dead reckoning" as it is known aboard a ship.

While this is largely a matter of experience and judgment, it is not a question of guesswork. It was a method that the old school of whaling captains were very skillful in using. The course was determined by the compass with allowances for drift and set of the current. The speed of the ship was largely a matter of judgment with the log as a check. The patent log had been invented at that time but our ship was equipped with the old-fashioned log which had been first used about 1750. Heaving the log during these sunless days was performed twice a day, in the morning and afternoon. I rarely missed being on hand to hold the sand glass although that honor was frequently claimed by my sister as being one thing a girl could do as well as a boy. The log consists of the "chip," which is a quadrant-shaped piece of wood weighted on the curve with lead and fastened to a flexible line by short pieces of line from the three corners of the chip, the one to the lower corner being fast to a plug that is inserted in a hole in the chip. A piece of white rag is fastened to the line about 68 feet from the chip and, at intervals of 50 feet 7 inches, a knot is made in the line which has a total length of about 500 feet, although this will vary with the size of the ship. This line is wound on a reel which a sailor holds in his hands facing the stern. Another person holds a sand glass which will run out in 30 seconds. When the officer gives the word "Heave," the chip is dropped over the stern in the wake of the ship and the line runs off the reel until the white rag marker reaches the taffrail, when the officer says "Turn" and the holder of the sand glass turns it over. When the sand runs out this time, he cries "Stop" and grabs the line, gives it a sharp jerk which pulls out the peg in the chip and allows it to skip over the surface of the water. He then notes the length of line that has run out, or the number of knots, which is the speed of the ship for an hour at the rate she was then traveling. The line is reeled up and put away.

We were very much disturbed by the leak although it was not increasing, but it took an hour morning and evening to pump her dry. This was not too bad as it was not a physical strain on the crew, but a leaky ship is a mental strain and, not knowing the cause or the location of the leak, you could not avoid thinking that it might suddenly increase. Such thoughts were often very insistent whenever it blew hard and the old ship rolled and pitched heavily. I still believed the leak was in the after end of the ship, so one day I again went through the scuttle in the cabin floor into the run and crawled around on the skin, or inner planking of the hull, listening for the sound of water trickling down the timbers which is quite different from the swish of the water rushing by on the outside. Finally, quite well aft on the starboard side, I caught the sound I was trying to find and, after assuring myself that I was not mistaken, I went on deck and told my father what I had discovered. Of course, he was greatly interested and immediately followed me into the run. After listening for a while, he sent for the cooper and they made an opening through the skin and found the leak, but this was not enough to account for the quantity of water that was being pumped out of the hold twice a day. This leak was plugged and I noted a considerable reduction in the number of strokes of the pump as I counted them the next morning.

SPERM WHALES

FORTUNATELY, a few days after the Kanaka ran amuck, we raised a school of sperm whales. The Kanaka boatsteerer, Harry, was lucky man in seeing the first spout and won the prize of twenty pounds of tobacco. As his musical "There blows — blows" floated down from aloft, we felt instinctively that we had raised a school of sperm whales. In a few minutes, they could be seen from the deck and orders were given to call all hands and clear away the three port boats. The courses were clewed up and the main yards squared. The boats got away in good order and set their sails. The whales were then off the lee bow about two miles away. The mainyards were braced forward and the ship put on a course a little to windward of the boats. My father then started to go aloft, telling me to follow. When I reached the fore-topgallant crosstrees, whales were spouting in every direction. It was a beautiful day with a nice whole sail breeze and a smooth sea and I never saw so many whales at one time. It did not seem possible that we could fail to get two and possibly three whales as we got that number out of a much smaller school in our previous cruise in these waters. These were mostly cow whales, and if one was struck, the whole school would stay with the fast whale. Bull whales do not run in schools, but when struck in a school with cow whales, the entire school deserts the fast whale.

Suddenly there was a spout right ahead of the third mate's boat, and not far off. Unless something unusual happened, they would surely fasten. My father was intensely excited and it was a critical moment; the boatsteerer stood up and there was a flurry of white water, the sail came down and with the mast was shifted aft. But something had gone wrong, a sperm whale either sounds, goes straight down, or runs but this one did not do either. My father was watching through his spyglass and evidently sensed the situation, from his remark: "He has either missed the whale or the iron has drawn." In a few minutes, the mast was again stepped and the sail set. I never saw a boat row onto a loose whale; after a boat has fastened, oars can be used. Our boats always sailed onto a whale except when the wind was very light and then they used paddles. The wonderful race for a whale with all the crews pulling and the officers exhorting them in stentorian tones, as described in *Moby Dick*, just never happened. While my father was expressing his views as to what had happened in the third mate's boat, I was wondering what would happen when they returned to the ship, because if the boatsteerer was seriously at fault he would be "broken"; that is, demoted and sent into the forecastle. I looked about to see what the other two boats were doing and then I realized there was not a spout to be seen. By what means those whales miles away learned of the attack and knew that it failed, I know not. It was a cow whale, and if the boat had fastened, the school would have stayed with her. It was a calamity and it had happened so suddenly that we could hardly realize the change.

Just then, a whale broke water just ahead of the second mate's boat and headed for the boat. The next moment, they were fast and my father announced that he would lower. As he started down the shrouds, it suddenly flashed in my mind that I pulled stroke oar in his boat and the thought did not fill me with joy. It was too late for regrets and I helped throw off the after gripe as the boat was swung clear of the cranes and followed down the side of the ship as the boat was lowered. We started to row what I thought was a short distance, as looked at from aloft, but I would have been as well pleased if it had been twice as far; but after pulling for fifteen minutes or more, I changed my mind. My father had apparently forgotten our relationship as he heaved against my oar with his right hand and handled his steering oar with his left while calling upon me to put my back into each pull. Finally, casting my eye over my shoulder, at the imminent risk of catching a crab, I saw that we were nearly up to the fast boat. In a few minutes my father sang out "Way enough" and then we had a chance to look the situation over.

The second mate was standing in the bow of his boat swearing a perfect stream of oaths at his crew because they were so paralyzed with fear they would not pull onto the whale so he could fire a bomb lance into it. The whale was acting queerly, moving around in a circle towing the boat after him, and we saw that the iron had entered his spout hole which explained why he remained on the surface. While we lay on our oars, waiting for the whale to come around to us, the first mate's boat got in the way of the second mate's boat and struck his steering oar, thus lifting the mate off his feet and landing him in the water. It struck me funny and I had a good laugh but they soon hauled the mate into his boat, pulled onto the whale and fastened. While the mate was going into the head of the boat and the boatsteerer going aft to the steering oar, the whale rolled over a few times, which completely fouled the lines of both boats so neither boat could haul onto the whale. Of course, they could pull up to him with their oars but both crews were so badly frightened that they would not do it. Both the mates and the boatsteerers had exhausted their vocabularies and were repeating themselves.

At this stage in the proceedings, my father gave the order to "give way" and we proceeded to pull up to the whale. The cooper, our boatsteerer, was given the order to stand up and then the order, "Give it to him," and his iron went into the whale to the hitches. "Stern all" was the next order but we were a little ragged in its execution and the boat's bow struck the whale's body before we got her going astern. The cooper now unhitched the bowline in the short warp around the whale line and stowed the second iron in its proper place against the side of the boat with the head under the box. It has been stated by some writers that the second iron is thrown overboard, if not used, to avoid serious injury to the boat's crew, which would be true if the second iron was attached to the line as they describe it, but such descriptions are not true and it would be very foolish to throw the iron overboard.

The cooper now went aft and my father went into the head of the boat and took out a hand lance as he did not carry a bomb gun. The order was given to "haul line" and my job was to hold the turn around the loggerhead and take in the slack as we hauled up to the whale lying quietly on the surface of the water. It was apparent that it was a very large whale. When close enough to the whale, my father thrust the lance well down into the side of the body just aft of the fin. Immediately, there was a violent commotion and we were ordered to "stern all."

Our crew had done well up to this time, considering it was a new experience for four of us, but the movements of the whale were disconcerting to state it very mildly. The net result of our efforts was that we stayed close to the whale in spite of the fact that nobody wanted to be there, and while we were struggling to get out of the mess, the whale settled and threw his head straight up out of the water so close that one on the starboard side of the boat could have touched it. The steerage boy jumped to his feet and had one foot on the rail in a mad desire to get away from that awful-looking object when my father jumped over a couple of thwarts, grabbed him by the collar of his shirt, and threw him into the bottom of the boat. He had been watching two of the men who showed the most fear, expecting one or both of them to try to jump overboard. It is not an unusual occurrence with a green crew but they no sooner get overboard when they want to get back and sometimes capsize the boat.

About the time the steerage boy was thrown to the bottom of the boat, the whale brought his head down so close to us that we shipped quite a quantity of water but were not struck. Then we found ourselves close to his flukes, but I doubt that he was seriously feeling for us although the smash with his head was typical of a sperm whale's method of attack as they prefer to attack with their head. Before we could get into action, the whale started to run and we were off on a "Nantucket sleigh ride," but it was not very fast. He made a great sweep that brought us across the course of the ship and, as we were the last boat in the line, it looked as if we might not get across but we went right under the bowsprit and then around to the stern and back to where we started.

The third mate was waiting for us and the whale was still on the surface but running slowly. The third mate's boat pulled up to the whale and he shot one bomb lance into the whale which exploded and the whale immediately began to spout blood. He went into a flurry in a few minutes, turned on his side and was dead. The lines were cleared and hauled into the boats they belonged to. The second mate went alongside the whale, cut a square hole through the corner of his fluke, made a line fast and, letting out five or six fathoms of line, made it fast around his loggerhead. The first mate's boat fastened the warp of the second mate's boat to their loggerhead and the other two boats did this same maneuver and we proceeded to tow the whale to the ship.

Now that the whale was alongside the ship, it was possible to get a fairly accurate measure of his size. His size did not impress me when I first saw him over my shoulder while pulling toward him because a whale floats low in the water, but when we were closing in for my father to lance him, I realized that he was a big whale. When he thrust his head out of water alongside the boat, I knew he was the largest living thing I had ever seen. No measurements were taken but judging by the length of the ship, the overall length of the whale was not less than seventy feet.

The whale was brought alongside with the flukes forward, the ship being hauled aback on the port tack, to bring the whale on the lee side for greater convenience in cutting in. The boats were hoisted and the fluke chain was passed around the small section of the body just ahead of the flukes, taken through a hawsehole and made fast. All hands then went to dinner.

When they returned to the deck, the fore- and main-topgallant sails were furled although the wind was light, the main topsail was clewed up and braced forward while the mainyard was braced sharply to port so as to give room to haul the cutting falls forward, by a guy from the foremast, to bring them over the main hatch. The fore-topsail had been hauled aback and the wheel put hard down so the ship made almost as much leeway as she did headway. The cutting stage was lowered over the side, long handled spades taken down from the racks under the spare boat skids, boarding knives removed from their sheaths, and all the rest of the gear required for cutting in a whale was laid out on deck where it would be handy when needed. The grindstone was brought out and placed a little aft of the waist where the cooper could keep the spades sharp for the officers on the stage. The main hatch was taken off and a few men detailed to handle the blanket pieces as they are lowered into the blubber room. A cask had been broken out and lashed near the main rigging with the head removed to receive the contents of the case when that stage of the proceedings is reached.

Now the windlass is manned and the Captain with the first and second mates go out on the stage and a long-handled spade is passed down to each of them. The whale now lies between the stage and the ship with his fins opposite the opening in the bulwarks made by the removal of the gangplank and the rail in the waist. A man goes over the side in a bowline and stands on the whale while passing a chain around the fin close to the body. One of the two cutting falls is swung over the side with a large hook on the block to which is attached the chain and the order is given to "heave away." As the falls tauten, the body rolls and the officers begin cutting through the blubber with their spades on the lower side of the fin and across the body, thus starting the blanket piece, so called. This is made a continuous operation by cutting on a diagonal line around the body, called the "scarf." The strain on the falls easily separates the blubber from the body as the cut next to the head and the scarf are extended. The blubber is wrapped around the body like a blanket, hence the name "blanket piece." The blubber of this whale was about eight inches thick and full of oil. Right or bowhead whales of that size would have blubber twice as thick.

As the whale rolled over in the cutting process, the lower jaw was disjointed and hoisted on deck but this operation was not performed with a boarding knife as described in some books. The tongue, which is very small for the size of the body, is taken aboard with the jaw. A peculiar feature of a sperm whale is its lack of lips on either jaw. The very narrow lower jaw carries one continuous row of teeth but there is no mouth in which food can be retained and there are no teeth on the upper jaw for mastication. The lower jaw would appear to be used for crushing the food into pieces which are then swallowed whole. I do not recall hearing anyone claim to have seen a sperm whale in the act of feeding. Bowheads and right whales are frequently seen feeding, which is called "scooping." Sperm whales are supposed to live on squid, the "devil fish" of fiction, which it is claimed grow to enormous size with many tentacles. It was a well-known fact among whalemen that a sperm whale in his dying flurry often ejected great chunks of undigested squid.

While the body of the whale is being rolled, deep cuts are made along the side of the head above the upper jaw for the separation of the junk from the case which is in the top of the head. When the blanket piece is hoisted to the limit of the falls, the windlass is stopped, an oblong hole is cut in the blubber a foot or two above the plank-sheer with a boarding knife, which looks something like a two edged sword without a guard. The eye of the lower block on the other set of falls is pushed through this hole and a long wood billet, called a "toggle," is inserted in the eye on the other side of the blubber. The blanket piece is then cut off above the toggle with the boarding knife after taking the strain on the second falls with the windlass. Heaving now starts on the second blanket piece, raising it, while the first piece is lowered into the blubber room.

After the incisions have been made on both sides of the head for the separation of the case and junk, a chain strap is passed through an opening made in the top of the whale's head vertically over the corner of his mouth. One of the cutting falls is hooked into this opening and the head is lifted while a heavy purchase is held on the junk by another strap through it which is led aft to the mizzen chains. These opposing pulls finally unjoint the head back of the eye at what might be called the neck, although a whale has no such part in the usual meaning of the word as he cannot move his head without moving his body. The head of this whale was so large that the case could not be hoisted on deck without first separating the junk. This is a spongy substance saturated with oil located below the case with a layer of tough, fibrous substance containing no oil, called "white horse," between it and the upper jaw. The junk is hoisted on deck and the white horse left for the sharks to dispose of. While these operations are being performed on the head, the blubber has been well removed from the body. The backbone is then unjointed a few feet from the flukes and the carcass is set adrift. In view of the fact that the water was fairly alive with sharks, it must have been picked clean in a very short time.

The head was hoisted as high as it was considered safe to stress the cutting gear and the mast, and the case, which is really a cavity filled with liquid spermaceti, was opened and the operation of baling out its contents with a bucket was begun. At first, the bucket was filled by pressing it into the case with a pole but, finally, a man got into the case and filled the bucket as it was lowered to him from the deck. The odor from this oily mess was not offensive. The wind was increasing, with evidence that it would soon be a gale, and the ship was rolling down rather hard so that the case would be nearly submerged one minute and threatening to tear loose or carry away the gear the next. Therefore the baling had to be hurried and given up, finally, as baling became too dangerous. The head was then cut loose, but we had recovered most of its contents.

When the case is opened, the spermaceti is liquid but it becomes a white crystalline mass which must be reheated in the trypots to run it into the casks in the hold. The junk is tried out at the same time and is mixed with the contents of the case; this oil is kept separate from the oil tried out from the blubber.

The head of a sperm whale is the most interesting feature of this whale and the entire whale family. It is radically different from the head of any other type of whale. Nobody really knows the purpose of the case in the head of a sperm whale. The bone, or baleen, which is suspended from the upper jaw of the bowhead and right whales and is found also in a very abbreviated form in the same location in the humpback, finback, sulphur-bottom, and California gray, or nearly every other type of whale, has a very definite and well understood purpose. The case must not be confused with the brain which is farther back in the head and, apparently, it has no connection with the circulation of the blood. It is thoroughly protected from injury by an extremely tough exterior cover or casing.

The location of the spout hole is another peculiarity of the sperm whale, compared with other species of the whale family. The whale breathes through this orifice which is on top of the extreme forward end of the sperm whale's head and it is well back on the head of the other types of whales. The air passageway must extend the entire length of the head to reach the lungs of the sperm whale.

The skin of the sperm whale is similar to that of every other whale and it is a dark gray but looks black when wet. There are no white patches like those under the lower jaw of a bowhead which, by the way, is very good eating when fried in whale oil, and tastes much like the white of a fried egg. The skin or outside of every part of the whale is a peculiar substance, varying in thickness according to its location, but being fully one half inch in thickness on the whale we had just caught. The skin of the bowhead is twice as thick and has a grain or fiber vertical to the surface. The sperm whale skin is not tough, can be easily cut with a knife, has no strength in tension, contains no blood vessels and is firmly attached to the blubber. The outer surface is covered with a very thin filmy substance that is readily abraded and when dry is brittle. This is a strange covering but no doubt wonderfully adapted to its purpose.

There is another product of the sperm whale which is known as ambergris, found floating on the water; it is an intestinal secretion in the whale. This substance is not produced by any other species of whales. It was not my good fortune to see any of this substance recovered from a sperm whale, and when I inquired why the body was not opened to see if it contained ambergris, I was told that it was found only in sick whales which condition would be indicated by the bloated body and frequently by the ejection of this substance during the death flurry of the whale. Ambergris is very valuable for its peculiar property of collecting the oil of perfumes from flowers and on account of its very uncertain supply.

When the boats had returned to the ship, it occurred to me that a sight for latitude would be in order as the sun was out for the first time since we left the Solomon Islands. I did this and worked it out and, in the afternoon between two and three o'clock, I took a sight for longitude using the chronometer I had always used, but I did not work this mathematically until a few days later, as there was too much going on that I wanted to see. It was like trying to watch a three-ring circus. If I went into the waist, the center of activity, I would be ordered away for fear that I might get knocked down the main hatch by a swinging blanket piece, so I climbed into the bow of the starboard boat where I had a fine view of the cutting-in operations and could practice darting a short-handled spade at the sharks swarming about the whale.

After the case was cut adrift, the jawbone was lashed to the rail and the deck was cleared as the wind was increasing, and it was decided that trying out would be postponed until the next day. The main-topsail was sheeted home and hoisted but the courses were furled. I was curious to learn why the third mate had failed to fasten to the whale as I knew he had made a report to my father, but I never learned the story. My father had decided that neither officer nor boatsteerer was seriously to blame, something went wrong; the third mate was very glum for a few days but, from the little I heard, I concluded that the boatsteerer was overanxious and darted too soon and the iron drew.

The manner the second mate had fastened to the whale we captured was most unusual and no one in the after gang had ever seen it happen before. The whale came at the boat head-on and the officer did not dare order the boatsteerer to hold his iron until the whale had run by so he could be struck in the body, hence he took the chance of striking him in the spout hole. If the iron had missed the mark by a few inches either way, it would not have entered the whale's head far enough to toggle, as the outer covering of the head is a tough gristle impervious to attack by any kind of a weapon. Taken all in all, it was a great day, especially for Harry the boatsteerer, and everybody was glad he won the prize as they all liked him.

It had been a strenuous day and everybody was tired but watches have to be maintained, and before the first night watch was relieved, they had double-reefed both topsails. I could hear from my bunk the cry of "Haul out to windward" as the sail was hauled into position for passing the weather earing around the end of the yardarm and, when it is properly secured, comes the order "Haul out to leeward." The sail is now stretched along the yard, and as fast as it is rolled up above the reef band, the reef points are passed around the roping of the head of the sail and tied in a square knot. Greenhorns always tie a "granny knot," which is almost impossible to untie after it has been under strain, while a square knot never jams and can be quickly released by pulling either end back on the standing part.

When I came on deck in the morning, the ship was close hauled under close reefed topsails and the decks were very sloppy. The wind moderated later in the day and hauled aft which permitted putting the ship on her course. The crew commenced cutting the blubber into rectangular sections called "horse pieces" which are laid lengthwise on a plank bench where a man facing the end cuts the blubber into thin slices to the skin, using a broad two-handled utensil called a "mincing knife." The horse pieces are thrown

into a tub and, when filled, it is drawn over the deck to the tryworks where the blubber is picked up by a two-tined fork on a
wooden handle and tossed into the trypots. The tryworks consist
of two cast-iron pots set in brick masonry, with a firebox under each
pot and smoke flues on the after end of each pot leading into short
sheet-iron stacks to carry the smoke clear of the bulwarks and create
the necessary draft. A wood fire is started and maintained until
scrap is available which is the tried out blubber and this keeps the
fires going as an excellent fuel. The oil is bailed from the pots as
it is tried out into a copper tank standing close to the starboard side
of the tryworks, called the "cooler." Care must be taken not to over-
cook or undercook the oil or burn the scrap which would affect
the color of the oil and its quality. Therefore, the tryworks are
tended by the boatsteerers with the officer of the watch checking the
operation occasionally to see that it is being properly carried on.
When the oil has cooled in the cooler, it is bailed into wooden casks
which are rolled against the cooler using a large funnel in the
bunghole.

The casks are secured to a lashing rail as they are filled which is
fastened to the stanchions of the bulwarks and allowed to cool the
oil further. The bung is knocked out when the oil is completely
cooled by a "bung starter" and striking the stave on each side of the
orifice. The cask is placed over an opening with a receptacle below
from which a canvas hose leads to the casks in the hold below. A
very simple device vents the casks as the oil is poured from them.
This is a piece of bent copper tubing about two feet long which is
inserted in the bung hole with the thumb closing the outer end until the tube is well within the cask. On removing the thumb, air
rushes into the cask while the oil flows out in a continuous and
steady stream. I was interested in this operation and always inserted
the vent tube when around at this operation. The thumb must be
removed at just the right time or the oil would run out of the tube
instead of air going into the cask. The tube must be removed and
cleaned, when this happens, and I missed out the first time I tried
but the fact that I was the "Old Man's" son never saved me from

criticism whenever I did anything wrong. This was a busy time for the cooper, especially when a new cask was to be used for the first time. Oak staves usually have a number of small wormholes which will leak a lot of oil, so they must be found and plugged. A very simple test is applied to be sure all holes are found. The cask is turned down on its bilge, a ladle of hot oil from the tryworks poured in and the bung replaced. The cask is rolled about until it is full of vapor from the hot oil which spurts out through the open wormholes. These holes are marked with chalk and then filled with wooden plugs, after being opened with a steel punch.

Our whale stowed down 85 barrels of oil of which 15 barrels were case oil and quite a little oil was lost owing to the delay in trying out. My father estimated 100 barrels would have been the result if all of it could have been saved. The teeth were removed from the lower jaw and portions of the jaw bone were kept for scrimshaw uses. The jaw had a total length, including the pans, of about twenty-five feet. It must have been an old whale as his teeth were worn down almost to the gum.

The deck and the paintwork were thoroughly cleaned, clothes washed and the ship restored to its usual neat and shipshape appearance. There was never any truth in the notion that a whaleship is dirty. There are plenty of men and literally an ocean of water, which being salt water does not take kindly to soap, but with the ashes from the tryworks a preparation is made that will remove anything known as dirt, including the skin on your hands. Every good first mate had an obsession for cleanliness; it helped to keep the crew busy and a busy crew had little time or inclination for plotting mischief.

PONAPE

We were approaching the Caroline Islands and it became important to know the ship's position. I had worked out my sight, taken the day we killed the sperm whale, and our position as plotted on the chart agreed closely with the results of the dead reckoning as computed by my father. The sky had been overcast ever since that day and we had not been able to get a sight of the sun. My father went over my calculations and found them correct. If we were on our course, we should raise Strong's Island [Kusaie], the most south-easterly island of the group, but we might miss it if we were much to the eastward and the whole island group. We would then have to keep on to the Ladrone or Marianas Islands. My father was particularly anxious to reach the island of Ponape because of its fine harbor. The only good harbor on Strong's Island is on the windward side and he was windbound there for several weeks on one voyage. The channel is very narrow and the ship could not be worked out against the wind which was too strong to tow the ship with the boats.

The day after our canvas of the situation opened with a thick fog and a fair wind. It suddenly cleared about ten o'clock and we got a sight of the sun, each using a different chronometer, and then it shut in foggy again. An astonishing situation confronted us when we worked out our sights. We had missed the group of islands by my father's calculation while Ponape was dead ahead, if my position was correct. My father checked my work and could find no error which showed that one chronometer was wrong, but which one? The fog lifted a little about noon and we had a brief glimpse of land off our starboard quarter. I claimed it was Strong's Island which agreed with my position but my father thought it was a small island east of Ponape. All uncertainty was dispelled about four o'clock by the sight of a bold and high point of land right over the jib boom which was immediately recognized as Chokach Cliff on the northern end of the island of Ponape and west of the entrance to Ascension harbor which was our destination. We arrived off the entrance to the harbor just before dark.

The pilot who came off in a whale boat with a Kanaka crew was a white man who ran away from a whale ship years before and had become quite a man of affairs. He said it was too late to take the ship in and we must wait until morning. The pilot and his crew stayed aboard and his boat was taken in tow while the ship lay off and on under reduced sail. Of course, we had no chart showing the harbors of Ponape, or of any of the islands we visited in the South Pacific, but that did not deter us from carrying out our plans. We were fortunate in this instance in securing the services of a man who knew the waters and could be trusted but, if he had been away, we would have gone in anyhow. Whalers had to learn to get along without pilots.

The island of Ponape is in Latitude 6:45 North and Longitude 158:15 East. It was discovered by a Spaniard about 1590 but for many years it was visited by American whalers only, traders and the American Missionary brig *Morning Star* later. The whalers called it Ascension but the native name was Kusaie and it was used by the resident missionary. It always appealed to me as more appropriate and euphonius than Ascension. Ponape is the most interesting of the Caroline Group; of volcanic origin, it has many high peaks and covers an area of about 340 square miles. The island is surrounded by a barrier reef with openings in six places forming as many harbors in the protected waters between the reef and the shore. The bottom is covered with coral formations which are wonderfully beautiful when seen on a clear day. The island is covered with tropical foliage far more varied in character than that on the small atolls we had visited. I could hardly wait for morning in my desire to reach the anchorage and get in closer touch with the shore and its wonderful sights. My mother and sister were fully as excited over the plans that were being discussed for our time while in port. Father and Mother were quite well acquainted with Mr. Edward T. Doane, a missionary who had lived there since 1855 and was to contribute much to the pleasure of our visit.

It is a debatable question as to how much the missionaries had benefited the natives of these islands. It is true that the whalers had brought them diseases of which they knew nothing and had taught them habits and tastes that they would have been much better without. The missionaries were honest in their faith and their efforts to christianize the natives but it is doubtful if they knew in what way this would make these natives happier or more useful. I can conceive of no more happy and carefree people than these natives were before the white man came on the scene. Nature had provided them with everything they needed, a climate that was never cold enough for clothing and not excessively warm, and food was always available and varied with no effort required to obtain it. They worshiped idols or rather spirits of good and evil powers, quarreled at times and even had tribal wars, but has christianity stopped conflicts among its most civilized believers? In many ways the Kanaka was but a child and needed friendly advice. The missionaries would have been more helpful and far more successful if they had known more of the human weaknesses of their own people. The awful thing to the missionary was the nakedness of the native but this meant nothing to the native except comfort and convenience. Their native dress was more sanitary and healthful than ours, which should have been obvious to the missionaries if they had not been obsessed with the notion that dress was essential to morality.

Soon after breakfast the next morning, we stood in for the opening with a nice breeze in beautiful sunshine to enter Ascension Harbor. There is no beach to a barrier reef, it is an abrupt wall of coral formation rising out of very deep water. The surf is not a series of rollers but one great breaker that marks the sea side of the reef with a never ending line of white foam and high-tossed spray. The pilot took his position on the foreyard where he could look down on the water ahead and pick out the channel by the color of the water, or bottom, as there were no buoys. As we passed out of the intense blue of the deep water, the bottom was suddenly so clear and distinct that it did not seem there was depth enough to float the ship, but it was probably fifty feet deep. We turned to the south and ran parallel to the shore as we approached, with a few small changes in our course as ordered by the pilot, until we ran into a basin about a mile wide where we anchored head to the reef and then laid a small anchor to keep the ship from swinging. We were so completely protected by land and reef that it was as smooth as a millpond no matter how hard the wind blew outside. We passed a few native houses on our way to the anchorage, low thatched structures near the shore, and numerous coconut trees with a dense background of foliage including many large trees. It was a beautiful prospect, intensely green and cool-looking, but it was rather humid as I was to learn later.

We were surrounded by canoes loaded with produce to trade as soon as the anchor was on the bottom and they wanted tobacco, calico, beads, knives, etc. Mr. Doane was an early visitor and he was pleased to learn my mother was aboard, so it was soon arranged that the family would stay at his house while the ship was in port.

I met the pilot's son who was about my age and size. His mother was a Kanaka and I never saw her but I had no illusions as to her looks; if there were any beautiful Kanaka women in the islands of the western Pacific, they had been kept out of my sight. The women mature young and grow to look old before they are out of their teens. This boy was good-looking and bright. He had dark eyes and black hair but he was much lighter in color than the full-blooded Kanakas. He stood very erect, which is characteristic of these natives, walked with an easy graceful swing and was a splendid shot with rifle or shotgun. He talked good English, in a low and pleasant voice, and could read and write which he had learned from his father. He was my companion on several trips through the country contiguous to the harbor while hunting wild pigeons. I did the hunting and he shot most of the pigeons we bagged. A wild pigeon is so near the color of the foliage that it was difficult for me to see them even when Harry pointed them out to me. They generally sat very still in the upper branches of the tallest trees. Our rambles led us through a heavily wooded country by narrow footpaths as there were no beasts of burden or any kind of vehicles in Ponape.

There were many kinds of ferns including the large and attractive tree fern. The ground was covered with a mass of low-growing bushes, vines and shrubs that were practically impenetrable except for the paths kept open by the natives. There were beautiful orchids and many colorful flowers and birds of attractive plumage, but Harry knew only the Kanaka names for all these new and novel things which I could not remember. The soil was extremely productive and everything seemed to grow wild as I saw no evidence of cultivation except a small garden belonging to Mr. Doane. There were many varieties of the banana growing wild, also plantains that are a kind of variety of banana which must be cooked. Yams of huge size were plentiful and pink-colored sweet potatoes which I was told were cultivated. There were several varieties of the breadfruit tree which is a very handsome tree and a remarkable provision of nature for the sustenance of man. The fruit I saw was practically round, about the size of a honeydew melon, but the outer cover or shell is hard with a rough pebbly surface, dark green in color. The natives cook it in hot ashes, and when broken open, it is a firm white substance that looks very much like the inside of a loaf of bread. It does not taste like bread but with butter and salt it is a very good substitute. The strange trait of the breadfruit tree is that it bears continuously, having blossoms and ripe fruit at the same time. There were several kinds of melon-shaped fruits that grew on trees. Their flavor was delicious, but they were filling and you could not eat as much as you wished to. Pineapples did not grow wild but Mr. Doane had a nice patch near his house that I discovered one day and again learned the filling quality of tropical fruit. I thought it would be easy to eat a whole pineapple and nearly busted myself before admitting I could not do it. This cured me of eating the luscious pineapples.

Bamboo grows plentifully in parts of the island, also a slender reed that may belong to that same family which is used for the side walls of the native houses. The reeds are placed close together vertically and held in position with a coarse twine made from the fibre of dried coconut husks. It is quite a rigid wall and keeps out the rain but allows the air to circulate through the joints. Their houses are interesting and well adapted to the climate. The floors are well compacted earth smoothed by the bare feet of the occu pants. On one side, and sometimes three sides, is a raised platform of bamboo about two feet above the floor where the family sit and sleep. The roof is a light frame structure covered with a thick thatch of pandanus leaves that is waterproof, which is quite important as the island has a heavy rainfall. There are no partitions or windows and the doorway may or may not have a reed screen but not a door. Cooking is done outdoors or in a rude structure whose chief duty is to keep the rain from putting out the fire. The natives do all their cooking on hot stones or in hot ashes. Fish are wrapped in green leaves and buried in hot ashes, the leaves being selected for their effect on the flavor of the fish. Dogs and pigs are roasted but I did not see this done as they are reserved for special occasions. The dog was considered quite a delicacy. Nothing could be boiled as they had only calabashes that would hold water but could not resist fire.

The calabash tree is another remarkable provision of nature for the convenience of the natives in providing a tough and durable vessel that makes a light bowl or jug of varying sizes for food and water and other housekeeping purposes. The natives were still using their own primitive method for starting a fire by rubbing a pointed stick of fairly hard wood against the grain of a very dry and soft-fibered piece of wood. Pushing the stick back and forth on the punkwood created a small pile of fine, fluffy fiber which was so hot from the friction that it would burst into flame from a puff of breath at the right moment. Dry grass and twigs were handy to feed the flame from the punkwood as that would last for an instant only. It was surprising how quickly they would make a fire; in fact it looked so very simple that I had to try it, and found that it was not as simple as it looked although I made a fire after a number of failures.

I spent some time aboard our ship each day as they were taking on firewood and fresh water and I went with the boats that towed the empty casks up a small river that emptied into the harbor. It was a beautiful stream, the water clear as crystal, and we took on an ample supply for the balance of the voyage. We got wood enough for the galley and for dunnage; that is, to stow between the casks in the hold to prevent them from shifting. The crew were busy searching for leaks and some were found, but it was evident that a complete overhauling in a dry dock was necessary if all the leaks were to be stopped, and that could be done only when we returned to 'Frisco. Another whaleship arrived in port and, a few days later, another whaler came in which gave the little harbor a very busy time and permitted the exchange of visits with a comparison of plans for the balance of the season.

At the suggestion of Mr. Doane, we took one of our boats on the afternoon of a pleasant day and with him as guest and a native as pilot we entered a passageway through a mangrove forest which was so narrow that paddles were substituted for oars. The mangrove grows in the water along stretches of the shore of this island and reddish-brown tendrils drop into the water from the branches and take root in the bottom. This process is repeated so that a dense forest is grown that is impassable except where the natives keep a passageway open by cutting off these tendrils as they drop down. There is a dense canopy of leaves overhead through which the sunlight filters in a subdued light that permits sight in a limited way. The breeze was entirely cut off so there was an uncanny stillness that I was glad to have end with our emergence into the clear water and sunshine on the other side of the forest.

We were now in a river with densely wooded shores and no habitations but it was very beautiful. After rowing upstream for a few miles, the river narrowed as though we were coming to its head and then we passed through an opening in the foliage of the shore into an almost circular amphitheater with the far side a vertical wall of rock rising fully one hundred feet and over the center was pouring a beautiful sheet of water. The water fell directly into the pool as the rock was that vertical and the shore was covered with dense foliage except at these falls. It was the most perfect piece of nature's handiwork that I have ever seen, not the largest or the grandest, but a gem in a perfect setting. The rock was an outcrop of basalt that, farther north, terminates in the great Cliff of

Chokach with a sea face nearly a thousand feet in height that can be seen for many miles at sea. We viewed this scene as long as possible before starting our return to the ship. There is no twilight in the tropics, when the sun goes down it is dark, so it was necessary that we get through the mangrove forest before sunset which we did. This beautiful day compensated for many of the discomforts of sea life.

During our evenings at Mr. Doane's house, one of the interesting subjects of conversation was some ancient ruins near the east shore of the island, some twelve to fifteen miles south of Ascension Harbor, which Mr. Doane said were built prior to the coming of the present race of Kanakas. He said a German scientist, J. S. Kubary, had visited these ruins a year or two before and had cleared away some of the vines and bushes that had nearly covered the ruins so that it was now possible to reach them by boat and see most of the more important and best-preserved parts. We became so interested in the subject that my father decided we would devote a day to visiting these ruins, which are a great mystery.

An Englishman named Christian examined these ruins later and described them quite fully in *The Caroline Islands* as well as much interesting information about the islands and their people. While Christian thinks the present race have certain traditions that account for the building of these ancient structures, I am inclined to accept the conclusions of Mr. Doane that they were built by a race that were extinct before the ancestors of the present race of Kanakas came to the island. Mr. Doane had lived on the island for over twenty years and knew the language spoken by the people, so he had exceptional opportunity to learn the native traditions. These ruins and any theory for their existence are absolutely inconsistent with the life and habits of the Kanaka. There must have been such a decadence in the people, if the ruins are to be considered their work, that amounts to a complete wiping out of the original race. These ancient ruins are not confined to Ponape as there are similar ruins on Strong's Island and on other islands of this group but not in such size and area as on Ponape. The present

Kanaka of these islands is not the immediate descendant of a highly developed and vigorous race. He is the product of conditions that do not make such qualities and is just what one might expect of any people who never had to struggle for anything essential to life. There is no natural enemy of man on these islands, no wild animals or snakes, a few scorpions and centipedes that everyone avoids. The Kanaka is soft and indolent and never had any of the white man's diseases and therefore had no resistance against them. They died like flies with our child diseases of chicken pox and measles while smallpox nearly exterminated the population of some islands. They were terribly superstitious and, for that reason, they kept away from the ruins we were about to visit. The Kanakas were a good-natured, likable people for all their weaknesses.

We made an early start on the day set for our trip with the Captain's boat and a full crew. I was not of the crew, perhaps my mother had something to say about it, for while it was probable we could make the trip under sail, the possibility of pulling a fourteen-foot oar for the distance back did not appeal to me. It was a beautiful day with a nice whole-sail breeze from the northeast which is the "trade wind" of that locality from October to May. The water was very clear and smooth as we were inside the barrier reef except while crossing the entrance to Middle Harbor where we had a modified ocean swell. We were sailing over a marine garden covered with coral and other marine growth of the most beautiful shapes and colors. The water was so clear that every detail of the bottom was as plainly visible as though it was at the surface instead of several feet below. There were a variety of shells in many colors and sponges of various sizes and colors. There were fish in a variety of colors so that it was literally a riot of color. The famous bêche-de-mer, or sea slug, was pointed out as it lay on the bottom apparently inanimate and not very attractive. This was one of the principal articles of export from the islands of the Pacific. It is highly prized as an article of food by the Chinese and Japanese after it has been cleaned, cooked, dried and smoked.

The ruins were built on small low islands or on the coral reefs in shoal water so they were surrounded by water and it was possible to land from the boat. The ruins are great monolithic walls of large blocks of stone laid dry in alternate courses of headers and stretchers having a thickness of eight to fifteen feet and a height of a few feet to nearly forty feet, enclosing rectangular areas of varying dimensions. The structures were scattered over a considerable area that was such a jungle of tropical growth it was impossible to define their limits. It would have taken days to make a complete examination of these structures. The largest and best preserved of those known to Mr. Doane, and which we visited, had an outer and inner wall covering an area about 100 by 200 feet, or roughly half an acre. The outer walls were about 15 feet in thickness and from 20 to 40 feet in height. There was a good-sized opening in one side and a raised platform along three sides of the enclosure close to the wall. Inside this enclosure was another similar structure, rectangular in shape, the walls parallel to the outer walls with the space between them about 50 feet in width. The walls of this interior structure were about half the thickness and height of the outer walls. Low walls crossed the space between the inner and outer walls at three places, two of them forming another enclosure on one side which could be entered from the central area only, and the third crossing on the opposite side. The central area had an opening in the wall opposite the one in the outer wall.

Within this chamber or enclosed area, there was a stone vault or tomb with an opening in one side. There were three similar but smaller vaults in the outer enclosure. These were built of large blocks of stone of the same general shape as those in the walls. The walls of this entire structure were in good condition generally, vertical with squared corners well bonded in both directions and the courses were fairly continuous with close joints for the manner in which the stones were laid. There was no sign of mortar or small stones used as pinners to fill in the joints. The stones were as long as twenty feet in some cases and preserved their cross section throughout their entire length. They were mostly five-sided, some eight-sided, but none were square or four-sided, and there were no tool marks on any of them. Mr. Doane said that the few white men who had seen these ruins were greatly impressed as to how they had been quarried and dressed to shape. What kind of tools had been used and what had become of them, but the most interesting question was, where did the stone come from? The stone must have come from the great outcrop of basalt at the north end of the island, twenty miles by water from the ruins, and there is ample evidence visible that it did come from there.

Basalt is a volcanic rock that frequently solidifies from its fused state in long polygonal sections with smooth sides. The Giant's Causeway on the northeast coast of Ireland is a well-known example of this peculiarity of basalt. The outcrop at Chokach is a similar formation. Therefore, there was no necessity for dressing the stone and tools were not needed. It is rather easy to break the stone so tools were not needed to cut them to any particular length, and this is confirmed by many broken pieces in the walls. The thickness of these stones varied from eight or nine inches to fifteen to eighteen inches. The transportation of these stones from the northerly end of the island to the site of the ruins at Nan Matal on the southeast coast was a huge task, even by water, which undoubtedly was the way it was done, but it was not insurmountable. Placing the stones in the structure was perhaps the simplest part of the operation although it was a big job but there must have been a large force of men with great energy and resourcefulness.

The real mystery is the purpose of these structures which no one has solved. They appear to be too scattered for tombs unless one assumes a large race of people living on the island but, in that event, they would have left some evidence of their occupation. It must have taken years to build those structures and many more years for a race of people to develop a desire for such huge monuments or tombs for their great men. They may have had a defensive purpose, not as the lair of pirates or for the protection of early Spanish discoverers which would appeal to a boy, but they are too large for such a transitory purpose. I think they were built by a powerful body of dominant and aggressive men who came from a far country by water and, finding these islands occupied by a large race of soft, unwarlike people, they proceeded to take possession. Being inferior in numbers and not certain of the length of their stay, they built these structures for defensive use if necessary and the work was performed by the natives under the direction of the invaders. The final chapter could have been that the invaders abandoned the enterprise and sailed away or, weakened by disease and deaths, the natives annihilated them. Either theory accounts for the lack of any descendants of the builders but we are still ignorant of their origin. My theory is that they came from South America.

We looked over some of the more accessible structures but none quite as large or complete as the one I have described. Some walls had fallen but, we could not determine whether from settlement of the foundations or the effect of the tremendous growth of trees, bushes and vines. Some of the canals were so choked with this growth that we could not enter them.

We had our lunch at the ruins and left in time to make the return trip in daylight. The wind was dropping with the sun and a good part of the return trip was made with the oars. It was after dark when we reached our ship and we stayed aboard that night, sending Mr. Doane ashore with the boat. It had been a wonderful day and the memory of it is with me almost as though it had just happened.

I had many opportunities to witness the swimming abilities of the natives and it was their most outstanding accomplishment. They were truly at home in the water and I envied them because I did not swim and never learned, a fact which always creates surprise because I was born at sea. Just why being born on a ship should insure ability to swim has never been clear in my mind. I fell overboard on a previous visit to Ponape when I was twelve years old and a sailor rescued me. My father was an excellent swimmer and he learned to swim in the regulation swimming hole in a country village in Connecticut. He sent me with the boat filling water casks with instructions to the officer to teach me to swim and, while his methods were rather rough, I might have learned in a few more lessons. The Kanaka never dove into the water but always went in feet first and they never cared to dive from a height such as jumping off the foreyard as many of our sailors would. They could stay under water much longer than any of our men and never seemed tired by swimming.

The natives make a very pleasant drink by fermenting the juice collected from the bud of a coconut palm which prevents the growth of a coconut, of course. This drink is called "toddy" and is not intoxicating but it is exhilarating in a mild way. By refermenting and concentrating in the sun, it can be made into a potent liquor. In the Ladrone Islands which we visited later, the Spaniards had taught the natives to distill toddy which made a liquor they called "argudente" that was the equal of the most powerful Jersey Lightning ever produced. The Kanaka makes a concoction from the kava root that grows wild on these islands which produces a physical effect that would seem to be partly narcotic and the drinker's legs get badly tangled while his brain remains fairly clear. In the day of my experience, the liquor was produced by old women masticating the root and expectorating the juice into a coconut shell or a calabash. After fermenting sufficiently, the clear liquor was decanted into another vessel which was then passed around the gathering with the highest in authority drinking first. It seemed to be a ceremonial affair of the older men but, it should be noted, that the white man did not teach the natives how to get intoxicated.

All good things must end and the day came for our departure. We had bought quite a number of hogs that were running about the deck and had obtained a boatload of dry coconuts from a small nearby island. We had yams and sweet potatoes and the mainmast and mizzenmast stays were festooned with bunches of bananas.

Another tragedy occurred before we could get underway and while the first table and the crew were having breakfast. The steward did not respond to his call and a careful search of the entire ship failed to locate him. It was first thought that he might have run away, although an arrangement had been made with the chief of the natives that no aid was to be given to any of our men trying to run away as without it they would have a hard time. It was discovered finally that a bag of shells and coral lying in the mate's boat was missing which lead to the assumption that the steward had committed suicide. It was recalled that he had been more quiet than usual and dropped remarks about not finishing the voyage, so we were forced to conclude that he had jumped overboard. A few days after we sailed, his body came to the surface with the bag of shells tied to his ankles. We all felt very badly at the loss of the steward and inwardly hoped he had deserted as he was a quiet, likable man and had been very nice to my mother and sister.

Preparations for getting under way include the removal of gaskets from topsails, foresail, headsails and spanker, the anchor was hove short and a kedge or light anchor was laid out on the reef with a line to the ship and a boat stood by to get it aboard as soon as the ship was underway. We had a fair wind coming in and the wind was from the same direction so that we would be close on the wind going out with no room to tack. There was no room to maneuver in the harbor with two other ships at anchor. Therefore, the anchor was hove and the ship hauled as close to the reef as the depth of water would permit and a second line run to the kedge from the starboard quarter. The topsails were sheeted home and hoisted with the maintopsail braced forward on the starboard tack and the fore-topsail squared. The line from the bow to the kedge was slacked as the line from the quarter was hauled in which swung the bow to port. The spanker was set and the fore-topsail braced forward, the jib was hoisted and the sheet hauled aft. The order to "belay all" was given and the ship was headed for the channel with her sails full. The line to the kedge was slacked and the kedge tumbled into the boat which was alongside in a few minutes, the falls were hooked on to it and the boat hoisted to its position. This maneuvering of the ship was beautifully executed without a slip or hitch and, although the audience was small, it could be very critical if there had been any opportunity. When the opening in

the barrier reef was off the weather quarter, we came about on the
other tack and the ship was soon bowing to the ceaseless swell of
the Pacific. The ship was hauled aback for the pilot to leave after
a short hitch offshore. I said good-by to the pilot's son with real
regret as he had been a likable and interesting companion and I
often wondered what became of him in the later changes of the
government of the island. Of course, he married a Kanaka girl
and the white blood may have reached the vanishing point in his
progeny after a few generations.

The question of who owned these islands had not been raised
but, if anyone had asked me who owned Ponape, I would have said
the Kanakas who lived there. If any nation had an interest in the
property, I would have said it was the United States because her
whaleships had been going there since 1830 and the American
Foreign Mission Board had missionaries on the island since about
1850, and also American traders had been visiting the island for
many years. Any other nation that knew about the island were
keeping very quiet about it but, some time after our visit German
traders visited Ponape and a naval vessel visited the island of Yap
in the Caroline Group and raised the German flag in 1885. This
action brought a protest from Spain who claimed to have discovered these islands in the sixteenth century. The matter was decided by the Pope in favor of Spain and their flag was raised in
Ascension Harbor on the island of Ponape in 1886 and hell was
turned loose on these harmless natives. The worst that could be
said against them was that, in defense of their birthright, they killed
a few foreign usurpers. The Spaniards accused Mr. Doane of in-
citing the natives to resist their authority and deported him to
Manila but, upon the intervention of our Government, he was returned to Ponape so broken in health that he went to Honolulu in
1890 there to die shortly thereafter. It was about this time that the
Germans acquired the Caroline Islands along with other islands
scattered about the western Pacific Ocean. To complete the history,
the treaty negotiated at Paris after the First World War gave the
Caroline Islands to Japan. Ponape now has roads, and other evi-

dences of civilization, including a government in which the native has no voice. I am glad that I saw it while it was still in its past as the present is colorless and the future not bright.

After rounding the northerly end of Ponape with its towering Cliff of Chokach, with its reminder of the ruins at Nan-Matal, we laid our course for the Ladrone group which is referred to by residents as the Marianas because Ladrone means a thief. It appears that the natives pilfered from the discoverer's ship, hence the title he gave to this group. We returned to regulation sea life, two men at masthead on the lookout for whales, anchor put on the bow and the chain stowed below as it was nine hundred miles from Ponape to Saipan our next port.

SAIPAN AND GUAM

THE loss of our steward made it necessary to promote the cook and take a man from the forecastle as cook. This was the second time the cook had been taken into the cabin to fill the vacancy of the steward but, in the other case which occurred on the *Monticello*, the vacancy was created by demoting the steward for incompetence. The cook was an exceptional ship's cook but he was not a good steward, strange as this may seem.

My father had taken a Kanaka boy on the recommendation of Mr. Doane, who was to act as cabin boy until we reached 'Frisco when he was to be general utility man in our home in Oakland. Joe, which was the English for his Kanaka name, was a well set-up youngster, good-natured and willing but not very ambitious. He lived with us about a year in Oakland when his longing for home became so strong that my father secured passage for him on a whaler making the between-seasons cruise in the South Pacific and returned him to Ponape.

The weather was good and the wind favorable, we saw no whales and touched at no islands. The foremast hands were becoming very much interested in Saipan as word had been given out that they were to have liberty at that island. It was customary on cruises of about a year's duration to allow the crew to go ashore for a day in some port where they could have a wild time without much opportunity or incentive for running away, if they so desired. One can readily understand that few ports met these conditions, and especially to the crew of a ship that had taken one whale and had a sizable leak. One of the stories told about the whalers of that day concerned a captain who never lowered for whales on Sundays and searched for a desert island on which to give his crew liberty. Saipan seemed to have the required qualifications; it belonged to Spain and had a governor with a small force of so-called soldiers who could be relied upon, at a price, to take care of any deserters. It had a reputation for a powerful brand of argudente, the women were said to be attractive and gracious, and the island was interesting.

We arrived at the island in due time and anchored on the lee side in an open roadsted. Immediately after breakfast the next morning, the starboard watch was landed on the beach and I went with them, partly because that was technically my watch but actually because I wanted to see the gang in action. I had listened for hours to what they would do on that day and now I was to see the program carried out. Several personal affairs were to be adjusted with no "damned officers" to interfere, then they would look the women over, then they would get "damned good and drunk." When the port watch came to take them aboard the "old hooker," they would give them a "helluva licking." They did get drunk which was the only part of the program they carried out and they did not waste any time about it. Furthermore, they stayed drunk all day so that the port watch had to pick them up along the beach and carry them to the boats. I was disgusted and left them when Frenchy, one of the crew, embraced a small tree and tried to sing the Marseillaise.

The village was rather interesting, there was more attention given to the layout of the houses with respect to the main thoroughfare than prevailed on the other islands we had visited. The houses were built better and there was at least one game cock in every one of them. The people were not like the Kanakas; in fact, they are so mixed with the Spanish and Philippinos that the original race has lost its identity. They are called Chamorros and speak a language containing many words derived from the Spanish. Those who have studied these people believe they had a language of their own and were fairly well advanced in the civilized arts. They are smaller than the Kanakas and of a lighter shade of brown. Their spoken language is soft with a musical tone and a prolongation of the vowels. Most of the natives of this village were quite well dressed which meant their bodies were fully covered. The men wore cotton trousers and a cotton or linen shirt with the tails outside, like the Chinese and Philippinos, and these shirts were elaborately pleated and carefully laundered in some cases. Most of the people were barefoot. The women wore Mother Hubbards and most of them were fat; if there were any beauties in the village, they had been locked up or moved to the interior. After seeing the exhibits, I felt a little better toward the men for deciding to get drunk before they looked them over. The children were naked, dirty and happy, with their swell-front tummies which seem to be a trade mark common to all the children of the islands.

The drunks were bundled into the boats late in the afternoon and taken aboard ship, and the boats took the port watch ashore the next day. I did not go with them but, from what I heard later, they followed closely the program of the starboard watch except that three men were missing when they were rounded up to return to the ship. The Governor came aboard the next morning to assure my father that he would have these men in a few days but my father had decided to go to Guam, about a day's sail to the south of Saipan, and touch at Saipan on our return.

Guam is quite a large island of volcanic origin with high land a short distance back from the shore and a large harbor protected by an outer coral reef similar to Ascension Harbor at Ponape. It was a Spanish possession at that time and was used as a penal station for Manila. It is now an island possession of the United States. We had a double purpose in going to this island; one was to dispose of some pickled salmon in trade, the other was to lay in a supply of lime juice or lemon juice to serve to the crew as antiscorbutic and thereby hangs a tale.

I have said that we had two or three possible sea lawyers in the forecastle and, as time passed, we were sure that Hank the literary cuss was the ringleader, but he skillfully avoided any issue with the officers and on the face of it, he was an honest, loyal seaman. One day, he headed a committee of the crew that obtained an interview with my father and he quite skillfully quoted the law about the protection of the crew from scurvy when on exceptionally long voyages. As a preventive, a daily allowance of lime or lemon juice was required when fresh vegetables were not available. They had the whiphand, in a way, because they knew we would be without fresh vegetables for six months or more unless we went into some port where such supplies could be bought. My father agreed to obtain a supply of lime or lemon juice but they could not furnish us with the quantity we wanted and they could not buy our pickled salmon.

The harbor of Guam, called Port Luiz, has room for quite a fleet of deep-draft vessels and is well protected in all directions but we were obliged to anchor about two miles from the landing owing to shoal water toward the shore. The principal town, called Agana, is located near the shore some seven to eight miles northeast of the harbor. This was the capital or headquarters of the Spanish Government's representative. The location was to get the benefit of the northeast trade winds which come off the sea at this place and make it cool and comfortable while it is very hot and humid at the harbor because these trades are cut off by the very high land behind it.

Shortly after we came to anchor, a white man and the headman of the town came aboard and invited the family to be his guests during our stay. He talked the native language as well as English and my father had business dealings with him on previous visits, so it was accepted and arranged that we would go to his house the next day. I was delighted with this program as I was not favorably impressed with what I could see of Guam. The land was covered with verdure but there was very little evidence of life ashore and no canoes came out to the ship which made it appear very lonely compared to Ascension Harbor. My mother recalled her first visit to Agana when I was a baby a bit over a year old. The ship did not enter the harbor that time but lay "off and on" under sail directly off the town and we came ashore in a boat to the surprise of the natives and the captain of another whaler whose boat was capsized in the surf shortly before we landed. He was very much interested when he saw a woman in the boat but he nearly passed out when he saw that she had a baby in her arms. My father admitted that it was rougher than he expected but my mother saw nothing to be disturbed about with my father at the steering oar and no record was kept of what I thought about it.

Trouble broke out the next morning in the after gang when the second and third mates got in an argument over some trivial matter and the third mate knocked the second mate down, probably from too many argudente drinks. The second mate went to my father and announced that one of them must leave the ship then and there. An investigation developed that there was bad blood between the two that could not be cured and one of them would have to go and, as the second mate was the more valuable to the ship, the third mate was given his discharge. It seemed as if Old Nick himself was directing the destinies of the ship and, while my father's decision was not questioned, the incident cast a gloom over the entire ship as the third mate was a good natured, likable man with a rather unusual career which he could discuss in an interesting way. He was a fairly well-educated man whereas the second mate signed his name with a cross and was inclined to be surly, but he was a great whaleman.

This episode made it necessary for me to remain aboard the ship when the family went ashore as the third mate and his personal effects were taken along which left no room for me. Arrangements were made for me to go ashore later and I was told there would be a conveyance at the landing to take me to the town. When I landed a few hours later, I found a two-wheeled cart with a bullock hitched to it and it looked like an undersized Mexican steer to me whose highest speed might be two miles an hour. The cart was the most primitive I had ever seen, wheels of solid wood and the body consisted of board slats laid across an extension of the shafts which were rigidly fastened to the wooden axle. I gave it one good look and decided to walk and, fortunately the road had a hard surface and followed the shore with no confusing intersections so there was no danger of getting lost. The first mate who brought me ashore was in favor of the bullock cart because he feared my father might not approve my making the trip alone, but I emphatically vetoed the cart, and it was one of the most delightful tramps I ever made.

The shore was bordered with coconut groves which did not obstruct the view of the ocean that was very beautiful. There were short stretches where low growing trees, bushes and ferns shut out the ocean view but it was a bright clear day and the flowers were gorgeous. I tried to find names for the flowers and unusual trees and plants that lined both sides of the road with small shrines attached to trees at rather frequent intervals and, I recalled, these people had adopted the Catholic faith. It seemed odd that the road was so good and they had no horses.

I became thirsty and wondered if I could climb a coconut tree like the Kanaka boy did on Ocean Island and get one for its cool and appetizing drink, but I did not dare try it. By the time my thirst was becoming acute, I came to a small stream of clear water where I quenched my thirst and rested for a few moments. I did not meet anyone for some distance and then, around a curve, came a file of men with an armed man at each end. I recalled, after first being startled, that this was a penal colony for Manila and these were probably prisoners being shifted for some reason. As we passed, the guards saluted and I said "It is a fine day" and noted with relief that they were inoffensive in appearance. I came to the village in due time and found the house where the family were staying and, learned to my surprise, that they came here in a carry-all drawn by two ponies that belonged to our host.

The house had two stories, or rather a high basement and one story containing the living quarters. The walls were of coral rock, whitewashed, and the roof was red tile which produced a very pleasing effect with its background of green foliage. The stairs were on the outside of the house and ended at a veranda on the floor level. The rooms were of good size, comfortably furnished and quite cool considering the outside temperature. My first request was for a drink of water and an unglazed clay carafe was taken from a recess in the outside wall of the house near the front door and a glass was filled with water which was quite cool, much to my surprise. I then learned that the rapid evaporation of the water in the carafe through its porous sides lowered the temperature of the water inside considerably below that of the outside air. The outside of the carafe was constantly covered with moisture which made it necessary to refill it at intervals but this was probably the oldest method known to man for cooling his drinking water, yet it was using the same fundamental principle that operates every apparatus invented by man for replacing nature in lowering temperatures.

Our host's wife was a native or Chamorro, good-natured and not bad looking for a stout woman but she talked very little English. They had plenty of servants and the food was good. We came with the expectation of staying a day or two, which my father thought would be ample time to transact his business, as it would have been to sell his pickled salmon for they went like hot cakes but, buying a large order of lemon juice was a horse of another color. It was Lent and there could be no business done until these religious ceremonies ended. My father was disgusted and said so in very profane language, but the order had gone out from the priest that there should be no gainful labor during Lent, and so we waited and had a most interesting experience. My mother recalled that her previous visit was during Lent but they were not buying lemon juice that time.

Everybody did all they could to entertain us, the Governor and his staff called and so did the head priest, who was fat and jolly and talked good English. He chatted with my mother about her previous visits, recalled little incidents such as the landing in the surf, and was a fund of information. He was the political head as well as the spiritual leader of the community and he exercised his power with good judgment and a human understanding of the weaknesses of the people he was dealing with. The Chamorro is more emotional that the Kanaka and has had a closer and longer association with the white man than the natives of the Caroline Islands as was apparent in their dress and manner of living. They had accepted the Catholic religion quite generally and observed its requirements on Sundays and church days during the forenoons but, in the afternoons, they gathered in the plaza and fought game cocks backing their birds with whatever cash they had. The padre was an interested witness which, no doubt, prevented serious disorder and reckless betting as these people are enthusiastic gamblers.

The Governor's staff included a doctor who was a full blooded Spaniard but he was a pronounced blond which was a great surprise to me, as I had assumed they were all brunets. He also talked English and did what he could to make our visit interesting and pleasant. The government officials lived in very comfortable residences built on the general plan of our host's house and surrounded with flowering plants and shrubs but no trees that would cut off the sea breeze. There was no green grass, therefore no lawns, but with such masses of foliage, it was not a serious loss.

The doctor invited me to dine with him alone, a day or two after we arrived, and I very promptly accepted and have remembered always the evening as one of my most interesting experiences. It was a nice thing for the doctor to do and it established him in my mind as a real fellow. Perhaps I should have absorbed more of the details of furnishings and the setting of the table but I was a hungry boy and have retained a somewhat hazy picture only of a cool, attractive room with comfortable furniture and dining table at which we were served by a native boy in white shirt and trousers. Some of the dishes were new to me but I ate them all through the skillful attention of my host without any feeling that I was abusing my opportunity. The doctor offered me a long Manila cheroot after dinner which I declined as not being a smoker but I did take a glass of wine upon his assurance that it was very mild, in fact, only a "lady's drink" although I thought he might have omitted the latter part of the description. However, it was very tasty and I allowed myself to be persuaded to have a second glass and then I stopped as I was not sure of the capacity of the ladies he referred to and I did not wish to create any suspicion as to my condition in my father's mind. We talked for some time after coffee on many subjects which, of course, I cannot recall but I remember that he did not remind me in any way that I was just a youngster. He had his servant escort me to my quarters because of the darkness and my lack of knowledge with the village streets.

I inspected the village carefully and found it rather neatly laid out around a central plaza with the church as its principal feature. The native houses were mostly one story but they were much more substantially built than those in Ponape. Some houses had wood floors but the general dirt floor was well packed and swept clean. There was always a chest of drawers with a bedstead and, at least, one game cock tethered to a leg of the bed by a cord fastened to the cock's leg. Of course, I attended a cock fight and found it quite exciting. I was surprised to learn that steel spurs were attached to the legs of the birds as I thought they were well equipped by nature. Some skill is shown in the handling of the birds but, after they are released in the ring, they cannot be touched until the fight is ended. The birds are fighters and skillful in their rapid movements. They fight entirely with their spurs and strike for the head or neck but the bodies often get hit, which makes some of the contests quite gory. The fights were well attended and, although the spectators were very partisan and backed their choices with their money, they were good natured about it.

I bought a young bird that came from a highly recommended strain of fighters and succeeded in having him delivered aboard the ship without my parents' knowledge as my mother thought it a brutal and degrading sport. I wished many times that I had left the bird in Guam. We had brought a few hens and a rooster from our home in Oakland and these were installed in a coop under the workbench just aft of the try works. They soon became so adjusted to sea life that they had the run of the ship and supplied enough eggs for my mother to treat the cabin to some of her famous cakes. The rooster was of the typical barnyard type and was fully three times the size of my game cock, so I concluded the odds were not too bad and a match was arranged one afternoon with the forehatch as the pit. One of the crew handled the rooster and I handled the game cock and it was clearly a case of weight against skill. The old rooster appeared anxious to fight and I was rather disturbed as to the outcome. However, it was too late for me to back out as I had talked too much about the skill and courage of my bird so, at the signal, the two were released. The little game cock looked at the rooster for a moment and then made a pass to draw him out. It was without doubt the largest fowl he had ever seen much less fought but, the old rooster was game and started to mix things when the little bird hopped into the air, struck once and his spur pierced the head of the rooster, and the next moment he was dead. I realized at once that I was in for a bad time as the killing of the rooster had to be explained to my mother and I had not thought that the little cuss could kill the rooster. Well, the thing was done so I picked up the rooster and carried it aft to my mother and told her the story. Instead of being turned over to my father for a good licking with a ropes end, she looked at me very quietly with an expression of sorrow rather than anger and said, "Willie how could you be so cruel?" That was all but it hurt far more than the ropes end and it ended my interest in game cocks.

Arrangements were rapidly shaping for the great religious procession that would be the culminating event of the week. It started in the forenoon with a band at the head of the line followed by a small body of soldiers with the Governor and his staff, then the mayor and town authorities, then the clerical organization with the head priest and his assistants and then came men and women in white carrying banners and four men carrying a glass case containing an effigy of Christ, followed by a large number of young girls dressed in white. The procession passed through the principal streets of the village which were lined with the residents and natives from other villages, and it seemed like several thousand people. It was an interesting and impressive sight. The procession ended at the church where everyone entered except our family as we had been informed that we were infidels in the eyes of the church and we would avoid any unpleasant manifestations by not entering. Our host had permission from the priest to take us up in the belfry where we could look down on the assemblage through a lattice partition and thus witness the ceremonies better than if we had been on the floor of the church. It was quite a large church and it was crowded with people who were on their knees most of the time. The interior fittings were simple except the altar which was really handsome and, we were told by our friend, that it came from Spain.

The large living room of the house was always filled evenings with an interesting gathering of the family and their friends as it was as much of an event to them as it was for us. Conversation was limited as most of these people could talk Spanish or Chemona and we could talk English only, but it was surprising how much information could be gathered by signs with a few words in either tongue. I enjoyed listening to the talk, especially the women, as their voices and their laughs are very musical. Some of the young women were rather good-looking; they are naturally indolent but their movements are graceful. The women smoked generally, mostly the long Manila cheroot, which was an awful shock to my mother but was very interesting to my sister and me. They inhaled skillfully and handled their cheroots like experts. I knew a little about cigarettes and I had several friends in Oakland who were quite proud of their ability to inhale deeply and exhale slowly but, compared with these women, they were novices.

The religious services ended and several kegs of lemon juice were delivered at the harbor and transferred aboard ship by our boat and the salmon was all sold and delivered ashore for which we took away about all the Spanish gold there was on the island. We took leave of our friends with real regret as they had made our visit very pleasant and I often look back on that week as the most unusual experience of my life. We reached the ship too late in the afternoon to sail that day but all preparations were made for an early departure in the morning. I noticed the ship looked very smart and, as we came alongside, I saw that she had been given a coat of black paint with a white stripe along the molding outside the planksheer. The deckwork had all been repainted which made her look very neat and clean. The mate had decided that the best way to keep the crew out of trouble was to keep them busy.

INSUBORDINATION

I was wandering around the deck that evening to get acquainted again when I noticed that none of the foremast hands was on deck and, as I started to look down the forecastle scuttle, I saw that the fore hatch was gone. I heard a peculiar sound in the water and looking over the rail near the fore rigging, I saw the fore hatch in the water secured by ropes to the fore-chains and it looked as if some of the crew were planning to run away. I ran aft and told the second mate who was on deck about the fore hatch and we went forward together. By that time, the men were coming on deck, some of them carrying bundles and quite a load of argudente, so the second mate hurried aft and reported the situation to my father who was in the cabin. My father came on deck and met the crew on the port side amidships and asked them where they were going. One of the men spoke up and said they had gone as far as they intended to and they were leaving the damned old hooker before she dropped from under them, also, he advised my father to step aside if he did not want to get hurt. That was the end of the conversation, my father went into action and ploughed through the front ranks of the group with both arms working like pistons of an engine and men going down like tenpins. The men in the rear took one look and bolted for the forecastle. One man stumbled and fell just as my father was about to hit him but, instead of waiting for the man to get up, he grabbed him with one hand around an ankle and the other in the seat of his pants and hove him down the forecastle scuttle in the rear of the last of those endeavoring to get below. It was all over, nobody was seriously hurt, several men had sore heads for a day or two and my father had a fine time. The officers and boatsteerers were gathered in the waist but they knew better than to butt in unless they were ordered to do so. An officer was ordered to get the fore hatch in its place and an anchor watch of an officer and a boatsteerer was detailed to take charge of the deck and to call my father if there were any further signs of insubordination but nothing happened.

I presume that this episode was a demonstration, to many people, of the brutality that it was claimed was so prevalent in American whale ships. I maintain that it was not brutal and it was probably the only method that could have prevented a very serious situation and possible loss of life. There is nothing that appeals to the type of men that made up that crew like physical courage. It is the only authority they will actually bow to although they will never admit being afraid of any man, but they are. While I do not pretend to analyze the mental attitude of weak men, it was the deduction of the captains of that day from their experiences, that in all cases of insubordination, authority must be asserted instantly and effectively. Experience had shown them also that nothing is more effective than physical force.

I have often wondered how the critics of physical force would have handled the situation I have just described. Perhaps they would have let the men take the boats and go ashore but what about the situation that would confront the Captain and the officers when the shore authorities had returned these men with orders to take them and get to sea. It should be apparent that the authority of the after gang must be enforced whenever it is disputed. Further, it must not be overlooked that in the background of concerted insubordination there lurks the danger of mob violence with its lust for blood. One thrust of a knife in the hand of an intoxicated man who, when sober would not think of refusing to obey an order, and there is an orgy of killing. There was never a serious mutiny that was not the result of failure by the captain to act promptly upon the first evidence of insubordination for once the crew takes possession of a ship, they are in a terrible predicament as this is mutiny on the high seas which is punishable by death. In the old days, they were hung and the fact that lives had been taken made this result inevitable.

The physical equipment of men is not always comparable with their courage and situations would arise when an officer was obliged to seek aid in the shape of a belaying pin or a bung starter and this was the primary cause of most of the brutality on shipboard. When an officer started to enforce discipline, he had to finish it. Of course, there were brutal captains and officers which could not be avoided under the system that controlled the selection of these men in those days, but they were the exception and not the rule. During my boyhood days at sea, including five different ships and crews, I never saw a case of brutal treatment of a member of the crew; I saw discipline enforced when the occasion required but with no more force than was necessary to insure its success. I hope my readers will realize that the period of the men I am writing about is of the past and I know very little of the men who follow the sea today and I draw no comparisons between them.

The American whaling captain of that day was a plain, rather reticent, serious minded man utterly devoid of show or swagger. He held no commission and wore no uniform but he could say with John Paul Jones, "By God sir I am captain of this ship because I am the best man in her."

The next morning, immediately after breakfast, all hands were called and we proceeded to sea. I thought the men were exceptionally alert and they sang a few chanteys at the windlass and no fault could be found with their execution of the orders for making sail. The affair of the night before was closed and I was happy as it was a terrible experience for me.

The discharge of the third mate led to the promotion of the

fourth mate and this vacancy was not filled as there was no need of a fourth officer while my father headed his own boat. A boat-steerer for the first mate's boat was found among the beachcombers and he was shipped for the balance of the voyage, this being necessary as the fourth mate had been boatsteerer in the first mate's boat. A native was shipped as steward and the cook went back to his job in the galley. The new steward did very well although I never liked him because he looked too much like a Chinaman and, in my day, no California boy liked a Chinaman, but why, I could never tell. Another native had been shipped as a foremast hand, a husky fellow who made a lot of trouble until a remedy was found for his complaint.

Our course was laid for Saipan after clearing the barrier reef with its constant roar of the surf and we arrived there the next day. The first boat to come alongside belonged to the Governor and it contained our three men looking well and not too sorry to be back. They had to submit to the gibes of their shipmates while they pounded rust off the anchor chain for a few days as penance for deserting. The story was told that, when they saw the ship sail, they returned to the village and were promptly locked up under arrest and it never occurred to them that the ship would return.

Having settled for the capture of the deserters, and bought what fresh supplies were offered, mostly sweet potatoes and a few chickens, we sailed for the Japan Sea. Masthead lookouts were set and the routine of sea life restored. Our course was "full and bye" with a wind that blew steadily for more than a week and all that we could carry, our topgallant sails and courses too. We had lost time at Guam and my father was anxious to get into the Japan Sea where we hoped to find right whales.

I have always remembered that passage of about two weeks as the most uncomfortable of our voyage and it gave me an understanding of a merchantman as they are always making a passage. As I have already stated, the *Florence* was very stiff and had a disagreeable roll to windward because she would not stay heeled over as she crossed the seas. She was wet most of the time, even on the poop deck, as she was throwing spray the entire length of her weather side. The deck watch kept under the topgallant forecastle as the only place they could find that was dry. No work could be done although halliards were set up and yards braced two or three times a day to keep the men alert. It was almost impossible to walk the deck because, if you let go of the weather rail for a moment, you would find yourself in the scuppers on the next lee roll unless you were fortunate enough to bring up against the booby hatch.

There was just one haven of refuge outside of the cabin, and that was stuffy, because the companionway door and the portholes were closed, and it was the room opening on deck used by the third mate and cooper. This room was on the lee side and it was protected from the spray by the spare boats over head so the door could be left open. I could watch the cooper scrimshawing and the third mate making half-models with his knife or fancy lanyards while they told me stories of their life at sea. The third mate was making a very fine blackjack with the lead covered with a finely woven net of cotton twine which continued in a braided lanyard with fancy knots and a loop at the end to go around the wrist. He was doing this to kill time as he was not the kind of man who would use such a weapon. This blackjack nearly killed the second mate a few days before the end of the voyage although by the hand of another man than the third mate.

I came on deck one morning right after turning out and I had just reached the waist when the ship gave a quick lurch as a sea hit her, my feet flew out from under me and I fell flat on my back as the top of the sea came over the rail and covered me. A loud bellow went up from the spectators which I decided from the volume of noise must have included every man in the watch. Fortunately I saw the funny side of the incident and joined in the laugh because I was not hurt although I had to change every stitch I had on.

We still had a number of hogs on deck and they had a bad time sliding back and forth in their efforts to keep their feet but, after a while, they got wise and just lay down in the lee scuppers with their head to windward. While we were shipping a lot of spray, we were not taking solid water so the hogs were in no danger of drowning and the weather was not cold. We tied short pieces of rope to the legs of the large hogs to keep them from spread eagleing so, when they skidded, all four legs went in the same direction.

When we left 'Frisco, it was my father's intention to stop at some port in Japan, probably Hakodate, as he had been there several times. We touched at Yokohama in the *Monticello* and this made me anxious to see our original plans carried through. But they had to be abandoned because my father did not think it would be wise to enter a port where there was a United States Consul who might be appealed to by the crew to order a survey of the ship on the complaint that she was unseaworthy. Many a ship has been condemned in a foreign port upon such a charge and that was in no worse condition than was the *Florence*. It could not be denied that she had a constant leak but it was not dangerous and it did not increase much in heavy weather since the overhauling at Ponape. Who could tell what the crew would swear to was the extent of the leak in a gale. It was too risky and, much to my regret, Japan was dropped from our visiting list although this fact was not known to the crew until shortly before the ship passed out of the Japan Sea. Hakodate is on the southerly end of Yezo near the northerly end of the Japan Sea. Our sea lawyer had been a little premature in making his claim for lime juice.

A sight was taken on the sun every day as it crossed the meridian for latitude and, in the afternoon, another sight for longitude by my father and myself and each worked out his own sights although we used the same chronometer now. It was a great satisfaction to me that we agreed substantially in our positions.

One day the cry of "Sail o" came from aloft and, in answer to the request from the deck of "Where away," came the reply "Dead ahead sir." My father motioned to the man at the wheel to "keep her off" and then looked through his spyglass along the weather rail for a moment. He laid the glass down in its place on the skylight, said "keep her full and by" and resumed his promenade on the weather side of the poop deck but I thought I saw a smile pass over his face. A little later, the lookout hailed the deck and announced that the sail was land and the smile was accounted for. It was "sail rock" and it is almost always taken for a ship. It was now plainly visible from the deck and I would have sworn it was a square-rigger coming down before the wind. In fact, it is about the size of the ship, a lone, absolutely barren pinnacle of rock surrounded by very deep water without a projecting shelf of rock at the water line. What a frightful thing for a ship to run into and I was glad when it was astern as I thought we went much too close. That was all we saw of land or sail until we passed into the passage through the Loo Choo Islands into the Yellow Sea.

Shanghai was not far away and I wanted to go there very badly but we were looking for whales and we began to work north for the Tsushima Straits. The weather moderated and our floating home became much more comfortable. I came on deck one very fine night with a full moon as we were passing astern of a large square-rigged merchantman. She was evidently bound for China and, as the wind was light, she had everything set including skysails. She looked beautiful as she slipped through the water with hardly a sound and no one visible except the man at the wheel. The little old *Florence* with her patched sails had little attraction for the watch on that splendid ship but the winds blew just as hard and the seas ran as high for the little whaler as they did for the big merchantman.

JAPAN SEA

In a few days, we worked our way through the Strait of Tsushima, with Korea in sight to the north and Japan to the east and south, and entered the Japan Sea. We were in the waters where years later the Japanese Navy destroyed a Russian fleet of warships. We slowly cruised through the Japan Sea with very good

weather most of the time which means that we were not hove to or
under close reefed topsails while in the sea. We raised right whales
three or four times but did not fasten once. It was very dishearten-
ing. I spent hours in the "crows-nest" as this structure had been
erected on the foretopmast crosstrees for the protection and comfort of the men who stood the masthead watches. I had never seen
a right whale taken and I was extremely anxious that we get at
least one, which seemed a very modest desire, but I was doomed to
be disappointed. We zigzagged back and forth across the Japan Sea
from Tsushima to Saghalien, never at anchor and never still except
when hauled aback to lower or hoist our boats or when there was
no wind. The few whales we did see had a date somewhere and
were late.

One day, a Korean fishing junk came alongside and the crew
came aboard. They wore a conglomeration of clothes that would
have made it difficult to tell whether they were men or women if
seen on land but being on a boat made it easier to assume that they
were men. They wore a queer turret shaped hat of woven straw
that certainly looked out of place with their jobs but, perhaps it
was in keeping with the whole outfit, which was anything but
nautical according to our standards. Their craft looked as though
it might founder any minute although I was assured by our mate
that it was seaworthy. It was high aft and the rudder was in
quite a deep recess formed by the overhang of the superstructure
and the extension of the sides of the hull beyond the stern post.
She was rather beamy with one mast and a square sail of very
course material fastened to horizontal slats and hung from a yard
that could be hoisted to the head of the mast. Ropes lead aft to the
rail from the ends of the yard and I assumed they were braces. I
concluded that the sail was reefed by lowering the yard and rolling
up one or more slats and tying ropes around the roll but, I might
have been wrong, nobody could answer my questions. The yard
was bamboo which is light and very strong and had my approval.
The mast had been fished and repaired to such an extent that it
was anybody's guess as to how it started, probably as a piece of

bamboo. There was no jib or any kind of a head sail and I doubt that she could make any headway with the wind forward of the beam, therefore, she could not beat to windward. I should add that ropes were attached to the lower corners of the sail for use as sheets. The ropes looked home made of very poor stuff but not out of keeping with the rest of the outfit. Fishing gear was scattered about the deck, long oars or sweeps and a mess of junk that might have been the accumulation of ages.

The visit reminded my mother of an experience she had when in those waters in the ship *Florida* and I was a baby, in long clothes. One day while the boats were off chasing whales, including my father, a junk came alongside. The native crew became very much interested in me and asked many questions with much gesticulation which my mother could not understand and she became alarmed, especially when the captain picked me up and proceeded to make an intimate examination that disclosed the fact that I was a boy, which was what they wanted to know. I was handed back to my mother with profuse smiles and many gestures of approval and they soon left the ship. I wonder what would have happened if I had been a girl, and what a relief it must have been to the fears of my mother.

Our progress through the sea brought us to a lone island inhabited by sea fowls only and, as the sea was smooth, a boat was sent ashore which returned in a few hours with a big supply of eggs. Of course, they had a fishy taste but the cook managed to make them into some very edible dishes. Such situations are the real test of a good cook.

OKHOTSK SEA

After what seemed to be a long period of time, actually about six weeks, we left the Japan Sea by way of the La Pérouse Strait and entered the Sea of Okhotsk. We laid our course for North East

Gulf which, as the name indicates, is at the extreme northeasterly corner of this sea, a matter of about 1200 miles in a straight line although sailing ships seldom sail in a straight line between such points. We had not caught a right whale and we were now in one of the three habitats of the bowhead whales, the others being the Bering Sea and the Arctic Ocean. If they exist anywhere else, the location is not known to the whalemen. It is a strange thing, that no one has seen a bowhead whale in the Pacific Ocean, yet the bowhead of the Okhotsk Sea is identical with the bowhead of the Bering Sea and the Arctic Ocean. The question is raised, which was the ancestral home and why have they ceased to exchange visits as it is only a short passage from one sea to the other. Scientists claim that the bowhead and the right whale are of the same family and the same whale. I have heard this subject discussed for hours by men who have killed more of these two types of whales than the scientists ever saw and I am accepting their conclusions that, while they are no doubt of the same family, they are very different in their habits and are never found in the same waters. Of course, some one will dispute this last statement because the right whale was caught in the Bering Sea before any bowheads had been seen there, but it was in the southeasterly part of this sea where the bowhead has never been seen and no right whale has ever been encountered in those parts of the sea that are frequented by the bowhead.

The first right whale was taken by the ship *Ganges*, Captain Barzillai T. Folger, of Nantucket in the year 1835 or 1836 on the "Kodiac Ground" which took its name from the small island of Kodiac on the south side of the Alaska Peninsula. It may be proper to call this the first northern right whale because there is sufficient difference between the northern and southern right whales for whalemen to declare most emphatically that they never cross the equator. The date of the first whaler entering the Bering Sea is not clear, it was soon after 1835, if not that year, and they were after the right whale. They whaled in the Kodiac Ground and in Bristol Bay which is on the Bering Sea side of the Alaska Peninsula. The right whale was rarely found north of St. Matthew Island, if ever, which is about latitude 61 north.

The first bowhead whale was taken in 1843 on the coast of Kamchatka which is the Asian side of Bering Sea. This capture was made by the ship *Janus,* Captain Turner, or the ship *Hercules,* Captain Ricketson. The date of the capture of the first bowhead in the Okhotsk Sea is not clear; it was probably in 1847 or 1848, by either the American ship *Huntsville* or the French ship *Asia.* The bowhead is a cold water whale and prefers waters in close proximity to ice. This does not agree with conditions in the Okhotsk Sea where there are long periods in the summer when there is no ice at all in that sea, but it may be that the bowhead is exterminated from those waters.

The hunt for the bowhead was confined to the Bering Sea for several years and many were taken off Karaginski Island in latitude 59 degrees on the coast of Kamchatka. Then they worked farther north and, for years, they were taken in the Gulf of Anadir on the Asia side. Finally, in 1848, the bark *Superior* of Sag Harbor, N.Y., Captain Royce, entered the Arctic Ocean and captured the first bowhead in those waters. No doubt, there was some of the spirit of adventure and exploration in this cruise as the resources of the Bering Sea had not been exhausted. My father entered these waters in the *South Boston* in either 1849 or 1850, probably both years, and took the last whale which filled every cask they had in the Bering Straits. So, the whalemen gradually worked further north and east until they reached Banks Island to the east of Mackenzie River. The number of these whales must have been tremendously reduced since 1843 but they are still taken in Bering Sea, on the Asian side, and they probably frequent the same regions that they always have.

The view of Captain H. H. Bodfish is interesting in this discussion, as he is both well read on Arctic literature and has been a close observer. It is his opinion that the bowhead never goes east of a line drawn from Cape Prince of Wales to the west end of St. Lawrence Island which is about in the center of Bering Sea. This is probably because of the shoal water on the easterly side of this line. He believes that the bowhead comes down into the Bering Sea in winter and remains on the Asian shore in the broken ice field and this is where they have been found in the spring. As soon as the ice permits, they move up the coast and into the Arctic Ocean where they cross to the American side and proceed east by Point Barrow. They go east to the Mackenzie River and then as far north as the ice will permit and, in August, they are seen coming from the north along the shore of Banks Island and Cape Bathurst. They work west as the ice makes and, if the "pack ice" is well down on the north coast, they go west earlier keeping close to the pack ice and stopping for a time off Herald Island. Then they go south through Bering Strait when the new ice forms and follow along the Asian coast to whatever point the solid ice ultimately makes.

The breeding grounds of the bowhead are not known definitely and it is doubtful if they are along the shore of Asia, for two reasons, they are there in the wrong season of the year and they are not seen in Bering Sea in the spring with young calves. There is good reason for believing that their breeding grounds are east of the Mackenzie River near Cape Bathurst which Sir John Franklin described as the "home of the black whale" many years ago. Captain Bodfish tells of seeing hundreds of the small black whales one year when whaling off the Mackenzie River which he, and most whalemen, thinks is a different breed although they are alike in looks, shape and habits. On this occasion, he states that a number of bowheads were in sight when the small whales first appeared but the bowheads were gone in a few minutes. In my opinion, they are the young bowheads returning to their first home.

In both of my trips to the Arctic Ocean, we entered the Bering Sea in May and made the ice well over to the Asian shore. The first voyage, in the ship *Hibernia* in 1870, we came directly from the Hawaian Islands and entered Bering Sea through one of the passes in the Aleutian Islands chain near the 180 degrees meridian. The second trip, in the bark *Monticello* the following year, we came from Yokohama, Japan, and entered the Sea near Copper

Island on the Asian side. There are plenty of codfish in the waters about the Aleutian Islands and we "hauled aback" on both trips and tried to catch some but were unsuccessful both times. Fish of various kinds are plentiful on the American side of Bering Sea and around the coast into the Arctic Ocean. There is an island a short distance north from Unimak Pass through the Aleutian Islands called Walrus Island which is a resort of fur seals and walrus but it is out of the course usually taken by whalers.

The whaleships look first for whales at the edge of the ice and, if the whales had found it possible to work north, the whalers were obliged to enter the ice and follow the whales. The ships rarely got out of the ice after entering it until they reached open water in the vicinity of St. Lawrence Island. As I recall, we were in the ice about four weeks in the *Hibernia* and about six weeks in the *Monticello*. This ice is much thinner than the ice in the Arctic Ocean and it is in smaller cakes. There was rarely any pressure of the ice against the ship and, as long as there were any "leads" open, sail was kept set and as much progress made north as possible. It was perfectly smooth whether the wind blew or not. The dazzling white of the ice in every direction as far as the eye could see was rather trying at first but one got used to it soon. It was a great relief to get out on the ice and stretch one's legs in a good long walk. Our little dog, in the *Monticello* cruise, was so glad at the opportunity for a long run that he started for 'Frisco but, as he did not know the difference between water and ice, he took a bath at the first hole he came to. He was a very surprised dog and it took some time to get him to go on the ice again.

We had built the "crow's-nest" before we reached the Sea, a canvas covered frame placed on the topmast crosstrees of the foremast, and regular masthead watches were stood by the officers and boatsteerers. We saw whales several times and the men went out on the ice to shoot them or fasten to them with an iron. We kept men at holes where whales might come up to breathe and several were shot with a bomb gun but lost. A dead whale was discovered one day from the masthead and men were sent out over the ice to claim possession in the name of our ship; we never did know who killed it. The ice was so thick that it took a number of days to get the ship to the whale and, by that time, the whale was badly "blasted." Whalemen speak of a dead whale as a "stinker" and it was unnecessary to ask why after this experience.

There was a hole of open water, one day, from about amidships for 100 feet astern and it was very calm with nearly everybody on deck. Suddenly, a big bowhead came up in this hole so close to the stern of the ship that one could have thrown a biscuit on him. Every one was immediately busy and two boats were lowered with my father and officers and boatsteerers as crews, with each officer carrying a bomb gun. It was very important to give the whale a death blow at once. The first mate, James Green, stood his gun against the stern sheets of his boat and leaned over it to unhook the falls when, in some way never accounted for, the gun went off and the lance cut through the flesh of his face from the lower jaw to a point above his eyebrow. He fell back into the arms of the officer next to him but he did not lose consciousness and, blinded with powder and blood, he came up the side of the ship practically un-aided. His wound was sewed up by my father without anesthetic or antiseptics, as they had none, and first, officers and finally my mother held his head while this sewing was done. The only scar in after years was at the lower eyelid which was severed and not exactly united. The bone was fractured above the eyebrow and a silver plate was inserted later and a scar remained here. There was one feature of this incident which I cannot overlook and that was the nerve and grit of one little woman compared to the big strong men. First one officer and then another, as they gave up sickened by the sight of blood, held Mr. Green's head while my father took the stitches but my mother had to take over and finish the job. The patient showed wonderful grit but could not keep from moving his head under the great pain. In my experience, a woman can be depended upon to show true nerve and grit at the crucial moment better than a man. Mr. Green stayed in his bunk for about four weeks and it was two weeks more before he went on active duty.

To return to the whale, the cause of all this trouble, he lay there and spouted for several minutes then "took a header and went down below" and that was the last we saw of him. We kept butting at the ice whenever the direction of the wind would permit us to carry sail. The *Monticello* was better prepared to butt ice as she had been a "Greenland whaler" and she had an extra course of oak planking for several feet above and below the water line the full length of the ship. She was protected further by iron plates at the bow for some distance back and she had heavy timber braces forward of the fore hatch and below the forecastle floor to resist crushing.

The *Hibernia* was a very strong built ship but had no extra reinforcing forward and we had knocked off all the projecting part of her stem. We tried various devices of mats of old hawsers and rafts of Southern California "iron" wood, lashed to the bow in front of the stem, but she was too heavy a vessel for such frail protection to be of real benefit. She was the largest ship in the whaling business at that time, being of 551 tons measurement. She was a full rigged ship with double topsails on each mast and she carried three royals, which made her a handsome sight under full sail. It is needless to say that every one knew it when she hit a cake of ice. My father never took things easy as with him time saved was time gained. We arrived in sight of Cape Navarin finally and, in a few days, we got into open water and passed between the shore of Asia and St. Lawrence Island.

We made a short call at Plover Bay on the Asia side to get what information we could from the natives as to when the whales went north and to trade for fur clothes, boots, etc. The officers and men wore as much of the native clothes from then on as they had been able to secure. I always wore the skin boots made of tanned seal skin with the hair on the inside and a thick layer of Manila oakum in the bottoms to take up the moisture, the natives use dry grass, but I never cared to wear the fur coats and shirts as the smell was too much for me. The natives are adepts at tanning skins and making garments and, in those days, they did all their sewing with sinew for thread.

We arrived at this same bay the following year just in time to assist the bark *Oriole* of New Bedford which had been stove by a cake of ice and the leak not discovered until a boatsteerer took off the fore hatch and jumped down into the hold to get an iron when he landed in water up to his waist. My father went aboard with a boat crew and several other ships sent men to help pump until they got her into Plover Bay where they put her on the beach to "heave her down" and to repair the leak. We afterward heard that they were obliged to abandon the ship as the leak could not be repaired. She was almost a new ship and was on the first season of her voyage and the owner's loss was great gain for the natives.

We raised whales about this time and got one, one boat going on to the whale under sail and the boatsteerer darted two irons into it. The sail and mast were taken down at once and passed aft out of the way and the exchange of places by officer and boatsteerer accomplished. If the officer can shoot a bomb lance into a vital place in the whale, he will spout quantities of dark red blood and soon roll over dead. The other boats took in their sails, got out their oars and went to the aid of the "fast boat" to tow the whale to the ship.

As I have described the cutting in of a sperm whale, I will add how the treatment of the head of a bowhead whale differs and not repeat the blubber part which is the same. The headchain is passed through the spout hole and the cutting block hooked on. Then a man goes down on the whale and cuts through the spinal column with an axe. The windlass heaves on the "head fall" and, if necessary, a purchase is hooked to the head from the after part of the ship and the head hauled aft. As soon as the head is thus unjointed, it is hoisted aboard and lowered on deck. Heaving on the blanket piece brought up the other lip and further heaving brought up the throat and tongue. The tongue of the bowhead is very large and full of oil. The skin of the outside of the throat near the end of the jaw is generally white and delicate, compared with the skin of the rest of the body, and when it is cooked in hot oil it tastes like the white of an egg. It is another process in cutting in a bowhead to cut off strips of "black skin" to be cooked in oil and eaten. When the carcass is unjointed from the flukes, that member is hoisted aboard to cut out the fluke chain and the flukes then thrown overboard. The fins are used in swimming but the flukes are the principal propelling power and also the rudder and weapon of defense. The flukes propel the whale by a sculling motion although the resemblance to a two-bladed propeller is quite striking.

The next operation is to remove the slabs of bone from the gum which secures them to the curved bone of the upper part of the head. This bone is entirely different from the bone that is the frame of the whale's body. It is more like horn and is very elastic, being laminar in structure flatways of the slab and it can be split into thin sections. The outer edge of each slab is curved forward about two inches in width near the butt, gradually flattening out to nothing at the end. The slabs are packed close together with the rounded part overlapping the slab in front. The inner edge of each slab is fringed with coarse hair several inches in length. There are more than 600 slabs of bone in a large whale which vary in length from about 14 feet to two feet more or less. The weight of this bone will vary from 2000 to 3000 pounds according to the size of the grown whale. The peculiar substance which attaches the slabs to the head, called "gums," fills the space between the slabs and fits into a concave cavity in the under side of the real bone frame of the head. This gum is bloodless, white and somewhat like very tough cheese. It is separated from the head with the spades and it is then divided into pieces containing five or six slabs and stowed in the hold. After the whaling is finished and the ship is bound for port, this bone is brought on deck and each slab cut out, the gum scraped off and the slab washed clean. They are then tied in bundles of convenient size to handle. This bone reached a value of four to five dollars a pound which explains why the later whaleships were interested in catching whales for the bone only.

The whale uses this great mass of bone suspended from the upper jaw to secure the food which is an animalcula that floats on the waters of the Bering Sea and Arctic Ocean in enormous quantities. It is very fine, no larger than grains of rice swollen in water. The whale swims close to the surface with his lower jaw dropped and the lips thrown out from the head and waving slowly so as to draw as much water as possible into the open mouth and the food with it. The water passes out of the mouth through the spaces between the slabs of bone but the fringe of hair retains the particles of food by acting as a sieve. When the whale has a mouthful, the lower jaw is closed, the lips pressed into place and the food swallowed. The combined use of tongue and lips helps to force the water out of the mouth. The tongue is enormous but the throat of the bowhead is no larger than a man's fist. The right whale lives upon similar food so, it must be evident, that neither species can be accused with swallowing Jonah.

The right whale and the bowhead are the two outstanding members of the baleen family because they have the baleen, or whale bone of commerce, in its most highly developed form. The sulpherbottom, finback, humpback and California gray have whale bone but it is so short that it has no commercial value.

The right whale of the northwest Pacific coast and the Bering Sea was a very large, fat whale. The largest output of oil that I have knowledge of, was produced by a right whale captured in Bristol Bay, on the Alaska side of Bering Sea, which stowed down 313 barrels of oil. It was evident that right whales of that area were unusually large and fat because right whales caught in other areas were not noted for their yield of oil.

The right whale of the Bering Sea area has a peculiar bony growth on the extreme outer end of the upper jaw, called a "bonnet" by whalemen, which nothing is known about. It is apparently completely extraneous with an uneven surface, like an enormous seed wart, with the substance similar to whale bone except it has no fibre. The upper part of the head of the right whale, to which the whale bone is attached, is not as curved as that of the bowhead whale. The spout of the bowhead is one straight column when the whale is on the surface to breathe but, the spout of the right whale is in two streams from the double spout hole, called a "forked spout" by whalemen. When the right whale goes down they always "turn flukes" which is throwing their tail out of the water. The bowhead does not always do this but some times does it.

The right whale when struck, that is fastened to by the iron from a boat, unless mortally wounded, will run very fast and for long distances, often compelling the boat to cut the line to avoid being taken out of sight of the ship. The right whale often fights hard with his flukes which is very dangerous to the boats. The bowhead rarely runs very fast for any distance although they generally make for the ice and often escape in that way. They seldom fight but they are wicked when they do so. I saw a bowhead bring his flukes down on a boat several times without doing any damage beyond breaking an oar or two. It was quite evident that the act was not malicious or the boat would have been destroyed.

The bowhead seldom defend their young and desert them on the first evidence of danger to themselves. The right whales always defend their young.

The right whale of the Japan Sea was quite apt to sink when dead while the bowhead seldom sinks, if ever, and I doubt that the right whale of the Bering Sea ever sinks after death. The cause of the sinking of whales is a much disputed point between whalemen. Some hold that it is caused by the rupture of an air sac or cavity in the whale while others claim that it is purely individual with the whales of different species. It is well known that the humpback whale nearly always sinks and, for that reason, is always sought in shoal waters. I do not recall hearing of a sperm whale sinking but, on the other hand, the finback and other species, namely the California gray, frequently do so. It depends upon the depth of the water whether the whale can be brought to the surface again. If it is not too deep for the ship to anchor near the whale so that the line to the iron can be brought aboard ship, the whale will come to the surface in a day or two when the gases of decomposition increase the flotation. If the iron is well toggled in tough tissue, a steady strain can be held on the line to hasten the flotation.

The right whale runs to windward after being struck, often at such a speed that it is difficult to haul up close enough to kill him even with a bomb lance. In many cases the iron drew or the line had to be cut on account of darkness or distance from the ship. The right whale is not a fighter, in the sense that he will attack a boat, he is extremely quick to strike with his flukes if the boat or an oar happens to touch the rear of his body. As I recall the many discussions that I have listened to between officers and captains concerning the traits and fighting qualities of the different whales, the conclusion is very clear in my mind that they had the greatest respect for the right whale. The California gray is more pugnacious but he is not so disposed to run away with the boat but, just to show how difficult it is to adopt a rule of conduct for any branch of the whale family, a California gray ran away with two of our boats fast to him and they had to cut their lines after firing eight or ten bomb lances into various parts of his body.

The sperm whale is not only a fighter but a vindictive cuss, on occasion, in that he will attack when he might run away. There are cases on record where they have attacked and destroyed the ship but the whalemen I knew were never much in awe of a sperm whale. They often try one stunt and that is to sound as soon as they are struck. We had one whale on the *Monticello* voyage take four tubs of line in a perpendicular dive but he came up within a very short distance of where he started and the boat that was fast to him pulled up and killed him with a bomb lance. Those very deep dives are usually followed by a long breathing spell during which the whale will not run fast. I do not want to give the impression that a sperm whale was not dangerous, because the records hold ample proof to the contrary, but the whalemen of my acquaintance had a wide experience as they had successfully hunted and killed all of the species that inhabit the seas. Each type was dangerous but these men had learned their ways and they were not inclined to magnify or belittle them. It was true that, comparing all the conditions then attached to the whaling business, the Arctic Ocean whaling was the most dangerous as an enterprise although the bowhead was probably the least dangerous of all the whales as an opponent.

The winter cruise in the South Pacific was a diversion and not a constant struggle for the safety of the ship and its crew. In fact, it was called the "between season" cruise to distinguish it from the real object of the voyage which was the Arctic Ocean or the Okhotsk Sea. The whalemen I have in mind were the last of the broadly experienced men in the business and, as they passed on, their places were not filled. In a few years, the "between season" cruise was abandoned and my father never went to the South Pacific again. The Arctic fleet finally concentrated their efforts on the cruise to the Arctic where many of them wintered at the mouth of the Mackenzie River. A few ships, mostly from New Bedford, made occasional cruises to the South Pacific and the Japan Sea either outward or homeward bound. Honolulu was entirely abandoned as a refitting port and San Francisco took its place. The business had even then started upon a series of changes that gradually robbed it of its color and romance and finally ended in its complete extinction. But strange to say, it did not leave a large body of employable men looking for jobs. The men who had created a great industry and, who had become the finest body of mariners the world has ever seen, passed on with the ships and left no successors.

Arctic Ocean whaling was extremely prosperous for a few years owing to the demand for whalebone, which finally reached such high prices that the whalers saved the heads only and let the bodies with the valuable blubber go, because it was claimed the opportunity to catch other whales would be lost if they stopped to try out the oil. This was an extravagant and wasteful decision by a management that had become money mad. Steamers had replaced the sailing ships and, with this great gain in speed and saving in time, they were still too short of time to cut in the whales as the trying out could have been done while under way. A comparison of the catches of these steam whalers with the old sailing ships shows how silly this practice was. For example, we came out of the Arctic Ocean in 1870 as ship wrecked passengers in the ship *Josephine*,

Captain Bernard Cogan, who had 26 whales for the season's catch and every one had been cut in and the oil tried out. I know of no catch by a steam whaler comparable with this one season's catch by the *Josephine* which was not an isolated case as many of the sailing ships made remarkably successful voyages to the Arctic Ocean.

This has been a digression and I will return to our progress through the Okhotsk Sea to North East Bay. Bearing out my previous assertion that life at sea was never monotonous, and shortly after leaving the Japan Sea, the first mate reported to my father that the foremast hands were seriously disturbed by the actions of the man we shipped in Guam. They said he was crazy and should be locked up, recalling the experience with the crazy Kanaka. The man was called aft and my father and the first mate tried to find out what was troubling him. He knew a few English words and was evidently distressed as to his future. Everything he could not understand was construed as a personal menace adding to his fears. He made no complaint against any of his shipmates and he was evidently in good physical condition as he had gained weight. The steward talked with him in his own tongue but could learn nothing more than that he thought his life was in danger. It is a nuisance to lock up a man aboard a ship for more than a few days and there is the danger of an investigation by the Court, either at the instigation of the man through his consul or by a charge by some member of the crew. The crew seemed honest in their fear of the man but how far they could be trusted was a question, however, it was a serious matter. My father decided to have the man watched carefully and to relieve him of going aloft.

A few days later, he came aft during the dog watch and went down on his knees before my father. He talked a lot of jargon that nobody could understand. My father talked to him and then sent him forward apparently satisfied that no one intended to harm him. He repeated this action in a few days and then it became a daily occurrence. I marvelled at my father's patience but I knew something would break soon. My father was walking back and forth on the poop deck when the Chamorro came aft and up the steps to the upper deck but, just as he started to drop on his knees, my father reached over and gripped him by the collar with his right hand. He then straightened the man up, whirled him around and gave him a vigorous shove forward, followed by the toe of his boot in the seat of the man's pants. When the man struck the deck, he was fully ten feet from the steps and he did not stop moving until he was forward of the tryworks. Strange as it may be, that was the end of his prayers and of all his doubts and fears. He was permanently cured and made no more trouble. Whether he had conceived the scheme in his own head or had been inspired to work the bluff by his shipmates, we never knew, but the episode was ended.

The crew had acquired a goat while we were at Saipan and they devoted quite a lot of time to teaching him tricks as he was a real pet. I knew something about billy goats as I owned one in Oakland until he took possession of the veranda one day and refused to let my mother enter the house until I came home from school, so he changed owners. There was one rule of the ship that Billy could not or would not learn, that he belonged forward of the waist. Perhaps, the fact that the galley was aft of the mainmast and he soon learned that the eats came from there because he was always hungry, was his trouble about this rule. In the course of time, Billy's primeval instincts aided by skillful coaching began to assert itself and, whenever a man stooped over to coil a piece of running gear, Billy took it as a challenge and would land with his head in the seat of the man's overalls. It was treated as a good joke but, as Billy gained weight and experience, it ceased to be funny to the recipient of this action. It always brought a laugh from the spectators and it was very destructive of discipline as Billy was thoroughly democratic and the southerly exposures of men all looked the same to him. Therefore, the inevitable happened, when the cook accidentally left the galley door open while he was conferring with the steward and Billy went in and ate a panful of dough that was ready to be baked for the men forward. He was the evidence of his guilt as he was swelled up as if he had swallowed a balloon.

This affair was duly reported to the first mate who promptly notified the watch that the goat would be thrown overboard the first time he came aft of the mainmast. Everybody felt sorry for Billy because we all knew he had an awful load on his stomach. Not long after this, the first mate, while facing aft to shield his pipe from the back draft of the mainsail, dropped his match and stooped to pick it up when a gray streak of goat landed where the mate intended to scratch the match and he nearly went through the cabin bulkhead. Billy was given a good licking and was kept tied up forward until he was given to some natives who came aboard at North East Gulf and thus ended his sea voyage.

One morning as I lay in my berth wondering if it was time to turn out, I noticed a peculiar sound to the water rushing by on the other side of the planking that indicated the old girl was slipping right along but I also observed that she was rolling very slowly and easy which did not fit with the swish of the water. I hurried into my clothes and then through the cabin still trying to interpret that steady, easy roll. As I reached the deck, I looked up over the combing of the cabin bulkhead to see the sky as I instinctively noted we were running before the wind under topsails, but I was now looking at a wall of water right astern of us and, as my eyes travelled up to find the top, I realized that it was a following sea whose crest appeared to be as high as the mizzen crosstrees and it looked about to fall on top of us. I have never come so near being paralyzed with fear in my life and could neither move nor speak, but I saw the crest of that wave was settling and it passed out of my sight below the combing of the cabin and a beautiful clear, blue sky took its place. How we had escaped that particular sea I could not tell and, then I turned around and looked forward, to see that we were about to make a dive to the bottom of the ocean. But the bow commenced to lift and presently the flying jib boom was reaching for the zenith. Then I looked aft again and there was the towering wall of water looking down on the ship but, once more the stern lifted, the sea passed out of sight and the phenomenon was explained to my intense relief. We were running dead before the wind in a moderate gale with an unusually long, and heavy sea, which was not curling or breaking. It had evidently been blowing very heavy but we had missed the full force of the wind. The seas were so long that the ship was simply sliding down the slope of one sea and sailing up the slope of the next, with the distance between seas considerably more than twice the length of the ship which enabled her to pass over them without shipping any water or rolling heavily. As a matter of fact, our decks were perfectly dry. A large ship might have had a hard time but the little *Florence* fitted the seas and had a comfortable time. The strength of the wind was not in keeping with the size of the seas, therefore, we had no difficulty in carrying enough sail to keep the ship ahead of the seas. We had a whole main-topsail, double reefed fore-topsail and the whole foresail.

When the ship was at the bottom of the hollow between the seas, the wind was entirely cut off from the sails by the sea astern and they either hung limp or came back against the mast but, as she came out of the hollow, the wind filled the sails again and as she went over the top of the sea they received the full force of the gale and we raced down the other side with the main topsail threatening to leave its bolt ropes. That sail was the principal driving force, the fore-topsail did very little, but the foresail got the wind from under the main topsail and helped to balance the forces that were trying to turn the ship on her heel. She was steering well with one man at the wheel while some ships would have kept two men spinning the wheel first one way and then the other. It was under such conditions that the old-fashioned tiller wheel used to exercise the legs of the helmsman as well as his arms as the tiller swept back and forth over the deck. The seas were the largest I had ever seen and they rose and fell with the regularity of a clock. I was fascinated with the following sea although I knew they were huge undulations of the water over which we were sailing and not rolling. I could not keep my eyes off that enormous wall of water as it towered above our little ship; it seemed to be chasing us and just missing by such a narrow margin that sooner or later we must be caught and then we would be swamped, but we always slipped away just in time to avoid such a catastrophe.

Running before a gale is more or less dangerous and much depends upon the ship as some run well and some very badly. The *Florence* was a flat-floored ship and never had to be hove to because she could not run. Certain writers of sea tales always have as a climax to a storm the ship scudding before the gale under bare poles regardless of whether or not that is in the direction of her destination. There are two difficulties that must be overcome in the operation of a ship running before a gale; first, she must be kept truly before the wind which is difficult with some ships that steer badly and, therefore, those ships are constantly in danger of "broaching to," that is to come up to the wind, which is a very dangerous maneuver as the ship must pass through the trough of the sea and that has foundered many a good ship. Second, the ship must be kept ahead of the seas in order that they will not come over the stern and cause a lot of trouble. Sometimes, the man at the wheel is washed overboard or seriously injured and the cabin is flooded and then the ship broaches to. To carry sail enough to keep the ship moving when down in the hollows between the seas and not have too much sail when she comes up on the crests of the seas is the problem that must be solved and experience is the only safe guide. Toward afternoon, the wind and the sea went down and we were again under full sail but the remembrance of that day will remain with me always. I had acquired a better appreciation of the weatherly qualities of the ship and I took back some of the mean things I had said about her on the passage from Guam.

We raised land the next morning and, that afternoon, we anchored in the upper part of North East Gulf with the shore of Kamchatka on the east and the mainland of Siberia on the west. A small island lay midway between the shores and a short distance to the north the Gulf opened into a bay which we were to enter later. There were several whale ships here and we had our first "gam" in several months. Following the usual custom, the captain of the other ship came aboard the *Florence* as we were a "lady ship" and our first mate returned to the other ship with their boat but his own crew manning it. I generally went with the mate as it gave me a change of scene and the opportunity to get new reading matter. I was treated to the best the ship had and was entertained with the recital of their experiences and the ships they had met.

There was quite a bit of curiosity as to how many ships had come to Okhotsk Sea and what would be the attitude of the Russian Government toward the American ships. A rumor had reached the ships that a Russian man-of-war had been ordered to drive all foreign whalers out of the sea and, while the captains rather expected it might happen, we did not meet any warships during the time we were in Russian waters. There was doubt as to the authority of the Russian Government because American whalers had been coming to the Okhotsk Sea for many years but it was agreed that it would be of little use to argue that question with the captain of a warship if his orders were to drive us out. Furthermore, the Okhotsk Sea is a large body of water and the captain of a warship might not find us, unless he knew the location of the whaling grounds. As a matter of fact, the whales were found in North East Gulf, South West Bay and Shantar Bay in the opposite corner of the Sea, at that time.

An interesting phase of the situation from our point of view, was the fact that my uncle, Captain Lewis Williams, was there in a Russian ship because it was partly his understanding that his ship would have Russian protection and he would have some influence in the selection of the ships that would be allowed to stay in Russian waters, and this was a factor in our being there in an American ship. No Russian ship appeared and all our fears were groundless but it continued to be an interesting subject of conversation between the captains and officers of the different ships whenever they met and, as no word was received by my uncle or any one else, we were in continual expectation of a visit from the Russians as long as we stayed in the Okhotsk Sea. It was rather tough luck for my uncle as his ship was the only one that did not get any oil and was the only ship with the legal right to be there. None of the ships in the fleet of seven or eight ships made a really good catch but the Russian ship *Tirgur* was white washed. My uncle had his wife with him which was of great interest to our family as we were all very fond of both of them but we knew that we would not see them until we went to South West Bay as they were not coming to North East Gulf. However, it gave our family something to look forward to eagerly.

Shortly after our arrival at the head of the Gulf, natives came aboard with fresh salmon which we bought and found it to be a most appetizing change from our diet of salt beef and pork. We were told that the streams were literally jammed with salmon but my father was more concerned with whales than fresh fish at that time so no provisions were made to increase the supply of our food. The natives reminded me of those we saw on the other side of the peninsula in the Bering Sea but we did not call them Eskimos. They wore fur clothing and were excessively dirty, but they were Siberians.

We discovered soon after anchoring that there was a very heavy current growing out of a rise and fall of over twenty feet in the tides. This was the heaviest tidal movement I had ever encountered and it had to be reckoned with in our plans for any movement of the ship. On one occasion, we undertook to work out of the upper bay against a head wind that unexpectedly grew into a fair sized gale just as we reached the narrowest part of the passage. The wind blowing against the tide kicked up a short undercut sea that gave us the worst mauling for a few hours that I can remember. The swinging cabin lamp burned kerosene oil and had a glass chimney which I had never known to be pitched off, but that night, she threw them on the cabin floor as fast as they could be replaced and we finally had to substitute a regulation oil lamp without a chimney to save the few glass chimneys that were left. The sea became normal as the turn of the tide approached and we worked down the gulf but the weather conditions were poor for whaling and we decided finally to run back to the head of the bay with the other ships. As we came up into the wind, we decided to anchor ahead of the *Arnolda* which gave us plenty of room to swing clear of two other ships already at anchor and placed us in a convenient position for gamming.

The ship commenced to drag as soon as our anchor hit bottom and chain was payed out to bring her up but she continued to drag under the combined effect of the tide and the seas that rolled in from the blow in the gulf. The bottom was rocky and smooth which prevented the anchor from holding although the man at the wheel was steering the ship after the anchor to give it a chance to catch but still we dragged with the chain shivering and shaking as the anchor bumped along over the rocky bottom. We then dropped the other anchor and gave it the same length of chain that had been payed out with the first anchor but still she dragged and we were bearing down on the *Arnolda* and it seemed a collision was inevitable. This ship was now directly astern and, as she rose and fell to the seas, it seemed that we were being drawn into a gigantic shears from which there was no escape. My father was pacing up and down on the quarter deck and my mother and sister were watching the *Arnolda* as her jib boom towered above us one moment and just missed our spanker boom the next. I was in a near panic as it seemed that nothing could be done and it was too late to take to the boats. It seemed certain that the next jump would bring the two ships together as we were still dragging with the anchors shaking the ship from stem to stern. All of a sudden, there was action and the *Arnolda* was off on our starboard quarter entirely removed from any possibility of a collision and, in another moment, our anchors caught on some projection of the bottom and the ship stopped dragging.

The change came about so quickly and smoothly that I could not realize what had happened and then it was all as clear as the beautiful sunshine about us. Captain Bouldry had waited until it was apparent that our ship would not swing either way and then he had his wheel put hard a-port and his ship swung to starboard picked up her anchor and dragged out of our way. The tide running by the ship had the same effect on the rudder as if she had been going through the water under sail. If our anchors had held for only a few minutes, so as to get the effect of the moving water on our rudder, we could have done the same thing to avoid a collision. Well, it was all over without any shouting of orders or any visible evidence of fear or serious concern on anyone's part as to the outcome of the situation. Just the same, there was one boy on the little old bark *Florence* who would have liked to give a real cheer for the resourcefulness of Captain Bouldry of the bark *Arnolda* but, of course, such evidence of hysteria was not to be thought of although I wondered if everybody felt as calm as they appeared to be. Aboard a ship is one place where you learn to control your emotions. You can bluff your fellow man but you cannot bluff the elements. I presume that is one reason why I heard very little boasting during my life on a whaleship. It is a strange side light of human nature that a calling which depended entirely upon individual skill, courage and resourcefulness should have so completely eliminated the boaster. The American whaleman had an unusual career; his success was due entirely to individual accomplishment and, yet the higher he climbed the ladder of success, the more reticent and reserved he grew as to his part in that career. My mind often drifts back to those clear eyed men of the sea when I am obliged to listen to the lurid description of the terrible fights some man thinks he has had to reach his goal, and I wonder what is his conception of a fight.

Captain Bouldry soon came aboard and I did not return to his ship with our mate as he was one of my father's cronies and, when they were together, the reminiscing was worth listening to. It was seldom that this Captain passed up an opportunity for a gam on our ship. On one occasion, he came aboard when both ships were under reefed topsails and getting a boat away from the ship and alongside another ship is some trick in moving ships but, in such weather, it seemed that it would be attemped only if obligatory. He came aboard just for an afternoon call. Such skill with a ship in distress and a crew to be saved has brought world wide acclaim to the fortunate participants. But no one would accuse a whaleman of making a grandstand play for the applause of the gallery because, to them, it was all part of the day's work. If a whale had been raised, they would have lowered and made a capture without a moment's hesitation.

This diversion reminds me of the last whale taken by the ship *Josephine* when on our way out of the Arctic, after we had lost our ship *Hibernia* at Point Barrow earlier in the season, some four years before this voyage, and we were guests of Captain Cogan. It was blowing quite a fresh gale from the north and we were running under easy canvas when a bowhead was raised close at hand. The first mate insisted on lowering as the signs were favorable for an easy capture and, although Captain Cogan would not have ordered an officer to lower under the conditions, he would not refuse his request to lower. The ship was hauled aback and the first mate's boat lowered, as it would be a quick job if successful, and one boat would be safer than two boats with the ship standing by to drop another boat if required. The whale was taking it easy, entirely unconscious of any danger, and the mate went on and fastened. The boatsteerer got his irons home in a vulnerable spot and, although the whale ran to windward for a short distance, they soon had him spouting blood and in a very short time he was alongside the ship. The boat's crew were literally encased in ice from their waist down and they had to be hoisted over the rail in bowlines, a type of knot that forms a loop. As an exhibition of courage and skill, it would seem to have merited some form of special recognition but, outside of a drink of hard liquor and an admonishment to get into dry clothes as quickly as possible, the event was closed when the crew came over the rail. It was just a part of the day's work.

Captain Bouldry had been in a Japanese port and told some interesting experiences ashore that recalled our visit to Yokohama three years before and intensified our regrets that we had been obliged to abandon our plans to visit Hakodate on this cruise. Comparison of our experiences to date revealed the information that, of the four ships present, no one had been particularly successful and the outlook was not bright as no one had seen any whales which seemed strange in view of the fact that the whalers had not visited those waters for several years. However, it was early in the season and, if the whales were not in the Gulf, they were in the bays in the opposite corner of the Sea, but these captains agreed that they would stay there a few days longer to be sure their conclusion was correct.

My attention was called to the presence of two sun dogs in the sky while we lay at anchor on a very quiet day. Actually, there appeared to be three suns quite clearly defined behind a thin covering of light gray clouds. The real sun was the central one with a dog on each side but there was no appreciable difference in their size, shape or illumination. It was rather a weird sight, although not unusual, but I had never seen one before and, in fact, I have not seen the sun with two dogs since. I have seen the sun with one dog on many occasions since then. Of course, some of the men said it was a sign of bad weather. The gale that followed verified their prediction and gave them an opportunity to remark to me that, if the old man had taken the warning, we would have missed a very uncomfortable night and all the trouble that followed.

There finally came a day when a bowhead whale was raised and the first and second mates lowered. Sails were set and both boats headed for the whale as directed by signals from the ship. It was a quiet day with a whole sail breeze and only one whale was in sight. The other ships were too far off to take any interest in the affair although their men at masthead had probably reported to the deck that the *Florence* had lowered two boats. It was an accepted understanding among whalemen that, when a lone whale was raised, he would be left to the ship whose boats were first in the water. Sometimes two ships would join forces, or "mate" as it was called, and then divide the proceeds. The ship nearest to the whale when killed would cut it in and try out the oil although the actual capture may have been by the boats of the other ship. Then later, the oil and bone, if there was any, would be divided. If a dead whale was picked up, it would be surrendered to the boats of the ship whose name was on the iron found in the whale, if they were on the spot before the iron could be cut out and thrown overboard. The old whalemen could tell some very interesting stories about dead whales that had been picked up and the irons cut out almost under the eyes of the boat's crew that had killed it but had lost their line shortly before the whale went into his flurry.

In one case, a boat went onto the dead whale and the boatsteerer darted an iron into him just as though he was alive and then he changed ends with the officer who fired a bomb lance into the dead whale, but it did not fool the Argus-eyed captain in the crow's-nest of the ship to whom the whale really belonged. One of their boats reached the scene before their iron could be cut out because the captain had noted that the whale died without spouting blood, a most unusual occurrence. The irons of every ship are marked on the side of the head with the name of the ship and the number of the boat cut into the metal with a die. The initials were used for the boats also and, on the *Florence* which was a four boat ship, they were designated by the initials B.W., W.B., L.B. and S.B. for bow boat, waist boat, larboard boat and starboard boat, respectively. The dead whales are known as "stinker" because they decompose rapidly and generate very offensive odors. One of the very successful captains picked up so many dead whales in one season that he was ever after referred to as "Stinker —— " by the whalemen.

BOWHEAD WHALE

THE whale our boats were chasing ceased blowing and went down apparently unaware of the presence of our boats, although they were near enough to note his course and speed. The boats proceeded along that course for about the time the whale might be expected to stay down, which is roughly a minute for each spout while on the surface, and then they slacked off their sheets and drifted. When the whale came up he was some distance from the boats but he was still moving leisurely and spouting with a regularity that indicated a peaceful state of mind. A bowhead has a single spout which rises fairly high with a slight pitch forward and has considerable volume so that it is readily visible for a considerable distance. On a quiet day, the intake of air following the spout makes a very distinctive noise that can be heard for a long distance. The boats hauled in their sheets again and laid their course for the whale but, again, he sounded before they could reach him and when he came up the next time, he was still farther away in another direction. Nobody knew what had happened but, evidently, he was not to be our whale and the first mate returned to the ship although the boats were not recalled. Suddenly, there was an excited cry of "There blows" from the crow's-nest followed almost immediately by the words "He's fast" and, sure enough, the second mate's boat was fast and the ship was headed for the spot. It was not an exciting affair and when the ship arrived, the whale was dead and a line was fast in his flukes ready to be picked up from the ship as we came alongside. Apparently, the whale had no particular objective which brought him back to the waiting boat as he aimlessly cruised about. It fitted with the reputation of the second mate to never leave a whale while there was any possibility of getting fast. Harry, his boatsteerer, was all smiles as he came over the rail as his boat was hoisted on to her cranes and, well he might feel good, as he had sunk two irons to their hitches in the body of the whale that now lay alongside the ship.

One look at the whale and I was satisfied that it would yield the largest amount of oil from any whale I had seen. The result verified this conclusion as he stowed down 160 barrels of oil and almost 2000 pounds of bone. The body was not as long as the sperm whale we caught in the Pacific but it was much more bulky and the blubber was twice as thick and full of oil. The color of the blubber was a dark yellow and the skin was blacker and much thicker than that of the sperm whale. While the head of a sperm whale is the most prominent feature, and constitutes about one third of his bulk, the head of a bowhead is even larger and also his most prominent feature. There is nothing in common between the heads of these two types of the whale family although each is specifically adapted to its purpose. The sperm whale, as I have already noted, lives on the deep sea squid and he is really a carnivora. The whale can chop up the squid and swallow the pieces whole as he cannot chew them. The bowhead might be called a vegetarian as they live on that very low form of life which is almost on the line between organic and inorganic. This gelatinous substance floats on the surface of Okhotsk Sea, Bering Sea and the Arctic Ocean in such masses that it discolors the water over large areas. The whale must have a large mouth and a convenient arrangement for separating the food from the water and that is just what the head of the bowhead and right whales is designed to accomplish.

The whale we had alongside gave me an opportunity to study the head more closely than any ideas formed from a discussion and I can enlarge on my previous description. The upper jaw has a very pronounced bow from the crown, or top above the eyes, to the nib end which is rather narrow. The spout hole is in the very top of the crown and has two passages separated by a tough membrane leading back into the lungs. The slabs of bone hanging from the upper jaw form a tent like structure as they slope outward and they varied in length in this whale from about eighteen inches at the throat to sixteen feet. This whale was unusually large and the bone would normally be about twelve feet in maximum length. There are between 300 and 400 slabs of bone in each side of the upper jaw. The lower jaw starts quite wide at the body end but narrows as it curves around the nib end and the lower lips are huge as they fold against the upper jaw and entirely enclose the slabs of bone, when the mouth is closed. The space between the two sides of the lower jaw is nearly filled with the huge tongue which is very rich in oil. One is awed by this huge mouth which is hard to visualize and, even when actually seen, it is hard to estimate its size. The head is about one third the length of the whale and it appears to be all mouth. The natural question of the novice is, why such a big mouth for such small food? The whale certainly takes a mouthful is one answer.

The eyes are just back of the corners of the mouth and the ears are a few inches back of the eyes. The head is taken aboard in four operations, first a lip from the lower jaw, then the throat and tongue, then the other lower lip and finally the upper jaw. The whale has been stripped of the blubber and is laying on his belly so the upper jaw can be disjointed just back of the spout hole and the entire head hoisted aboard, that is, the jaw, two rows of slabs of whalebone hanging from it and the upper mass of gum and top of the head. The tongue of this whale was as large as a ten-barrel cask and about as near the shape of a cask as anything I can think of.

The skin at the nib end is as white as milk and is called "white skin" to distinguish it from the black skin of the rest of the body. Every whale has skin of the same structure, as far as I am able to judge from my observations, although it varies in thickness. The skin of this bowhead was the thickest I had ever seen. I have already stated that the skin of a whale is entirely different from that of any animal known to man. It has no strength in comparison with the skin of any land animal or of any large members of the fish family, such as the shark. It is easily scratched or scored with any hard implement and it contains no blood vessels. However, it is firmly attached to the blubber which must assist in carrying any unusual stress upon the skin from either internal or external causes. The Eskimo is very fond of black skin as it seems to take the place of bread while white skin is a delicacy. This white skin of the throat is very palatable even when cooked in oil in the trypots but, if fried in lard, it is really good eating. All in all, the skin of a whale is a remarkable substance and it has always seemed strange to me that scientists have had so little to say about it. Whale meat is not very different from the meat of any animal except in the coarseness of the grain. It is dark red and not bad eating, if soaked in water thoroughly to extract the oily flavor that is rather unpleasant, if the meat is cooked as it comes from the body. We were very busy for several days trying out and stowing down the oil and separating the bone into sections of eight or ten slabs for convenience in stowing the bone in the hold.

We saw more whales but they were shy and always got away. It was tantalizing as we disliked to leave as long as there were whales and we might catch one any day. My father lowered every time a whale was raised. The cooper finally objected to going in his boat as boatsteerer and I was promoted to his position. I was greatly pleased, of course, as I was sure my father would not have given me the place unless he believed that I could fill it. I had been growing very fast and was strong so that I was undoubtedly physically fit and I knew as much about a boat as any of the crew for I was always in one. My father's boat was in the water as often as any of the boats, taking gamming into account. I also had taken the place of any man in the other boats when he was ill. Life took on a more interesting and important outlook and I prayed for an opportunity to show that I could dart an iron as far and true as any of the boatsteerers. Of course, I had to stand some joking by the officers but I got by the preliminary tests, such as shipping my oar in coming alongside the ship at the order "Ship in forward" when the oar is tossed out of the oarlock with the blade forward and then slipped aft over the thwarts without interfering with the men. The next duty is to throw the boat's warp in a neat coil so that the end lands on deck in easy reach of the man waiting for it. Then the forward tackle is hooked on at the order of the officer in the stern sheets and the boat is fended off the side of the ship as it is hoisted to position. It all sounds very simple but it is liable to mishaps in rough water. I had seen it done a great many times and the weather was moderate during the first days of my apprenticeship which gave me time to practice.

My father finally decided to leave the Gulf, which was called Ohijinsk or Penjinsk by the Russians depending whether you were on the west or east side, and we laid our course for South West Bay which took us through the entire length of the Sea and out of the sight of land. We had been in sight of land all the time in the Gulf and the bay at its head, sometimes quite close, but we did not go ashore as it was rather barren and unattractive. I was sorry that we did not stop at Okhotsk City which was the capital, so to speak, of that part of Siberia and had an official representative of the Russian Government known as the Governor, but there was more than a suspicion that he was an exile.

It had more than a passing interest for my mother as she had visited at the Governor's house for about two weeks when I was a baby and I had taken this opportunity to have the croup, for the first and only time in my life. My father was away on the ship at that time and my mother was terribly worried. There was no doctor available and no medicine that she knew anything about. The Governor and his family were very much disturbed also and, although anxious to do something to relieve my distress, they could not talk English and my mother could not talk Russian. The situation began to be serious when my mother remembered the old New England remedy of a hot onion poultice applied to the throat and chest and she recalled that she had seen onions growing in the garden near the house. The next problem was to get the onions but, finally, she made the family understand that what she wanted grew in their garden and they brought in the products of the garden until they came with the onions. The poultice was made very soon and applied and, in a very short time, I was breathing normally and the excitement was over. All things considered, it was not the proper time for the master of an American whaleship to be calling on a Russian official even though he might be an old friend.

One afternoon, we raised two devil fish, or California grays, and my father lowered with the third mate as boatsteerer as he intended to use a darting gun. I had no experience with this gun and my father did not consider it wise to let me try it with my first attempt in the head of the boat. I was terribly disappointed but I realized that he would be taking a long chance with me, not only on account of the unwieldy nature of the darting gun but because of the necessity of striking the whale near a vital spot to secure any advantage from the bomb lance. The gun carried an iron as well as a loaded chamber with a bomb lance. The first and second mates also lowered their boats. My father and the first mate went onto the two whales at almost the same moment and the second mate fastened to the mate's whale so that all three boats were fast. The whale my father was fast to was badly hurt by the bomb lance and, as my father got a lance into him at once, he soon commenced to spout blood and soon rolled fin out and sunk. The other went off at a fast clip with the two boats trying to haul onto him. The ship was maneuvered alongside the Captain's boat and the line to the whale taken aboard. The whale came to the surface very un-expectedly, in a short time, and was secured to the ship with the usual fluke chain.

I was in the crow's-nest watching the efforts of the other two boats to kill their whale. It was late in the afternoon and they went out of sight in the haze on the horizon. I came down from the mast-head and reported to my father that it looked as though the two boats would have to cut from their whale as he was still running strong. The ship was kept after the boats under easy sail and no concern was felt for their safety as the wind was light and the sea smooth. A devil fish is not a pleasant fellow to be fast to even in daylight and, therefore, we were not surprised when, a little later, they pulled alongside and reported that they had to cut as they had shot all their bomb lances into the whale without any effect, ex-cept to increase his speed and it was impossible to haul up close enough to lance him. Throwing the line out of the bow chock into the side chock so as to breast the boat off while hauling up to get the lance into his vitals aft of the fin is a very risky operation with a devil fish, because if the boat comes within his vision, he will surely reach it with his flukes and one blow will wreck it. My father's only comment when the officers came aboard was "I ex-pected you would get run away with, you had too many bomb guns," which was a little satire he could not resist as the officers frequently joked him about his aversion to a bomb gun and the fact that he never carried one in his boat. The fact that the third mate went as boatsteerer on the occasion just recorded accounted for the bomb lance in this case and, of course, my father must have agreed to it. There was no question but what my father loved to kill his whale with a lance. It was much more of a sporting proposition than shooting him with a bomb lance and there was far more danger in using the lance and it called for greater skill and more prompt action. My father's height, long reach and great strength gave him an advantage with a hand lance which was not possessed by many men in the business.

The whale was cut in the next day and we proceeded on our way as the blubber was tried out. The only variation in cutting in was that the head was not saved. The devil fish belongs to the baleen family but the mouth bone is very short and has no commercial value. These species with the shorter slabs must feed on coarser food than the bowhead and right whales although the bone hangs in the upper jaw on both sides. The oil of these short-bone whales was not considered as valuable as that of the sperm, right and bowhead whales but they were worth catching when the opportunity offered. This statement does not include the sulphur-bottom as this species were not caught by American whalers, at least, not to my knowledge. The devil fish or California gray has especially good lines for speed and is quite graceful to look at compared with the other members of that family. Their head is rather short and rounded at the end and the body tapers symmetrically from the head to the flukes. Our whale was in good condition and stowed down something over thirty barrels of oil.

One day, we spoke the *Bartholomew Gosnold,* Captain Willis, who had his wife and two sons aboard. One son steered the Captain's boat, which was interesting to me although I think he was older. This was one of the largest ships then in the whaling business and she carried five boats. The rig had recently been changed from a ship to a bark; that is, the mizzenmast was changed to fore-and-aft-rigged, while the foremast and mainmast remained as square-rigged. She had painted ports which was typical of the New Bedford ships. I liked this as it gave the ship a more distinctive appearance, and made her look larger than when painted black or any plain color. There is the impression of gun ports in these painted ports which may have been used as an excuse by Confederate cruisers to fire on whaleships.

We set our colors, as we were to windward of the *Gosnold*, which in the language of the sea indicated that we wished to speak her and she acknowledged by clewing up her courses and hauling aback. Our ship was then swung off before the wind and headed directly for the other ship. My father was on the poop deck directing the man at the wheel and Captain Willis was walking back and forth on the house as the *Gosnold* had that typical New Bedford superstructure over the after part of the ship. When it would have seemed to a novice that we could not possibly avoid ramming the *Gosnold*, we swung off a trifle and crossed her stern so close that the two captains talked to each other in their ordinary tones of voices. After inquiring as to each other's health and the health of the ladies and their children, Captain Willis remarked that, as their ship was the larger, he would be glad if Captain Williams and his family would come aboard and dine with them. His invitation was accepted and we passed under his lee and hauled aback which brought our ship to a standstill.

Speaking a ship was always a most interesting event to me. I think that I preferred the speaking part to the receiving end as I could never feel entirely comfortable watching the other ship coming down the wind headed directly for us until it would seem impossible for her to go clear, and then she would swing off just a trifle, to go rolling by so close you could almost touch her boats from the taffrail. It was wonderful seamanship and none understood it better than the American whalemen. Merchant ships in my day rarely spoke each other and rather avoided it, preferring to do their talking by signals. It saved time and involved no risk of a collision, time being the essence of their business.

As soon as the family were ready, the starboard quarter boat was swung clear of the cranes and lowered level with the rail when my father and I took our places at the falls, my mother and sister stepped in and sat down on a temporary seat in the stern sheets, and the boat was lowered into the water with the crew following her down the side of the ship and taking their places in the boat as she struck the water. It happened to be a very smooth time but the procedure would have been the same if it had been rough. Getting a boat away from a ship in rough water is not quite as dangerous as coming alongside and getting the occupants aboard the ship. The transfer is always made on the lee side. Our usual method when my mother was in the boat was to lower the port quarter boat just to the surface of the water when the ship was rolled down on that side, then the boat with my mother in it would come alongside and the crew would transfer her to the port boat while it was down. As soon as this transfer was made, the boat would be hoisted to the level of the rail and my mother would step out. This may sound very simple but there were times when it was a trying experience and I think everybody concerned breathed deeper when it was over. My mother always did as she was told, therefore, she never had any trouble. The fact that she was small and surefooted was a great help but the main thing was her complete confidence in the men who had her in charge.

We had a very pleasant gam with Captain Willis and his family as they were old friends of my parents. The ship had a large cabin and was a very comfortable home at sea. The *Florence* looked as good when we returned later in the day in spite of the fact that she was leaking rather badly.

We eventually entered Shantar Bay on the west side of the Okhotsk Sea in Siberia. We then had our first meeting with my uncle and aunt in the Russian bark *Tirgur,* which was a red letter day for the entire family.

We were to try our luck at "Bay whaling" and the ship was anchored in a nice landlocked harbor. The boats were provisioned and equipped with a camping outfit and sent off for a week at a time to look for whales among the islands of that locality. The whales were scarce, at least as far as our successes were concerned, and we did not get any whales. The weather was very stormy, sudden squalls coming up when we would get up anchor and sail around to the lee side of the island, after we had left our first pleasant harbor to follow our boats north toward Shantarskie [Shantar] Islands. My mother recalled her visit to Ayan, a city further up the coast, but we had no intention of being involved with Russian officials and kept away from inhabited areas.

On one of the fair, calm days, one of the boats was sent to a rocky island, high and barren, which was covered with birds, similar to the island we had obtained eggs from in the South Pacific. The crew brought back a good supply of eggs which was welcome food for every one except me as I still had my fill of eggs. On another good weather day, the family went ashore on the mainland where it was quite wild and uninhabited. We had a good chance to stretch our legs and found edible berries much to the delight of my mother and sister.

HOMEWARD BOUND

IT was a very discouraging situation that whales were so difficult to raise and more of a problem to catch. The weather was getting worse rather than improving and, it finally became so bad, that my father decided to recall the boats. This was done by signals consisting of the code flags set in the rigging. Everything was put in order for the "homeward bound" voyage. As the news passed from officers to boatsteerers to crew, evidences of joy were seen expressed in various ways which is unusual aboard a ship.

The day for departure arrived, the anchor was raised after the sails had been set, the man at the wheel held her for the wind to fill the sails and the ship was on her way. The course was southeast which would take the ship through one of the passages between the Kuril Islands. We were under short sail most of the time and the lookout at the masthead was maintained for whales.

While the ship was passing through the Kuril Island Strait, she suddenly trembled violently from stem to stern and the water, which had been quite smooth, became agitated into small, sharp pointed waves that were not like a tiderip so often experienced in these passages between islands. My father remarked that it was an earthquake, a waterquake for us, but there was evidently an earthquake somewhere among the islands. It was soon over and we sailed into the Pacific Ocean.

I have already made the statement that the two weeks passage from Saipan to the Yellow Sea was the most uncomfortable part of this voyage but the trip across the Pacific Ocean was almost as rough. The wind blew hard most of the days and the ship was under short sail, foresail, jib and double-reefed mainsail. When it moderated, we shook the reefs out of the mainsail. The seas broke over the bow and swept the full length of the ship. I counted the strokes of the pump in the mornings after the heavy nights and it was a relief if the number was about the same as had become normal.

It had been a very disappointing season for the whale ships we had encountered. We had 80 barrels of sperm oil and 200 barrels of whale oil, also 2000 pounds of whalebone. The other ships remained on their voyages for more seasons and, eventually, had a good catch. The *Bartholomew Gosnold,* Captain James M. Willis, returned to New Bedford on March 30, 1876 with 950 barrels of sperm oil, 1200 barrels of whale oil and 12,500 pounds of whalebone. The *Arnolda,* Captain George F. Bouldry, returned to New Bedford on May 1, 1876, with 620 barrels of sperm oil, 1175 barrels of whale oil and 16,200 pounds of whalebone. These ships had been whaling for a year and a half after we returned to port but they had better success in that time than during the season of 1874. The amount of oil and bone taken for a season varied greatly as, for example, my father had a catch of 1300 barrels of oil and 10,000 pounds of whalebone in the one season of 1872 in the Arctic Ocean and northern seas, besides salvaging the bark *Minerva* that had been abandoned in the Arctic loss of 1871. The season of 1875 was also a fair one with 1250 barrels of oil in a seven months voyage and the amount of bone has been omitted from the records. It will be seen from these figures that my father had nearly as large a catch in one seven months season as the above ships had in voyages of four and a half years. However, whaling was a profitable business until the end of the nineteenth century.

Our trip across the Pacific "homeward bound" was spoiled by one more serious incident that marked this voyage as one of unusual tragedies. I have pointed out the grudges that develop aboard a ship and the danger of one man causing trouble as an individual or by arousing the crew to insubordination. The feeling against an officer is quite common and this happened to my father when he had his first voyage as a mate. He first shipped as a "greenhand" in the forecastle of the ship *Albion* from Fairhaven on May 28, 1840. Andrew Potter of New Bedford claimed to have shipped this big boy and he always took an interest in him. My father next sailed as blacksmith and boatsteerer in the ship *South Carolina* on June 30, 1842, from New Bedford and Mr. Potter was again his shipping agent. My father took his discharge in Lahaina, Sandwich Islands, and then shipped as boatsteerer on the *Gideon Howland*. This ship returned to New Bedford on November 11, 1844, and my father shipped as second mate on the ship *Chili*, Captain H. H. Ricketson, sailing from New Bedford on July 10, 1845. He returned June 29, 1848 and sailed as second mate of the *South Boston*, Captain Soule, on September 5, 1848. The first mate was discharged at a port in Chili because of some difficulty with the Captain and my father was promoted to first mate. This was a rapid rise from greenhand to first mate in eight years and it is logical that some of the seamen may have thought he was young and inexperienced for this position. It is evident that he did not exert his physical ability in handling the crew during this voyage as they did not know how powerful he was.

Andrew Potter told the story when the ship returned to New Bedford on June 29, 1848, and he boarded the ship in Buzzards Bay as was the custom for agents. While he was about the deck on the way into port, he overheard the remark of a crewman that they were going to give that long-legged mate the licking of his life when the sails were furled. Mr. Potter communicated this situation to my father and advised him to slip over the side as soon as the ship came to anchor and get away in a shore boat and possibly out of town, until the men forgot their grievances. My father thanked him for his advice and suggested that Mr. Potter stay around and see him get his licking. The anchor was dropped, the sails furled, and the crew gathered forward with the evident intent to carry out their threat. My father then walked to the forecastle deck, took off his coat, faced the crew with no weapon, and made approximately this statement: I understand you feel that I have not treated you fair during the voyage and you now propose to give me a thrashing; very well, I am ready for you. To the astonishment of Mr. Potter, not a man advanced and, with a few muttered threats, they crept into the forecastle to make their preparations to go ashore.

Now, to return to our trouble between the second and third mates which was settled by the discharge of the third mate and the fact that the third mate was likable while the second mate was inclined to be surly, although he was a more valuable whaleman. There was a sailor who resented the second mate for some unknown reason and he armed himself with the blackjack that the third mate had made during the voyage. Being a coward at heart, he made an opportunity to get near the second mate during the night watch and hit him with the blackjack. As so often happens with these frenzied men, he hit him too hard and nearly killed him so that we had another serious injury to handle. We were only a few days from San Francisco and the sailor was put in irons to be turned over to the authorities when we arrived in port. The mate was taken care of to the best of our ability and he was able to leave the ship for better attention ashore.

So, we sailed through the beautiful Golden Gate into our home port on November 12, 1874. This was the end of my ambitions, if ever very serious, to be a whaleman. I had been about three years in five ships during my boyhood, after the child stage which was in whaleships except during the Civil War. I decided that I had enough of the sea. I studied hard and entered the School of Mines, Columbia University, in 1878 to become an engineer. My mother and sister remained ashore, living in Oakland, California, while my father continued to make one-season voyages to the Arctic Ocean. On his last voyage, he took a small steam craft on the ship, a sort of tugboat, and used it to cruise in the ice fields looking for whales. He would be gone for days at a time and suffered hardships from exposure, poor food and water, besides worries which broke his health, and he died August 26, 1880. This was the first steamboat used in the Arctic for whaling.

CAPTAIN THOMAS WILLIAM WILLIAMS

THE WILLIAMS family of this book were originally from the town of Hay on the river Wye in Wales, British Isles. They migrated to the United States in 1829 as steerage passengers in a sailing packet and, after spending a year or so on the eastern end of Long Island, they settled in Wethersfield, Connecticut.

The family were employed in the local woolen mill as weavers and the son, born on December 21, 1820 learned the weaving trade, but his mother thought the mill was injuring his health and had him learn the toolmaker's trade as apprentice at the local blacksmith shop.

Thomas William Williams, the first son, was named Thomas after the custom for this family. He was big and strong and he ran away from home to go to sea, although he told his mother what he intended to do. He shipped as a "greenhand" on the whaleship *Albion,* Captain Austin Smith, which sailed from New Bedford, Massachusetts, on May 28, 1840, and returned to that port on May 16, 1842.

Mr. Andrew Potter of New Bedford claimed he shipped the boy and remembered him as a very tall and slender youth. He boarded the ship upon her return in the lower bay, as was the custom, and greeted the boy who had contracted "moon blindness" from sleeping on deck in the tropics. The young man had no money and did not want to wait for the voyage to be settled, as he was anxious to see his mother, so he begged Mr. Potter to loan him the money to take him home. Mr. Potter was impressed with the youth and loaned him the money, which he received by the first mail after Thomas reached Wethersfield. This was the beginning of a friendship that lasted throughout their lives.

After about a month at home, Thomas returned to New Bedford and presented himself to Mr. Potter for another voyage. He was shipped as blacksmith and boatsteerer on the whaleship *South Carolina*, Captain Ansel Stewart, which sailed from New Bedford on June 30, 1842, for the Pacific Ocean. Thomas took his discharge at Lahaina, Sandwich Islands, on October 3, 1843, and shipped as boatsteerer on the *Gideon Howland*, Captain Arthur Cox, and this whaleship returned to New Bedford on November 11, 1844.

Thomas William Williams became a citizen of the United States on April 5, 1845.

He sailed as second mate of the whaleship *Chili*, Captain Henry H. Ricketson, which left New Bedford on July 10, 1845, and returned June 29, 1848. He next sailed as second mate of the whaleship *South Boston*, Captain Soule, which left New Bedford on September 5, 1848, but he became first mate when some difficulty caused the discharge of the first mate in a port of Chili on the voyage around South America. This voyage ended on January 28, 1851, with the return of the ship to New Bedford.

Thomas W. Williams married Eliza Azelia Griswold of Griswoldville at the Wethersfield Congregational Church on April 22, 1851.

He sailed as master of the whaleship *South Boston* from New Bedford on July 15, 1851, and returned April 3, 1854, with a voyage valued at $140,000, which established him as a lucky captain. He was owner of 1/16th of this ship. Upon his return to Wethersfield, he found a son awaiting him; Thomas Stancel, born February 13, 1852. Captain Williams remained in Wethersfield for more than six months during which time he bought a farm of one hundred acres and established a herd of cattle, driving them from Vermont himself. This land had been owned at one time by his wife's father, Horace Griswold, who inherited the land from the earliest Griswold settler of Colonial days.

Captain Thomas W. Williams was master of the whaleship *Florida* sailing from Fairhaven, Massachusetts, October 11, 1854, and returning April 6, 1858. A second son was born while he was away; Henry Ricketson, born January 10, 1855.

He sailed as master of the *Florida* again on September 7, 1858, and took his wife with him. She wrote a daily journal during this voyage which is Part I of this book. The voyage ended in San Francisco, owing to the Civil War, on October 26, 1861, and the ship was sold for $16,000, of which Captain Williams was 1/4 owner. Two children were born during this voyage and the family returned to Wethersfield where the mother and her four children remained during the war.

Captain Williams sailed as master of the bark *Jireh Swift* from New Bedford on September 2, 1862, and he owned 3/32 of this vessel. He went to the Azores hoping he could enlist some more men but learned that there was a Confederate privateer in the vicinity that had captured eight ships in two weeks so he crowded on sail and went to Brava in the Cape Verde Islands. The *Jireh Swift* was a fast sailer with near clipper ship speed. He went around Cape Horn and cruised in the Pacific Ocean, arriving at San Francisco on November 12, 1864, and discharged his cargo worth $100,000. He sailed from San Francisco on December 9, 1864, and the ship was captured after a chase by the Confederate cruiser *Shenandoah* and burned in the Arctic Ocean on June 22, 1865. Captain Williams with officers and crews of other whalers destroyed were sent to San Francisco on the whaler *Milo* and arrived there on July 21, 1865.

On arrival in San Francisco, Captain Williams was asked to take the *Florida* on a whaling voyage and he went east to buy whaleboats and other gear not available in San Francisco. The ship had not been successful as a freight ship after she was sold there in 1861. Captain Williams returned to San Francisco with his wife and daughter in March, having traveled by the Isthmus route from New York. This voyage began in April 1866 and ended in San Francisco in the fall of 1867. Their second daughter was born on April 11, 1867, in the Japan Sea. The family established their residence in Oakland and the Captain went east in 1867 to settle his business affairs in Wethersfield and New Bedford and he returned to Oakland early in 1868 with his two sons. He went into business in Oakland.

He went to Honolulu late in 1869 and sailed as master of the *Hibernia* on December 6, 1869, and returned on March 16, 1870, to get his family who arrived by steamer from San Francisco. He sailed again on March 19, 1870, and the ship was wrecked by a submerged ram of an ice floe on August 28, 1870, at Point Barrow in the Arctic and they returned to Honolulu, Sandwich Islands, on the whaler *Josephine*, Captain Cogan, on November 3, 1870.

Captain Williams sailed on November 24, 1870, as master of the ship *Monticello* and she was one of the thirty-two whalers lost in the Arctic in 1871. The family returned to Honolulu in the whaler *Progress*, Captain Dowden. The story of this disaster is Part II of this book as written by the son, William Fish Williams, born on the voyage of the *Florida* in Part I.

Captain Williams fitted out the whaleship *Florence* and returned to Point Belcher in 1872 on his theory that some of the whaleships would have survived. He found the *Minerva* was the only ship in seaworthy condition and he salvaged her, putting his son Stancel in command with part of his large crew which he had recruited in preparation for this prospect. Oil and whalebone were salvaged from the wrecks and these two whalers returned to San Francisco in the fall of 1872 with a good salvage season.

He sailed in April, 1873, with the *Florence*, in which he was part owner, returning to San Francisco November 8, 1873. He sailed again on December 25, 1873, and took his family with him. The story of this voyage is Part III of this book as written by the son, William Fish Williams. They returned to San Francisco November 12, 1874.

Voyages followed in 1875 and 1876 while the family remained in Oakland so the two children could complete their schooling. The second daughter had died in Oakland in 1869. In 1876, his brother, Lewis Williams, was in command of the *Florence* and Captain

Thomas W. Williams was master of the bark *Clara Bell* which was wrecked by the ice and the crew was saved by Captain Lewis Williams. There were twelve whalers lost in the Arctic Ocean that season, which was another serious blow to the industry.

Captain Thomas W. Williams took the bark *Francis Palmer,* of which he was the owner, to the Arctic for eight months in 1879. He took a small steam craft on deck with which he chased whales in the leads between ice floes where the ship could not go. (This was the idea of "catchers" which is now the method used in the Antarctic by the modern whale factories.) This was his last voyage. He acted as agent and fitted out the bark *Dawn,* of which he was ½ owner, for voyages from 1877 to 1880, and his brother, Lewis Williams, was master of the *Florence* in 1876-78 voyages until she was lost in the Arctic in 1878 but her cargo was saved.

It was a well-known trait of seafaring men to buy a piece of land with good intentions of retiring from the sea to live ashore. Captain Thomas W. Williams had this desire to own land. He bought the farm in Wethersfield in 1854, and other parcels of land in Wethersfield over the years.

When he returned from his third voyage on June 29, 1848, he bought the tool shop where he had learned his trade of blacksmith and tool maker. He continued this business under the original owners as the "I. H. Bailey Tool Shop" and acquired water rights with the purchase of this factory.

In 1866, he built a mill on the stream below the Tool Shop for John Chapman to manufacture woolen goods. He was an inventor with stockinette machines of his own development but they had a mechanical defect and were unsuccessful. The mill was shut down in 1868.

In 1868, Captain Thomas W. Williams was in the coal and wood business in Oakland, California, which appeared to be an attempt to establish some business other than whaling which was suffering from the Civil War losses of whale ships and the drilling of petroleum wells.

In 1872, he became associated with George A. King in the carriage making business in Oakland and remained a partner until 1875 when he put his son, Stancel, into this business in his place. The Captain's training as a blacksmith may have been the reason he selected the carriage business.

He invested in other enterprises in Wethersfield and New Bedford but they did not prosper after the war and were eventually shut down.

Captain Thomas W. Williams died in Oakland August 26, 1880, and he is buried in Wethersfield Church Cemetery.

ELIZA AZELIA WILLIAMS

ELIZA AZELIA GRISWOLD was born December 11, 1826, in the Griswoldville section of Wethersfield, Connecticut, where she lived. Her ancestry goes back to 1645 in Wethersfield. She married Captain Thomas W. Williams at the Congregational Church in Wethersfield on April 22, 1851.

She was a small woman, weighing less than one hundred pounds, and she could stand erect under her husband's outstretched arm without touching it. She was timid and did not like the duties forced upon her by her husband's long absences. He made investments which required her to collect interest and principal and to invest money. She was annoyed by the treatment she received from her husband's brother-in-law who was a sharecropper on the Captain's farm in Wethersfield.

Like the older New Englanders, she was reticent and she followed the formalities of actions and speech which were the custom of those days.

She was five months pregnant when she sailed on her first voyage, September 7, 1858, but she never wrote one word in her journal about her condition and she never blamed her seasick spells on this possibility. She went gamming in Banderas Bay, Mexico, the night before her daughter was born in February 1861.

Women followed their men in the pioneering days and this was true of the whaling period. The Captain made plenty of money and she wanted him to give up his whaling life but these men with the urge for whale fishery could not be satisfied with life in a small town, so she went to sea with him. She wrote to her husband when he was away that she did not want him to write sympathetic letters to her but this did not stop him from writing how much he missed her.

Her first voyage covered thirty-eight months and her second voyage was eighteen months long. After that, voyages were for the season and always of less than one year in duration. She was in two ship losses in the Arctic when they returned in other whale ships to Honolulu.

The family moved from Wethersfield to Oakland, California, in March 1866, going by way of the Isthmus route, a 26-day trip by ships. The two boys were left with two of the Captain's sisters to attend school in Boston while five-year-old Mary went with her parents. They sailed in the whaleship *Florida* soon after their arrival in 1866 and their daughter Flora was born in the Japan Sea during this voyage. They returned to Oakland in the fall of 1867 and Captain Williams went east to close out his business affairs in Wethersfield. He returned to Oakland in February 1868 and brought the two boys to unite the family there. The family made their home in Oakland from then on, except when they were on whaling voyages. The last voyage was in 1874; after that school kept the family at home.

After the Captain died in Oakland, his wife returned to Wethersfield with her daughter Mary in 1881 and she died February 17, 1885, and is buried with her husband in the Village Cemetery, Wethersfield.

LEWIS WATKINS WILLIAMS

LEWIS, the brother of Captain Thomas W. Williams, was born in Wethersfield in February 1838, and he was the youngest of that generation. He completed his education at the English High School in Boston, Mass., at sixteen years of age. He chose whaling instead of going to college as his family wished him to do. He sailed with his older brother, who was master of the *Florida,* as a seaman on October 11, 1854 and returned to New Bedford on April 6, 1858.

He sailed as boatsteerer on his next voyage in the whale ship *Gratitude,* Captain William Davis, Jr., from New Bedford on August 25, 1858 and was in the Okhotsk Sea in the summer of 1859 but the two brothers did not meet. He took his discharge that winter, probably in the Sandwich Islands, and sailed as mate on the *Othello,* Captain Charles B. Killmer, and the brothers met in the Okhotsk Sea in the summer of 1860 as recorded in the journal which is Part I of this book. The *Othello* returned to New Bedford on March 12, 1863.

Lewis Williams sailed as mate in the *E. Swift,* Captain Reuben Pontius, on November 12, 1863, from New Bedford and the two brothers met in Banderas Bay, Mexico, in the month of December 1864. Lewis took his discharge from this ship and returned to Wethersfield to marry Hannah C. Woodhouse there on February 4, 1866. Late in 1867, he and his wife went to Oakland, California, and returned to Wethersfield in April 1869.

He sailed from New Bedford as captain of the whaler *Fanny* on July 21, 1869, and took his wife with him. This ship was abandoned in the Arctic in the big loss of September 1871. The two brothers with their families returned to Honolulu in the whaling bark *Progress* and from Honolulu to San Francisco in the steam packet *Moses Taylor* late in October 1871.

Captain Lewis Williams was master of the Russian whaler *Tirgur* in the season of 1874 and the two families met in the Okhotsk Sea as recorded in Part III of this book.

In 1876, Lewis Williams sailed as master of his brother's whaleship *Florence* from San Francisco on March 3rd and Captain Thomas Williams took the *Clara Bell* to the Arctic, sailing from San Francisco on April 18. This was another disastrous year in the whaling industry with twelve ships lost including the *Clara*

Bell and they were saved by the prompt return of the *Florence* to the aid of his brother Thomas. It is to be noted that these two brothers had stopped taking their wives to the Arctic Ocean.

The *Florence* returned to San Francisco on October 22, 1876, and Captain Lewis Williams sailed in her on November 29, 1876, for another voyage which ended October 27, 1877. He sailed again on April 18, 1878, and the *Florence* was lost in the Arctic but her cargo was saved with a value of $11,500, which was fair for the one-season voyages then being made.

Captain Lewis Williams then sailed as master of the whaling brig *Hidalgo* from San Francisco on one-season voyages from 1879 to 1895, with a few years in which he remained at his home in Oakland.

He was captain of the whaler *Andrew Hicks*, sailing from San Francisco for an eleven-month voyage in 1903.

He made his last voyage in command of the whaler *California*, owned by William Lewis & Son, which sailed from San Francisco on March 17, 1906, and returned on November 16, 1906. The Williams and Lewis families were now united by marriage and they saw each other often in San Francisco.

Captain Lewis Williams died in Oakland, California, on December 16, 1916, and his wife returned to live with her relatives in Wethersfield and Newington, Connecticut. They are buried in the Newington Cemetery. They did not have any children.

THOMAS STANCEL WILLIAMS

The eldest son of Captain Thomas William Williams and Eliza Williams was born February 13, 1852 and he was more than two years old when his father returned from the whaling voyage following his marriage. The boy was named Thomas Stancel Williams as the first son in this family was always named Thomas.

It was the desire of Captain Williams that his children should be provided with a good education and Stancel was sent to school in Boston at an early age. He lived with his Aunt Esther Howe and her husband who was an expert pattern maker.

Captain Williams came east in the fall of 1867 to settle business affairs with the intention of moving the family to Oakland, California. Upon his return in February 1868, he took his sons Stancel and William with him. His second son, Henry, died of scarlet fever in April 1864 at the age of nine years. Stancel attended school in Oakland and he was considered smart so that it appears his father did not intend that he should follow in the whaling business. He did not go with the family on the whaler *Hibernia* in 1870 but he joined them at Honolulu to sail on the whaleship *Monticello* November 24, 1870. This was the voyage that ended with the loss of whaleships east of Point Belcher in the Arctic Ocean in September 1871. The record does not state whether Stancel was an officer on this voyage but he probably was the third or fourth mate.

When Captain Williams went to the Arctic in 1872 with the hope of salvaging an abandoned whaleship, he took Stancel with him and made him Captain of the salvaged whaler *Minerva*. Stancel brought this ship back to San Francisco with her salvage cargo of oil and bone.

It appears that Captain Williams wanted Stancel to give up whaling and he put him in the carriage business in Oakland with George A. King in 1875. Stancel married Edith King, the daughter of his partner, on September 9, 1875. This marriage ended with divorce in July 1886.

Stancel wanted to follow whaling and he took their whaleship *Francis Palmer* from San Francisco on March 17, 1880, as the Captain and returned from the Arctic in September, with a good catch. His father died during his absence and his mother allowed him to continue as captain of this whaler in 1881 to 1884.

These voyages did not pay the cost of fitting out the whaler except in the voyage of 1882 and the estate of Captain Thomas Williams could not afford to send him out in 1885. This ship was sold in January 1886 after lying in Oakland Estuary since the fall of 1884.

The family had returned to live in the East by this time and no record exists about any further whaling voyages by Stancel Williams, as he was called by the family. He had no children by his marriage to Edith King and he did not remarry. He died July 9, 1917, in San Francisco and he is buried in the family plot in Wethersfield.

Stancel was struck in the leg by a bomb lance on one of his voyages and he had a wooden leg as a result of this accident. This handicap probably prevented Stancel from following the sea life he desired.

WILLIAM FISH WILLIAMS

THIS third son of Captain Thomas W. Williams and his wife Eliza was born on the whale ship *Florida* on January 12, 1859, during the crossing of the Tasman Sea enroute to New Zealand. He was three years old before he went ashore to live during the Civil War. These years of his life are recorded in the journal which his mother wrote on her voyage from 1858 to 1861, and is Part I of this book.

He sailed with the family on three voyages after the war, surviving two shipwrecks in the Arctic, the loss of the *Hibernia* in 1870 and of the *Monticello* in 1871. His description of the loss of the thirty-one whalers in the ice in 1871 forms Part II of this book.

He was a boatsteerer on the bark *Florence* during his last voyage from December 25, 1873, to November 12, 1874. His story of this voyage is Part III of this book.

At fifteen years of age, he decided that he did not want to follow the sea but wished to become an engineer. It is apparent that his education was not neglected during the whaling voyages as he entered the School of Mines, Columbia University, in New York City on February 10, 1878, and he graduated with the degree of Civil Engineer on June 8, 1881, and on June 14, 1882, he received the degree of Engineer of Mines.

He followed both engineering professions for several years in various sections of the United States, but after marrying Anna L. Cornor of Oakland, California, on April 7, 1883, and having four children, he decided mining towns were not good for raising a family. With many friends of the family in New Bedford, he settled there and became the first City Engineer. He designed the bridge across the harbor between New Bedford and Fairhaven, during his service to the city from 1894 to 1912.

In 1912, he went to the State of Massachusetts as Engineer of the Harbor and Land Commission and had charge of construction of the Cape Cod Canal. He held various engineering titles as the Department of Public Works was organized and finally Engineer of the Department. On December 6, 1922, Governor Channing H. Cox appointed him Commissioner, at his request, and he was reappointed December 9, 1925, by Governor Alvin T. Fuller for a second term of three years. He retired at the end of this term, December 1928, with a fine record of achievements.

His account of the 1871 disaster was published in 1902. In 1929 he wrote the story of his voyage in the *Florence* (unpublished until now), and in February he told a reporter from the New Bedford *Sunday Standard* about his reasons for writing it. "It is a notion I have had for years, without getting to the point of doing any definite work," he is quoted as saying. "The history of whaling as it is being written today is irritating to me. The writers in their desire to be thrilling have stressed the brutal side beyond what the realities warrant. They have enlarged overmuch on certain aspects in which they assumed interest centers, and created a distorted picture. The truth itself, I think, would prove far more interesting than these 'dreams.' "

He died October 1, 1929, at his home in New Bedford and was buried in the family plot, Wethersfield, Conn.

MARY WATKINS WILLIAMS

MARY WILLIAMS was the daughter born in 1861 on board the *Florida*. She went on four voyages with the family after her birth voyage, 1866, 1870, 1871, 1873–74, and was in the wrecks of the *Hibernia* and *Monticello* when they were lost in the ice. On the 1866 voyage she celebrated her fifth birthday at sea en route to California via the Isthmus route.

Mary Williams attended schools in Oakland, California, and graduated from the High School.

On April 8, 1897, Mary Williams married Edgar R. Lewis of the whaleship firm William Lewis & Son of New Bedford. Edgar R. Lewis was born in Chilmark, Martha's Vineyard, son of the whaling captain William Lewis and Lucretia Hancock Lewis. His family moved to New Bedford when he was seven years old. Edgar Lewis became known as "The Whalebone King." He added to the catch of his own whaleships much of the whalebone brought back by other whalers for which he acted as agent. New Bedford became the whalebone market of the world, and the Lewis warehouse often contained 100,000 pounds of whalebone, practically the world supply. The markets were principally the quality dress and corset makers of Paris, New York and other metropolitan centers. The price was fixed at five dollars a pound for many years, and this continued until celluloid came in as a substitute.

After their marriage, the Lewises traveled from New Bedford to San Francisco in the spring and fall of each year to fit out the ships for the season's voyages to the Arctic and to handle their catches and lay them up in Oakland Creek for the winter. The officers and crews were mainly from New Bedford and they made this same migration.

The firm of William Lewis & Son owned many whalers during the last half of the century, until the passage of the Seaman's Act in 1909 which Edgar Lewis thought would make the cost of crews too expensive for whaling. Captain William Lewis built the steam whaler *Mary and Helen* in 1879 and she was the first steam whaler in the Arctic Ocean in 1880. She had auxiliary engines that gave her a speed of eight knots. The engines enabled her to get into the leads in the ice and to get out of them without dependence upon the winds. Her voyage was successful; Captain Lewis followed her with the *Lucretia* and other shipowners built steamships. This revolutionized Arctic whaling, although ship losses continued to be severe.

Edgar Lewis also had a ship chandlery business which was burned out by the San Francisco earthquake in 1906. He sold his ships in 1909 and retired from the whaling business completely in 1915. Then he went to live on an apple ranch in the Prosser Valley in the state of Washington, where he died in 1932.

Mary Williams Lewis was a remarkable old lady who took up golf in the early 1900's. Very reticent about her age, she used to claim February 29 as her birthday. She returned to New Bedford after her husband's death and lived with her nephew, named Thomas William Williams for his grandfather, until her death March 3, 1938. She is buried with her husband in the Williams family plot in Wethersfield. She was the last of this "One Whaling Family" and, probably, about the last one who was born on a whaleship.

WHALING HISTORY

The WHALING industry is a good example of the changes that took place in the United States because the country became a leader in progress. The building of the transcontinental railways and the industrial age changed the maritime East into a manufacturing area. New Bedford from the leading whaling port became a great cotton mill city, financed with the receipts from whaling.

The peak of the whaling industry was in 1846 with 735 vessels engaged in this trade in the United States. There were 230 foreign whaleships, making a total of 965 vessels in the world fleet. About 30 percent of the oil catch was exported thereby bringing a good revenue to the new country.

There were 678 ships in this fleet of 735 whalers and the total tonnage was 233,189 tons with a value of $21,075,000. The catch of whale oil amounted to 428,000 barrels in 1851 and whalebone was 5,652,000 pounds in 1853. The value of these two products exceeded $10,000,000 in 1851, 1853, 1854 and 1857 and then started to decline. The practice of three and four year voyages in those days is reflected in these catch figures for years later than 1846. The highest catch of whale oil was reported for 1845 as 11,593,483 gallons but the value was not as high for that year. Whalebone was reported as 5,652,300 pounds in 1853 which was the peak catch.

Significant as these figures were, the modern whaling industry far surpasses these days of wooden sailing ships and iron men. The large steel steamships of today, called "floating factories," are owned in Norway, Great Britain, Holland, Russia and Japan. Twenty of these ships total 406,656 tons which is nearly double the tonnage of the 1846 fleet in the United States.

The catch in the 1961-62 season was 2,074,000 barrels of whale oil and 665,000 bbls. of sperm oil. The values at the year's highest prices in total were $82,750,000, which is eight times the value of the whaling catch in the 1851-57 period in the United States.

The size of the catch is regulated in these days by the Whaling Commission and the actual catch varies from year to year. Prices for the oil vary also just as they did in the old days of whaling. Recent prices compare as follows: sperm oil $1.36 vs. $1.32 and whale oil $0.83 vs. $0.53 with prices in the 1851–57 period. However, the price of the whale oil reached $1.45 per gallon during the Civil War while sperm oil went to $2.25 per gallon.

The main catch of today is from whaling in the Antarctic and their season is from mid-December until the end of March. Some whaling is done from shore stations in many parts of the world, including the west coast of the United States, but the annual catch is small compared to the old whaling days in the Pacific and Arctic Oceans. The United States does not import oil in recent years.

The entire whale is used, blubber, meat and bones, in the modern process to extract the oil. The residue is meat meal for livestock feed. Meat extract goes into soup in England while the oil is used for margarine and cooking fats. The Japanese eat whale meat. There is no modern use for the short whalebone from the Antarctic whales.

The processing of whales is much more efficient today in keeping with industrialization but demand has not raised prices as might have been expected. It would be interesting to know how profits compare today with the 1841–1860 period when the whaler *Lagoda* made 98 percent profit in six voyages and from 219 percent to 363 percent during the Civil War. This is no proof that all voyages were profitable and there was always the danger of losing the ship. Alexander Starbuck states in his *History of the American Whale Fish-*

ery that 68 whalers were expected to return to New Bedford in 1858 and 44 of these voyages would be a loss totaling $1,000,000. His book reports the whaler *Pioneer* of New London, Connecticut, as making the highest catch of $150,060 on her return September 18, 1865.